# READINGS IN EVIDENCE-BASED SOCIAL WORK

# READINGS IN EVIDENCE-BASED SOCIAL WORK

Syntheses of the Intervention Knowledge Base

Michael G. Vaughn
*Saint Louis University*

Matthew O. Howard
*University of North Carolina, Chapel Hill*

Bruce A. Thyer
*Florida State University College of Social Work*

Los Angeles • London • New Delhi • Singapore • Washington DC

*For information:*

 SAGE Publications, Inc.
2455 Teller Road
Thousand Oaks,
    California 91320
E-mail: order@sagepub.com

SAGE Publications India Pvt. Ltd.
B 1/I 1 Mohan Cooperative
    Industrial Area
Mathura Road, New Delhi 110 044
India

SAGE Publications Ltd.
1 Oliver's Yard
55 City Road
London EC1Y 1SP
United Kingdom

SAGE Publications Asia-Pacific
    Pte. Ltd.
33 Pekin Street #02-01
Far East Square
Singapore 048763

Printed in the United States of America

*Library of Congress Cataloging-in-Publication Data*

Readings in evidence-based social work : syntheses of the intervention knowledge
base/edited by Michael G. Vaughn, Matthew O. Howard, Bruce A. Thyer.
    p. cm.
Includes bibliographical references and index.
ISBN 978-1-4129-6323-7 (cloth)
ISBN 978-1-4129-6324-4 (pbk.)
    1. Evidence-based social work. 2. Social service--Practice. 3. Social work
education. I. Vaughn, Michael G. II. Howard, Matthew O. III. Thyer, Bruce A.

HV10.5.R415 2009
361.3′2—dc22                                        2008031848

This book is printed on acid-free paper.

08   09   10   11   12   10   9   8   7   6   5   4   3   2   1

| | |
|---|---|
| *Acquisitions Editor:* | Kassie Graves |
| *Editorial Assistant:* | Veronica K. Novak |
| *Production Editor:* | Kristen Gibson |
| *Copy Editor:* | Bill Bowers |
| *Typesetter:* | C&M Digitals (P) Ltd. |
| *Proofreader:* | Caryne Brown |
| *Indexer:* | Holly Day |
| *Cover Designer:* | Gail Buschman |
| *Marketing Manager:* | Carmel Schrire |

# Contents

# Preface _____

Much has been written in recent years about evidence-based social work practice. Indeed, entire journal issues have been devoted to conceptual discourse surrounding the implementation, appropriateness, and teaching of evidence-based approaches for social work. While these discussions are important as the field wrestles with its future, few compilations have synthesized what is known for the benefit of social work students. This volume is an attempt to begin to address this gap. We use systematic reviews and meta-analyses that have been published in *Research on Social Work Practice,* the primary evidence-based practice journal in social work, to accomplish this goal. These types of formal reviews have been an important methodology for reviewing sets of research studies as a critical link between research and practice. This type of volume is badly needed in order to subsume evidence-based practice knowledge within the professional curriculum of social work. Thus, this book is practical in that it attempts to expose students and scholars to what works across a range of practice domains relevant to the field of social work. Our objective is not to gather everything that is known across multiple fields (e.g., psychology, medicine, public health) via systematic reviews and meta-analyses. Instead, our aim is a far more modest one: to begin the engagement of students in evidence-based practice by exposing them to the evidence. One efficient way to begin this effort is to compile a volume of research syntheses across the intervention knowledge base derived from social workers. Thus, this book is explicitly a pedagogical tool for students. At the same time, we hope that social work scholars may find this work useful as well.

This volume is organized around three major sections. At the beginning of each section is a brief overview, as well as several questions to consider with respect to the chapters. At the end of each section there is a summary for social work practice that attempts to do additional lesson drawing. An introductory chapter on the relevance of systematic reviews and meta-analyses for social workers provides an overview of these methods. A concluding chapter that assesses the way forward for advancing evidence-based social work education completes this volume.

There are several people we would like to acknowledge. First, we greatly appreciate the help of Kassie Graves at Sage Publications, who was open to such a book and helped coordinate this effort.  Also, we would like to thank doctoral student Lisa Schelbe of the University of Pittsburgh for her organizational prowess and general assistance with the volume. Finally, our thanks to all of the fine social work researchers who contributed to this work, for without their scholarship no such volume could exist.

# Introduction to Systematic Reviews and Meta-Analyses in Social Work

## On the Importance of Syntheses of Intervention Research for Effective Practice

*Matthew O. Howard, Michael G. Vaughn, and Bruce A. Thyer*

In 1963, the distinguished physicist, applied mathematician, and historian of science Derek de Solla Price published his seminal work, *Little Science, Big Science,* establishing the field of scientometrics—the science of science—and proposing a mathematical model for the growth and "half-life" of published scientific literature. De Solla Price conjectured, on the basis of his review of nearly 200 years of British science published in the *Philosophical Transactions of the Royal Society,* that scientific knowledge accumulated exponentially (de Solla Price, 1963).

## _____ Dramatic Accumulation of Scientific Research

Although current findings do not support de Solla Price's specific predictions vis-à-vis the growth function characterizing scientific publication activity over the past half century, they do reveal notable increases in the accumulation of scientific knowledge. To wit: in 1963, PubMed, the publicly available biomedical database maintained by the National Library of Medicine, indexed 141,719 scientific papers. Comparable figures for later years were 1973 (228,824), 1983 (303,271), 1993 (415,794), 2003 (585,822), and 2007 (757,873). These numbers reflect proportional increases of 61 percent

(1963–1973), 33 percent (1973–1983), 37 percent (1983–1993), 41 percent (1993–2003), and 29 percent (2003–2007). The 757,873 new scientific reports indexed in PubMed during 2007 constituted an increase of 535 percent over the 141,719 reports indexed in 1963. In absolute terms, it is remarkable that more than 750,000 scientific reports were indexed in one bibliographic database in 2007 alone; in relative terms, it is striking that 172,051 more new scientific reports were indexed in 2007 than in 2003, a growth rate of nearly 30 percent.

PsycINFO, the leading computerized bibliographic database for the retrieval of psychological research, indexed 9,433 reports in 1963, 27,865 in 1973, 42,449 in 1983, 63,914 in 1993, 95,715 in 2003, and 110,309 in 2007. The number of scientific reports indexed in PsycINFO in 2007 was 1,169 percent greater than the comparable number of reports indexed in 1963. Taken together, PubMed and PsycINFO indexing figures for the past 45 years clearly indicate that growth of the biomedical and psychological scientific literature, while not exponential in nature, has been substantial.

## Failure to Utilize Practice-Relevant Scientific Literature

Despite considerable scientific advances, professionals in the health care and psychosocial practice areas have often failed to apply current knowledge to pressing practice concerns. Local area studies have documented widespread unexplained variations in the methods by which common human conditions, such as lower back pain, depression, and end-of-life care are treated (e.g., Wennberg, Fisher, Goodman, & Skinner, 2008). Serious lags in the adoption of scientifically supported interventions by professional practitioners, recurrent failures of practitioners to draw upon basic science findings in applied practice settings, and basic science research that itself has been less than ideally responsive to the needs of practitioners have led to the promotion of a "translational science" initiative by the National Institutes of Health (Office of Portfolio Analysis and Strategic Initiatives, 2008).

Although the notable growth of empirical knowledge may ultimately serve to reduce the glut of scientifically unsupported (if not patently fraudulent) practices that currently characterize many professional fields, the sheer mass of published scientific studies presents significant problems of its own for scientifically inclined practitioners. How, they ask, given the time constraints and other exigencies of modern practice, is it possible to remain current with the relevant science in their professional practice areas? One way is to utilize systematic reviews and meta-analyses of scientific studies that attempt to take stock of areas of intervention research and provide an assessment of the magnitude of effects across multiple studies.

## Efforts to Promote Evidence-Based Practice

Recognizing the problems posed by an increasingly large and sophisticated practice-relevant scientific literature, researchers have made attempts in recent years to promote more scientifically informed professional practices. Pedagogical efforts have included the promotion of evidence-based practice in medicine and allied health and psychosocial professions (Sackett, Straus, Richardson, Rosenberg, & Haynes, 2000; Howard, McMillen, & Pollio, 2003; Howard, Allen-Meares, & Ruffolo, 2007). Evidence-based practice pedagogy involves teaching student and professional practitioners effective and efficient methods for accessing, appraising, and applying recent scientific findings to their professional practice efforts in direct, mezzo, and macro practice settings (Chan, Morton, & Shekelle, 2004).

Organizational initiatives, such as the Cochrane and Campbell Collaborations, have also exerted significant effects on current efforts to increase scientifically supported practices. The Cochrane Collaboration (CC) was established in 1993 and produces a quarterly collection titled the *Cochrane Database of Systematic Reviews*. According to the Cochrane Collaboration Web site (www.cochrane.org), the CC is a ". . . not-for-profit . . . independent organization, dedicated to making up-to-date, accurate information about the effects of healthcare readily available worldwide. It produces systematic reviews of healthcare interventions and promotes the search for evidence in the form of clinical trials and other studies of interventions . . . Those who prepare the reviews are mostly healthcare professionals who volunteer to work in one of the many Cochrane Review Groups, with editorial teams overseeing the preparation and maintenance of the reviews as well as application of the rigorous quality standards for which the Cochrane Reviews have become known" (Cochrane Collaboration, 2008, homepage).

The Campbell Collaboration (www.campbellcollaboration.org) is an offshoot of the CC, established in 2000 to produce systematic reviews in the areas of education, crime and justice, and social welfare, and to address methodological issues in the preparation of systematic reviews in psychosocial practice areas. Perhaps the most important contributions of the Cochrane and Campbell Collaborations are their development of key methods for the preparation of systematic reviews of the scientific literature and widespread promotion of the utility of such reviews for scientists and practitioners alike. Although a number of published products, such as codified practice guidelines (i.e., algorithms, clinical pathways, options, standards, and so on) have been developed to encourage more scientifically based professional interventions (Howard & Jenson, 1999a; 1999b), many practitioners prefer systematic reviews, given the substantial heterogeneity in the rigor of methods by which practice guidelines are developed. Many practice guidelines are more consensually than scientifically based.

# Definitional Issues

*Systematic reviews* attempt to answer one or more clearly formulated questions by using ". . . systematic and explicit methods to identify, select, and critically appraise relevant research, and to collect and analyze data from relevant primary studies. Statistical techniques (meta-analysis) may or may not be used to summarize the results of included studies" (Cochrane Collaboration, 2008). *Meta-analysis* involves ". . . the use of statistical techniques to integrate the results of primary studies (usually randomized controlled trials) in order to obtain a more precise estimate of clinical effect" (Hind & Booth, 2007, p. 1). The effect size metric is the magnitude of treatment effect in standard deviation units (e.g., standardized mean difference). Typically, the effect size statistic (usually expressed as Cohen's d in intervention research) has been interpreted as small (.20), medium (.50), or large (.80) (Cohen, 1988). It is important to point out, however, that small effects can be meaningful, particularly if a treatment is low in cost and can be used on a large scale.

Greenhalgh (2006) has provided a succinct description of eight successive steps involved in systematic review development: (1) objectives of the review of controlled trials are stated and study eligibility criteria adumbrated; (2) a comprehensive search for relevant published and unpublished trials is then undertaken; (3) attributes of each relevant trial are systematically identified and recorded, including those reflecting methodological rigor and magnitude and direction of substantive findings; (4) excluded trials and the reasons for their exclusion are carefully noted; (5) a complete database of relevant trial findings is assembled (which may involve directly contacting investigators for additional trial information); (6) results of included trials are analyzed, using statistical syntheses (i.e., meta-analysis) if appropriate; (7) sensitivity and other analyses of the data set are then conducted; and (8) a critical summary of the review, containing a complete statement of the review's aims, methods, and findings, is published.

Compared to traditional narrative reviews, systematic reviews have many strengths. Robinson, Dellavalle, Bigby, and Callen (2008) observed that narrative reviews frequently fail to adequately describe literature search and data extraction methods; adopt inconsistent approaches to the critical appraisal of incorporated studies; rarely pool data across similar studies; and frequently take a desultory approach to the identification and discussion of study implications. Conversely, systematic reviews address a clearly stated and explicitly formulated question; carefully explicate literature search and data extraction methods; systematically evaluate study quality using predefined criteria; and interpret findings in light of the quality, magnitude, and precision of the data derived from the review.

Other advantages of systematic review methods identified by Greenhalgh (2006) were that:

1. Explicit methods *limit bias* in identifying and rejecting studies.

2. Conclusions are hence more *reliable* and *accurate*.

3. Large amounts of *information* can be assimilated quickly by health care providers, researchers, and policymakers.

4. Delay between research discoveries and *implementation* of effective diagnostic and therapeutic strategies is reduced.

5. Results of different studies can be formally compared to establish *generalizability* of findings and *consistency* (lack of heterogeneity) of results.

6. Reasons for *heterogeneity* (inconsistency of results across studies) can be identified and new hypotheses generated about particular subgroups.

7. Quantitative systematic reviews (meta-analyses) increase the precision of the overall result.

Given the clear benefits associated with their application, it is not surprising that systematic reviews are increasingly prevalent in the scientific literature. Moher, Tetzlaff, Tricco, Sampson, and Altman (2007) estimated that more than 2,500 systematic reviews are published annually in the biomedical area. Unfortunately, far fewer such reviews are published in areas relevant to psychosocial practice, including social work. Widespread adoption of systematic review methods has led to a growing concern with the quality of published reviews.

## Systematic Review Quality

Evaluations of systematic reviews and meta-analyses indicate that they are frequently of marginal quality (e.g., Shea, Moher, Graham, Pham, & Tugwell, 2002). Comparisons of Cochrane Collaboration and non-Cochrane systematic reviews vis-à-vis quality generally favor the former because they are more commonly and frequently updated and for other reasons, but shortcomings are noted across the plethora of published systematic reviews (e.g., Jadad, Cook, Jones, Klassen, Tugwell, Moher, & Moher, 1998). The seriousness of this situation cannot easily be overstated, given the growing reliance of consumers, health policymakers, and practitioners on systematic reviews for readily accessible and easily digested information regarding potential treatments and other practice interventions (Shea, et al., 2002).

A number of efforts are under way to enhance the quality of health research reporting generally and that of systematic reviews specifically. Altman, Simera, Hoey, Moher, & Schulz (2008) announced the funding of the Enhancing the Quality and Transparency of Health Research (EQUATOR) project by the United Kingdom's National Knowledge Service. EQUATOR will promote improved reporting of health-related research through a series of related projects, including an EQUATOR Web resource (www.equator-network.org), which includes a number of research reporting guidelines specific to select scientific publication types. Among the guidelines included in

EQUATOR are the Quality of Reporting of Meta-Analysis (QUOROM) standards (Moher, et al., 1999; 2000), soon to be known as the Preferred Reporting Items for Systematic Reviews and Meta-Analyses (PRISM) standards (Moher, et al., 2007). Although the QUOROM standards are the best established measures for the assessment of systematic review quality, a number of other such measures are available, including the Overview Quality Assessment Instrument (Oxman, Guyatt, Singer, Goldsmith, Hutchinson, Milner, & Streiner, 1991) and the Quality Assessment Checklist (Sacks, Berrier, Reitman, Ancona-Berk, & Chalmers, 1987). QUOROM standards require the inclusion of approximately 30 specific items of information in published systematic reviews. For example, methods sections of systematic reviews conforming with QUOROM guidelines must describe specific study inclusion and exclusion criteria; methods for assessing clinical heterogeneity; data abstraction protocols; principal measures of effect; strategies for combining results, including statistical testing and confidence intervals; handling of missing data; and means by which statistical heterogeneity was assessed. They must also provide a rationale for any *a priori* and subgroup analyses that are reported.

As many commentators recognize, merely promulgating best practices guidelines for the conduct and reporting of systematic reviews will not, in itself, lead to widespread changes in how systematic reviews are prepared. It is encouraging, then, to note that the editors of many leading journals are requiring adherence to the QUOROM standards as a prerequisite for publication of systematic reviews in their journals (e.g., Needleman, Grace, & Sloan, 2002; Robinson, et al., 2008). These and other recent developments pertinent to systematic reviews may portend their greater use in many practice areas.

## Emerging Issues

A number of issues have arisen coincident with efforts to promote more broad-based development and use of systematic reviews. Several studies have assessed the effects of excluding "gray literature" (i.e., previously unpublished trials) and publication bias on the validity of conclusions of systematic reviews, noting that the effect sizes of published trials tend to be larger than those of unpublished trials (Hopewell, McDonald, Clarke, & Egger, 2008; Preston, Ashby, & Smyth, 2004).

Theorists have also called for systematic reviews to incorporate the fruits of qualitative investigations (Barbour & Barbour, 2003; Thomas, Harden, Oakley, Oliver, Sutcliffe, Rees, Brunton, & Kavanagh, 2004) and described diverse approaches to integrating divergent data sources other than meta-analysis, including quantitative methods such as Bayesian analysis and qualitative approaches such as meta-synthesis (Dixon-Woods, Agarwal, Young, Laver, & Sutton, 2004).

Current concerns relevant to systematic reviews also include whether and how best to involve stakeholders in review development; preferred approaches to the incorporation of economic analyses in prepared reviews; how often and under which conditions systematic review updating should occur; which approaches to updating are most cost-effective (Moher, Tsertsvadze, Tricco, Eccles, Grimshaw, Sampson, & Barrowman, 2008); proper roles and expectations for authors of primary studies and journal editors in promoting enhanced systematic review quality; efforts to populate an international Web-based register of clinical trials in the social, behavioral, criminological, and educational areas to subserve systematic review development activities in psychosocial areas; and considerations of a future time when systematic reviews of meta-analyses and other meta-meta-analytic methods may be appropriate (e.g., Moriarty, Manthorpe, Wilcock, & Iliffe, 2007; Turner, Boruch, Petrosino, Lavenberg, de Moya, & Rothstein, 2003).

## Discussion

The past half century has witnessed the remarkable growth of practice-relevant scientific research, and there are clear indications that this impressive growth will continue or accelerate for the foreseeable future. In an effort to reduce the lamentably slow rate at which scientific progress is translated into practice innovations with real benefits for clients, a number of pedagogical approaches (e.g., evidence-based practice) and clinical products (e.g., practice guidelines) have been promoted as means to increase scientifically based practice. Systematic reviews hold perhaps the most promise in this respect and have proliferated widely across medicine and allied health professions over the past decade. Relatively few systematic reviews and meta-analyses have been published in social work; thus, we hope that the reports included in this volume will encourage social work professionals both to engage in the process of systematic review development and to use available systematic reviews in their professional practice efforts.

## References

Altman, D. G., Simera, I., Hoey, J., Moher, D., & Schulz, K. (2008). EQUATOR: Reporting guidelines for health research. *Lancet, 371,* 1149–1150.

Barbour, R. S., & Barbour, M. (2002). Evaluating and synthesizing qualitative research: The need to develop a distinctive approach. *Journal of Evaluation in Clinical Practice, 9,* 179–186.

Chan, K. S., Morton, S. C., & Shekelle, P. G. (2004). Systematic reviews for evidence-based management: How to find them and what to do with them. *The American Journal of Managed Care, 10,* 806–812.

Cochrane Collaboration (2008). Glossary of Cochrane Collaboration terms. Retrieved April 18, 2008 from http:www.cochrane.org/resources/glossary.htm.

Cohen, J. 1988. *Statistical power for the behavioral sciences.* (2nd ed.) Hillsdale, NJ: Lawrence Erlbaum Associates.

de Solla Price, D. (1963). *Little science, big science.* New York: Columbia University Press.

Dixon-Woods, M., Agarwal, S., Young, B., Jones, D., & Sutton, A. (2004). *Integrative approaches to qualitative and quantitative evidence.* London, UK: Health Development Agency.

Greenhalgh, T. (2006). *How to read a paper: The basics of evidence-based medicine* (3rd ed.). Oxford, UK: Blackwell, BMJ Books.

Hind, D., & Booth, A. (2007). Do health technology assessments comply with QUOROM diagram guidance? An empirical study. *BMC Medical Research Methodology, 7,* 1–9.

Hopewell, S., McDonald, S., Clarke, M., & Egger, M. (2008). Grey literature in meta-analyses of randomized trials of health care interventions. (Review). *The Cochrane Library, Issue 1.*

Howard, M. O., & Jenson, J. M. (1999a). Clinical practice guidelines: Should social work adopt them? *Research on Social Work Practice, 9,* 283–301.

Howard, M. O., & Jenson, J. M. (1999b). Barriers to development, utilization and evaluation of social work practice guidelines: Toward an action plan for social work. *Research on Social Work Practice, 9*(3), 347–364.

Howard, M. O., Allen-Meares, P. A., & Ruffolo, M. (2007). Teaching evidence-based practice: Strategic and pedagogical recommendations. *Research on Social Work Practice, 17*(5), 561–568.

Howard, M. O., McMillen, J. C., & Pollio, D. (2003). Teaching evidence-based practice: Toward a new paradigm for social work education. *Research on Social Work Practice, 13,* 234–259.

Jadad, A. R., Cook, D. J., Jones, A., Klassen, T. P., Tugwell, P., Moher, M., & Moher, D. (1998). Methodology and reports of systematic reviews and meta-analyses: A comparison of Cochrane reviews with articles published in paper-based journals. *Journal of the American Medical Association, 280,* 278–280.

Moher, D., Tetzlaff, J., Tricco, A. C., Sampson, M., Altman, D. G. (2007). Epidemiology and reporting characteristics of systematic reviews. *PLoS Med, 4*(3). Retrieved July 24, 2008, from http://medicine.plosjournals.org/perlserv/?request=get-document&doi=10.1371%2Fjournal.pmed.0040078&ct=1.

Moher, D., Tsertsvadze, A., Tricco, A. C., Eccles, M., Grimshaw, J., Sampson, M., & Barrowman, N. (2008). When and how to update systematic reviews (Review). *The Cochrane Library, Issue 1.*

Moher, D., Cook, D. J., Eastwood, S., Olkin, I., Rennie, D., & Stroup, D. F. (1999). Improving the quality of reports of meta-analyses of randomized controlled trials: The QUOROM statement: Quality of reporting of meta-analyses. *Lancet, 354,* 1896–1900.

Moriarty, J., Manthorpe, J., Wilcock, J., & Iliffe, S. (2007). Consulting with stakeholders: Using the expertise of researchers, professionals, carers, and older people in systematic reviews. *Dementia: The International Journal of Social Research and Practice, 6,* 449–452.

Needleman, I., Grace, M., & Sloan, P. (2002). QUOROM and systematic reviews. *British Dental Journal, 192,* 605.

Office of Portfolio Analysis and Strategic Initiatives, National Institutes of Health (2008). NIH Roadmap for Medical Research. Retrieved April 19, 2008, from http://nihroadmap.nih.gov/clinicalreserach/overview-translational.aasp.

Oxman, A. D., & Guyatt, G., Singer, J., Goldsmith, C. H., Hutchinson, B. G., Milner, R. A., & Streiner, D. L. (1991). Agreement among reviewers of review articles. *Journal of Clinical Epidemiology, 44*, 1271–1278.

Preston, C., Ashby, D., & Smyth, R. (2004). Adjusting for publication bias: Modeling the selection process. *Journal of Evaluation in Clinical Practice, 10*, 313–322.

Robinson, J. K., Dellavalle, R. P., Bigby, M., & Callen, J. P. (2008). Systematic reviews: Grading recommendations and evidence quality. *Archives of Dermatology, 144*, 97–99.

Sackett, D. L., Straus, S. E., Richardson, W. S., Rosenberg, W., & Haynes, R. B. (2000). *Evidence-based medicine: How to practice and teach EBM.* Philadelphia: Churchill-Livingstone.

Sacks, H., Berrier, J., Reitman, D., Ancona-Berk, V. A., & Chalmers, T. C. (1987). Meta-analysis of randomized controlled trials. *New England Journal of Medicine, 316*, 450–455.

Shea, B., Moher, D., Graham, I., Pham, B., & Tugwell, P. (2002). A comparison of the quality of Cochrane reviews and systematic reviews published in paper-based journals. *Evaluation & The Health Professions, 25*, 116–129.

Thomas, J., Harden, A., Oakley, A., Oliver, S., Sutcliffe, K., Rees, R., Brunton, G., & Kavanagh, J. (2004). Integrating qualitative research with trials in systematic reviews. *British Medical Journal, 328*, 1010–1012.

Turner, H., Boruch, R., Petrosino, A., Lavenberg, J., de Moya, D., & Rothstein, H. (2003). Populating an international web-based randomized trials register in the social, behavioral, criminological, and education sciences. *Annals of the American Academy of Political and Social Sciences, 589*, 203–223.

Wennberg, J. E., Fisher, E. S., Goodman, D. C., & Skinner, J. S. (2008). Tracking the care of patients with severe chronic illness. *The Dartmouth Atlas of Health Care, 2008.* Dartmouth, NH: The Dartmouth Institute for Health Policy & Clinical Practice, Center for Health Policy Research.

# PART I

# Children and Families

## *Overview and Key Questions*

The family is one of the primary institutions in society. Some of the major roles of the family include socialization, protection, and the provision of material resources. Although families function within a wider context that includes community and political and economic forces, there is little doubt that family influences provide an important avenue for facilitating successful development of children. Many family factors such as parenting style (e.g., warmth, involvement, monitoring), family size, conflict and disruption, and support have been widely studied. Many interventions targeting childhood problems have been developed that specifically address family processes. Much still needs to be learned about what specific family process mechanisms are best to target in order to produce effective results for children and families alike.

Here in Part I, Brad W. Lundahl, Janelle Nimer, and Bruce Parsons focus on synthesizing results of parent training programs designed to prevent child abuse (Chapter 1). Their meta-analysis is important due to the critical need to identify effective prevention-oriented solutions for child abuse. Attention deficit hyperactivity disorder (ADHD) is a condition that is very difficult for parents to manage. In Chapter 2, Jacqueline Corcoran and Patrick Dattalo use meta-analytic techniques to examine studies of parental involvement in treatment of ADHD. Next, in Chapter 3, Ashley M. Austin, Mark J. Macgowan, and Eric F. Wagner present findings from a systematic review of family-based interventions designed to induce change for adolescents who have exhibited substance-use problems. Finally, in Chapter 4, Patricia Ann Craven and Robert E. Lee systematically evaluate therapeutic interventions for foster care children.

As you read these selections, consider the following questions:

1. What social policy recommendations would you make regarding families, based on the results of the research syntheses presented in these chapters?

2. How can effective family-based treatments be implemented in systems of care?

3. How can social work practitioners who work with families incorporate the findings presented in these chapters?

# 1 Preventing Child Abuse

## A Meta-Analysis of
## Parent Training Programs

*Brad W. Lundahl, Janelle Nimer, and Bruce Parsons*

Decreasing the frequency of child abuse is a moral imperative with clear
benefits to children and society. Children who have been physically
abused or neglected are much more likely to experience emotional, social,
and behavioral problems that can undermine their immediate and long-term
well-being (Cicchetti & Rogosch, 1994; Hildyard & Wolfe, 2002).
Researchers and clinicians have long been aware of problems associated with
child abuse and have responded by developing many interventions aimed at
preventing abuse and helping victims heal. Despite such efforts, abuse occurs
at alarming rates and, generally speaking, affects families of all backgrounds.

Prevention of physical abuse or neglect, or its further perpetration, is clearly
preferable to attempting to ameliorate the sequelae of abuse. Programs
designed to prevent abuse and neglect are based on models that attempt to
explain why some individuals abuse. There is wide agreement that the perpetration of abuse results from complex interactions among characteristics of
parents, children, cultures, and environmental influences (Belsky, 1984;
DiLauro, 2004; Gaudin & Kurtz, 1985). Of the many influences associated
with abuse, characteristics of parents, such as their information processing ten-
dencies, are considered centrally important because they mediate the more dis-
tal influences, for example, child effects (Belsky, 1984). Thus, parents are often
the target of interventions designed to reduce the frequency of child abuse.

Of the many programs designed to reduce child abuse, we examined the
impact of parent training and parent education programs. Such programs

Originally published in *Research on Social Work Practice* 2006; 16; 251. DOI: 10.1177/
1049731505284391 The online version of this article can be found at: http://rsw.sagepub.com/
cgi/content/abstract/16/3/251

are widely relied on in instances where a parent is considered to be at risk of abusing a child (Altepeter & Walker, 1992; Dore & Lee, 1999; Sanders, Cann, & Markie-Dadds, 2003). Parent training programs operate on the premise that parents will be less likely to abuse if they improve and expand their child-rearing skills, rely less on coercive child management strategies, and modify attitudes linked to harsh parenting. In addition, many parent training programs include supplemental components designed to enhance parents' emotional well-being, such as anger and stress control, out of recognition that preventing child abuse is not simply accomplished through transmitting knowledge about child development and child management skills.

Although several meta-analyses have investigated the effectiveness of parent training for other populations (e.g., Cedar & Levant, 1990; Lundahl, Risser, & Lovejoy, 2006; Serketich & Dumas, 1996), no known meta-analysis has specifically examined the effectiveness of parent training programs targeting parents judged to be at risk for abusing a child. In a previous broad banded meta-analysis of programs aimed to decrease child maltreatment, five parent training programs, among other interventions, were identified (MacLeod & Nelson, 2000). The average effect size ($d = 0.36$) for these five studies was in the moderate range. This initial meta-analysis provided the first step in understanding the general impact of parent training programs designed to prevent abuse, yet many questions remain. Confidence in the average effect, for example, is undermined because it is derived from only five studies. Moreover, the low number of studies prevented analyses of possible moderators of this effect, such as characteristics of the treatment or participants. These weaknesses limit the utility of the finding in guiding future research and making informed clinical decisions. The primary contributions of meta-analytic reviews are that they can identify how stable an outcome is across a variety of studies and assess conditions under which the intervention is most beneficial. In the present meta-analysis, we sought to overcome the limitation of the study conducted by MacLeod and Nelson (2000) by formally assessing the stability of effectiveness indicators and investigating characteristics theoretically associated with outcomes.

# Method

## Study Selection

Six criteria were used to select studies for inclusion. Studies were included if they (a) reported on parent training programs designed to reduce or prevent physical child abuse, child neglect, or emotional abuse of a child (i.e., programs aimed at sexual abuse were excluded), (b) involved actual parent training rather than analogue procedures, (c) treated families in which parents or children were not developmentally or cognitively delayed, (d) reported pretreatment and posttreatment data on at least 5 participants, (e) were published in English in a peer-reviewed journal, and (f) provided sufficient data to compute an effect size.

Computer searches of articles listed between 1970 and August 2004 in the following databases were conducted: ERIC, PsycINFO, and Social Work Abstracts. To avoid a high rate of false rejections, the following broad search terms were used: *child abuse, child neglect,* and *parent training.* This strategy identified 186 studies that were screened based on the six inclusion criteria, leaving 23 studies for final analysis.

## Dependent Measures

Parent training programs are designed to reduce child maltreatment by changing parental factors associated with child abuse. For example, increasing parents' healthy child-related attitudes, child-rearing skills, and emotional well-being presumably lowers the risk of child abuse. The parent training programs we evaluated generally assessed some aspect of parents' personal functioning and/or indicators of child-rearing skills. We organized such parental outcomes into four outcome classes: emotional adjustment, child-rearing attitudes linked to abuse, child-rearing behaviors, and documented abuse. As can be expected, studies differed in what and how they measured behaviors within these outcome classes. Thus, these four classes served to organize varied responses.

### Parents' Emotional Adjustment

A range of emotions are associated with risk for child abuse (DiLauro, 2004; Dix, 1991). In our sample, negative affect was frequently assessed and included emotions such as anger, anxiety, depression, or stress. Other studies attempted to increase parents' feelings of competence or efficacy in child rearing. Although not always the case, studies frequently used standardized measures of emotions. A nonexhaustive list of commonly used measures includes the Parent Stress Index (Abidin, 1990), the Novaco Child Anger Scale (Novaco, 1978), the Parents Sense of Competence (Johnston & Mash, 1989), the Beck Depression Inventory (Beck, Steer, & Garbin, 1988), and the State-Trait Anxiety Inventory (Spielberger, Gorsuch, & Lushene, 1970).

### Child-Rearing Attitudes

Cognitions and attitudes empirically linked to child abuse were also frequently assessed in our sample of studies. For example, beliefs about the value of harsh parenting practices, expectations about children's developmental competencies, perceptions of children's needs, and beliefs about children's level of responsibility were often assessed. Some of the standardized measures included the Adult-Adolescent Parenting Inventory (Bavolek, 1984), the Child Abuse Potential Inventory (Milner, 1986), and the Parent Opinion Questionnaire (Azar & Rohrbeck, 1986).

### Child-Rearing Behaviors

Unlike parents' self-reported emotions and attitudes, child-rearing behaviors were often assessed directly as parents interacted with their children. Parent behaviors of interest included the use of aggression, praise, criticism, communication patterns, corporal discipline, or warmth. Examples of commonly used observational systems included the Nursing Child Assessment Teaching Scale (Barnard, 1978) and the Dyadic Parent-Child Interaction Coding System (Robinson & Eyberg, 1981).

### Documented Abuse

Very few studies examined documented abuse, probably because gathering such data is both difficult and fraught with ethical issues (Ammerman, 1998). The studies that did examine actual abuse looked at recidivism rates (Gershater-Molko, Lutzker, & Wesch, 2002) or state records indicating a need for further monitoring or care (Barth, Blythe, Schinke, & Schilling, 1983).

## Moderator (Independent) Variables

Characteristics of parent training programs and participant characteristics were coded to assess whether such factors influenced outcomes.

### Characteristics of Parent Training Programs

We coded seven features of parent training programs: (a) location of parent training, (b) use of a home visitor, (c) mode of parent training delivery, (d) length of treatment, (e) use of a control group, (f) theoretical underpinnings of the intervention, and (g) methodological rigor.

The location of parent training was most often in an office setting or home setting, though some programs delivered services in both settings. To supplement parent training, some programs employed a home visitor who would occasionally meet with the family in their home to reinforce principles taught in parent training, assess the environment, or provide other support. With regard to the mode in which parent training was delivered, studies typically delivered the intervention in either a group or an individual format, though some programs engaged parents in both modes. The amount of time parents spent in parent training varied across programs; we formed two groups, shorter and longer, by calculating a median split. Those in the shorter group received fewer than 12 sessions. To assess whether effect sizes were inflated in studies that did not employ a control group, the presence of a control group was coded.

Parent training programs are guided by a theoretical framework to explain the causes, supporting conditions, and ameliorative factors associated with disruptive child behaviors. Although we found diversity in the theoretical underpinnings and intervention strategies of parent training programs, most could be classified by whether the guiding philosophy was behavioral or non-behavioral intervention. Serketich and Dumas (1996) provide an excellent overview of the assumptions of behavioral programs. To be coded as a behavioral parent training program, we adopted their third assumption, which states, "Therapy seeks to establish a shift in social contingencies such that children's prosocial behaviors obtain positive parental reinforcement, and their aversive behaviors are consistently punished or ignored" (p. 172). If a study included additional interventions that supplemented the teaching of social contingencies, it was still coded as a behavioral program. If the intervention did not conform to this definition of behavioral parent training, it was coded as a nonbehavioral program. Nonbehavioral programs tended to emphasize communication styles and to promote an authoritative parenting style.

### Participant Characteristics

Four participant characteristics expected to influence parent training effectiveness were coded: (a) whether parents were identified as actual abusers or of a group at risk to abuse, (b) children's ages, (c) parents' ages, and (d) the percentage of single parents in the study.

Studies clearly reported whether participants were drawn completely from a pool of identified abusers or from a pool of individuals identified as at risk to abuse. Studies that targeted participants identified as having abused a child generally recruited parents who had been convicted of child abuse by a state agency. By contrast, studies that classified participants as being at high risk of abusing a child generally targeted samples known to face or possess factors associated with abuse, such as families referred to child protective service centers without confirmation of abuse or parents who scored high on the Child Abuse Potential Inventory (Milner, 1986, 2000). Of course, parents judged to be at high risk to abuse may have perpetrated equal or higher rates of child abuse than the identified abusers without coming to the attention of child protective services. However, moderator analyses were only conducted on groups identified to be abusers or at risk rather than mixed groups to investigate if differences emerged. Ages of children and parents were coded when available to assess whether parent training works better for children of a certain age group and whether younger parents benefit less than do older parents. Last, the percentage of participating single parents was recorded, and the median was used to categorize studies with a relatively high percentage or low percentage of single parents.

### Rigor

Methodological rigor of studies was coded on an 8-point scale. Each study received 1 point for including each of the following: a control group, blind coders of observational data, a treatment manual, assessment of fidelity to the manual, at least three descriptions of the sample (e.g., age of child, ethnicity, percentage of single parents), and standardized measures of dependent variables of interest. In cases where random assignment was not made but a control group was used, a study could receive 1 point if it reported statistical equivalence between the groups. Lastly, studies received 1 point by providing sufficient data to directly calculate an effect size, Cohen's *d*, from means and standard deviations rather than indirectly from other indicators (i.e., *t* test, *p* value).

## Reliability

All studies were independently coded by the first and second authors. Intraclass correlation alphas were computed for continuous variables, and Cohen's kappa (κ) was calculated for dichotomous variables. Among the four continuous moderator variables, alphas were all in excess of .90, with an average of .95. Interrater reliability for all effect sizes exceeded .95. For the dichotomous variables, κs were above .87 for all variables. Disagreements were resolved through consulting the studies and discussion.

## Effect Size Organization and Calculation

To organize our findings, four meta-analytic data files were constructed, one for each dependent variable class. Each study could potentially contribute an effect size to each file, though none did. Many studies provided multiple measures of a dependent variable within one or more outcome constructs. In this case, the average effect from the multiple measures was taken to limit an individual study's contribution to a given construct (Lipsey & Wilson, 2000). We also calculated effect sizes for follow-up data, though there were so few studies that separate files were not created.

We used Cohen's *d* as the measure of effect size (see Lipsey & Wilson, 2000). Cohen's *d* reflects the differences between the posttreatment means of the treatment group and the control group, divided by the pooled standard deviation, adjusted for sample size. Or, in the case of a study that did not use a control group, *d* reflects the difference between the pretreatment and posttreatment scores, divided by a pooled standard deviation. Thus, *d* represents differences in means expressed in standard deviation units. Effect size computations and summary analyses were done using a meta-analytic software program, DSTAT (Johnson, 1993). When possible, *d* was calculated directly from means and standard deviations because this is the most precise method. If this was not possible, *d* was calculated from *F* or *t* values; *p* values were used as a last resort. If studies indicated nonsignificant findings, we assigned an effect size of 0.00. Some indices of interest examined desirable behaviors, whereas others examined undesirable behaviors. An increase in desirable or a decrease in undesirable behaviors in the treatment group, relative to the control group, resulted in a positive $d$ statistic. A decrease in desirable or an increase in undesirable behaviors in the treatment group, relative to control group, resulted in a negative $d$ statistic. As a guide, effect sizes around 0.80 have been described as large in magnitude, whereas those around 0.50 are considered to be moderate, and those in the neighborhood of 0.20 are considered to be small though significant (Cohen, 1988).

Within each data file, we tested for and corrected extreme values as recommended by Lipsey and Wilson (2000). Correcting for extreme values in quantitative reviews is consistent with the purpose of meta-analyses, specifically to "arrive at a reasonable summary of the quantitative findings of a body of research studies" (p. 107). This was done by identifying $d$ values that were greater than 2 standard deviations from the mean of the sample of $d$ values obtained within a particular construct and time frame. These outlying values were assigned a value equivalent to 2 standard deviation units from the mean (i.e., Windorizing). Three $d$ values within the immediate impact of parent training and one follow-up study underwent this procedure.

## Meta-Analytic Strategy

In addition to reporting overall effects, which gives an impression of the average effect size across all studies regardless of variability in treatment or participant characteristics, meta-analysis methodology allows for tests of moderator effects. Moderator analyses provide a more specific assessment of the strength of effect based on predefined parameters (i.e., independent variables) expected to influence outcomes and are pursued when a set of studies is not homogeneous. Homogeneity was tested using the within-class goodness-of-fit statistic, or $Q_w$ (Johnson, 1993). A significant $Q_w$ statistic suggests heterogeneity within a set of studies and the need for moderator analyses. The presence of statistical differences between categories of parent training program characteristics was tested with the between-class goodness-of-fit statistic, or $Q_w$. A significant $Q_b$ statistic indicates the magnitude of the effect differs between categories of the moderator variable. Investigating the presence of moderators, then, occurs when there is significant heterogeneity and a sufficient number of studies to make meaningful comparisons.

The order in which moderator analyses are pursued is often theoretically driven. In this study, we first examined the effect of including a control group based on the assumption that studies that do not employ a control group are less rigorous and may present inflated outcomes relative to those that do. For the second set of moderator analyses, we simultaneously present the influence of several different characteristics of parent training programs because there is not a clear theoretical hierarchy of importance to justify a

**Table 1.1**     Characteristics of Parent Training Interventions

|  | Control Group | No Control Group |
|---|---|---|
| Home visitor |  |  |
|    Yes | 7 | 8 |
|    No | 1 | 9 |
| Location |  |  |
|    Office only | 2 | 8 |
|    Home only | 3 | 9 |
|    Mixture | 3 | — |
| Number of sessions |  |  |
|    Low | 3 | 6 |
|    High | 5 | 7 |
| Theoretical orientation |  |  |
|    Behavioral | 3 | 5 |
|    Nonbehavioral | 4 | 6 |
|    Mixture | — | 6 |
| Delivery mode |  |  |
|    Group | 2 | 9 |
|    Individual | 4 | 2 |
|    Mixture | 2 | 6 |
| Abuse status of targeted parents |  |  |
|    Identified abusers | 2 | 6 |
|    At risk to abuse | 6 | 4 |
|    Mixture | — | 7 |

NOTE: In cases where the sum of studies with in a moderator class does not equal 25, data were missing from a study.

step-down analysis. In cases where significant homogeneity remained after conducting between-category analyses of program characteristics, we examined whether the study targeted identified abusers or individuals deemed to be at risk to abuse as the third moderator. Moderator analyses for the long-term benefit of parent training were not conducted because of the limited number of studies investigating the durability of effects.

# Results

## Study Characteristics

Of the 23 studies that met the inclusion criteria, 17 used pre-post only designs, 4 studies compared one treatment group to one control group, and 2 studies compared two treatment groups to one control group, resulting in a total of 25 parent training treatment groups. The number of studies employing certain parent training program characteristics is summarized in Table 1.1, and specific information about moderators and effect sizes immediately following parent training for each study can be found in Table 1.2. As can be expected, studies differed in their focus, method of parent training, and choice of dependent variables. The result of such variability, which is unavoidable in meta-analytic reviews, is uneven distribution of program characteristics and dependent variables. This, in turn, limits the testing of some hypotheses because of a low number of studies to make comparisons.

## Effects Immediately After Treatment

Immediately following parent training, parents evidenced moderate, but significant, positive gains in all outcome constructs. As can be seen in Table 1.3, the average effect size for attitudes linked to abuse was 0.60 (number of studies, $k = 11$), 0.53 ($k = 11$) for emotional adjustment, 0.51 ($k = 13$) for child-rearing skills, and 0.45 for documented abuse ($k = 3$). None of these values, however, were homogeneous, as evidenced by significant $Q_w$ statistics.

The first moderator analysis tested the influence of including a control group, though moderator analyses could not be conducted within the documented abuse class because there were only three studies that examined this outcome (see Table 1.3). The only significant difference employing a control group made was in indicators of emotional adjustment. Parents in studies that did not employ a control group ($d = 0.62$, $k = 8$) reported significantly higher levels of emotional adjustment, compared with those where a control group was used ($d = 0.30$, $k = 5$), $Q_b = 4.96$, $p < .05$.

The average effect size for studies using a control group was homogeneous and therefore considered to be a stable indicator of the impact of treatment, but this was not the case for the eight studies not using a control group, which contained significant heterogeneity, $Q_w = 32.11$, $p < .01$, suggesting a need for further moderator analyses. For emotional adjustment, secondary analyses were not interpretable because for each of the moderators, at least one of the comparison groups involved two or fewer studies, thereby limiting confidence in the findings. However, when these eight studies were submitted to the tertiary moderator analysis, risk group status, a significant difference emerged, $Q_b = 18.42$, p < .01. Studies targeting identified abusers (d = 1.26, k = 4) showed greater emotional gains compared with parents considered to only be at risk of abusing a child (d = 0.45, k = 4). This moderator removed significant heterogeneity only for studies involving identified abusers; further analyses for the studies including at-risk participants, however, were not pursued because only four studies remained.

The use of a control group did not produce a significant difference in parents' child-rearing attitudes linked to abuse or their child-rearing behavior outcome classes, $Q_b$s = 0.32 and 0.02, $p$s < .50, respectively. Thus, second-level moderator analyses were conducted on the entire set of

**Table 1.2**     Study Characteristics and Effect Sizes

| | Study Characteristics | | Effect Sizes | | | |
|---|---|---|---|---|---|---|
| Author | n | Moderators | Child-Rearing Skills | Emotional Adjustment | Attitude to Abuse | Actual Abuse |
| Acton (1992) | 29/— | 2/3/1/2/1/3/1/2 | — | 1.10 | 0.85 | — |
| Barth (1983) | 9/9 | 1/1/3/1/1/3/1/2 | 0.53 | 1.62 | — | — |
| Barth (1988) | 24/26 | 1/2/2/1/2/1/2/2 | — | 0.17 | 0.22 | 0.78 |
| Bredehoft (1990) | 27/— | 2/3/1/2/1/2/2/1 | — | 1.61 | — | — |
| P. S. Cohen (2001) | 190/— | 2/3/3/1/3/2/—/2 | — | — | 1.03 | — |
| Duggan (1999)[a] | 373/270 | 1/2/2/1/2/3/2/2 | 0.10 | 0.09 | — | 0.06 |
| Fetsch (1999) | 75/— | 2/2/1/2/1/1/1/1 | 0.49 | 0.40 | — | — |
| Gershater-Molko (2002) | 41/— | 1/1/2/1/2/3/—/2 | — | — | — | 0.78 |
| Gershater-Molko (2003) | 33/— | 2/1/3/1/2/3/—/1 | 1.54 | — | — | — |
| Golub (1987) | 40/— | 2/3/1/2/1/2/2/2 | 0.35 | — | 0.27 | — |
| Huebner (2002) | 34/— | 2/2/1/2/1/2/2/1 | 0.31 | 0.74 | — | — |
| Irueste-Montes (1988) | 22/1 | 2/1/3/1/3/1/—/— | 0.68 | — | — | — |
| Irueste-Montes (1988) | 20/1 | 2/1/3/1/3/1/—/— | 0.70 | — | — | — |
| Iwaniec (1977) | 10/— | 2/1/3/1/2/3/1/1 | — | 0.87 | — | — |
| Iwaniec (1977) | 10/— | 2/1/3/1/3/3/1/1 | — | 1.78 | — | — |
| Moore (2001) | 26/— | 2/2/1/2/1/2/—/— | — | — | 0.65 | — |
| Peterson (2003)[a] | 42/57 | 1/2/3/1/3/3/2/2 | 0.60 | 0.24 | 0.78 | — |
| Schinke (1986)[a] | 11/09 | 1/2/1/2/1/1/1/1 | 1.31 | 1.23 | 0.95 | — |
| Taylor (1988)[a] | 14/14 | 1/2/1/2/1/1/1/1 | 1.23 | — | 1.03 | — |
| Thomasson (1981)[a] | 42/— | 2/2/1/2/1/3/—/2 | — | — | 0.82 | — |
| Thompson (1997) | 267/— | 2/2/1/2/1/1/1/1 | — | — | 0.18 | — |
| Weinman (1992)[a] | 56/— | 2/2/3/1/1/2/2/2 | — | 0.00 | 0.50 | — |
| Whipple (1996)[a] | 34/— | 2/2/3/2/3/3/1/— | — | 0.38 | — | — |
| Wolfe (1988)[a] | 16/14 | 1/2/1/1/3/1/2/1 | 0.51 | — | — | — |
| Wolfe (1981)[b] | 5/— | 2/1/3/1/3/1/—/2 | 1.54 | — | — | — |

NOTE: For study characteristics, n is the number of participants who completed parent training in the treatment or control groups. Because some studies did not provide precise data, ns were occasionally estimated. Information about eight moderators for each study are listed. The codes are as follows: (a) use of a control group, 1 = yes, 2 = no; (b) abuse status, 1 = identified abuser, 2 = atrisk, 3 = mixture; (c) location of intervention, 1 = office, 2 = inhome, 3 = mixture; (d) use of a home visitor, 1 = yes, 2 = no, 3 = mixture; (e) delivery type, 1 = group, 2 = individual, 3 = mixture; (f) theoretical background, 1 = behavioral, 2 = nonbehavioral, and 3 = mixture; (g) percentage of single mothers, 1 = less than 40%, 2 = more than 40%; and (h) number of sessions, 1 = fewer than 12,2 = more than 12 sessions. A dash indicates the primary study in question did not report such information.

a. Follow-up data were collected.

b. Wolfe (1981) employed a control group, yet the nature of the data required the effect size to be calculated as if it were a pre-post contrast.

studies within each of these two outcome constructs irrespective of whether a control group was used. Table 1.4 simultaneously presents the influence of five different parent training program characteristics for child-rearing attitudes and behaviors.

**Table 1.3**  Overall Findings Immediately Following Treatment

| Outcome Variable | d | k | Confidence Interval (95%) | $Q_w$ | $Q_b$ |
|---|---|---|---|---|---|
| Attitudes linked to abuse | .60 | 11 | .47/.73 | 25.00** | |
| No control group | .58 | 7 | .44/.72 | 20.85** | |
| Control group | .67 | 4 | .39/.96 | 3.83 | 0.32 |
| Emotional adjustment | .53 | 13 | .40/.65 | 47.51** | |
| No control group | .62 | 8 | .47/.77 | 32.11** | |
| Control group | .30 | 5 | .07/.54 | 10.43 | 4.96* |
| Child-rearing behaviors | .51 | 13 | .38/.64 | 27.35** | |
| No control group | .52 | 7 | .36/.68 | 17.37* | |
| Control group | .50 | 6 | .27/.74 | 9.96 | 0.02 |
| Documented abuse | .45 | 3 | .19/.72 | 6.99* | |
| No control group | — | — | —/— | — | |
| Control group | .45 | 3 | .19/.72 | 6.99* | — |

*$p < .05$. **$p < .01$.

**Table 1.4**  Moderators Associated With Immediate Effects

| | Outcome Construct | | | | | |
|---|---|---|---|---|---|---|
| | Attitudes Linked to Abuse | | | Child-Rearing Behavior | | |
| Moderator | d | k | $Q_w$ | d | k | $Q_w$ |
| Home visitor | | | | | | |
| Yes | .76* | 5 | 9.03 | .64*** | 9 | 19.90* |
| No | .46* | 6 | 10.66 | .40*** | 4 | 4.23 |
| Location | | | | | | |
| Office only | .46** | 6 | 10.66 | .41** | 5 | 4.29 |
| Home only | .22 | 1 | — | .10 | 1 | — |
| Mixture | .82** | 4 | 4.98 | .85** | 7 | 9.38 |
| Number of sessions | | | | | | |
| Low | .33* | 3 | 5.85 | .57 | 6 | 20.34* |
| High | .70* | 7 | 13.01 | .38 | 5 | 4.66 |
| Theoretical orientation | | | | | | |
| Behavioral | .24** | 3 | 2.46 | .61*** | 6 | 3.49 |
| Nonbehavioral | .69 | 4 | 9.57* | .32*** | 2 | 0.02 |
| Mixture | .80 | 3 | 0.03 | .58 | 4 | 16.78* |
| Delivery | | | | | | |
| Group | .46** | 7 | 10.69 | .41 | 5 | 4.28 |
| Individual | .49*** | 2 | 2.68 | .67 | 3 | 18.84* |
| Mixture | .94*** | 2 | 0.92 | .64 | 5 | 0.95 |

NOTE: $d$ is effect size; $k$ is number of studies.

*$p < .05$. **$p < .01$. ***$p < .10$.

Two of the five moderator variables were consistently related to variation in the child-rearing attitudes and child-rearing behavior constructs: the presence of a home visitor and location of delivery. Studies using a home visitor produced significantly more change in attitudes, $Q_b = 5.31$, $p < .05$, and a trend in child-rearing behaviors, $Q_b = 3.23$, $p < .10$. Also, delivering parent training through a mixture of both office and home settings was significantly better than office only delivery in changing attitudes and behaviors, $Q_b s = 7.45$ and $8.85$, $ps < .01$, respectively. Two moderator variables significantly influenced changes in child-rearing attitudes but not child-rearing behaviors. Specifically, studies using a higher number of parent training sessions changed attitudes more than those with fewer sessions, $Q_b = 6.12$, $p < .05$. Also, studies that delivered parent training through group and individual modes changed attitudes more than those that relied on individual only or group only parent training, $Q_b = 2.97$, $p < .10$, and $Q_b = 10.48$, $p < .01$, respectively. The remaining moderator, theoretical orientation, showed inconsistent results across the two outcome constructs. Programs that involved either a nonbehavioral or a mixture of nonbehavioral and behavioral components changed child-rearing attitudes significantly more than did those that relied on behavioral only programs, $Q_b s = 8.37$ and $9.71$, $ps < .01$, respectively. By contrast, behavioral parent training programs tended to change child-rearing practices more than nonbehavioral programs, $Q_b = 3.36$, $p < .10$. abusers ($d = 0.93$, $k = 5$) changed child-rearing behaviors more than did those targeting at-risk individuals ($d = 0.45$, $k = 4$), $Q_b = 5.94$, $p < .05$. This analysis reduced significant heterogeneity in each case.

## Participant Characteristics

Our ability to test the relationship between participant characteristics and parent training effectiveness was limited because few studies provided the information needed to assess this relationship and because characteristics of parent training programs accounted for most of the variance in outcomes. To provide an impression of how participant characteristics were related to outcomes, correlational analyses were conducted with awareness that such analyses are based on assumptions of the general linear model that do not apply to meta-analyses (Lipsey & Wilson, 2000). Thus, the following results can provide only an impression. For each relationship, the number of studies (i.e., $k$) and the $r$ value with the corresponding $p$ value are provided in parentheses. Correlations with documented abuse could not be conducted because only two studies provided sufficient information. Parents' age was correlated with the three outcomes in the following manner: Of the studies that provided sufficient information on parents' age and child-rearing behavior ($k = 7$, $r = .25$, $p = .58$), emotional adjustment ($k = 8$, $r = .63$, $p = .09$), and child-rearing attitudes toward abuse ($k = 7$, $r = .00$, $p = .99$), the average correlation was $r = .30$. Children's age was correlated with the three outcomes in the following manner: child-rearing behavior ($k = 7$, $r = .55$, $p = .20$), emotional adjustment ($k = 4$, $r = .92$, $p = .09$), and attitudes toward abuse ($k = 5$, $r = -.37$, $p = .54$). The average correlation between children's age and parents' child-rearing behavior ($k = 7$), emotional adjustment ($k = 4$), and child-rearing attitudes ($k = 5$) was $r = .37$. Last, the percentage of single parents in a study was correlated with the three outcomes in the following manner: child-rearing behavior ($k = 9$, $r = -.51$, $p = .16$), emotional adjustment ($k = 13$, $r = -.43$, $p = .15$), and attitudes toward abuse ($k = 8$, $r = -.29$, $p = .48$). Correlations between participant characteristics and documented abuse were not meaningful as there were only three studies in this group.

## Follow-Up Effects

None of the studies examined the long-term impact of parent training in reducing actual abuse; five studies assessed the long-term effect on child-rearing behaviors, and six studies examined child-rearing attitudes and parents' emotional adjustment. Encouraging results were found for the durability of changes in child-rearing attitudes, $d = 0.65$. More tempered results were found for the durability of changes in emotional adjustment and child-rearing behaviors, $ds = 0.28$ and $0.32$, respectively. Tests of homogeneity suggested that the only unstable group of studies involved those examining parents' emotional adjustment, $Q_W = 17.21$, $p < .01$.

## Rigor

Correlational analyses were also run between rigor ratings and three outcomes immediately following treatment: child-rearing behaviors ($k = 13$, $r = -.35$, $p = .24$), emotional adjustment ($k = 13$, $r = -.52$, $p = .09$), documented abuse ($k = 3$, $r = -.90$, $p = .28$), and attitudes toward abuse ($k = 11$, $r = .16$, $p = .63$). The average of these three correlations was in the low negative range, $r = -.24$. Although the interpretation of such analyses is open to debate, there is concern that a negative relationship between study rigor and outcome may mean that the real impact of parent training is somewhat overestimated.

## Fail-Safe *n*

As in other research designs, confidence in the results of a meta-analysis is influenced by the potential of sampling bias. Publication bias, the tendency for studies presenting statistically significant results to be published more often than those presenting less significant results, is frequently cited as problematic for meta-analytic reviews because the results may be inflated when the so-called fugitive literature is not actively sought and secured (see Begg, 1994; Greenhouse & Iyengar, 1994). One method for assessing the stability of meta-analytic results is to calculate the fail-safe $n$ statistic proposed by Rosenthal and adapted by Orwin (see Lipsey & Wilson, 2000). This statistic estimates the number of unpublished studies with an effect size of 0.00 needed to reduce an overall obtained effect size to a certain level.

We calculated the fail-safe $n$ for results within each outcome class presented in Table 1.3. We were interested in knowing how many potential unpublished studies would be needed to reduce the overall effect size to .20, which is considered to be a small effect. For the parental attitudes, emotional adjustment, and child-rearing behavior outcome classes, the fail-safe $n$s were 22, 21, and 20, respectively. Thus, there would need to be almost twice as many unpublished parent training studies targeting the risk to abuse a child to move the findings of our study from a moderate effect to a small effect in these domains. For the documented abuse outcome, the fail-safe $n$ was only 3.75, suggesting the results from the articles we sampled are not robust.

# Discussion and Applications to Research and Practice

When a child is at risk for being physically abused or neglected by a parent, a variety of intervention options are available. At the extreme end, children may be temporarily removed from their parents' custody with the possibility of termination of parental rights. In other cases, children may remain with their parent, provided certain conditions are met. Although not universal, some form of parent education or training is likely to be considered as an option for preventing child abuse (Sanders et al., 2003). Thus, it behooves the treatment community to understand the conditions under which parent training can be most effective in reducing the risk of future abuse or neglect. The results of this study help elucidate such conditions and provide general support for parent training with this population.

Our results indicate parent training is effective in reducing the risk that a parent will physically abuse, verbally abuse, or neglect a child. Immediately following parent training, parents reported significant and meaningful changes in attitudes and emotions linked to abuse and observed child-rearing behaviors and substantiated abuse.

Parents completing parent training likely developed more child friendly beliefs and attitudes, which may have resulted in an increased willingness to understand and accept children's developmental capabilities, emotions, or intentions. In addition, parent training programs changed parents' beliefs that corporal punishment is an effective long-term socialization strategy. Even a minor shift in parents' attitudes toward their children or child rearing is expected to influence parents' perceptions of child behavior, interpretations of such behavior, related emotions, and, ultimately, parenting choices (Milner, 2000). Thus, the introduction of authoritative information on child development, child socialization strategies, and/or the role of children and parents seems to be an effective means of changing attitudes linked to abuse. Parents' emotional well-being was also strengthened through parent training. Targeted emotions often included some form of negative affect, such as anger or stress, or parents' confidence in the parenting role. Compared to child-rearing attitudes and beliefs, which, theoretically speaking, are directly linked to parental behavior, emotional well-being acts as a moderating factor. Said differently, certain emotional states, such as negative affect, have been shown to increase the likelihood of abuse. Many of the programs in our study had designed complementary interventions that aimed to promote parents' emotional well-being guided by the premise that increased emotional stability will promote parents' willingness or ability to apply adaptive child management practices rather than rely on power assertion or abuse. Although evidence that undesirable beliefs and emotions can be modified is certainly encouraging, the ultimate test is whether parents change how they interact with their children. Unfortunately, only three of the studies in this sample examined the effectiveness of parent training on identified abusers. Of these, two showed strong effects (Barth, Hacking, & Ash, 1988; Gershater-Molko, Lutzker, & Wesch, 2002), whereas the other showed almost no benefit (Duggan et al., 1999). Parent training was moderately effective in promoting desirable and reducing undesirable child-rearing behaviors. That is, parents who completed parent training were more likely to rely on noncoercive strategies, such as expression of warmth and democratic reasoning, when interacting with their children and were less likely to rely on coercive strategies, such as the use of physical force or threats.

The abovementioned general findings offer generic support for providing parent training to parents considered to be at risk to abuse a child. Yet, such generic findings do little to guide the design of future parent training programs. Examining the influence of certain predefined characteristics of the programs across studies can, however, yield information that can guide the design of future parent training programs.

From the studies in our sample, there is evidence to suggest that home visitors make a substantial positive impact on parents. How home visitors promote more desirable changes in parents' attitudes and child-rearing behaviors is not clear; theory suggests visitors can provide parents with emotional support and help them individualize information learned in parent training (DiLauro, 2004). In a similar manner, programs that provided interventions through a mixture of office and home settings were more successful than were those offering parent training in only one setting. Involving a home visitor and delivering parent training through a combination of settings may seem cost and labor intensive; however, others have shown that this may not be the case as creative use of in-home and on-site services may actually reduce overhead expenses associated with an office. More important than considerations of convenience and economics, of course, is delivering the best possible intervention when the welfare of children is at stake. Although our results revealed a clear advantage for the use of a home visitor and delivering parent training in a mixture of home and office settings, they were mixed with regard to other variables. As predicted, a higher number of sessions was associated with greater changes in attitudes linked to abuse but not with child-rearing behaviors. Although speculative given that this mixed finding is inconsistent with predictions, it may be that parents' attitudes and beliefs are more difficult to change compared to child-rearing practices. Parents may readily adopt the child management skills taught in parent training because teaching them is straightforward and parents may welcome new strategies that promise to make parenting more desirable. By contrast, changing long-held attitudes and beliefs is difficult and may require more time (Bargh & Chartrand, 1999). A degree of support for this hypothesis may come from the results involving the mode of delivering parent training. Parental attitudes changed more through a mixture of group and individual delivery than either mode alone. It may be that individual and group delivery modes have unique mechanisms through which attitudes and beliefs are challenged. Individual delivery may pinpoint specific beliefs and trace their history or challenge them through commonly used therapy methods such as cognitive behavioral therapy. Group delivery, on the other hand, may challenge parents' long-held attitudes through the power of group consent on what is "correct" (e.g., children's developmental capacities) or because willingness to change attitudes may be higher if provided by a peer parent compared to a professional.

Parent training programs that relied solely on group delivery were less effective in changing child-rearing practices compared to those that involved some amount of individual delivery, though this finding was not statistically significant in the present study but has been documented elsewhere (Lundahl et al., in press; Wekerle & Wolfe, 1993). The combined results from the present study, where individual delivery is related to improved outcomes, and this same finding in a previous meta-analysis (Lundahl et al., 2006) suggest parent training programs should include an individual component. Individual delivery may provide a means to conduct a more thorough functional assessment of the steps leading to abuse, whereas group delivery offers general strategies that may not apply to certain parent-child dyads. In addition, it may be that the one-on-one time available in individual delivery provides a healthy relationship in which parents can begin to examine and change their beliefs and behaviors.

Theoretical orientation of parent training programs also influenced the degree to which parents modified child-rearing practices and attitudes. Programs that included behavioral principles showed more positive changes in parental behavior compared to studies that did not. Physical child abuse occurs more often in families where a child is difficult to manage because parents begin to rely on harsh, domineering child management practices. Behavioral programs teach specific child management skills that may explain the relative success over nonbehavioral programs in changing parents' child-rearing practices. By contrast, nonbehavioral programs were more successful in changing attitudes linked to abuse possibly because such programs stress the importance of adopting democratic or authoritative parenting philosophies. Thus, different outcomes reflected the unique principles and assumptions emphasized by behavioral and nonbehavioral programs. Nonbehavioral programs shifted parental attitudes more than did behavioral programs, and behavioral programs taught child management skills better than did nonbehavioral programs. Rather than choosing between a behavioral or nonbehavioral program, elements of both should be considered. Indeed, our data suggest that mixing these two theoretical orientations does not result in undesired outcomes and tends to promote positive outcomes.

Investigating the influence of parental characteristics on parent training outcomes could not be thoroughly pursued because of the small number of studies. From the correlational analyses we conducted, there was some indication that older parents and older children enjoyed stronger outcomes and that single parent status undermined outcomes. These findings are, however, exploratory and require replication.

Understanding the long-term success of parent training programs in reducing abuse is important; unfortunately, few studies examined this question. Of those that did, desirable changes in parents' child-rearing attitudes were stable, whereas positive changes in emotional well-being and child-rearing behaviors slipped toward pretreatment levels by approximately 40%. Despite such slippage, all changes at follow-up were meaningful and support the use of parent training.

Just as no two families are the same, parent training programs differ in their approach to preventing child abuse and neglect. This meta-analysis sought to understand how such differences influence outcomes. Compared to the only other known quantitative analysis of parent training programs targeting child abuse, our results offer a more optimistic outlook (MacLeod & Nelson, 2000). Our findings complement and extend the work of MacLeod and Nelson (2000) by being based on more studies and conducting moderator analyses.

Our findings revealed that success is more likely in programs that include a home visitor or offer treatment in a combination of office and home settings. Also, including an individualized component, as opposed to group-only treatment, increases the likelihood of success. The guiding assumptions of behavioral and nonbehavioral programs offer different strengths in helping to reduce the risk of child abuse, and our results indicate that combining elements of both can capitalize on the unique strengths of both approaches.

Child abuse results from complex, transactional interactions among characteristics of children, parents, culture, and the immediate environment. Of the myriad influences on parental behavior, parent training attempts to strengthen parents' abilities to raise their children without violence. To assist in this goal, all parent training programs teach child-rearing skills or provide information designed to modify unhealthy child-rearing beliefs. Many programs also include components designed to enhance parents' emotional well-being that appear to be successful. Training improved multiple aspects of parents' lives, including their attitudes, emotions, child-rearing behaviors, and actual abuse. Such changes lower the risk that these parents will abuse in the future. Thus, we argue parent training should continue to be considered as one of many approaches to reducing the risk of child abuse and neglect.

Several limitations need to be considered when evaluating the results of this study. For example, this sample of studies was based on groups identified as abusers and those deemed to be at risk to abuse. Although both groups responded positively to parent training, only a minority of studies examined families known to have actually abused a child. Unfortunately, determining whether these groups would respond differently based on intervention characteristics could not be determined. Also, we note that the studies in this sample defined abuse broadly with little or no differentiation between physical abuse, neglect, or verbal abuse. This lack of specificity may undermine decision making at the individual case level. Also, study rigor may have influenced effect size estimates. Rigor ratings were negatively associated with effect sizes, which suggests that the obtained values may be slightly inflated. That is, the lower a study's rigor, the higher its reported effect size. It may be that high-quality studies provide a more realistic, discouraging picture of the influence of parent training. Last, our sampling strategy relied on a computer search and eliminated unpublished studies. Although computer searching technologies have improved greatly, there is a chance that we missed some studies. The high fail-safe $n$ values for three of the four outcome classes suggest our results are robust against the possibility of missing studies. By contrast, the low fail-safe $n$ value for the documented abuse outcome class suggests this value could easily be overturned, and confidence in this value is tentative.

# References

References marked with an asterisk indicate studies included in the meta-analysis.

Abidin, R. R. (1990). *Parent Stress Index* (3rd ed.). Charlottesville, VA: Pediatric Psychology Press.

*Acton, R. G., & During, S. M. (1992). Preliminary results of aggression management training for aggressive parents. *Journal of Interpersonal Violence, 7,* 410–417.

Altepeter, T. S., & Walker, C. E. (1992). Prevention of physical abuse of children through parent training. In D. J. Willis & E. W. Holden (Eds.), *Prevention of child maltreatment: Developmental and ecological perspectives* (pp. 226–248). Oxford, UK: Wiley.

Ammerman, R. T. (1998). Methodological issues in child maltreatment research. In J. R. Lutzker (Ed.), *Handbook of child abuse research and treatment* (pp. 117–132). New York: Plenum.

Azar, S. T., & Rohrbeck, C. A. (1986). Child abuse and unrealistic expectations: Further validation of the Parent Opinion Questionnaire. *Journal of Consulting and Clinical Psychology, 54,* 867–868.

Bargh, J. A., & Chartrand, T. L. (1999). The unbearable automaticity of being. *American Psychologist, 54,* 462–479.

Barnard, K. E. (1978). *Nursing child assessment teaching scale.* Seattle: University of Washington.

*Barth, R. P., Blythe, B. J., Schinke, S. P., & Schilling, R. F. (1983). Self-control training with maltreating parents. *Child Welfare, 62,* 313–324.

*Barth, R. P., Hacking, S., & Ash, J. R. (1988). Preventing child abuse: An experimental evaluation of the Parent Enrichment Project. *Journal of Primary Prevention, 8,* 201–217.

Bavolek, S. J. (1984). *Adult-adolescent parenting inventory.* Eau Claire, WI: Family Development Resources.

Beck, A. T., Steer, R. A., & Garbin, M. G. (1988). Psychometric properties of the Beck Depression Inventory: 25 years of evaluation. *Clinical Psychology Review, 8,* 77–100.

Begg, C. B. (1994). Publication bias. In H. Cooper & L. V. Hedges (Eds.), *The handbook of research synthesis* (pp. 399–410). New York: Russell Sage.

Belsky, J. (1984). The determinants of parenting: A process model. *Child Development, 55,* 83–96.

*Bredehoft, D. J. (1990). An evaluation study of the self-esteem: A family affair program with high-risk abusive parents. *Transactional Analysis Journal, 20,* 111–117.

Cedar, B., & Levant, R. F. (1990). A meta-analysis of the effects of Parent Effectiveness Training. *The American Journal of Family Therapy, 18,* 373–384.

Cicchetti, D., & Rogosch, F. A. (1994). The toll of child maltreatment on the developing child: Insights from developmental psychopathology. *Child & Adolescent Psychiatric Clinics of North America, 34,* 759–776.

Cohen, J. (1988). *Statistical power analysis for the behavioral sciences* (2nd ed.). Hillsdale, NJ: Lawrence Erlbaum.

*Cohen, P. S. (2001). Effectiveness of a parent education intervention for at-risk families. *Journal of the Society of Pediatric Nurses, 6,* 73–82.

DiLauro, M. D. (2004). Psychosocial factors associated with types of child maltreatment. *Child Welfare, 83,* 69–99.

Dix, T. (1991). The affective organization of parenting: Adaptive and maladaptive processes. *Psychological Bulletin, 100,* 3–25.

Dore, M. M., & Lee, J. M. (1999). The role of parent training with abusive and neglectful parents. *Family Relations, 48,* 313–325.

*Duggan, A. K., McFarlane, E. C., Windham, A. M., Rohde, C. A., Salkever, D. S., Fuddy, L., et al. (1999). Evaluation of Hawaii's Healthy Start Program. *Future of Children, 9,* 66–90.

*Fetsch, R. J., Schultz, C. J., & Wahler, J. J. (1999). A preliminary evaluation of the Colorado Rethink Parenting and Anger Management Program. *Child Abuse & Neglect, 23,* 353–360.

Gaudin, J. M., & Kurtz, D. P. (1985). Parenting skills training for child abusers. *Journal of Group Psychotherapy, Psychodrama, & Sociometry, 38,* 35–54.

*Gershater-Molko, R. M., Lutzker, J. R., & Wesch, D. (2002). Using recidivism data to evaluate Project SafeCare: Teaching bonding, safety, and health care skills to parents. *Child Maltreatment, 7,* 277–285.

*Gershater-Molko, R. M., Lutzker, J. R., & Wesch, D. (2003). Project SafeCare: Improving health, safety, and parenting skills in families reported for, and at-risk for child maltreatment. *Journal of Family Violence, 18,* 377–386.

*Golub, J. S., Espinosa, M., Damon, L., & Card, J. (1987). A videotape parent education program for abusive parents. *Child Abuse & Neglect, 11,* 255–265.

Greenhouse, J. B., & Iyengar, S. (1994). Sensitivity analysis and diagnostics. In H. Cooper & L. V. Hedges (Eds.), *The handbook of research synthesis* (pp. 383–398). New York: Russell Sage.

Hildyard, K. L., & Wolfe, D. A. (2002). Child neglect: Developmental issues and outcomes. *Child Abuse & Neglect, 26,* 679–695.

*Huebner, C. E. (2002). Evaluation of a clinic-based parent education program to reduce the risk of infant and toddler maltreatment. *Public Health Nursing, 19,* 377–389.

*Irueste-Montes, A. M., & Montes, F. (1988). Court-ordered vs. voluntary treatment of abusive and neglectful parents. *Child Abuse & Neglect, 12,* 33–39.

*Iwaniec, D. (1997). Evaluating parent training for emotionally abusive and neglectful parents: Comparing individual versus individual and group intervention. *Research on Social Work Practice, 7,* 329–349.

Johnson, B. T. (1993). DSTAT 1.10: *Software for the meta-analytic review of literatures* [Computer software and manual]. Hillsdale, NJ: Lawrence Erlbaum.

Johnston, C., & Mash, E. J. (1989). A measure of parenting satisfaction and efficacy. *Journal of Clinical Child Psychology, 18,* 167–175.

Lipsey, M. W., & Wilson, D. B. (2000). *Practical meta-analysis.* London, UK: Sage Publications.

Lundahl, B. W., Risser, H. J., & Lovejoy, M. C. (2006). A meta-analysis of parent training: Moderators and follow-up effects. *Clinical Psychology Review, 26,* 86–104.

MacLeod, J., & Nelson, G. (2000). Programs for the promotion of family wellness and the prevention of child maltreatment: A meta-analytic review. *Child Abuse & Neglect, 24,* 1127–1149.

Milner, J. S. (1986). *The Child Abuse Potential Inventory: Manual.* Webster, NC: Psytec.

Milner, J. S. (2000). Social information processing and child physical abuse: Theory and research. In D. J. Hansen (Ed.), *Nebraska Symposium on Motivation: Motivation and child maltreatment* (Vol. 45, pp. 39–84). Lincoln: University of Nebraska Press.

*Moore, J., & Finkelstein, N. (2001). Parenting services for families affected by substance abuse. *Child Welfare, 80,* 221–238.

Novaco, R. W. (1978). Anger and coping with stress: Cognitive behavioral interventions. In J. P. Foreyt & D. P. Rathjen (Eds.), *Cognitive-behavioral therapy: Research and applications* (pp. 82–97). New York: Plenum.

*Peterson, L., Tremblay, G., Ewigman, B., & Saldana, L. (2003). Multilevel selected primary prevention of child maltreatment. *Journal of Consulting and Clinical Psychology, 71,* 601–612.

Robinson, E. A., & Eyberg, S. M. (1981). The dyadic parent-child interaction coding system: Standardization and validation. *Journal of Consulting and Clinical Psychology, 49,* 245–250.

Sanders, M. R., Cann, W., & Markie-Dadds, C. (2003). Why a universal population-level approach to the prevention of child abuse is essential. *Child Abuse Review,* *12,* 145–154.

*Schinke, S. P., Schilling, R. F., Kirkham, M. A., Gilchrist, L. D., Barth, R. P., & Blythe, B. J. (1986). Stress management skills for parents. *Journal of Child and Adolescent Psychotherapy, 3,* 293–298.

Serketich, W. J., & Dumas, J. E. (1996). The effectiveness of behavioral parent training to modify antisocial behavior in children: A meta-analysis. *Behavior Therapy, 27,* 171–186.

Spielberger, C. D., Gorsuch, R. L., & Lushene, R. E. (1970). *Manual for the State-Trait Anxiety Inventory.* Palo Alto, CA: Consulting Psychology Press.

*Taylor, D. K., & Beauchamp, C. (1988). Hospital-based primary prevention strategy in child abuse: A multi-level needs addressment. *Child Abuse & Neglect, 12,* 343–354.

*Thomasson, E., Minor, S., McCord, D., Berkovitz, T., Cassle, G., & Milner, J. S. (1981). Evaluation of a family live education program for rural high-risk families: A research note. *Journal of Community Psychology, 9,* 246–249.

*Thompson, R. W., Ruma, P. R., Brewster, A. L., Besetsney, L. K., & Burke, R. V. (1997). Evaluation of an Air Force child physical abuse prevention project using the Reliable Change Index. *Journal of Child and Family Studies, 6,* 421–434.

*Weinman, M. L., Schreiber, N. B., & Robinson, M. (1992). Adolescent mothers: Were there any gains in a parent education program? *Family Community Health, 15,* 1–10.

Wekerle, C., & Wolfe, D. A. (1993). Prevention of child physical abuse and neglect: Promising new directions. *Clinical Psychology Review, 13,* 501–540.

*Whipple, E. E., & Wilson, S. R. (1996). Evaluation of a parent education and support program for families at risk of physical child abuse. *Families in Society: The Journal of Contemporary Human Services, 77,* 227–239.

*Wolfe, D. A., Edwards, B., Manion, I., & Koverola, C. (1988). Early intervention for parents at risk of child abuse and neglect: A preliminary investigation. *Journal of Consulting and Clinical Psychology, 56,* 40–47.

*Wolfe, D. A., Sandler, J., & Kaufman, K. (1981). A competency-based parent training program for child abusers. *Journal of Consulting and Clinical Psychology, 49,* 633–640.

# 2

# Parent Involvement in Treatment for ADHD

## A Meta-Analysis of the Published Studies

*Jacqueline Corcoran and Patrick Dattalo*

Rates of attention-deficit/hyperactivity disorder (ADHD) in school-age children have been estimated at 3% to 7% (American Psychiatric Association [APA], 2000). Given its prevalence, effective treatments are critical. Several reviews and meta-analyses have been conducted on the ADHD treatment literature. Medication has been the source of many meta-analyses and reviews throughout the years (e.g., Connor, Glatt, Lopez, Jackson, & Melloni, 2002; Faraone & Biederman, 2002; McClellan & Werry, 2003; Schachter, Pham, & King, 2001; and for a comprehensive review, see Jadad et al., 1999). DuPaul and Eckert (1997) and Robinson, Smith, Miller, and Brownell (1999) focused their meta-analyses on school-based interventions.

Baer and Nietzel (1991) conducted a meta-analysis of cognitive-behavioral treatments for their impact on child impulsivity, which was not restricted to those diagnosed with ADHD but also included those with conduct disorders, behavior disorders, and learning disabilities. Interventions were found to be successful in reducing impulsivity with an overall mean effect of .77. Klassen, Miller, and Raina (1999) published a systematic review of different management strategies for ADHD, although they did not conduct a meta-analysis. They found that psychosocial interventions were not effective according to parent and teacher reports on reducing ADHD symptoms when compared to control and/or comparison groups. Although they did not study the range of outcomes beyond ADHD symptoms, they concluded that behavioral therapies

Originally published in *Research on Social Work Practice* 2006; 16; 561. DOI: 10.1177/1049731506289127 The online version of this article can be found at:http://rsw.sagepub.com/cgi/content/abstract/16/6/561

may be most helpful, not for ADHD symptoms, but for associated features, including peer problems and academic difficulties.

Pelham, Wheeler, and Chronis (1998) reviewed psychosocial treatments for ADHD according to the American Psychological Association Task Force criteria. They found that behavioral parent training met the criteria for a "probably efficacious treatment." Because the review focused on ADHD, it is assumed that ADHD symptoms were the outcome, although this was not made explicit in their review.

Purdie, Hattie, and Carroll (2002) conducted a meta-analysis of a range of interventions for ADHD that were published in the 1990s, including parent training (a total of four studies). They found the effect of parent training on hyperactivity, impulsivity, and attention to be low, although the impact on what they defined as "general cognition," comprising academic performance, memory, and IQ, was much more robust (.53 effect size).

As the current research study was drawing to a close, Bjornstad and Montgomery (2005) published in the *Cochrane Collaboration* a systematic review of cojoint family therapy for children with ADHD examining the outcomes of ADHD symptoms, disruptive behaviors, and school performance. Following *Cochrane Collaboration* standards, only randomized controlled trials were included and only two studies met the rigorous criteria established. The authors acknowledged that it was difficult to draw conclusions based on the limited number of studies.

This review of the literature indicates that a comprehensive meta-analysis of all interventions involving parents—not necessarily family therapy or parent training and not limited to a certain time frame—is still an area of knowledge that needs to be synthesized. Parent involvement in intervention for child ADHD has been recommended (Barkley, 1998). First, parents of children with ADHD often experience distress and frustration with their children's behavior. Interventions targeting the interactions between the child and caregivers may be essential to prevent coercive parent-child interactions, which are linked to the development of conduct problems (Patterson, 1982; Patterson, DeBaryshe, & Ramsey, 1989). Second, the problems children with ADHD have with self-regulation of behavior appear to rest more with performance rather than knowledge (Barkley, 1998). Therefore, self-regulation may have to be achieved through the efforts of people in the child's environment, such as parents. Given recommendations that parents be involved in treatment of ADHD in children, a meta-analysis was undertaken to determine the effect of parent involvement on child symptoms.

# Research Objectives

The primary objective of the current meta-analysis was to determine the magnitude and the direction of the difference of the effect size (ES) of the various outcomes associated with parent-involved treatment of ADHD. Outcomes were divided into 21 categories according to the particular informant involved—child, parent, or teacher reports of the following: (a) child internalizing problems, (b) externalizing problems, (c) ADHD, (d) social competence, (e) family functioning, (f) self-control, and (g) academic performance.

A secondary objective was to determine whether certain moderators influenced the ESs for these 21 categories of psychosocial outcomes. The current study examined five moderator categories, including the particular outcome involved, treatment characteristics, design type, key design characteristics, and sample demographics.

# Method

## Search Criteria and Procedures

To identify studies Medline/PubMed, PsycINFO, CINAHL, Social Work Research Abstracts, and Infotrac were searched from 1970 to 2003 with the following terms: *attention-deficit/hyperactivity disorder* (ADHD), *attention deficit disorder* (ADD), *hyperkinesis,* and *treatment, therapy, intervention.* Studies had to be written in English and published in refereed journals or books. Excluded were single-subject designs, case studies, and unpublished studies and interventions that were reported only at meetings or conferences. Reference sections of articles were also reviewed.

Inclusion criteria for studies involved the following:

• The study focused on a parent-involved psychosocial treatment for ADHD in a child (ranging in age from 0 to 18). As long as parents were a part of treatment, studies were included; it was not necessary, for instance, for parents and children to be seen cojointly. Another necessary criterion was that the treatment had to be clearly defined. For instance, studies in which participants received different types of psychosocial interventions, including family treatment, depending on their need (e.g., Satterfield, Cantwell, & Satterfield, 1979) were excluded. In addition, studies that only focused on treatment of the child were excluded.

• Children had to be screened for ADHD either by meeting diagnostic criteria or by scoring in the clinical range on established measures of ADHD symptoms.

• Although it was not necessary for designs to be randomized controlled, a comparison or control group design was a criterion.

• Of vital importance was that the current study contained sufficient statistical information to calculate a Cohen's *d* ES.

Hundreds of studies were screened for inclusion into the current study. Ultimately, the search yielded 16 published articles, which were published from 1980 to 2003.

## Coding of Studies

All studies were coded independently by the first author and a trained doctoral student in social work, and disagreements were discussed to consensus. Table 2.1 presents the detailed coding system used to describe

**Table 2.1**        Coding Scheme

| Category | Values |
|---|---|
| Outcome(s) | Child, parent or teacher reporting on the child's: |
| | Internalizing problems |
| | Externalizing problems |
| | Attention-deficit/hyperactivity disorder symptoms |
| | Social competence |
| | Family functioning |
| | Self-control |
| | Academic and/or learning disorders |
| Treatment characteristics | Modality: |
| | Individual |
| | Group |
| | Family |
| | Day treatment |
| | Other medication vs. no medication |
| | Number of sessions |
| Design type | Random treatment and control |
| | Random treatment and comparison |
| | Nonrandom treatment and control |
| | Nonrandom treatment and comparison |
| | One group pre- and posttest |
| | One group posttest only |
| Key design characteristics | Overall quality |
| | Sample size |
| | Type of experiment, control, and comparison groups |
| | Number of respondents in experiment, control, and comparison groups |
| | Follow-up |
| Sample demographics | Race |
| | Gender |
| | Socioeconomic status |
| | Household composition |

each study, which comprised treatment aspects, demographic characteristics of the sample, the research design, and the overall quality of the study. Quality was dependent on the following criteria: type of design with more points assigned for randomization and control conditions, the presence of follow-up, if the sample size was at least 30 participants per condition, and if there was the necessary information provided to code all the demographic information. Quality scores ranged from 2 to 6.

## Data Analysis

Separate ESs were calculated in each study for each outcome measure. The 21 outcomes categories were—according to the child, parent, or teacher report—(a) child-internalizing problems, (b) externalizing conduct problems, (c) ADHD, (d) social competence, (e) family functioning, (f) self-control, and (g) academic and/or learning disorders. Each type of outcome measure was also used as a potential moderator of ES.

The ES index reported is Cohen's $d$, defined as the difference between the means for experimental group and control and/or comparison group outcomes divided by the pooled within-group standard deviation (Cohen, 1988). Cohen's $d$ is a widely accepted measure to use when reporting group differences on outcomes research because it is readily interpretable, referring to differences between the groups in standard deviation units. An ES of .20 indicates two-tenths of a standard deviation unit difference between experimental participants and control comparison participants. Usually, an ES of .20 is described as small, .50 as medium, and .80 as high.

Effects were given a positive sign to indicate hypothesized change, and a negative sign to indicate change in the direction that is opposite to what was hypothesized. Therefore, positive values for $d$ signify greater treatment success by experimental group participants than by control and/or comparison group participants.

Meta-analytic procedures assume independence of the individual hypothesis tests included in the meta-analysis. One source of nonindependence is the use of multiple hypothesis tests located within a single study (Strube & Hartman, 1983). Use of nonindependent results in a meta-analysis tends to inflate the Type I error rate for an analysis and should be avoided (Wolf, 1986). Various strategies have been used to avoid the problem of nonindependence of effects for the same study. Mullen (1989) suggested that it is preferable to collapse the different results into one global hypothesis test than to consider separate hypothesis tests derived from the same study as if they were independent. Therefore, an overall ES (Cohen's $d$) was calculated for studies with multiple outcome measures; that is, within each study, ESs were averaged so that each study yielded no more than one ES. No study or participant was counted more than once. The rationale for averaging measures into a single index was supported because a nonsignificant difference in ESs was obtained when individual measures were compared.

The resulting single ES for each study was inserted into Borenstein and Rothstein's (2001) Comprehensive Meta-Analysis (CMA) program. Following Hedges and Olkin (1985), ESs were adjusted to correct for bias to small sample size. Weighting procedures were used to combine ESs from different studies to give greater weight to studies whose effects were based on larger sample size. This weighting procedure is important because ESs that are based on a small sample (fewer than 30 respondents) in the original study yield overestimates of true effects and, consequently, must be reduced accordingly. CMA also computed Confidence Intervals (CIs) around the point estimate of an ES. Because all studies proposed directional hypotheses predicting that the intervention would have a positive effect, the 95% CIs (with one-tailed alphas of .05) are presented.

Fixed-effects models are appropriate when meta-analysts wish to make inferences only about the ES parameters in the reviewed studies or about an identical set (Hedges & Vevea, 1998). In fixed-effects models, the study effects estimate the population effect with the only error being from the random sampling of participants within the studies. In contrast, random-effects models are appropriate when analysts wish to make inferences that generalize beyond the specific set of reviewed studies to a broader population. These models assume that variability between ESs emerges from participant-level sampling error and from random differences between studies that are associated with variations in experimental procedures and settings. It has been argued that random-effects models more adequately mirror the heterogeneity in behavioral studies and use noninflated alpha levels when the requirement of homogeneity has not been met (Hunter & Schmidt, 2000; Mullen, 1989; Rosenthal, 1984). The CMA program computed fixed- and random-effect model parameters, and fixed-effects and random-effects models are reported.

To account for the "file drawer problem," the tendency for studies supporting the null hypothesis to remain unpublished (Rosenthal, 1984), a fail-safe $N$ was calculated. The fail-safe $N$ is the number of undiscovered or unpublished studies with ESs of zero that would raise the overall ES above a critical value of $p = .05$ (Wolf, 1986).

Heterogeneity was analyzed by computing Corcoran's $Q$, which has an approximate chi-square distribution with $p - 1$ degrees of freedom, where $p$ is the number of categories within each moderator variables (Hedges & Olkin, 1985). Because the $Q$ statistic for all reviewed studies combined indicated heterogeneity, a moderator variable analysis of ESs was conducted to identify sources of heterogeneity.

There is support for using meta-regression analysis to explore sources of heterogeneity if, as it is in this analysis, an initial overall $Q$ test for heterogeneity is significant (Berkley, Hoaglin, Mosteller, & Colditz, 1995; Hardy & Thompson, 1998, Harwell, 1997; Higgins & Thompson, 2002). The term *meta-regression* is used to indicate the use of study-level covariates, as distinct from regression analyses that are possible when individual data on outcomes and covariates are available. The $Q$ tests for general "overdispersion" of trial results and does not address whether heterogeneity relates to particular covariates. Furthermore, $Q$ only examines main effects and does not control for the explanatory effects of other possible moderators.

The appropriate regression model is a random-effect model where the weight for each trial should be equal to the inverse of the sum of the within-study variance and the residual between-studies variance. This random-effects model is consistent with the aforementioned model used to calculate an overall ES, $d$ (Hunter & Schmidt, 2000; Mullen, 1989; Rosenthal, 1984; Thompson & Higgins, 2002). Stata's METAREG module (Steichen & Harbord, 2005) was used to perform a random-effects regression analysis for the following reasons:

1. In addition to testing whether ESs are related to the values of a single moderator, multiple regression can be used to perform more complicated analyses.

2. The multiple regression model provides a control for the total number of tests, and consequently, reduces the likelihood of a Type I error.

The procedure for multiple regression was as follows:

1. Dummy variables were created for categorical moderators.

2. The set of moderator variables was tested for multi-collinearity.

3. The regression was performed using the reciprocal of the variance as the case weight.

4. The parameter estimates were tested and interpreted. Recall that tests on the individual parameters examine the unique contributions of each predictor.

5. An overall test of the model was performed.

# Results

## Sample

Table 2.2 presents study characteristics, and Table 2.3 describes ES findings. The sample consisted of 16 studies, of which nine were published in the 1990s, four were published in the 1980s, and three in the 2000s. In terms of designs, 13 utilized random treatment and control and/or comparison groups, and 3 employed nonrandom treatment and control and/or comparison groups. Eleven of the 16 studies reported more than one measure of treatment outcome. Sample sizes ranged from 16 to 443 with a mean of 91 and a median of 67. Most treatments focused on school-age children and relied on group services. The average length of treatment was 32 sessions, although most interventions were categorized as between either 1 and 8 or 9 to 16 sessions in length.

## Effect Size (Objective #1)

Separate ESs were calculated in each study for each outcome measure, and then each type of outcome measure was used as a potential moderator of ES. Table 2.4 summarizes the aggregate mean ESs by type of outcome measure for the 16 studies. Overall, the child's academic performance had the largest expected overall ES (8.2041), followed by the child's family functioning (.6730), and internalizing (.6349). Teacher-reported outcomes had the largest ESs (.7473), and child-reported outcomes had the smallest ESs (.1094). The overall $Q$ statistic was significant, and within-group homogeneity was not found for any group of ESs based on the type of outcome measure. Therefore, the mean ES for each study was used to calculate an aggregate fixed effect and random ES for the 16 studies.

Based on the value of Q, the requirement of homogeneity was not met ($Q = 331.49$, $df = 15$, $p < .01$), and consequently, the 16 individual ESs were combined within the context of random-effects model ($d = .4208$, $SE = .2727$, $p = .0617$, 95% CI = $-.1145$ to $.9662$). (For reference, the result of the fixed-effect model is $d = .1876$, $SE = .553$, $p < .001$, 95% CI = $.0791$ to $.2961$.) The fail-safe $N$ for this analysis is 264. In other words, 264 studies averaging null results (mean $z$-Score of zero) must be "crammed into file drawers" before one could conclude that the overall $d$ was due to sampling bias in the studies summarized in the current meta-analysis (Rosenthal, 1984).

## Moderator Variable Analysis (Objective #2)

A test for heterogeneity examines the null hypothesis that all studies are evaluating the same effect. Cochran's Q, the usual test statistic, is computed by summing the squared deviations of each study's estimate from the overall meta-analytic estimate, weighting each study's contribution in the same manner as in the meta-analysis.

$P$ values are obtained by comparing the statistic with a chi-square distribution with $k - 1$ degrees of freedom, where $k$ is the number of studies (Egger, Davey, Schneider, & Minder, 1997).

Because the $Q$ statistic indicated heterogeneity for all reviewed studies combined, an analysis was conducted to identify characteristics that could have influenced study outcomes. A random-effects meta-regression analysis was conducted to explore sources of heterogeneity. The Stata module

**Table 2.2**    Description of Design and Treatment

| Study Name and Year | Design of Study | Modality | Number of Sessions |
|---|---|---|---|
| Anastopoulos, Shelton, DuPaul, & Guevremont (1993) | Randomization to treatment and control groups with follow-up | Individual with parents | 9 |
| Barkley, Guevremont, Anastopoulos, & Fletcher (1992) | Randomization to treatment and comparison groups with follow-up | Parent-only for behavioral, family for problem-solving/ communication & structural family therapy | 8 to 10 |
| Barkley, Shelton, Crosswait, & Moorehouse (1996) | Randomization to treatment, comparison, and control groups | Group | 10 |
| Barkley, Edwards, Laneri, Fletcher, & Metevia (2001) | Nonrandomization to treatment and comparison groups with follow-up | Family for problem-solving and/or communication skills, parent-only for behavioral | 18 |
| Bloomquist, August, & Ostrander (1991) | Nonrandomization to reatment, comparison, and control groups with follow-up | Group | 7 |
| Bor, Sanders, & Markie-Dadds (2000) | Randomization to treatment, comparison, and control groups | Individual with parents | 10 to 12 |
| Firestone, Crowe, Goodman, & McGrath (1986) | Randomization to treatment, comparison, and medication groups with follow-up | Group | 9 |
| Gittelman et al. (1980) | Randomization to treatment and comparison groups | Individual with parents | 8 |
| Horn, Ialongo, Greenberg, Packard, & Smith-Winberry (1990) | Randomization to treatment and comparison groups with follow-up | Group | 12 |
| Horn, Ialongo, Popovich, & Peradotto (1987) | Randomization to treatment and comparison groups with follow-up | Group | 8 |
| Klein & Abikoff (1997) | Randomization to treatment, comparison, and medication groups | Individual parents | 8 |
| McNeil, Eyberg, Eisenstadt, Newcomb, & Funderburk (1991) | Nonrandomization to treatment and control group | Parent-Child | 14 |

*(Continued)*

**Table 2.2** (Continued)

| Study Name and Year | Design of Study | Modality | Number of Sessions |
|---|---|---|---|
| Multi-Modal Treatment Study of Children With Attention-Deficit/ Hyperactivity Disorder Group (1999) | Randomization to treatment, comparison, and community control groups with follow-up | Group | 360 |
| Pfiffner & McBurnett (1997) | Randomization to treatment, comparison, and control group with follow-up | Group | 8 |
| Strayhorn & Weidman (1989) | Randomization to treatment and control group | Parent-Child | 7 |
| Tutty, Gephart, & Wurzbacher (2003) | Randomization to treatment and comparison groups with follow-up | Group | 8 |

METAREG was used for random-effects meta-regression. The regression model consisted of the following potential moderator variables: (a) treatment characteristics (modality, medication vs. no medication, number of treatment sessions), (b) design type (e.g., randomly assigned treatment and control groups), (c) key design characteristics (overall quality, sample size, type of experimental treatment, control and comparison groups, number of respondents in the aforementioned groups, whether there was a follow-up measure of the outcome), and (d) sample characteristics (race, gender, socioeconomic status, household composition).

A bivariate correlation analysis was performed to identify potential sources of collinearity. Significant collinearity was suggested among the aforementioned moderator variables, and redundant variables were removed from the model. When variables appeared to be collinear, the final model includes variables that had relatively large part correlation (Pearson's $r$) with ES but had moderate-to-low zero-order correlations with other moderator variables ($r = .50$).

Figure 2.1 presents a funnel plot of ES by research design (for reference), mean age of children in the sample, and household composition. Table 2.5 summarizes the final meta-regression model. The $I^2$ for the model is .8120. The $I^2$ statistic indicates the percentage variability due to between-study (or interstudy) variability as opposed to intrastudy variability (Higgins, Thompson, Deeks, & Altman, 2003). Values of $I^2$ equal to 25%, 50%, and 75% representing low, moderate, and high heterogeneity, respectively. The tau-squared value is .2694. Tau squared is a measure of the residual variance after controlling for the effects of the moderator variables in the

**Table 2.3**     Study Effect Sizes According to Outcome (Sorted by Largest d First)

| Study | Quality Rating | Outcomes | d | n | SE |
|---|---|---|---|---|---|
| Barkley, Guevremont, Anastopoulos, & Fletcher (1992) | 4 | Ext | 1.7670 | 61 | .1811 |
| Bloomquist, August, & Ostrander (1991) | 2 | Int | 1.7210 | 52 | .2108 |
| Pfiffner & McBurnett (1997) | 4 | Ext, ADHD | 1.3650 | 27 | .2136 |
| Klein & Abikoff (1997) | 2 | ADHD | .9370 | 86 | .2695 |
| Firestone, Crowe, Goodman, & McGrath (1986) | 3 | Ext, ADHD | .8780 | 73 | .3542 |
| Barkley, Shelton, Crosswait, & Moorehouse (1996) | 5 | Ext, ADHD, Soc Comp | .8420 | 205 | .2850 |
| Horn, Ialongo, Greenberg, Packard, & Smith-Winberry (1990) | 3 | ADHD | .7670 | 42 | .2033 |
| Horn, Ialongo, Popovich, & Peradotto (1987) | 2 | Int, Ext, ADHD | .1980 | 24 | .5000 |
| Strayhorn & Weidman (1989) | 4 | Ext, ADHD | .1840 | 90 | .3273 |
| Anastopoulos, Shelton, DuPaul, & Guevremont (1993) | 4 | Int, Ext, Fam Func | −.1010 | 34 | .2727 |
| Multi-Modal Treatment Study of Children With Attention-Deficit/ Hyperactivity Disorder Cooperative Group (1999) | 5 | Ext, Int, ADHD, Fam Func, and Self-Cont | .0030 | 579 | .2500 |
| McNeil, Eyberg, Eisenstadt, Newcomb, & Funderburk (1991) | 1 | Ext, ADHD | −.0070 | 30 | .3200 |
| Barkley, Edwards, Laneri, Fletcher, & Metevia (2001) | 3 | Int, Ext, Soc Comp | −.0110 | 92 | .4082 |
| Gittelman et al. (1980) | 2 | Int, Ext, ADHD, Soc Comp, Aca Probs | −.3930 | 61 | .2281 |
| Bor, Sanders, & Markie-Dadds (2002) | 4 | Ext, ADHD | −.5060 | 63 | .2327 |
| Tutty, Gephart, & Wurzbacher (2003) | 5 | Int, Ext, ADHD, Fam Func, Self-Cont | −.9650 | 100 | .1013 |

NOTE: Ext = externalizing; Int = internalizing and/or conduct disorders; ADHD = Attention-deficit/hyperactivity disorder; Soc Comp = social competence; Fam Func = family functioning; Aca Probs = academic problems; Self-Cont = Self-control

model. The estimated between-study variance has been reduced from .8120 to .2694.

The model consisted of three variables: household composition (unstandardized beta coefficient = 1.7373, $p$ = .044), age (coefficient = .02057,

**Table 2.4**     Outcome Category and Mean Effect Size (Sorted by Largest d First)

| Outcome Type | Perspective Parent | Perspective Child | Teacher Perspective | Totals— Outcomes | Mean Effect Size —Outcome Type |
|---|---|---|---|---|---|
| Child academic performance | (0) | 43% (3) | (0) | 6% (3) | 8.2041 |
| Child self-control | (0) | 14% (1) | (0) | 2% (1) | −1.6683 |
| Child family functioning | 6% (2) | (0) | (0) | 4% (2) | .6730 |
| Child internalizing | 15%(5) | % (0) | 27% (3) | 16% (8) | .6349 |
| Child attention-deficit/ hyperactivity disorder | 30% (10) | 14% (1) | 45% (5) | 31% (16) | .3970 |
| Child externalizing | 36% (12) | 14% (1) | 27% (3) | 31% (16) | .3611 |
| Child social competence | 12% (4) | 14% (1) | (0) | 10% (5) | .0710 |
| Totals—perspective | (33) | (7) | (11) | (51) | |
| Mean effect size—perspective | .4327 | .1094 | .7473 | | .4208[a] |

a. Random effects model, $SE$ = .2727, $p$ = .0617, 95% Confidence Interval = −.1145 −.9662

| Research Design | Mean Age Sample | Household Comp | Effect | −1.00   0.00   1.00   2.00 |
|---|---|---|---|---|
| random comparison | 10 | two parent | 1.759 | |
| nonrandom control | 4 | single parent | 1.706 | |
| random control | 15 | two parent | 1.154 | |
| random comparison | 8 | - | 0.925 | |
| random comparison | 8 | two parent | 0.856 | |
| random control | - | two parent | 0.829 | |
| random comparison | 9 | two parent | 0.761 | |
| random comparison | 5 | - | 0.187 | |
| random control | 9 | single parent | 0.181 | |
| random comparison | 7 | single parent | 0.003 | |
| random control | 3 | two parent | −0.009 | |
| random comparison | 9 | two parent | −0.011 | |
| nonrandom control | 14 | single parent | −0.100 | |
| posttest only | 8 | single parent | −0.389 | |
| random control | 3 | single parent | −0.501 | |
| random control | 8 | two parent | −0.963 | |
| Fixed   Combined (16) | | | 0.1876 | |
| Random   Combined (16) | | | 0.4208 | |
| − = missing | | | | Reverse              Expected |

**Figure 2.1**     Funnel Chart Effect Sizes by Moderator Variables

$p$ = .049), and socioeconomic status (coefficient = 1.3876, $p$ = .100). Therefore, household composition is the strongest, statistically significant predictor of ES, followed by age; that is, larger ESs are predicted for two- versus single-parent households, and for older versus younger child clients. Although not statistically significant, the model also suggests that larger ESs are predicted for children from families with higher socioeconomic levels.

# Discussion and Applications to Research and Practice

A number of limitations characterize the current study. Ultimately, only a small number of studies—16—were eligible for inclusion in the meta-analysis. In general, studies are "not meta-analysis ready" because ESs are not routinely reported. Furthermore, researchers are sometimes unable to compute ESs because the information necessary for these calculations is omitted. Important methodological data are the research design and the specific sample size for each statistical test, the type of sampling, data collection techniques, and psychometric information for all instruments and outcome measures. In reporting data analyses, it is crucial to identify not only each statistical test but also equally important the exact value of the test with its corresponding $p$ value, whether it is one-tailed or two-tailed, as well as the degrees of freedom for each test. Incomplete reporting of research data and statistics may preclude the inclusion of a study in a meta-analysis. This could erroneously bias meta-analysis results, and its generalizability, as studies with missing data may have insignificant findings or be of poor quality. Another problem with studies was missing data for the moderator variables. Examples of pertinent population characteristics include (a) gender, (b) age, (c) ethnicity and/or race, (d) household composition, and (e) socioeconomic status.

Studies were restricted to cognitive-behavioral theoretical orientations, not because of inclusion criteria but by the type of treatment outcome studies that had been published. However, cognitive-behavioral treatment may not be routinely practiced in clinical practice outside university and laboratory research settings (Weisz, Weiss, & Donnenberg, 1992). Therefore, the published studies may not be representative of clinical practice and the way parents are involved in these settings.

With these caveats in mind, the overall results of the current meta-analysis should be considered suggestive of low-to-moderate intervention success moderated by household composition and age. Studies constituting the current meta-analysis focused on a wide range of outcomes, including academic performance, child self-control, family functioning, internalizing symptoms, externalizing symptoms, ADHD symptoms, and social competence. It is not surprising to note that ADHD and externalizing symptoms were represented in all the studies included in the current meta-analysis. The overall ESs were .3970 and .3611 for ADHD and externalizing, respectively, which are considered in the low range of ESs. However, this ES for ADHD symptoms was higher than the meta-analysis of parent training studies in the 1990s (Purdie et al., 2002).

At the same time, the ESs demonstrating the impact of medication on these symptom constellations have been higher. ESs for medication on ADHD symptoms have been reported for Ritalin as .82 (Swanson, McBurnett, Christian, & Wigal, 1995), for the tricyclics as .44 (Fletcher & Connor, as cited in Connor, Fletcher, & Swanson, 1999), and for Clonidine as .58 (Connor et al., 2002). Similarly, Connor et al. (2002) found that the stimulants have a positive effect on aggression, with ESs of .84 for overt and .69 for covert aggression.

Child internalizing was the next largest outcome category with one-half of the studies reporting on internalizing symptoms. It has been established that mood disorders are comorbid with ADHD in about 15%–75% of cases (Pliszka, 2000). The current meta-analysis indicates that parent-involved treatment may have a moderate effect on internalizing symptoms. The other outcomes had only a few studies represented within each category; thus, findings in these areas must be considered tentative. In general, the findings reflect Klassen et al.'s (1999) suggestion that the behavioral therapies may be effective, not so much for ADHD symptoms as for associated features, such as academic problems. Indeed, the current meta-analysis indicated that academic problems were strongly affected by parent-involved treatment, an interesting finding because generalizability of treatments across settings has been a problem. However, it must be noted that this finding is based on a total of only three studies. Purdie et al. (2002) also demonstrated the moderately strong effect of parent training on "general cognition," although this result stemmed from only two studies.

Of interest is that child social competence, a purported thrust of many of the parent-involved treatments in the current meta-analysis, were barely affected by intervention. Child social functioning, a problem often noted for children with ADHD, does not appear to respond well to parent treatment.

In examining ESs by informant, the largest ESs were found for teacher reports. This finding was similar to Purdie et al.'s (2002) meta-analysis involving various interventions for ADHD. The validity of teacher reports in the diagnosis of ADHD have further been demonstrated through long-term follow-up (Mannuzza, Klein, & Moulton, 2002). The low ES for child report might call into question the advisability of spending time having children fill out measures. It has been found that children tend to underreport externalizing symptoms (Loeber, Green, Lahey, Frick, & McBurnett, 2002). In general, studies tended to rely on a multitude of outcome measures completed by various informants and would do well to streamline their measurement process with outcomes that are theoretically linked to the intervention and that are well established in the field.

The regression of the moderator variables indicated that household composition and age were low-to-moderate predictors of overall ES. None of

**Table 2.5**   Moderator Variable Analysis

| Model | β | SE | t |
|---|---|---|---|
| Household composition: 1 = two-parent, 0 = single-parent | 1.7373 | .5978 | 2.91* |
| Socioeconomic level: 1 = low, 2 = middle, 0 = upper | −1.3876 | .6504 | −2.13 |
| Age | .2057 | .0834 | 2.47* |
| Constant | −1.2861 | 1.3661 | −.94 |

*$p < .05$.

the other moderator variables tested, including medication versus no medication, modality, number of treatment sessions, study quality, design type, race, and gender, were significant predictors. In the current study, the older the child the more benefits conferred by parent-involved psychosocial intervention. This result is contradictory to findings in the conduct disorder literature that younger children tend to do better than do older children when their parents receive parent training (Fonagy & Kurtz, 2002). Estimates indicate that oppositional defiant disorder and/or conduct disorder are present in 40% to 70% of children with ADHD (Newcorn & Halperin, 2000).

A consistent finding in the literature has been that living in a single-parent home is a risk factor for treatment outcome (Fonagy & Kurtz, 2002). The current meta-analysis, too, indicated that children in single-parent homes did not do as well in parent-involved treatment as those who were from two-parent homes.

## Conclusion

Overall, ADHD and externalizing symptoms are not affected by family involvement beyond a low-to-moderate effect, although child-internalizing symptoms are moderately affected. Other outcomes must be viewed as tentative because of the few studies in each category; however, academic performance and family functioning may be domains that family involvement positively benefits.

## References

American Psychiatric Association. (2000). *Diagnostic and statistical manual of mental disorders* (4th ed., text rev.). Washington, DC: Author.

Anastopoulos, A. D., Shelton, T. L., DuPaul, G., & Guevremont, D. C. (1993). Parent training for attention-deficit hyperactivity disorder: Its impact on parent functioning. *Journal of Abnormal Child Psychology, 21,* 581–596.

Baer, R. A., & Nietzel, M. T. (1991). Cognitive and behavioral treatment of impulsivity in children: A meta-analytic review of the outcome literature. *Journal of Clinical Psychology, 20,* 400–412.

Barkley, R. (1998). Attention-deficit/hyperactivity disorder. In E. J. Mash & R. A. Barkley (Eds.), *Treatment of childhood disorders* (pp. 55–110). New York: Guilford.

Barkley, R., Edwards, G., Laneri, M., Fletcher, K., & Metevia, L. (2001). The efficacy of problem-solving communication training alone, behavior management training alone, and their combination for parent-adolescent conflict in teenagers with ADHD and ODD. *Journal of Consulting and Clinical Psychology, 69,* 926–941.

Barkley, R., Shelton, T., Crosswait, C., & Moorehouse, M. (1996). Preliminary findings of an early intervention program with aggressive hyperactive children. In C. F. Ferris & T. Grisso (Eds.), *Understanding aggressive behavior in children. Annals of the New York Academy of Sciences* (Vol. 794, pp. 277–289). New York: New York Academy of Sciences.

Barkley, R. A., Guevremont, D. C., Anastopoulos, A. D., & Fletcher, K. E. (1992). A comparison of three family therapy programs for treating family conflicts in adolescents with attention-deficit hyperactivity disorder. *Journal of Consulting and Clinical Psychology, 60,* 450–462.

Berkley, C. S., Hoaglin, D. C., Mosteller, F., & Colditz, G. A. (1995). A random-effects regression model for meta-analysis. *Statistics in Medicine, 14,* 395–411.

Bjornstad, G., & Montgomery, P. (2005). Family therapy for attention-deficit disorder or attention-deficit/hyperactivity disorder in children and adolescents. *Cochrane Database of Systematic Reviews, 2,* CD005042.

Bloomquist, M., August, G., & Ostrander, R. (1991). Effects of a school-based cognitive-behavioral intervention for ADHD children. *Journal of Abnormal Child Psychology, 19*(5), 591–605.

Bor, W., Sanders, M. R., & Markie-Dadds, C. (2002). The effects of the Triple P-Positive Parenting Program on preschool children with co-occurring disruptive behavior and attentional/hyperactive difficulties. *Journal of Abnormal Child Psychology, 30,* 571–587.

Borenstein, M., & Rothstein, H. (2001). *Comprehensive meta-analysis.* Englewood, NJ: Biostat.

Cohen, J. (1988). *Statistical power analysis for the behavioral sciences* (2nd ed.). Hillsdale, NJ: Lawrence Erlbaum.

Connor, D. F., Fletcher, K. E., & Swanson, J. M. (1999). A meta-analysis of Clonidine for symptoms of attention-deficit hyperactivity disorder. *Journal of the American Academy of Child and Adolescent Psychiatry, 38,* 1551–1559.

Connor, D., Glatt, S., Lopez, I., Jackson, D., & Melloni, R. (2002) Psychopharmacology and aggression. I: A meta-analysis of stimulant effects on overt/covert aggression-related behaviors in ADHD. *Journal of the American Academy of Child and Adolescent Psychiatry, 41,* 253–262.

DuPaul, G. J., & Eckert, T. L. (1997). The effects of school-based interventions for attention deficit hyperactivity disorder: A meta-analysis. *School Psychology Review, 26,* 5–27.

Egger, M., Davey, S. G., Schneider, M., & Minder, C. (1997). Bias in meta-analysis is detected by a simple, graphical test. *British Medical Journal, 315,* 629–634.

Faraone, S. V., & Biederman, J. (2002). Efficacy of Adderall® for attention-deficit/hyperactivity disorder: A meta-analysis. *Journal of Attention Disorders, 6,* 69–75.

Firestone, P., Crowe, D., Goodman, J. T., & McGrath, P. (1986). Vicissitudes of follow-up studies: Differential effects of parent training and stimulant medication with hyperactives. *American Journal of Orthopsychiatry, 56,* 184–194.

Fonagy, P., & Kurtz, Z. (2002). Disturbance of conduct. In P. Fonagy, M. Target, D. Cottrell, J. Phillips, & Z. Kurtz (Eds.), *What works for whom? A critical review of treatments for children and adolescents* (pp. 106–192). New York: Guilford.

Gittelman, R., Klein, D. F., Abikoff, H., Katz, S., Pollack, E., & Mattes, J. (1980). A controlled trial of behavior modification and methylphenidate in hyperactive children. In C. K. Whalen & B. Henker (Eds.), *Hyperactive children: The social ecology of identification and treatment* (pp. 221–243). New York: Academic Press.

Green, S. M., Lahey, B. B., Frick, P. J., & McBurnett, K. (2002). Findings on disruptive behavior disorders from the first decade of the Developmental Trends Study. *Clinical Child and Family Psychology Review, 3,* 37–60.

Hardy, R. J., & Thompson, S. G. (1998). Detecting and describing heterogeneity in meta-analysis. *Statistics in Medicine, 17,* 841–856.

Harwell, M. (1997). An empirical study of Hedges's homogeneity test. *Psychological Methods, 2,* 219–231.

Hedges, L. V., & Olkin, I. (1985). *Statistical methods for meta-analysis.* Orlando, FL: Academic Press.

Hedges, L. V., & Vevea, J. L. (1998). Fixed- and random-effects models in meta-analysis. *Psychological Methods, 3,* 486–504.

Higgins, J. P., Thompson, S. G., Deeks, J. J., & Altman, D.G. (2003). Measuring inconsistency in meta-analyses. *British Medical Journal, 327,* 557–560.

Higgins, J. P. T., & Thompson, S. G. (2002). Quantifying heterogeneity in a meta-analysis. *Statistics in Medicine, 21,* 1539–1558.

Horn, W. F., Ialongo, N., Greenberg, G., Packard, T., & Smith-Winberry, C. (1990). Additive effects of behavioral parent training and self-control therapy with attention deficit hyperactivity disordered children. *Journal of Clinical Child & Adolescent Psychology, 19,* 98–110.

Horn, W. F., Ialongo, N., Popovich, S., & Peradotto, D. (1987). Behavioral parent training and cognitive-behavioral self-control therapy with ADD-H children: Comparative and combined effects. *Journal of Clinical Child Psychology, 16,* 57–68.

Hunter, J. E., & Schmidt, F. L. (2000). Fixed vs. random effects meta-analysis models: Implications for cumulative research knowledge. *International Journal of Selection and Assessment, 8,* 275–292.

Jadad, A., Booker, L., Gauld, M., Kakuma, R., Boyle, M., Cunningham, C., et al. (1999). The treatment of attention-deficit hyperactivity disorder: An annotated bibliography and critical appraisal of published systematic reviews and meta-analyses. *Canadian Journal of Psychiatry, 44,* 1025–1035.

Klassen, A., Miller, A., & Raina, P. (1999). Attention-deficit hyperactivity disorder in children and youth: A quantitative systematic review of the efficacy of different management strategies. *Canadian Journal of Psychiatry, 44,* 1007–1016.

Klein, R., & Abikoff, H. (1997). Behavior therapy and methylphenidate in the treatment of children with ADHD. *Journal of Attention Disorders, 2,* 89–114.

Mannuzza, S., Klein, R., & Moulton, J. (2002). Young adult outcome of children with "situational" hyperactivity: A prospective, controlled, follow-up study. *Journal of Abnormal Child Psychology, 30,* 191–198.

McClellan, J., & Werry, J. S. (2003). Evidence-based treatments in child and adolescent psychiatry: An inventory. *Journal of the American Academy of Child and Adolescent Psychiatry, 42,* 1388–1400.

McNeil, C., Eyberg, S., Eisenstadt, T., Newcomb, K., & Funderburk, B. (1991). Parent-child interaction therapy with behavior problem children: Generalization of treatment effects to the school setting. *Journal of Clinical Child Psychology, 20*(2), 140–151.

Mullen, B. (1989). *Advanced BASIC meta-analysis.* Hillsdale, NJ: Lawrence Erlbaum.

Multi-Modal Treatment Study of Children with Attention-Deficit/Hyperactivity Disorder Cooperative Group. (1999). A 14-month randomized clinical trial of treatment strategies for attention- deficit/hyperactivity disorder. *Archives of General Psychiatry, 56,* 1073–1086.

Newcorn, J., & Halperin, J. (2000). Attention-deficit disorders with oppositionality and aggression. In T. Brown (Ed.), *Attention-deficit disorders and comorbidities in children, adolescents, and adults* (pp. 171–207). Washington, DC: American Psychiatric Press.

Patterson, G. (1982). *Coercive family process.* Eugene, OR: Castalia.

Patterson, G., DeBaryshe, B., & Ramsey, E. (1989). A developmental perspective on antisocial behavior. *American Psychologist, 44,* 329–335.

Pelham, W. E., Jr., Wheeler, T., & Chronis, A. (1998). Empirically supported psychosocial treatments for attention deficit hyperactivity disorder. *Journal of Clinical Child Psychology, 27,* 190–205.

Pfiffner, L., & McBurnett, K. (1997). Social skills training with parent generalization: Treatment effects for children with attention deficit disorder. *Journal of Consulting Clinical Psychology, 65,* 749–757.

Pliszka, S. (2000). Patterns of psychiatric comorbidity with attention-deficit/hyperactivity disorder. *Child and Adolescent Psychiatric Clinics of North America, 9,* 525–540.

Purdie, N., Hattie, J., & Carroll, A. (2002). A review of the research on interventions for attention deficit hyperactivity disorder: What works best? *Review of Educational Research, 72,* 61–99.

Robinson, T. R., Smith, S. W., Miller, M. D., & Brownell, M. T. (1999). Cognitive behavior modification of hyperactivity-impulsivity and aggression: A meta-analysis of school-based studies. *Journal of Educational Psychology, 91,* 195–203.

Rosenthal, R. (1984). *Meta-analytic procedure for social research.* Beverly Hills, CA: Sage Publications.

Schachter, H., Pham, B., & King, J. (2001). How efficacious and safe is short-acting methylphenidate for the treatment of attention-deficit disorder in children and adolescents? A meta-analysis. *Canadian Medical Association Journal, 165,* 1475–1488.

Steichen, T. J., & Harbord, R. (2005). *METAREG: Stata module to perform meta-analysis regression.* Retrieved May 3, 2005, from http://ideas.repec.org/c/boc/bocode/s446201.html.

Strayhorn, J. M., & Weidman, C. S. (1989). Reduction of attention deficit and internalizing symptoms in preschoolers through parent-child interaction training. *Journal of the American Academy of Child and Adolescent Psychiatry, 28,* 888–896.

Strube, M. J., & Hartman, D. P. (1983). Meta-analysis: Techniques, applications, and functions. *Journal of Consulting and Clinical Psychology, 51,* 14–27.

Swanson, J., McBurnett, K., Christian, D., & Wigal, T. (1995). Stimulant medications and the treatment of children with ADHD. *Advances in Clinical Child Psychology, 17,* 265–322.

Thompson, S. G., & Higgins, J. P. T. (2002). How should meta-regression analyses be undertaken and interpreted? *Statistics in Medicine, 21,* 1531–1558.

Tutty, S., Gephart, H., & Wurzbacher, K. (2003). Enhancing behavioral and social skill functioning in children newly diagnosed with attention-deficit hyperactivity disorder in a pediatric setting. *Developmental and Behavioral Pediatrics, 24,* 51–57.

Weisz, J., Weiss, B., & Donnenberg, G. (1992). The lab versus the clinic: Effects of child and adolescent psychotherapy. *American Psychologist, 47,* 1578–1585.

Wolf, F. M. (1986). *Meta-analysis: Quantitative methods for research synthesis* (Sage University Papers Series on Quantitative Applications in the Social Sciences Series, 07–59). Thousand Oaks, CA: Sage Publications.

# Effective Family-Based Interventions for Adolescents With Substance Use Problems

## 3

## A Systematic Review

*Ashley M. Austin, Mark J. Macgowan, and Eric F. Wagner*

Treatment for adolescent substance use problems is effective in reducing substance use and related problems among adolescents (Catalano, Hawkins, Wells, & Miller, 1991; Williams, Chang, and the Addiction Centre Adolescent Research Group, 2000). However, there is insufficient evidence to determine what interventions work for whom and under what conditions (Williams et al., 2000). Moreover, it is unclear which types of interventions may be the most effective for different subpopulations of adolescent substance abusers. In addition, treatment for adolescent substance use problems continues to be plagued by high rates of treatment dropout and post treatment relapse to substance use. Specifically, research suggests that nearly half of adolescents never complete substance abuse treatment (Office of Applied Studies, 2000). Of those who do complete treatment, nearly two thirds relapse to substance use by three months to six months post treatment (S. A. Brown, 1993; S. A. Brown, Myers, Mott, & Vik, 1994; Cornelius et al., 2003). There is need for research to identify effective treatments for addressing adolescent substance use problems, including interventions that reduce treatment dropout and post treatment relapse.

The purpose of this article is to offer a systematic review of empirically supported, family-based interventions for adolescent substance use problems.

Originally published in *Research on Social Work Practice* 2005; 15; 67. DOI: 10.1177/1049731504271606 The online version of this article can be found at: http://rsw.sagepub.com/cgi/content/abstract/15/2/67

Initially used to describe traditional family therapy models based on family systems theory, the term *family-based* has evolved and expanded with time to reflect advances in treatment research (Ozechowski & Liddle, 2002). At present, family-based describes multiple adolescent substance abuse intervention approaches that are influenced by family systems theory as well as principles from numerous sources, including cognitive behavior theory, attachment theory, developmental theory, and social-ecological theory (Ozechowski & Liddle, 2002). In the present review, family-based adolescent substance abuse interventions will apply to any intervention that aims to address adolescent substance use and related problems through therapeutic interactions with both the adolescent and one or more family members. This review will assess the level of empirical support, as well as clinical support, of the identified family-based interventions. Recommendations for future research and applications to social work practice will be discussed.

Family-based interventions were selected for this review because they represent promising approaches to adolescent substance abuse treatment. A recent comprehensive review of the adolescent substance abuse treatment effectiveness research, which included all adolescent treatment outcome studies that reported substance use outcomes at discharge or post treatment, was conducted by Williams et al. (2000). Findings from this review suggest that family-based interventions may have better treatment outcomes relative to other outpatient substance abuse treatment approaches. These findings were consistent with earlier review findings indicating that family-based treatments, when compared to nonfamily modes of adolescent outpatient treatment, appear to be the superior treatment approach (Waldron, 1997).

In addition to increasing empirical support for family-based treatments, family-based interventions for adolescent substance use problems are appealing because of their consistency with social work values. In particular, family-based approaches address adolescent substance use problems from an ecosystems perspective, which includes attention to relevant developmental, family, social, neighborhood, community, and cultural needs (Ozechowski & Liddle, 2002). Current family-based interventions acknowledge the important role of the family system in the development and maintenance of adolescent substance use problems (Muck et al., 2001). Furthermore, contemporary family-based approaches to adolescent substance abuse treatment recognize the potential importance of targeting a variety of familial factors, including communication skills, contingency management, and conflict resolution (Ozechowski & Liddle,2002; Waldron, Slesnick, Brody, Turner, & Peterson, 2001), as well as multiple domains of adolescent functioning that may influence and are affected by adolescent substance use (Ozechowski & Liddle, 2002). Thus, family-based interventions for adolescent substance use problems are consistent with both developmental and social-ecological perspectives of adolescent functioning.

Despite findings that suggest the potential effectiveness of family-based interventions for the treatment of adolescent substance use problems, there remains a dearth of rigorous research in this area (Wagner, Brown, Monti,

Myers, & Waldron, 1999). As such, the present study will address several limitations of earlier reviews of family-based treatments for adolescent substance use problems. Previous reviews of interventions for adolescent substance use problems (Waldron, 1997; Williams et al., 2000) do not include the most recent treatment outcome studies (i.e., studies published since the latter half of 1999), which may represent some of the most rigorous research conducted in the area of treatment for adolescent substance use problems. Specifically, only one of the five intervention studies (Azrin, Donohue, Besalel, Kogan, & Acierno, 1994) included in the present review was also included in previously cited adolescent treatment research reviews. Moreover, results of previous reviews indicate that family-based interventions for adolescent substance use problems vary significantly across many factors, including therapeutic approach, target population, treatment duration and intensity, location of treatment, and types of services offered (Williams et al., 2000). Thus, there remains little known about which family-based interventions and what treatment characteristics associated with these interventions may be the most effective for treating adolescents with substance use problems. Finally, previous comprehensive reviews of family-based interventions for adolescent substance use problems have not examined issues related to effective implementation and delivery of empirically supported interventions in social work practice settings. This article will expand on previous reviews of family-based treatments for adolescent substance use problems by providing (a) an in-depth evaluation of only the most current and rigorous research of family-based interventions for adolescent substance use problems, (b) a systematic assessment of both empirical and clinical aspects of the identified intervention studies, and (c) a review focus that attends to issues relevant to social work theory and practice.

## AIM

The primary aim of the present study is to examine the level of efficacy and effectiveness of the most current, empirically supported family-based treatment approaches for adolescent substance use problems. This aim is addressed through a systematic review designed to answer the following three questions: (a) Does the intervention include treatment components associated with effective treatment for adolescent substance use problems? (b) What is the level of empirical support for each intervention as an efficacious treatment of adolescent substance use problems? (c) What is the level of clinical change associated with each intervention?

## Method

To answer the first question, a substantive evaluation of the family-based interventions will be conducted. To build on previous research related to developing and implementing effective treatment for adolescent substance use problems, the current review will use a composite of guidelines for effective treatment for adolescent substance use problems adapted from recommendations by Williams et al. (2000) and Wagner and Kassel (1995) to assess the extent to which each identified intervention meets the established guidelines (Table 3.1). Although the National Institute on Drug Abuse (NIDA) has put forth *Principles of Effective Treatment* (NIDA, 1999), these principles apply to substance abuse treatment in general and not treatment for adolescent substance use problems specifically. Research indicates that adolescents with substance use problems are a unique population with distinct treatment needs (Etheridge, Smith, Rounds-Bryant, & Hubbard, 2001), and federal guidelines recommend that special programs and treatment services be designed to meet the specific needs of adolescents (Center for Substance Abuse Treatment, 1999). As such, we elected to use the guidelines for effective treatment for adolescent substance use problems set forth by experts in the area of adolescent substance abuse treatment research (Wagner & Kassel, 1995; Williams et al., 2000) rather than NIDA's (1999) general substance abuse treatment principles.

To answer the second question, each intervention will be evaluated according to the standards for empirically validated therapies set forth by Chambless et al. (1998). The evaluation criteria developed by Chambless et al. (1998) are based on the American Psychological Association's Division 12 Task Force on Psychological Intervention Guidelines, which defined well-established and probably efficacious treatments. According to these criteria, well-established treatments:

1. have at least two good between-group design experiments demonstrating efficacy in at least one of the following ways:
   (a) superior (statistically significantly so) to placebo or another treatment or
   (b) equivalent to an already established treatment in experiments with adequate statistical power (about 30 per group);

2. must be conducted with treatment manuals;

3. must specify the characteristics of the client samples; and

4. have effects that have been demonstrated by at least two different investigators or investigating teams.

In addition, Chambless and Hollon (1998) specified methodological issues to be considered when determining efficacy. Using such criteria, the rigor of each family-based intervention study will be examined using the following methodological criteria:

1. Use of outcome assessment measures with demonstrated reliability and validity

2. Use of multiple methods of assessment (favored but not required)

3. Inclusion of follow-up results that demonstrate the enduring effects of different interventions, especially for disorders that have variable courses

4. Inclusion of all clients initially assigned to treatment in final analysis (especially when attrition is high)

5. Report on treatment adherence (favored but not required)

6. Report findings of between-group differences rather than draw conclusions based on pretest to posttest differences within each condition.

**Table 3.1**   Treatment Components Associated With Effective Treatment for Adolescents With Substance Use Problems Using Criteria by Williams et al. (2000) and Wagner and Kassel (1995)

| Guideline Criteria | Intervention | | | | |
|---|---|---|---|---|---|
| | BSFT | FBT | FFT | MDFT | MST |
| Treatment is easily accessible | N | N | N | Y | Y |
| Incorporate procedures to minimize treatment dropout | Y | Y | Y | Y | Y |
| Successful in minimizing treatment dropout | N | Y | N | N | Y |
| Provide comprehensive services | Y | Y | Y | Y | Y |
| Employ empirically validated techniques | Y | Y | Y | Y | Y |
| Include a family therapy component | Y | Y | Y | Y | Y |
| Offer parent support regarding the nonuse of substances | Y | Y | Y | Y | Y |
| Offer peer support regarding the nonuse of substances | Y | N | N | Y | Y |
| Focus on meeting the individual needs of each youth | Y | Y | Y | Y | Y |
| Focus on key curative or protective factors | Y | Y | Y | Y | Y |
| Address developmental issues related to adolescence | Y | Y | Y | Y | Y |
| Provide or arrange after-care services | N | N | N | N | N |

NOTE: BSFT = Brief Strategic Family Therapy; FBT = Family Behavior Therapy; FFT = Functional Family Therapy; MDFT = Multidimensional Family Therapy; MST = Multisystemic Treatment; N = no; Y = yes.

Finally, to answer the third question, we will evaluate the clinical significance of the changes in substance use associated with each intervention. As our definition of clinically significant change, we will use Kendall and Flannery-Schroeder's (1998) suggestion of a minimum criterion of 1.5 standard deviations from the dependent variable mean prior to treatment. In addition, the effect sizes associated with substance use changes will be evaluated according to the threefold classification proposed by Cohen (1988): small (.20 to .49), medium (.50 to .79), and large (.80 and above). We will calculate uncontrolled pre-treatment to post treatment and follow-up effect sizes using the following formula (mean substance use behavior at pretreatment minus mean substance use behavior at post treatment, or follow-up or pooled divided by standard deviation). Thus, this article evaluates the family-based outcome literature using several sets of criteria that assess both their efficacy and effectiveness.

## Selection Criteria

Intervention studies for family-based treatment of adolescent substance use problems were identified by consulting previous reviews of treatment for adolescent substance use problems and by conducting keyword searches of the electronic databases ERIC, PsycINFO, MEDLINE, Social Services Abstracts, and Social Work Abstracts, using the terms *adolescent, youth, teen, substance abuse, drug abuse, alcohol abuse, treatment outcome, intervention,* and *efficacy.* In addition, a review of the Campbell Collaboration and Cochrane databases was undertaken to determine if relevant reviews or studies that met the criteria below were included.

The studies included in this review were required to meet the following six criteria: (a) To make determinations of treatment efficacy, only randomized clinical trials were included in this review; (b) Although substance use problems frequently co-occur with other problem behaviors during adolescence, treatment for substance use problems addresses multiple issues specific to the use and abuse of substances; as such, only intervention studies with a primary objective of reducing adolescent substance use and substance use problems were included; (c) To provide a timely and current review of treatment research in the area of adolescent substance use problems, only the most up-to-date intervention studies were included. Specifically, only peer-reviewed studies published in the past 10 years (1994 through March 2004) were included in the review; (d) Because of the previously discussed strengths of family-based treatment as a treatment approach that is consistent with developmental and ecological perspectives inherent in social work practice, the selected studies were those examining the efficacy of family-based interventions for adolescent substance use problems; (e) The focus of the current review is to identify effective interventions for the treatment of existing substance use problems among adolescents. As a result, only studies testing treatment interventions for adolescent substance use problems were included in the review (no prevention studies were reviewed); (f) As identifying effective treatment for adolescents with substance use problems is the primary aim of this review, only studies examining treatments for youth ages 12 to 18 were included in the review.

# Results

A comprehensive search identified five family-based approaches reported in five studies that met the criteria discussed above. The intervention studies included in the review are as follows: Multidimensional Family Therapy (MDFT; Liddle et al., 2001), Functional Family Therapy (FFT; Waldron et al., 2001), Family Behavior Therapy (FBT; Azrin et al., 1994), Brief Strategic Family Therapy (BFST; Santisteban et al., 2003), and Multisystemic Treatment (MST; Henggeler, Pickrel, & Brondino, 1999). Although the efficacy of both MST and FFT has been demonstrated in previous clinical trials with juvenile offenders (Alexander, Pugh, Parsons, & Sexton, 1999; Bourdin et al., 1995; Henggeler, Melton, Brondino, Scherer, & Hanley, 1997), these studies did not have a primary focus of treating adolescent substance use problems and, as such, did not meet Criterion B. This is an important distinction noted by both Wagner et al. (1999) and Henggeler et al. (1999). Waldron (1999) cites the absence of previous research evaluating the efficacy of FFT as a treatment for adolescents with substance use problems. In addition, despite previous positive outcome studies of MST with juvenile offenders (Bourdin et al., 1995; Henggeler et al., 1997), the described aim of the Henggeler et al. (1999) study is to "examine the potential viability of MST in treating substance-abusing and -dependent adolescents . . . [and] effectiveness of MST in reducing drug use, criminal behavior, and out-of-home placements in a sample of substance-abusing and -dependent juvenile offenders and their families" (p. 172). Additionally, although the efficacy of BSFT has been demonstrated in early clinical trials (Szapocznik, Kurtines, Foote, Perez-Vida1, & Hervis, 1983; Szapocznik, Kurtines, Foote, Perez-Vidal, & Hervis, 1986), consistent with Criterion 3, only recent research (studies published in the past 10 years) was examined in the present review. Thus, although there may be other published studies of the identified family-based interventions, in an effort to review only the most current and rigorous research related to treating adolescent substance use problems, only studies meeting all of the specified inclusion criteria are reviewed in the present study.

    In the following review, each intervention will be described, along with a discussion of each study's characteristics, followed by a critical assessment of the extent to which the studies meet the criteria noted above regarding support for their efficacy and whether they include components associated with effective treatment for adolescent substance use problems.

## Descriptive Review of Family-Based Interventions for Adolescent Substance Use Problems

### BSFT

BSFT is a time-limited, family-based approach to adolescent substance use and related problems that relies on both strategic and structural interventions (Robbins & Szapocznik, 2000). BSFT is delivered to the youth and the entire family through Conjoint-Family Therapy or with the youth and one caregiver, One-Person Family Therapy, when engagement of the entire family is not possible. Both methods have been equally successful in achieving positive outcomes (Szapocznik et al., 1983; Szapocznik et al., 1986).

According to Robbins and Szapocznik (2000), BSFT is based on the fundamental assumption that family is the foundation of child development. As such, family interactions are assumed to play a critical role in the development of adolescent behavior problems, including substance use. Following these assumptions, family interactions are identified as a primary target for intervention in the BSFT model (Robbins & Szapocznik, 2000). BSFT also focuses on multiple domains of adolescent and family functioning, including relationships with the school, neighborhood, peers, and community resources. BSFT was developed initially to treat Hispanic youths and families, but ongoing efforts focus on assuring that the intervention can be individualized to meet treatment needs of youth and families across different ethnic and cultural groups (Robbins & Szapocznik, 2000).

BSFT is composed of three intervention processes: joining, diagnosis, and restructuring. A variety of empirically supported techniques are employed to facilitate each of the three phases. As the name implies, BSFT is a short-term intervention; however, the approach is individualized to meet the diverse needs of families, and treatment length is extended whenever necessary.

Further efforts to individualize treatment, facilitate accessibility, and retain clients include the option to deliver treatment in the home or community. Additionally, research focused on improving family engagement in BSFT resulted in the development of an empirically supported engagement strategy, Strategic Structural Systems Engagement (SSSE; Santisteban et al., 1996). SSSE aims to increase engagement of the entire family by using the tenets of BSFT (diagnosing, joining, and restructuring) before treatment officially begins (i.e., from initial phone contact to the start of treatment). There is no aftercare included in the BSFT model.

Santisteban et al. (2003) conducted a clinical trial that compared BSFT to a participatory-learning group treatment condition (GC) that had a problem-solving focus. This study included 126 predominately male (75%) Hispanic adolescents ages 12 to 18 from Miami, Florida. The overall attrition rate was 32%, with 30% of youths dropping out of BSFT and 37% of youths dropping out of the GC condition. In the study, youths received between 4 and 20 1-hour per week therapy sessions ($M = 11.2$, $SD = 3.8$), with the number of sessions determined by their level of need. Four outcome measures were used to assess functioning across the following domains: psychiatric and psychosocial functioning (this measure includes drug use), problem behavior, structural aspects of family functioning, and family environment. Findings included statistically significant post treatment differences for behavior problems (decreased rates of conduct disorder and socialized aggression; $p < .01$), marijuana use ($p < .05$), as well as family functioning ($p < .05$), with youths that received BSFT having better outcomes than youths in the GC. There were no significant effects for alcohol use. Changes were assessed at post treatment only. Study characteristics are presented in Table 3.2.

Calculations reveal no clinically significant changes for alcohol or drug use associated with either BSFT or the GC condition. In addition, effect sizes associated with BSFT were small for both alcohol use (.21) and drug use (.25). Effect sizes associated with each intervention are presented in Table 3.3.

The statistically significant outcomes from this study are consistent with findings associated with earlier clinical trials of BSFT (Szapocznik et al., 1983, 1986) supporting the usage of BSFT for the treatment of substance use problems among Hispanic adolescents. However, changes in substance use were not clinically significant, and effect sizes associated with these changes were small. Another limitation is the failure to include follow-up assessments. As such, the longevity of treatment effects remains unknown. Finally, the dropout rate was high (32%), and no intent-to-treat analyses were conducted.

## FBT

FBT is an intervention that addresses adolescent drug use and associated behavioral problems (Donohue & Azrin, 2001). As the name implies, FBT is based on a behavioral conceptualization of substance use and the development of substance use problems, whereby drug use is considered a strong primary reinforcer, as it is reinforced by both physiological stimuli (i.e., dependence, tolerance) and situational stimuli (i.e., peer acceptance, stress).

The FBT approach uses multiple empirically validated techniques with an emphasis on contingency management and communication skills training to target multiple domains of functioning: drug use, conduct, problem-solving skills, family interactions, and communication skills.

Standardized components of this program include the following: pretreatment engagement strategies, an assessment with the adolescent and the parents, drug analysis, dissemination of assessment and drug analysis results to the youth and parents, intervention selection by youth and family,

**Table 3.2**    Study Characteristics

| Characteristic | Intervention Study | | | | |
|---|---|---|---|---|---|
| | BSFT | FBT | FFT | MDFT | MST |
| Comparison conditions | GC | SC | CBT, CBT and FFT, and group therapy | MEI and AGT | US |
| Sample size | 126 | 29 | 120 | 152 | 118 |
| Gender of participants | | | | | |
| Male | 75% | 77% | 80% | 80% | 79% |
| Female | 25% | 23% | 20% | 20% | 21% |
| Race and ethnicity of participants | | | | | |
| Hispanic | 100% | 19% (including Blacks) | 47% | 15% | 1% |
| Black | 0% | 0% | 18% | 50% | |
| White | 0% | 0% | 15% | 16% | 2% |
| Other | 0% | 0% | 15% | 16% | 2% |
| Age of participants | 12 to 18 | 13 to 18 | 13 to 17 | 13 to 18 | 12 to 17 |
| Mean | 15.6 | 16 | 15.6 | 15.9 | 15.7 |
| Attrition rate | 32% (overall) 30% BSFT 37% GC | 10% (overall) 0% FBT 10% SC | 14% (overall) | 37% (overall) 30% MDFT 35% MEI 47% AGT | 2% MST 78% US never entered treatment |
| Delivery of treatment | Clinic | Clinic | Clinic | Home or community | Home or community |
| Follow-up | post tx | post tx | post tx, 3 months | post tx, 6 and 12 months | post tx, 6 months |
| Outcomes of the clinical trial: substance use | Decreased marijuana use (past 30 days); no effect for alcohol use | Decreased drug and alcohol use by post tx (days per month and months used)* | Decreased marijuana use at post tx**; no between-group differences | Decreased substance use (past 30 days) at post tx and 12 months * | Decreased alcohol and other substance use at post tx** but not at 6 months |
| Outcomes of clinical trial: related problems | Decreased behavior problems*; improved family functioning* | Improved school attendance, parent satisfaction, behavior problems, and depression*; no effect for legal contacts or placement in an institution | No effect for internalizing or externalizing behavior; no effect for family conflict | Increased family competence at post tx*; GPA at 12 months**; no effect for acting-out behaviors at any assessment period | Decreased number of days in out-of-home placements at 6 months*; no effect for self-reported criminal activity or arrests at post tx or 6 months |

NOTE: BFST = Brief Strategic Family Therapy (Santisteban et al., 2003); FBT = Family Behavior Therapy (Azrin et al., 1994); FFT = Functional Family Therapy (Waldron et al., 2001); MDFT = Multidimensional Family Therapy (Liddle et al., 2001); MST = Multisystemic Treatment (Henggeler et al., 1999); GC = group treatment control; SC = supportive counseling; CBT = Cognitive Behavior Therapy; MEI = Multifamily Educational Intervention; AGT = Adolescent Group Therapy; US = Usual community services; GPA = grade point average; tx = treatment.

*p < .05 (significant between-group differences). **p < .05 (significant within-group changes).

**Table 3.3**    Effect Sizes Associated With Each Intervention

| Intervention | Sample | Duration and Intensity | Effect Size Value[a] | Degree of Effect Size |
|---|---|---|---|---|
| BSFT | 126 | 4 to 20 sessions, 1 session per week (M = 11.2, SD = 3.8) | Post tx<br>alcohol = 0.21<br>drugs = 0.25 | Post tx<br>alcohol = small<br>drugs = small |
| FBT | 29 | Tx episode = 6 months, 2 sessions per week, then decrease to 1 session per week | Post tx<br>alcohol = 0.30<br>drugs = 0.84 | Post tx<br>alcohol = small<br>drugs = large |
| FFT | 120 | 12 sessions, 1 session per week for FFT, CBT, and group; 24 sessions, 2 sessions per week for joint CBT and FFT | Post tx<br>marijuana = 1.00<br>3 months<br>marijuana = 0.41 | Post tx<br>marijuana = large<br>3 months<br>marijuana = small |
| MDFT | 152 | 16 sessions, 1 session per week | Post tx<br>AOD = 1.46<br>6 months<br>AOD = 1.28<br>12 months<br>AOD = 1.66 | Post tx<br>AOD = large<br>6 months<br>AOD = large<br>12 months<br>AOD = large |
| MST | 118 | 12 to 187 hours of tx provided for 3 to 6 months (individualized; M = 40 hours, M = 130 days) | Post tx<br>alcohol and marijuana = 0.38<br>other drugs = 0.22<br>6 months<br>alcohol and marijuana = 0.34<br>other drugs = 0.19 | Post tx<br>alcohol and marijuana = small<br>other drugs = small<br>6 months<br>alcohol and marijuana = small<br>other drugs = small |

NOTE: BFST = Brief Strategic Family Therapy (Santisteban et al., 2003); FBT = Family Behavior Therapy (Azrin et al., 1994); FFT = Functional Family Therapy (Waldron et al., 2001); MDFT = Multidimensional Family Therapy (Liddle et al., 2001); MST = Multisystemic Treatment (Henggeler et al., 1999); CBT = Cognitive Behavior Therapy; AOD = alcohol and other drug use.

a. Effect sizes according to Cohen (1988) are as follows: small = 0.20 to 0.49, medium = 0.50 to 0.79, and large = 0.80 and above.

and implementation of the selected interventions. In further efforts to affect multiple domains of adolescent functioning, adolescents in FBT are encouraged to involve siblings and peers in the therapy process. Although FBT is a standardized program, it is designed to accommodate a diverse population of youths with a variety of cultural, behavioral, and individual preferences. In the FBT program, youths and families are able to select from a list of intervention strategies, those strategies that will best meet their individual needs.

FBT is delivered in an office-based setting, which may be a limit to accessibility. As such, the FBT model includes an empirically validated method for increasing treatment engagement (Donohue & Azrin, 2001). This process consists of manualized telephone contact with both the youth and primary guardian by the interviewer 3 days prior to the first session and 2 days after the first meeting with the therapist. The initial phone interview serves as both a reminder of the upcoming session and a rapport building process. The second phone interview serves to identify problems or concerns the youth or family might have and to verify the time and date of the second session. Food and beverages are also used to engage the youth and family during the initial assessment. Although there is a large focus on initial engagement and retention, there is no aftercare component included in the FBT approach.

FBT was examined in a clinical trial comparing FBT to supportive group counseling treatment (Azrin et al., 1994). The sample included 29 adolescents ages 13 to 18. Most of the adolescents in this study were White (81%) and male (77%; see Table 3.2). Treatment attrition was 10% and occurred only in the supportive counseling condition. Outcome domains examined in this study include drug and alcohol use, behavioral problems, depression, school attendance, and parent-child satisfaction with one another. FBT was provided during a 6-month time period. Initially, 1 hour of treatment was provided two times per week, but the frequency of sessions was decreased because it was determined that youths were making progress in treatment. None of the youths receiving FBT dropped out of treatment; however, the small sample size ($N = 15$) limits the utility of this finding. Post treatment findings indicated statistically significant differences between the FBT and supportive counseling conditions for both (a) the number of youths using illicit drugs and (b) the mean number of days of illicit drug use per month. Several other statistically significant differences were found between the two groups, with the youth in the FBT condition having better outcomes with respect to depression, school attendance, family relationships, problem behaviors, and alcohol use. There were no differences found for legal contacts or institutionalization. Calculations of clinical significance reveal no clinically significant changes for alcohol or drug use associated with either FBT or the supportive group. Similarly, effect size calculations for alcohol use indicate only small changes associated with FBT (effect size = 0.30). However, effect size calculations for drug use reveal large changes from pretreatment to post treatment (effect size = 0.84; see Table 3.3).

Although the study findings suggest that FBT may be an effective intervention for reducing substance use and related behaviors among adolescents, there are several noteworthy limitations. This study did not include any follow-up assessments, so it is impossible to know if the positive effects of treatment were maintained over time. Additionally, findings should be interpreted with caution as the study was conducted with a very small sample ($N = 29$) and, as such, has inadequate power.

## *FFT*

FFT is a short-term family-based intervention program used to treat high-risk youths and their families in a variety of contexts (Sexton & Alexander, 2000). The basic tenets of FFT, as described by Sexton and Alexander (2000) and the applicability of FFT to adolescent substance use problems discussed by Waldron et al. (2001), will be briefly summarized. FFT is based, in large part, on family systems theory, which assumes that problem behaviors occur in the context of family relationships and serve some core function within these family relationships. In addition to a family systems perspective, the FFT model relies heavily on cognitive behavioral theory and techniques. FFT takes a multisystemic approach to intervention by focusing on the multiple domains and systems in which the adolescent lives.

The intervention process in the FFT model is divided into two primary phases: (a) engagement and motivation of the youth and family and (b) behavior change for the youth and family. For substance-abusing youths, the main objectives of treatment are to (a) reduce or eliminate problematic substance use, (b) reduce or eliminate other problem behaviors within the family, and (c) improve family relationships. Therapeutic efforts in the FFT model are aimed at identifying the functions served by substance use and helping the youth and family replace maladaptive behaviors (substance use and other problem behaviors) with safer, more adaptive behaviors.

In the initial phase of FFT, the engagement and motivation phase (Sexton & Alexander, 2000), the intervention focus is on developing alliances, reducing resistance, improving communication, minimizing hopelessness, reducing dropout potential, developing a family focus, and increasing motivation for change (Sexton & Alexander, 2000). Efforts to achieve these goals include attention to issues of accessibility, availability, and cultural sensitivity of services, as well as the usage of positive interpersonal skills (validation, reframing, and reattribution) by FFT clinicians (Sexton & Alexander, 2000). To increase accessibility and engagement, FFT can be implemented in the home, the school, or the office depending on the individual needs of the youth and family (Sexton & Alexander, 2000). During the second phase, there is a focus on behavior change and improving family interaction patterns through communication-skills training, problem-solving-skills training, conflict resolution, parenting and contingency management skills, and relapse prevention skills. When appropriate, emotional regulation, relaxation training, self-esteem building, and assertiveness training may also be provided.

FFT is an individualized approach that targets multiple risk and protective factors related to family life, school, social network, community, resource availability, developmental level, and psychological and emotional needs (Sexton & Alexander, 2000). The FFT model is a comprehensive approach to substance abuse treatment that intervenes with the youth and family to change behaviors, improve relationships, and increase accessibility to and relationships with resources in the community (i.e., probation, schools), which will promote the maintenance of adaptive youth and family changes.

Waldron et al. (2001) conducted a clinical trial to examine the efficacy of FFT in treating adolescent substance use and related problems with family functioning. In the study, FFT was compared to Cognitive Behavior Therapy (CBT), a combination of FFT and CBT, and a psychoeducational group. This study was conducted with a sample of 120 multiethnic adolescents (see Table 3.2). The majority of participants were male (80%). Fourteen percent of the participants dropped out of the study; the dropout rates associated with each condition are not reported.

In the Waldron et al. (2001) study, FFT, CBT, and the group condition consisted of 12 sessions, 1 hour per week, during a 3- to 4-month time period. The joint FFT-CBT condition consisted of 1 hour of both CBT and FFT per week, for a total of 24 sessions. Outcome domains included substance use, internalizing and externalizing behaviors, and family conflict and were assessed at post treatment as well as at a 3-month follow-up. Findings indicated that only youth in the FFT and the joint conditions demonstrated reductions in marijuana use from pretreatment to post treatment. However, by the 3-month follow-up, reductions in marijuana use were significant for the joint condition but not for FFT. There were no statistically significant between-group differences for marijuana use for any of the conditions. There were no significant effects for family functioning (family conflict scores) or adolescent internalizing and externalizing behaviors. These findings are inconsistent with positive outcomes obtained in previous studies of FFT with non-substance-abusing juveniles (Sexton & Alexander, 2000).

Finally, calculations of clinical significance reveal no clinically significant changes in marijuana use associated with any of the treatment conditions. However, the effect size for changes in marijuana use at post treatment was large (effect size = 1.00). By the 3-month follow-up, the effect size for changes in marijuana use was much smaller (effect size = 0.41; see Table 3.3).

Strengths of the study include the use of manualized treatment as well as the inclusion of an ethnically diverse sample. FFT evidenced statistically significant reductions in marijuana use at post treatment as well as a large effect size associated with these changes. Positive substance use outcomes were maintained at the 3-month follow-up for the joint FFT-CBT condition but not for FFT alone. Because participants in the joint FFT-CBT condition received treatment twice as much as participants in the other three conditions, it is unclear whether positive outcomes are related to the intervention or the higher dose of treatment received by youths in this condition. Moreover, there were no statistically significant differences in marijuana use between treatment conditions at any of the assessment periods. Finally, neither long-term follow-up assessments nor intent-to-treat analyses were conducted.

## MDFT

MDFT is an outpatient, family-based treatment developed for adolescents with substance use and related behavioral and emotional problems (Liddle, 1999; Ozechowski & Liddle, 2002). MDFT is delivered in the home or community to facilitate accessibility to treatment. The MDFT approach combines aspects of several theoretical frameworks, including family systems theory, developmental psychology, ecosystems theory, and the risk and protective model of adolescent substance abuse. MDFT is a comprehensive approach that works to modify multiple domains of functioning by intervening with the youth, family members, and other members of the youth's support network. MDFT is designed to affect multiple risk and protective factors. Treatment focuses on individual characteristics of the adolescent, the parents, and other key individuals in the adolescent's life, as well as on the relational patterns contributing to the adolescent's substance use and other problem behaviors. To accomplish this, the approach employs a variety of well-supported therapeutic techniques to improve the behaviors, attitudes, and functioning across a variety of domains (Liddle, 1999).

MDFT is divided into three phases. Engaging both the youth and family is one of the main emphases in the first phase of MDFT (Liddle et al., 2001). Engagement strategies include the formulation of therapeutic alliances with the adolescent, family members, and other extrafamilial support systems. Furthermore, there is a focus on individualizing treatment for each of the family members involved. This is accomplished through the development of personal and individualized treatment objectives for each participant. The use of culturally specific themes is also cited as a useful tool for engaging diverse youths and families (Liddle, 1999). The second phase is more behaviorally focused and includes efforts to increase the youth's prosocial behaviors, positive social networks, and antidrug behaviors and attitudes. There is also an emphasis on developmental issues, including a focus on increasing developmentally appropriate family interactions. Teaching problem-solving and decision-making skills and modifying defeating parenting beliefs and behaviors through a process called enactment are the primary techniques used by MDFT clinicians during Phase 2. During Phase 3, the clinician works with the youth and family to generalize newly acquired skills and behaviors to future situations to maintain positive changes. MDFT does not include an aftercare component.

In the clinical trial conducted by Liddle et al. (2001), MDFT was compared with Adolescent Group Therapy (AGT) and Multifamily Educational Intervention (MEI). As noted in Table 3.2, the sample included 152 multiethnic adolescents ages 13 to 18 from Miami, Florida. The sample was primarily male (80%). In the clinical trial, 16 weekly treatment sessions were provided during an average of 5 months. Outcomes were measured across several domains considered relevant to improved adolescent functioning: treatment attrition, youth drug and alcohol use, problem behaviors, school performance, and family functioning. MDFT evidenced positive outcomes across several of these domains. Specifically, MDFT was associated with statistically significant differences in youth drug use at post treatment. Differences in drug use between MDFT and MEI, but not MDFT and AGT, were present at the 12-month follow-up (Liddle et al., 2001). Additionally, compared to the other two conditions, adolescents receiving MDFT demonstrated statistically significant improvements in family functioning at post treatment. Differences in GPA were marginally significantly different between MDFT and MEI ($p$ = .08). There were no significant findings for acting out behaviors at post treatment or the follow-up periods. Treatment dropout rates were different among the three conditions. Although there was treatment dropout in all three conditions, the dropout rate from AGT was disproportionately high (47%, compared to 35% for MEI and 30% for MDFT).

Calculations of clinical significance related to substance use reveal clinically significant changes in substance use between pretreatment and the 12-month follow-up for youth in the MDFT condition. Changes in substance use were not clinically significant for any of the other time periods within MDFT. No clinically significant changes were found for AGT or MEI. Effect sizes associated with MDFT were large for substance use changes at all three time periods (for post treatment, effect size = 1.46; for 6-month follow-up, effect size = 1.28; and for 12-month follow-up, effect size = 1.66; see Table 3.3). This study has several strengths, including the statistically significant between-group differences in substance use at post treatment and at the 12-month follow-up period, clinically significant changes at 12-months post treatment, and large effect sizes associated with all three assessment periods. Furthermore, the study included an ethnically heterogeneous sample and used standardized treatment that included the use of treatment manuals. The limitations include the small number of female participants as well as the failure to complete intent-to-treat analyses with treatment dropouts.

## MST

MST is a comprehensive, individualized, home-based therapy approach to treating adolescent antisocial behavior, including conduct disorder, delinquency, and substance abuse (Henggeler, Schowenwald, Bourdin, Rowland, & Cunningham, 1998). MST is based on the systems and social-ecological theories of human behavior and holds that the development of antisocial behavior in youth is the result of various individual, peer, family, community, and school factors. As such, MST is a child-focused family-centered intervention in which strategies are aimed at multiple known determinants of problem behavior that is, individual, family, peer, school, and community factors (T. A. Brown, Henggeler, Schoenwald, Brondino, & Pickrel, 1999). To address the multiple needs of youth and families, MST uses a combination of empirically supported intervention techniques based on strategic family therapy, structural family therapy, behavioral parent training, and cognitive behavior therapy.

A key element of MST is the focus on addressing complex problems in a comprehensive, intense, and individualized manner. Specifically, treatment is individualized in that the family and the MST therapist work together to target problems and select intervention strategies. MST capitalizes on youth and family strengths, emphasizing family empowerment and accessing needed family and community resources. Moreover, the service delivery model used with MST was developed with a focus on increasing accessibility and engagement and minimizing treatment dropout (T. A. Brown et al., 1999). The MST model includes the following treatment components: (a) Services are provided in home and community-based settings to facilitate cooperation, engagement, and retention in treatment; (b) low caseloads enable the therapist to be available 24 hours a day, 7 days a week to meet the diverse needs of youths and families; (c) treatment meetings are scheduled according to the needs of the youth and family, including evening and weekend sessions; and (d) responsibility for youth and family engagement and treatment outcome is assumed by all members of a treatment team, and treatment strategies are modified as needed to meet the needs of each youth and family (T. A. Brown et al., 1999).

The study conducted by Henggeler et al. (1999) compared outcomes of adolescents who received MST with adolescents who received usual community services (US) condition. Available to youths in the US condition were community outpatient, residential, and inpatient substance abuse programs and mental health services; however, 78% of the youths in the US condition received neither substance abuse nor mental health treatment during the time of the study (Henggeler et al., 1999). This study included a sample of 118 juvenile offenders ages 12 to 17. The sample consisted of primarily African American and White youths (Table 3.2). Treatment retention was very high, with 98% of youths in the MST condition completing the full course of treatment. Within the MST intervention, treatment length and intensity varied greatly among participants. In the reviewed study, treatment time ranged between 12 and 187 hours ($M = 40$ hours) for 3 to 6 months ($M = 130$ days). Outcomes were assessed for the following domains: treatment retention, drug and alcohol use, criminal activity, and out-of-home placements.

Results indicated statistically significant decreases in reported drug and alcohol use immediately following treatment; however, the changes were not maintained at the 6-month follow-up. Moreover, there were no statistically significant between-group differences at either post treatment or the 6-month follow-up. Inconsistent with findings from previous research examining the efficacy of MST for reducing juvenile delinquency (Henggeler et al., 1997), reductions in criminal activity were not significantly different for youth in the MST condition. There was, however, a significant reduction in out-of-home placement for youths in the MST condition, compared with youths in the US condition. Calculations of clinical significance related to substance use reveal that the changes in substance use were not clinically significant for either MST or the US condition. Similarly, effect sizes were small for substance use changes at both post treatment and the 6-month follow-up assessment (Table 3.2). One strength of the Henggeler et al. (1999) study was the high retention (98%) of youths in the MST condition. In general, however, the changes in substance use were modest, and the substance use outcomes disappeared by 6 months post treatment. Moreover, there were no between-group differences found for substance use. This is particularly concerning because 78% of youths in the US condition received no treatment at all. An additional limitation is the lack of standardization associated with MST in the reviewed study. Specifically, treatment dose (duration and intensity of services) varied substantially among participants. Furthermore, the fidelity assessment indicated that treatment adherence was low. Finally, because only 22% of the youths in the comparison condition received any treatment and the specific interventions they received were unclear, future replications of this study will be precluded.

## Critical Review of Family-Based Interventions for Adolescent Substance Use Problems

### Substantive Review Findings

A review of treatment components associated with each intervention indicates that each of the five family-based interventions are consistent with the majority of guidelines for effective treatment for adolescent substance use problems suggested by Williams et al. (2000) and Wagner and Kassel (1995). The extent to which the interventions meet each of the guidelines will be discussed below and summarized in Table 3.1:

1. Be easily accessible. In two of the five intervention studies (MST and MDFT), interventions were delivered in home-based or community-based settings in efforts to maximize accessibility. Although BSFT and FFT were developed to be delivered in multiple settings, including the home, school, and community, treatment was provided in clinic-based settings in the studies reviewed. FBT was provided in a clinic, and there is no mention of adapting the intervention to facilitate delivery in the home or community.

2. Incorporate procedures to minimize treatment dropout. All five interventions incorporate engagement strategies aimed at increasing treatment retention; however, treatment dropout appears to have been a problem across most of the interventions, except MST, where 98% of participants receiving MST were retained, and FBT, where all youths in the FBT condition were retained.

3. Provide comprehensive intervention services. All five interventions were comprehensive in that interventions addressed problems across multiple domains of adolescent functioning (i.e., family, social, legal, and community) through a variety of intervention strategies.

4. Employ empirically validated techniques. All five interventions employ intervention strategies based on empirically supported research (e.g., cognitive behavioral strategies, social skills training, contingency management, reframing).

5. Include a family therapy component. This criterion is inherent in all five interventions, as this review examined only family-based interventions for treatment of adolescent substance use problems.

6. Offer parent and peer support regarding nonuse of substances. All five interventions provide parent support through the therapeutic interventions with family members. Efforts aimed at increasing peer support of substance use changes made by the youth in treatment were less common. Only MST, MDFT, and FBT include peers in the therapeutic process.

7. Focus on meeting the individual needs of each youth. All five of the reviewed interventions were developed to be flexible and adaptable to meet the individual needs (i.e., cultural, psychosocial, economic, and legal) of each youth and family.

8. Focus on key curative or protective factors. All five interventions broadly describe aims to target multiple protective as well as risk factors identified as relevant to the development and maintenance of adolescent substance use problems, including psychological and emotional problems, family conflict, academic performance, peer relationships, and neighborhood and community support (Hawkins, Catalano, & Miller, 1992).

9. Address developmental issues relevant to adolescence. Developmental issues are addressed to some extent in all five interventions, as evidenced by therapeutic interventions aimed at family functioning, parenting skills, as well as peer- and school-related issues. Furthermore, all five interventions use specific therapeutic strategies that are developmentally appropriate for adolescents (i.e., communication skills training, conflict resolution, and contingency management).

10. Provide or arrange aftercare services. None of the interventions include an aftercare component, and they do not include strategies aimed at linking the youth and family with aftercare services.

Thus, although the five interventions are distinct from one another, they share multiple characteristics associated with recommendations for effective treatment of adolescent substance use problems. The review revealed that the interventions provide comprehensive yet individualized treatment for the youth and family, which includes the use of empirically validated intervention strategies relevant to the developmental needs of adolescents with substance use problems, and a focus on targeting specific risk and protective factors associated with the development and maintenance of substance use problems among teenagers. Moreover, as research consistently cites the important influence of peer substance use on adolescent substance use behavior and substance use treatment outcomes (S. A. Brown, Vik, & Creamer, 1989; Jainchill, Hawke, De Leon, & Yagelka, 2000), a significant strength of MST, MDFT, and FBT is the inclusion of peers in the therapeutic process.

Some interventions are not consistent with the recommended treatment guidelines. For instance, accessibility to treatment is critical to effectively engaging and retaining youth and families with complex needs. However, FBT was not developed for implementation in settings such as client homes or schools, which may maximize accessibility for economically disadvantaged and culturally diverse subgroups of adolescents with substance use problems. As these are the types of clients and settings typical of social work practice, this is an important limitation of FBT. Another notable exception is the high rate of treatment dropout for all of the interventions, except MST and FBT. Each of the interventions aims to address issues of treatment accessibility and engagement, yet dropout rates remain high. This is problematic because treatment dropout has been consistently associated with poor treatment outcomes among adolescents with substance use problems (Jainchill et al., 2000; Winters, Stinchfield, Opland, Weller, & Latimer, 2000). Finally, it was determined that none of the interventions address the issue of aftercare. This is very concerning because of the high post treatment relapse rates among adolescents with substance use problems (S. A. Brown et al., 1994; Cornelius et al., 2003). Thus, it is suggested that these intervention models may be improved by including aftercare services, increasing the involvement of peers in the therapeutic process, and addressing issues related to improving accessibility and minimizing treatment dropout.

### Empirical Review Findings

In addition to evaluating the extent to which an intervention includes treatment components associated with effective treatment for adolescent substance use problems, it is necessary to evaluate treatment efficacy. The methodological issues associated with each of the studies will be reviewed below, and the level of empirical support for each of the five family-based interventions will be assessed using the criteria outlined by Chambless and colleagues (Chambless & Hollon, 1998; Chambless et al., 1998). A discussion of the major findings will follow.

Each study was a controlled clinical trial comparing at least two treatment conditions. None of the studies used random sampling procedures. Instead, adolescents were obtained through referrals from the Department of

Juvenile Justice, schools, family, and health and mental health agencies. In general, the samples were small but varied in size considerably across studies, ranging from 29 to 152. When evaluated for adequate power (i.e., at least 25 to 30 participants per treatment condition; Chambless et al., 1998), four of the five studies—MST (N = 118), MDFT (N = 152), FFT (N = 120), and BSFT (N = 125)—had adequate power. In contrast, the study of FBT failed to achieve adequate power with a sample of only 29 participants divided among two treatment conditions. With regard to ethnic and racial composition, only three of the studies (MST, FFT, and MDFT) included an ethnically heterogeneous sample. The BSFT study included only Hispanic adolescents, and the FBT study used a sample that was primarily (81%) non-Hispanic White. In addition, females were conspicuously under-represented in all of the studies, with no more than 25% of the participants being female in any sample. As such, treatment efficacy for any of the interventions is much less clear for female adolescents with substance use problems than for males. Treatment attrition was considerable in all of the clinical trials, except the studies of MST and FBT, where treatment dropout associated with the treatment conditions was very low (2% and 0%, respectively). None of the studies included treatment dropouts in the analyses. Thus, positive outcomes may be inflated in that they reflect the outcomes of the subsample of substance-abusing adolescents who remained in treatment. The youths who remained in treatment may represent a subgroup of adolescents who were more amenable to treatment (i.e., more motivated for change, fewer environmental and psychosocial barriers to treatment) than those adolescents who dropped out of treatment.

The primary target of intervention in each of the studies was adolescent substance use. However, all studies assessed multiple areas of adolescent and family functioning. The assessment of outcomes across multiple domains of adolescent functioning is consistent with recommendations for effective treatment outcome studies in child and adolescent services (Chambless & Hollon, 1998). Moreover, each of the intervention studies assessed treatment outcomes using reliable and valid measures. It should be noted, however, that neither outcome domains nor outcome measures were uniform across studies. Rather, there was a great deal of variation in the measures used to assess substance use and other behaviors. For example, each study assessed substance use using a different measure. MDFT used a combination of youth and parent reports of past 30-day alcohol or drug use as well as urinalyses; FFT used the Timeline Follow-back (Sobell & Sobell, 1992), collateral reports from family members, as well as urine drug screenings; BSFT used the Addiction Severity Index (McLellan et al., 1985); FBT used youth and parent reports of youth substance use at each session as well as urinalyses at each session; and MST used the Personal Experience Inventory (Winters & Henly, 1989). In addition, the study of FFT measured only marijuana use because it was the primary drug of choice, whereas in the four other studies (MDFT, FBT, BSFT, and MST), alcohol and other substance use was measured.

The level of treatment standardization also varied across the studies. Only the study of MST included treatment fidelity checks. However, findings suggested that treatment adherence was a problem in the study. The duration and intensity of treatment varied across all the studies as well as within MST, BSFT, and FBT. In particular, treatment length and intensity varied greatly among participants in the study of MST, with a range of 12 to 187 hours of treatment being provided during a 3- to 6-month time period. In contrast, in the studies of MDFT and FFT, treatment regimens were delivered in specified amounts. However, as previously mentioned, in the study of FFT, youth in the joint condition received twice as much treatment as youth in the other three conditions. As treatment doses were not consistent across studies, and in some cases within studies, there remains little known about the interaction between treatment dose and treatment type on treatment outcomes. First, for the studies without standardized doses of treatment, it remains unclear what dose (i.e., how many sessions during what period of time) of treatment is associated with successful outcomes. Second, it is difficult to compare intervention findings across studies when interventions vary in length and intensity.

Follow-up periods vary notably across the five intervention studies. Three of the five studies (MDFT, FFT, and MST) included at least one follow-up interview after the post treatment assessment, whereas two of the studies assessed outcomes at post treatment only. Waldron et al. (2001) assessed outcomes of FFT at post treatment and at a 3-month follow-up. Follow-up data were gathered for MST shortly following termination from treatment and 6 months post treatment (Henggeler et al., 1999). The MDFT outcome study reported outcomes gathered at both 6- and 12-month follow-up periods (Liddle et al., 2001). Azrin et al. (1994) and Santisteban et al. (2003) assessed outcomes only at the end of treatment and included no follow-ups.

Each of the interventions demonstrated changes in substance use from pretreatment to post treatment; however, for MST and FFT, within-group differences in substance use were no longer significant by the follow-up periods. Only BSFT, MDFT, and FBT demonstrated statistically significant between-group differences in substance use outcomes, and of these studies, only MDFT demonstrated that substance use changes were maintained at follow-up. With the exception of the FFT study, findings indicated statistically significant between-group differences associated with other outcome domains as well. As noted, long-term treatment effects for BSFT and FBT are unclear because of the failure to include follow-up assessments.

The clinical significance of changes in substance use differed substantially across the five studies. MDFT is the only intervention that demonstrated substance use changes that were clinically significant according to Kendall and Flannery-Schroeder's (1998) criterion of 1.5 standard deviations from the dependent variable mean prior to treatment. The effect sizes associated with MDFT also reveal large changes in substance use at post treatment, as well as the 6- and 12-month follow-up assessments. Large effect sizes were found for FFT (for marijuana use) and FBT (for drug but not alcohol use) at post treatment. Effect sizes related to changes in substance use were small for both BSFT and MST.

The results from the methodological review identify meaningful differences in the level of empirical support associated with each intervention. None of the treatments met the standards for well-established treatment (Table 3.4). This is primarily a result of Criterion 4, which requires that

**Table 3.4** Level of Empirical Support Using Evaluation Criteria Developed by Chambless et al. (1998) and Chambless and Hollon (1998)

|  | Intervention | | | | |
|---|---|---|---|---|---|
|  | BSFT | FBT | FFT | MDFT | MST |
| Positive results from one or more between-group studies with specified population | Y | Y | N | Y | N |
| Positive results from two or more between-group studies with specified population | Y | N | N | Y | N |
| Effects replicated by two or more independent investigators with specified population | N | N | N | N | N |
| Adequate power (25 to 30) per condition | Y | N | Y | Y | Y |
| Clearly defined population | Y | Y | Y | Y | Y |
| Reliable and valid outcome measures | Y | Y | Y | Y | Y |
| Intent to treat analyses | N | N | N | N | N |
| Effects demonstrated at follow-up | No follow-up | No follow-up | N | Y (at 6 and 12 months) | N (effects disappear by 6 months) |
| Used treatment manuals | Y | Y[a] | Y | Y | Y[b] |
| Well-established treatment | N | N | N | N | N |
| Probably efficacious treatment | Y | N | N | Y | N |
| Promising treatment |  | Y | Y |  | Y |

NOTE: BSFT = Brief Strategic Family Therapy (Santisteban et al., 2003); FBT = Family Behavior Therapy (Azrin et al., 1994); FFT = Functional Family Therapy (Waldron et al., 2001); MDFT = Multidimensional Family Therapy (Liddle et al., 2001); MST = Multisystemic Treatment (Henggeler et al., 1999); Y = yes; N = no.

a. Use of treatment manuals not reported in published study but was verified via personal communication (B. Donohue, personal communication, February 17, 2004).

b. Use of treatment manuals not reported in published study but was verified via personal communication (S.W. Henggeler, personal communication, February 14, 2004).

an intervention be examined in randomized clinical trials with at least two distinct investigating teams. Two of the five interventions (MDFT and BSFT), however, met criteria consistent with probably efficacious treatment. It should be noted that the study of BSFT did not include follow-up assessments. This is a significant limitation as research suggests a majority of adolescents relapse in the first 90 days post treatment (S. A. Brown et al., 1994; Cornelius et al., 2003). The other three interventions (FFT, MST, and FBT) did not meet criteria for probably efficacious treatment. The study of FBT did not have adequate power because the total sample was very small ($N = 29$); in addition, this study did not assess substance use at follow-up. Although findings indicated that both FFT and MST demonstrated statistically significant changes in substance use from pretreatment to post treatment, these changes disappeared by the follow-up periods. Furthermore, neither FFT nor MST demonstrated statistically significant between-group differences for substance use at post treatment or follow-up.

Thus, findings from the empirical review indicate that two of the five interventions (MDFT and BSFT) are probably efficacious treatments for adolescent substance use problems and thus have the best evidence to date. However, it should be recognized that only the study of MDFT included follow-ups (6 and 12 months post treatment) necessary to demonstrate the long-term efficacy of the intervention. Moreover, MDFT was the only intervention that demonstrated clinically significant changes in substance use (at the 12-month follow-up) and large effect sizes at post treatment, as well as the two follow-up assessments. Although they did not meet full criteria for probably efficacious treatments, empirical review findings indicate that FFT, MST, and FBT each represent a promising intervention for treating adolescent substance use problems. Overall, MDFT emerges as the only family-based intervention with empirical support for changes in substance use behaviors that are both statistically significant and clinically significant immediately following treatment and at 1 year post treatment. Review findings have implications for future research and applications for social work practice.

# Directions for Future Research

There are several aspects of treatment research in the area of adolescent substance use problems that require further attention. First, to strengthen the level of empirical support for MDFT and BSFT, study findings must be replicated by different investigators and/or investigating teams. Positive findings from such studies would increase the level of empirical support for these interventions from probably efficacious to well-established treatments.

To ascertain longevity of treatment effects, studies must include adequate follow-up intervals. Findings from previous research suggest that two thirds of adolescents relapse to substance use in the first 6 months post treatment (S. A. Brown et al., 1994; Cornelius et al., 2003). At minimum, the inclusion of 3- and 6-month follow-up assessments is necessary to ascertain long-term treatment efficacy. In addition, the review revealed the lack of attention given to aftercare services in research of treatments for adolescent substance use problems. None of the reviewed family-based intervention studies examined the issue of aftercare. In light of the relapse rates discussed above, aftercare services clearly deserve attention in future empirical research. Specifically, future studies should examine the efficacy of interventions for adolescent substance use problems that include an empirically supported aftercare component, such as the Assertive Aftercare Protocol (Godley, Godley, & Dennis, 1999).

Additionally, future outcome studies of treatment for adolescent substance use problems should include intent-to-treat analyses for all adolescents who enter treatment, not just those who successfully complete the treatment episode. This may provide more accurate findings related to treatment effects and increase knowledge around the issue of treatment dropout among adolescents with substance use problems. Moreover, as treatment dropout was a problem associated with several of the interventions included in this review, it is recommended that future research explore pretreatment and treatment factors that may be associated with treatment engagement and treatment retention among diverse groups of adolescents with substance use problems.

Future treatment research should also examine the effects of client-treatment matching across different subgroups of adolescents with substance use problems. For example, future studies could match adolescents who differ across demographic factors (i.e., ethnicity, acculturation, gender, age, family structure) and psychosocial needs (i.e., comorbidity, juvenile delinquency, history of sexual or physical abuse) with specific family-based interventions. Such studies may yield findings about which interventions are most useful for which subgroups of adolescents with substance use problems.

Finally, research should be conducted on successfully implementing efficacious interventions for adolescent substance use problems in social work practice settings with potentially limited resources. Suggested study foci include cost effectiveness, therapist training and treatment adherence, and treatment duration and intensity. Effectiveness studies that address these issues are necessary for a successful transition from research to social work practice.

# Discussion and Applications to Social Work Practice

Findings from the present review can be used to improve decision making about the types of interventions implemented in social work practice settings with adolescents with substance use problems. Adolescents with substance use problems are a heterogeneous population with diverse psychosocial, cultural, legal, and developmental needs. Providing effective treatment for adolescent substance use problems can be daunting. Service providers face multiple challenges, including engaging difficult-to-reach adolescents, minimizing treatment dropout, and improving treatment response. One important step toward successfully treating adolescents with substance use problems is identifying and implementing effective interventions that are consistent with social work practice.

Contemporary family-based interventions view adolescent substance use problems from an ecosystems perspective, intervening with relevant social systems, including the individual, family, peer, school, neighborhood, community, and culture (Ozechowski & Liddle, 2002). As such, comprehensive family-based treatments for adolescent substance use problems, such as the five reviewed in this study, are congruent with social work values and theoretical perspectives. It is imperative, however, that we identify family-based interventions that have substantial empirical support and thus represent efficacious treatments for adolescents with substance use problems.

The findings from the present review can be used to guide the selection and implementation of empirically supported family-based interventions in practice settings with diverse subgroups of adolescents with substance use problems. Specifically, the current review identified (a) two interventions (MDFT and BSFT) that have demonstrated efficacy in treating multiproblem adolescents with substance use problems; (b) three interventions (FFT, MST, and FBT) that meet several criteria associated with efficacious treatment and thus represent promising approaches to treatment of adolescent substance use problems; (c) two interventions (FBT and FFT) associated with large reductions in substance use at post treatment and one intervention (MDFT) associated with large reductions in substance use immediately following treatment and at 6 and 12 months post treatment; (d) two interventions (MST and FBT) that have been particularly successful in minimizing treatment dropout; (e) four family-based interventions (MDFT, MST, FFT, and BSFT) that were developed for delivery in multiple social work practice settings, including homes, schools, and communities, in an effort to improve treatment accessibility and engagement; and (f) the specific therapeutic components of MDFT, FFT, FBT, BSFT, and MST that are consistent with guidelines for effective treatment for adolescents with substance use problems (Wagner & Kassel, 1995; Williams et al., 2000).

Barriers to effectively implementing interventions in a real-world social work practice setting must also be considered. Time-intensive and labor-intensive interventions that require a great deal of therapist training and supervision may create insurmountable challenges in traditional social work practice settings with limited funding. BSFT, MDFT, and MST all require lengthy and potentially costly training for practitioners. In the only study that examined the importance of therapist treatment adherence, Henggeler et al. (1999) found that poor adherence to MST protocol was associated with poor treatment outcomes. Thus, if social work practice settings cannot support the time-intensive and cost-intensive training necessary to implement a specific intervention, the treatment may not be effective. It follows that to increase the provision of effective, empirically supported treatment for adolescent substance use problems, research findings should be used to guide the implementation of interventions in social work practice settings, with particular attention to the feasibility and reliability of effective transportability of interventions across clients and communities.

# References

Alexander, J. F., Pugh, J. F., Parsons, B. V., & Sexton, T. L. (1999). Functional family therapy. In D. S. Elliot (Ed.), *Blueprints for violence prevention* (2nd ed.). Boulder, CO: Center for the Study and Prevention of Violence, Institute of Behavioral Science, University of Colorado.

Azrin, N. H., Donohue, B., Besalel, V. A., Kogan, E. S., & Acierno, R. (1994). Youth drug abuse treatment: A controlled outcome study. *Journal of Child & Adolescent Substance Abuse, 3*(3), 1–16.

Bourdin, C. M., Mann, B. J., Cone, L. T., Henggeler, S. W., Fucci, B.R., Blaske, D. M., et al. (1995). Multisystemic treatment of serious juvenile offenders: Long-term prevention of criminality and violence. *Journal of Consulting and Clinical Psychology, 63,* 569–578.

Brown, S. A. (1993). Recovery patterns in adolescent substance abuse. In J. S. Baer, G. A. Marlatt, & R. J. McMahon (Eds.), *Addictive behaviors across the life span* (pp. 160–183). London, UK: Sage Publications.

Brown, S. A., Myers, M. G., Mott, M. A., & Vik, P. W. (1994). Correlates of success following treatment for adolescent substance abuse. *Applied and Preventative Psychology, 3,* 61–73.

Brown, S. A., Vik, P. W., & Creamer, V. A. (1989). Characteristics of relapse following adolescent substance abuse treatment. *Addictive Behaviors, 14,* 291–300.

Brown, T. A., Henggeler, S. W., Schoenwald, S. K., Brondino, M. J., & Pickrel, S. G. (1999). Multisystemic treatment of substance abusing and dependent juvenile delinquents: Effects on school attendance at post treatment and 6-month follow-up. *Children's Services: Social Policy, Research, and Practice, 2*(2), 81–93.

Catalano, R. F., Hawkins, J. D., Wells, E. A., & Miller, J. (1991). Evaluation of the effectiveness of adolescent drug abuse treatment, assessment of risks for relapse, and promising new approaches for relapse prevention. *The International Journal of the Addictions, 25*(9A & 10A), 1085–1140.

Center for Substance Abuse Treatment. (1999). *Treatment of adolescents with substance use disorders* (CSAT Treatment Improvement Protocol Series No. 32. DHHS Pub. No. SMA 99–3283). Rockville, MD: Substance Abuse and Mental Health Services Administration.

Chambless, D. L., Baker, M. J., Baucom, D. H., Beutler, L. E., Calhoun, K. S., Crits-Christoph, P., et al. (1998). Update on empirically validated therapies II. *The Clinical Psychologist, 51*(1), 3–16.

Chambless, D. L., & Hollon, S. D. (1998). Defining empirically supported therapies. *Journal of Consulting and Clinical Psychology, 66*(1), 7–18.

Cohen, J. (1988). *Statistical power analysis for the behavioral sciences*. Hillsdale, NJ: Lawrence Erlbaum.

Cornelius, J. R., Maisto, S. A., Pollock, N. K., Martin, C. S., Salloum I. M., Lynch, K. G., et al. (2003). Rapid relapse generally follows treatment for substance use disorders among adolescents. *Addictive Behaviors, 28,* 381–386.

Donohue, B., & Azrin, N. (2001). Family behavior therapy. In E. F. Wagner & H. B. Waldron (Eds.), *Innovations in adolescent substance abuse interventions* (pp. 205–227). New York: Pergamon.

Etheridge, R. M., Smith, J. C., Rounds-Bryant, J. L, & Hubbard, R. L. (2001). Drug abuse treatment and comprehensive services for adolescents. *Journal of Adolescent Research, 16*(6), 563–589.

Godley, S. H., Godley, M. D., & Dennis, M. L. (1999). The assertive aftercare protocol for adolescent substance abusers. In E. F. Wagner & H. B. Waldron (Eds.), *Innovations in adolescent substance abuse interventions* (pp. 313–331). Oxford, UK: Pergamon.

Hawkins, J. D., Catalano, R. F., & Miller, J. Y. (1992). Risk and protective factors for alcohol and other drug problems in adolescence and early adulthood: Implications for substance abuse prevention. *Psychological Bulletin, 112*(1), 64–105.

Henggeler, S. W., Melton, G. B., Brondino, M. J., Scherer, D. G., & Hanley, J. H. (1997). Multisystemic therapy with violent and chronic juvenile offenders and their families: The role of treatment fidelity in successful dissemination. *Journal of Consulting and Clinical Psychology, 65,* 821–833.

Henggeler, S.W., Pickrel, S.G., & Brondino, M. J. (1999). Multisystemic treatment of substance abusing and dependent delinquents: Outcomes, treatment fidelity, and transportability. *Mental Health Services Research, 1*(3), 171–184.

Henggeler, S. W., Schowenwald, S. K., Bourdin, C. M., Rowland, M.D., & Cunningham, P. B. (1998). *Multisystemic treatment of antisocial behavior in children and adolescents*. New York: Guilford.

Jainchill, N., Hawke, J., De Leon, G., & Yagelka, J. (2000). Adolescents in therapeutic communities: One-year post treatment outcomes. *Journal of Psychoactive Drugs, 32*(1), 81–94.

Kendall, P. C., & Flannery-Schroeder, E. C. (1998). Methodological issues in treatment issues for anxiety disorders in youth. *Journal of Abnormal Child Psychology, 26,* 27–38.

Liddle, H. A. (1999). Theory development in a family-based therapy for adolescent drug abuse. *Journal of Clinical Child Psychology, 28*(4), 521–532.

Liddle, H. A., Dakof, G. A., Parker, K., Diamond, G. S., Barett, K., & Tejeda, M. (2001). Multidimensional family therapy for adolescent drug abuse: Results of a randomized clinical trial. *American Journal of Drug and Alcohol Abuse, 27*(4), 651–688.

McLellan, A. T., Luborsky, L., Cacciola, J., Griffith, J. E., McGahan, P., & O'Brien, C. P. (1985). *Guide to the Addiction Severity Index: Background, administration, and field testing results*. Rockville, MD: U.S. Department of Health and Human Services.

Muck, R., Zempolich, K. A., Titus, J. C., Fishman, M., Godley, M. D., & Schwebel, R. (2001). An overview of the effectiveness of adolescent substance abuse treatment models. *Youth & Society, 33*(2), 143–168.

National Institute on Drug Abuse. (1999). *Principles of drug addiction treatment: A research based guide*. Retrieved January 16, 2004, from http://www.nida .nih.gov/PODAT/PODAT1.html

Office of Applied Studies. (2000). *National survey of substance abuse treatment services (N-SSATS)*. Retrieved February 17, 2003, from http://www.samsha.org

Ozechowski, T. J., & Liddle, H. A. (2002). Family-based therapy. In C.A. Essau (Ed.), *Substance abuse and dependence in adolescence: Epidemiology, risk factors, and treatment* (pp. 203–226). East Sussex, UK: Brunner-Routledge.

Robbins, M. S., & Szapocznik, J. (2000). Office of Juvenile Justice and Delinquency Prevention. *Brief Strategic Family Therapy*. Retrieved March 1, 2003, from http://www.ojjdp.ncjrs.org/pubs/ alpha.html

Santisteban, D. A., Coatsworth, J. D., Perez-Vidal, A., Kurtines, W.M., Schwartz, S. J., LaPierre, A., et al. (2003). Efficacy of brief strategic family therapy in modifying Hispanic adolescent behavior problems and substance use. *Journal of Family Psychology, 17*(1), 121–133.

Santisteban, D. A., Szapocznik, J., Perez-Vidal, A., Kurtines, W. M., Murray, E. J., & LaPerriere, A. (1996). Efficacy of intervention for engaging youth and families into treatment and some variables that may contribute to differential effectiveness. *Journal of Family Psychology, 10*(1), 35–44.

Sexton, T. L., & Alexander, J. F. (2000). Office of Juvenile Justice and Delinquency Prevention. *Functional family therapy*. Retrieved March 1, 2003, from http://www.ojjdp.ncjrs.org/pubs/alpha.html

Sobell, L. C., & Sobell, M. B. (1992). Timeline follow-back. In R. Litten & J. Allen (Eds.), *Measuring alcohol consumption* (pp. 41–72). Totowa, NJ: Humana.

Szapocznik, J., Kurtines, W. M., Foote, F. H., Perez-Vidal, A., & Hervis, O. (1983). Conjoint versus one-person family therapy: Some evidence of effectiveness for conducting family therapy through one person. *Journal of Consulting and Clinical Psychology, 51*(6), 889–899.

Szapocznik, J., Kurtines, W. M., Foote, F. H., Perez-Vidal, A., & Hervis, O. (1986). Conjoint versus one-person family therapy: Further evidence for the effectiveness of conducting family therapy through one person with drug abusing adolescents. *Journal of Consulting and Clinical Psychology, 54*(3), 395–397.

Wagner, E. F., Brown, S. A., Monti, P. M., Myers, M. G., & Waldron, H. B. (1999). Innovations in adolescent substance abuse intervention. *Alcoholism: Clinical and Experimental Research, 23*(2), 236–249.

Wagner, E. F., & Kassel, J. D. (1995). Substance use and abuse. In R. T. Ammerman & M. Hersen (Eds.), *Handbook of child behavior therapy in the psychiatric setting* (pp. 367–388). New York: John Wiley.

Waldron, H. B. (1997). Adolescent substance abuse and family therapy outcome: A review of randomized trials. In T. H. Ollendick & R. J. Prinz (Eds.), *Advances in clinical child psychology* (Vol. 4, pp. 199–234). New York: Plenum.

Waldron, H. B., Slesnick, N., Brody, J. L., Turner, C. W., & Peterson, T. R. (2001). Treatment outcomes for adolescent substance abuse at 4- and 7-month assessments. *Journal of Consulting and Clinical Psychology, 69*(5), 802–813.

Williams, R. J., Chang, S. Y., & Addiction Centre Adolescent Research Group. (2000). A comprehensive and comparative review of adolescent substance abuse treatment outcome. *Clinical Psychology, Science, and Practice, 7*(2), 138–166.

Winters, K. C., & Henly, G. (1989). *The Personal Experiences Inventory*. Los Angeles: Western Psychological Services.

Winters, K. C., Stinchfield, R. D., Opland, E., Weller, C., & Latimer, W. (2000). The effectiveness of the Minnesota Model approach in the treatment of adolescent drug abusers. *Addiction, 95*(4), 601–612.

# 4

# Therapeutic Interventions for Foster Children

## A Systematic Research Synthesis

*Patricia Ann Craven and Robert E. Lee*

Foster care is a service under siege (National Commission on Family Foster Care, 1991). Currently, more than 500,000 children are in foster care (U.S. Department of Health and Human Services, National Clearinghouse on Child Abuse and Neglect Information, 2001). Because of factors such as AIDS, drug abuse, homelessness, and child maltreatment (Barbell & Freundlich, 2001), children are placed in foster care more often than any time in history. The contexts that result in out-of-home placement for many children are associated with negative life experiences and manifold challenges. Foster care, especially multiple placements, can exacerbate these challenges (e.g., Rosenfeld et al., 1997; Stone & Stone, 1983; Sumner-Mayer, 2007). Children in foster care are known to exhibit posttraumatic stress symptoms (Perry, Pollard, Blakely, & Vigilante, 1995) and a wide range of other mental and emotional disorders (Clausen, Laudsverk, Ganger, Chadwick, & Litronwnik, 1998; dosReis, Zito, & Safer, 2001; McIntyre & Keesler, 1998; Perry, Conrad, Dobson, Schick, & Ryan, 2000; Pilowski, 1995), behavioral problems (e.g., Chernoff, Combs-Orme, Risley-Curiss, & Heisler, 1994), and developmental problems such as cognitive deficits (Rosenfeld et al., 1997), learning disabilities (Naastrom & Koch, 1996; Stein, 1997), and adaptive behavior deficits (Horowitz, Simms, & Farrington, 1994). Moreover, extended stays in foster care are also known to be associated with short- and long-term bio-psychosocial problems (see reviews by Garwood & Close, 2001; Haury, 2000; Lee & Lynch, 1998; Lee & Stacks, 2004; Lee & Whiting, 2007). Because of all these circumstances, children in foster can be expected to demonstrate emotional, behavioral, and developmental disorders 2.5 times the rate in the

Originally published in *Research on Social Work Practice* 2006; 16; 287. DOI: 10.1177/1049731505284863 The online version of this article can be found at: http://rsw.sagepub.com/cgi/content/abstract/16/3/287

general population (Garwood & Close, 2001). Effective, multitargeted treatments for challenged foster children are needed.

Despite the need for empirically validated psychotherapeutic interventions, the literature is largely anecdotal. Therefore, our purpose has been to cull the foster care literature to find psychotherapeutic treatments that recognized the unique experiences of foster children, including promising interventions that are currently being applied to at-risk children. The overall number of therapeutic interventions found for children with behavioral problems was beyond the scope of this research.

Inclusion of interventions to be utilized in this systematic research synthesis (SRS) focused on the following criteria: (a) treatment utilized specifically with foster children, (b) interventions that mentioned utilization with foster children, and (c) interventions that targeted children with numerous risk factors. Because the amount of interventions specifically for foster children was sparse, articles that targeted at-risk children were included to provide possible therapeutic interventions that may be applied to foster children. Other inclusion criteria included empirical articles that described an intervention and a report of an empirical study of a treatment.

Because of the outpouring of new scientific knowledge and innovative interventions, a SRS was conducted utilizing the four features described by Rothman and Thomas (1994). The four features of a SRS include (a) planful structuring, (b) conceptual rather than statistical data integration (pertinent to a given area of study), (c) a very broad range of evidence on any given issue, and (d) seeking to aid in practice and policy development and accumulate new knowledge. The result is one or more hypotheses or "promising hunches" about means to solve a given behavioral or social problem. Because foster care is well documented as a cause of a plethora of problems for children, this SRS was an attempt to offer new insight and suggest future directions for therapeutic interventions targeted for foster children (Rothman & Thomas, 1994).

A total of 18 interventions and related empirical studies were reviewed in terms of their aims, outcomes, and methodological strengths and shortcomings. In addition, the intervention and empirical studies were categorized according to their theoretical, clinical, and empirical support utilizing a treatment protocol classification system (see Table 4.1; Saunders, Berliner, & Hanson, 2004). Although foster care is well documented as a difficult and challenging time for our youth, a gap in the literature relating to an insignificant amount of empirically validated interventions specifically for foster children that address the unique experience and culture of the foster child and the challenging dynamics of the foster family was found.

# Review of Literature

## Developmental Theory and Foster Family Dynamics

Childhood is characterized by change, transition, and reorganization and involves rapid growth and development (Hoagwood & Olin, 2002). This period of rapid change can contribute to increased vulnerability at this significant time in a child's life. Simultaneously, families also go through developmental transitions. According to Carter and McGoldrick (1999), stress is often greatest at transition points from one stage to another in the developmental process as families rebalance, redefine, and realign their relationships. Although children and families vary greatly in this developmental process, individual human development goes through an expected trajectory of stages depending on the availability of resources, cultural influences, and the period in history in which children grow up. Typical developmental transitions that family members experience during their life span involve changes in family structure, normative tasks of family members at each stage of development, emotional climate within the family, boundaries, patterns of interaction, and communication patterns. The foster child is faced with the task of adjusting to these normative tasks while transitioning to a new home environment.

Foster families provide a temporary substitute family structure ultimately driven by a contract with the state. Well-meaning foster parents are oftentimes faced with unrealistic tasks. The foster child is unsure of his or her future and lives in a world of uncertainty. A normal child's development trajectory would include the stability of what will occur from day to day based on the structure of his or her home life and stability of the family. On being placed in a foster home, a child is unsure of his or her future. The foster child is usually under the impression that he or she will eventually return home, regardless of what circumstances have removed him or her from his or her biological family. Adults cope with impermanence by building on an accrued sense of self-reliance and by anticipating and planning for a time of greater constancy. Young children have limited life experiences on which to establish themselves. Their sense of time focuses exclusively on the present, and this precludes any meaningful understanding of temporariness versus permanence. For very young children, periods of weeks or months are not comprehensible (American Academy of Pediatrics, Committee on Early Childhood, Adoption, and Dependent Care, 2001).

## Foster Children Experiencing Multiple Placements

Children are remaining in foster care longer than in the past, averaging 30.0 months in the District of Columbia, 35.6 months in Illinois, and 32.1 months in New York (Barbell & Freundlich, 2001). It is estimated that the longer the child stays in foster care, the more likely the child will have multiple placements (Barbell & Freundlich, 2001). In 1998, 21% of all foster children had three or more placements (U.S. House of Representatives, 2000). The number of placements a child experiences has been found to be directly related to the level of hostility he or she displays (Fanshel, Finch, & Grundy, 1989). In California, New York, and Pennsylvania, the number of infants younger than 36 months in foster care doubled from 1986 to 1991, twice the rate of increase in youth of all ages in foster care (U.S. General Accounting Office, 1994).

**Table 4.1**      Treatment Classification Criteria

*Category 1: Well-supported, efficacious treatment*

1. The treatment has a sound theoretical basis in generally accepted psychological principles.

2. A substantial clinical, anecdotal literature exists indicating the treatment's efficacy with at-risk children and foster children.

3. The treatment is generally accepted in clinical practice for at-risk children and foster children.

4. There is no clinical or empirical evidence or theoretical basis indicating that the treatment constitutes a substantial risk of harm to those receiving it, compared to its likely benefits.

5. The treatment has a manual that clearly specifies the components and administration characteristics of the treatment that allows for replication.

6. At least two randomized, controlled outcome studies have demonstrated the treatment's efficacy with at-risk children and foster children. This means the treatment was demonstrated to be better than placebo or no different or better than an already established treatment.

7. If multiple outcome studies have been conducted, the large majority of outcome studies support the efficacy of the treatment.

*Category 2: Supported and probably efficacious*

1. The treatment has a sound theoretical basis in generally accepted psychological principles.

2. A substantial clinical, anecdotal literature exists indicating the treatment's efficacy with at-risk children and foster children.

3. The treatment is generally accepted in clinical practice for at risk children and foster children.

4. There is no clinical or empirical evidence or theoretical basis indicating that the treatment constitutes a substantial risk of harm to those receiving it, compared to its likely benefits.

5. The treatment has a manual that clearly specifies the components and administration characteristics of the treatment that allows for implementation.

6. At least two studies utilizing some form of control without randomization (e.g., wait list, untreated group, placebo group) have established the treatment's efficacy over the passage of time, efficacy over placebo, or found it to be comparable to or better than already established treatment.

7. If multiple treatment outcome studies have been conducted, the overall weight of evidence supported the efficacy of the treatment.

*Category 3: Supported and acceptable treatment*

1. The treatment has a sound theoretical basis in generally accepted psychological principles.

2. A substantial clinical, anecdotal literature exists indicating the treatment's efficacy with at-risk children and foster children.

3. The treatment is generally accepted in clinical practice for at-risk children and foster children.

4. There is no clinical or empirical evidence or theoretical basis indicating that the treatment constitutes a substantial risk of harm to those receiving it, compared to its likely benefits.

5. The treatment has a manual that clearly specifies the components and administration characteristics of the treatment that allows for replication.

6a. At least one group study (controlled or uncontrolled), or a series of single subject studies have demonstrated the efficacy of the treatment with at-risk children and foster children;

or

6b. A treatment that has demonstrated efficacy with other populations has a sound theoretical basis for use with at-risk children and foster children, but has not been tested or used extensively with these populations.

7. If multiple treatment outcome studies have been conducted, the overall weight of evidence supported the efficacy of the treatment.

*Category 4: Promising and acceptable treatments*

1. The treatment has a sound theoretical basis in generally accepted psychological principles.

2. A substantial clinical, anecdotal literature exists indicating the treatment's efficacy with at-risk children and foster children.

3. The treatment is generally accepted in clinical practice for at-risk children and foster children.

4. There is no clinical or empirical evidence or theoretical basis indicating that the treatment constitutes a substantial risk of harm to those receiving it, compared to its likely benefits.

5. The treatment has a manual that clearly specifies the components and administration characteristics of the treatment that allows for implementation.

*Category 5: Novel and experimental treatments*

1. The theoretical basis for the treatment is novel and unique, but with reasonable application of accepted psychological principles.

2. A small and limited clinical literature exists to suggest the efficacy of the treatment.

3. The treatment is not widely used or generally accepted by practitioners working with at-risk children and foster children.

4. There is no clinical or empirical evidence or theoretical basis suggesting that the treatment constitutes a substantial risk of harm to those receiving it, compared to its likely benefits.

*Category 6: Concerning treatment*

1. The theoretical basis for the treatment is unknown, a misapplication of psychological principles, or a novel, unique, and concerning application of psychological principles.

2. Only a small and limited clinical literature exists suggesting the efficacy of the treatment.

3. There is a reasonable theoretical, clinical, or empirical basis suggesting that, compared to its likely benefits, the treatment constitutes a risk to those receiving it.

4. The treatment has a manual or other writings that specify the components and administration characteristics of the treatment that allows for implementation.

SOURCE: Saunders, Berliner, and Hanson, 2004.

Foster children may become vulnerable when they are removed from their homes and placed in different environments. When a child enters foster care, he or she may experience a variety of emotions including shame because his or her parents were unable to care for him or her (Williams, Fanolis, & Schamess, 2002). The effects of foster care may also exacerbate the existing problems or life experiences prior to placement. Rosenfeld and colleagues (1997) believe that most foster children carry permanent emotional scars from repeated multiple separations from parents, neighbors, and friends and remain reluctant to attach to substitute caregivers. When a foster child experiences multiple foster home placements, it can be traumatic and may interfere with the child's later formation of intimate relationships (Rosenfeld et al., 1997; Stone & Stone, 1983).

## Emotional and Behavioral Problems in Foster Children

The high prevalence of mental health problems among children in foster care is well documented (Clausen et al., 1998; McIntyre & Keesler, 1998; Pilowsky, 1995). Environmental, social, biological, and psychological risk factors have been used to explain foster children's vulnerability to the development of emotional or behavior disorders. Most foster children come from impoverished environments and were vulnerable to a myriad of risk factors associated with poverty, such as inadequate access to prenatal care, homelessness, and limited educational opportunities (McIntyre & Keesler, 1998).

## Academic, Peer, and Social Problems of Foster Children

Because of a focus on emotional and behavior issues, the essential educational, speech, and language acquisition of foster children may be neglected. The emotional trauma of transitioning to foster care can interfere with cognitive abilities (Rosenfeld et al., 1997). Because of multiple foster home placements and transferring to different schools, the emotional drain can affect the quality of foster children's schoolwork. Studies of maltreated children in foster care have shown higher rates of learning disabilities (10%—Nasstrom & Koch, 1996; 40%—Stein, 1997), achievement problems (41%—Chamberlain, Moreland, & Reid, 1992), and adaptive behavior deficits (73%—Horowitz et al., 1994). Common problems in school are falling behind academically, failing classes, failing to do homework, cheating, and disrupting class. Because of stigmatization, foster children may be picked on by classmates, develop school phobia, or engage in truancy (Noble, 1997).

Many foster youth end up homeless as adults, without acquiring the social and work skills needed to survive independently. Parents who grew up in foster care as children and who experienced homelessness as adults are almost twice as likely to have their own children placed in foster care as are parents who were homeless but were never in foster care (Roman & Wolfe, 1997).

## Foster Children and Trauma

In all, 22% of foster children of all ages were reported to suffer severe posttraumatic stress symptoms (Perry et al., 1995). Children exposed to trauma may have a wide range of symptoms such as posttraumatic stress disorder (PTSD), behavior disorders, anxieties, phobias, and depressive disorders (Perry et al., 2000). Maltreatment involving abuse and neglect poses grave risks for foster children. To complicate investigations of effects of foster care on children, the majority of these children have been abused or neglected prior to entering foster care (Stein, 1997). Dale, Kendall, and Sheehan (1999) screened 152 foster children between the ages of 6 and 8 for PTSD, and one third met the criteria. This includes children who have witnessed violent crime or experienced abuse, separation from caregiver, or other traumatic experiences. The majority of foster children have at least one psychiatric disorder, and approximately 33% have three or more diagnosed psychiatric problems (dosReis et al., 2001). Trauma unacknowledged in foster children may express itself in the development of internalizing (e.g., depression, anxiety) or externalizing (e.g., aggression, hyperactivity) disorders (Perry et al., 1995).

## Attachment Issues With Foster Children

A healthy attachment style can play a crucial role in the psychological effects of foster children (Haury, 2000). Attachment theory holds that attachment styles are developed in childhood and continue to affect the ability to form intimate and healthy relationships as adults (Ainsworth, 1982, 1989). Bowlby (1969) believed that the infant-caregiver relationship forms an internal working model that later influences interpersonal perceptions, attitudes, and expectations. This invokes trust and a secure base for the child to develop. Repeated experiences become encoded in our implicit memory as expectations and then as schemas of attachment to create a haven of safety (LeDoux, 1996).

Infants constitute a large and increasing proportion of children in out-of-home placement. Young children from birth to 3 account for 44% of all youth entering foster care (George & Wulczyn, 1999). Experiences in the first years of life have been defined as crucial to later personality development (Lieberman & Zeanah, 1995). Dozier, Higley, Albus, and Nutter (2002) have identified three critical challenges that infants and young children in foster care face. The three primary areas of concern are that (a) as a result of previous relationship failures, children often behave in alienating ways toward their caregivers (Stovall & Dozier, 2000; Tyrell & Dozier, 1999); (b) some caregivers are not nurturing even when infants signal their needs for reassurance clearly (Stovall & Dozier); and (c) even when previous caregivers have not provided adequate care, separations from these caregivers cause children to become deregulated behaviorally and physiologically (Fisher, Gunnar, Chamberlain, & Reid, 2000).

The foster care system may be problematic to assess attachment relationships by its own nature of complexity. Foster care facilitates the act of disrupted attachments, and professionals need to thoroughly understand the consequences of this interruption. James (1994) states that foster parents are in a unique position to deal with a child's specific needs when a child displays hostility, resentment, and ingratitude. Parent-child separation and the making and breaking of attachments are issues central in the life of a foster child and affect his or her emotional well-being. Foster children experience ambiguous loss as a result of the removal of significant family members from their internal family structure. Drawing on family systems theory, this ambiguous loss may leave them confused about who is in or out of their internal family system (Gardner, 1996). To develop into a psychologically healthy human being, a child needs a relationship with an adult who is nurturing and protective and who fosters trust and security (Werner & Smith, 1982).

Foster parents' understanding of the attachment cycle and the subsequent development of disordered attachment are imperative if the foster family is going to welcome a challenging child into their home (Wilson, 2001).

Although the purpose of this review was to gather current interventions used with foster children, reviewing conceptual literature was necessary to discover if the intervention research addressed these important issues that challenge foster children. Considering the current state of foster children, developmental and foster family dynamics, risk factors, emotional and behavioral problems, academic problems, trauma, and attachment issues, clinical implications indicate a need for adequate therapeutic interventions to address the multiple problems that result from foster care placement.

# Method

## Search Parameters

A comprehensive electronic search on First Search, PsychLit, Lexus-Nexus, ERIC, and MEDLINE was conducted. These search engines were chosen based on the wide range of disciplines addressed, such as psychology, sociology, social work, education, and medicine. The following keywords were searched: *foster care , foster children, foster families, children, family, surrogate family, out-of-home care, counseling, therapy, family therapy,* and *interventions.* Also *foster care* was linked to other terms, such as *attachment, trauma, emotional and behavioral disorders,* and *homelessness.* Specific boundaries were placed on the literature search including those keywords that would relate to foster care and current interventions. Included in the search were investigations of interventions with children at risk for removal to out-of-home care. Boundaries were initially broad, focusing on literature published the past 10 years. Because of the dynamic nature of contemporary society, only intervention studies conducted in the past decade (1994–2004) were reviewed. Historical and conceptual literature was also reviewed to integrate the current state of foster care with current available interventions.

## Evaluation Criteria

In the process of evaluating the interventions, two distinct categories emerged: Category 1 included interventions that focus on a specific treatment protocol that addresses a problem behavior or behaviors that exist for foster children, and Category 2 included interventions that focus on the prevention of future problem behaviors. Each study referencing the intervention is described in Table 4.2 (interventions that focus on treatment) and in Table 4.3 (interventions that focus primarily on prevention).

Empirical articles were evaluated based on the following criteria: literature review or theory; sample characteristics; design or sampling method; measures, data analysis, or effect size; focus of treatment or prevention; treatment integrity; and results or follow-up. Empirical articles with their related interventions were also evaluated using the treatment protocol classification system. The treatment protocol classification system (see Table 4.1) is to help establish a clear, criteria-based system for classifying interventions and treatments according to theoretical, clinical, and empirical support. The guidelines reflect the knowledge at the time of writing. As additional studies of testing the effectiveness of existing protocols will be conducted, classifications will change over time as more research is completed (Saunders et al., 2004).

## Results

## Overview of Interventions

As a result of the search, many articles focused on the numerous problems that foster children experience.

Many interventions that were specific to foster children were limited to technological explanatory literature describing interventions that have not been tested for their overall effectiveness. A total of 18 studies were included in this review to critique. Each intervention described and outlined in Tables 4.2 and 4.3 is a study that investigates the effectiveness and utilization of that intervention. The studies in this review include 2 studies in 1994, 1 in 1995, 4 in 1998, 2 in 1999, 2 in 2000, 2 in 2001, 1 in 2002, 3 in 2003, and 1 in 2004. Although 7 qualitative studies were found, only quantitative studies were evaluated using the criteria described above. Although the importance of qualitative studies was acknowledged, primarily only empirical articles were reviewed, and an inclusion of qualitative studies was beyond the scope of this research.

Only those studies that were found in peer-reviewed journals were included in this review. Interventions that included children who faced various risk factors (e.g., abuse, neglect, minority, poverty, no prenatal care, behavior problems) were also included in the search for effective interventions. Empirical

**Table 4.2** Characteristics of Studies of Interventions Focusing on Treatment

| Intervention and Referenced Study | Literature Review Yes or No, Theory or Model | Sample Size Age or Gender | Design or Sampling Method | Measures or Data Analysis, Effect Size | Focus of Treatment | Treatment Fidelity | Results and Follow-up |
|---|---|---|---|---|---|---|---|
| Dyadic Developmental Psychotherapy; Becker-Weidman (2004) | Yes; attachment theory | $n = 113$, ages 10–17, M/F | NR; 1 group | RADQ; CBCL; DDP; $t$ tests; effect size not mentioned | Affective attunement, PLACE, cognitive restructuring, psychodramatic enactments | Not mentioned | RADQ: $T = 12.822$, $p < .0001$; CBCL; t test, subscales range (4.897-10.57); $p$ value range ($< .0001$-.006); no follow-up |
| Hand in Hand; Whitemore, Ford, and Sack (2003) | Yes; family preservation | $n = 129$, ages 2-6, M/F | NR; 1 group; HH | TRF, CBCL, PPVT EOW; MANOVA frequency tables; graphs; effect size not mentioned | Special education, intensive case management, academic and developmental skill building, individual and family therapy, proctor care | Extensive screening of proctor patients | TRF: $F(9, 113) = 7.031$, $p < .01$; CBCL: $F = 10.746$, $p < .001$; BDI: $F = 25.64$, $p < .01$; PPVT: $t(59) = 5.66$, $p < .001$; EOW: $t(84) = 11.725$, $p < .001$; follow-up: intake, discharge, and 4 years |
| Dina Dinosaur; Webster-Stratton (2003) | Yes; Developmental theory | $n = 97$; ages 4–8; M/F | R; 4 groups | CSPS, NCM, CBCL, CT, PT, PT+CT, WLC; $t$ tests, frequency tables | Emotional literacy, empathy, friendship, communication skills, anger problem solving, school success | Treatment manuals, session protocols, checklists, video tapes | CSPC; CT vs. WLC, $d = .79$, $p < .05$; PT+CT vs. WLC, $d = .69$, $p < .05$, PT vs. WLC, $d = .25$, $p < .05$, NCM; CT vs. WLC, $d = .58$, $p < .05$; PT + CT vs. WLC, $d = .54$, $p < .05$; PT vs. WLC, $d = .46$, $p < .05$, CBCL; CT vs. WLC, $d = .38$; PT = CT vs. WLC, $d = .73$, $p < .05$; PT vs. WLC, $d = .89$, $p < .05$; follow-up: baseline, 2 months, 1 year, and 2 years |

| Intervention and Referenced Study | Literature Review Yes or No, Theory or Model | Sample Size or Age or Gender | Design or Sampling Method | Measures or Data Analysis, Effect Size | Focus of Treatment | Treatment Fidelity | Results and Follow-up |
|---|---|---|---|---|---|---|---|
| Foster Care Clinic; Horowitz, Owens, and Simms (2000) | Yes; multidisciplinary program | $n = 120$, ages 11–74, M/F | NR; 2 groups; FCC, CG | CBCL, C-GAS, PPVT, ESP, VABS; multifactor stratified logistic regression polycotomous; effect size not mentioned | Medical exam, developmental, psychological speech or language and motor assessments | Not mentioned | CBCL, C-GAS, PPVT, ESP, VABS; no significant differences; FCC were more likely to be identified with developmental and mental problems vs. CG; (56.5% vs. 8.6%; 37.1% vs. 13.8%); follow-up: baseline, 6 months, and 12 months |
| Parent-Child Interaction Therapy; Borrego, Urquiza, Rasmussen, and Zebell (1999) | Yes; social learning theory | $n = 1$, mother 35, male 3 | Single case Study | DPICS, ECBI, CBCL, PSI, CAPI; $t$ test, frequency tables; effect size not mentioned | Social reinforcement, operant model, increase positive interactions between mother and child | Training in PICT, treatment checklists | DPICS; increased positive interactions, ECBI; pre-152 vs. post-65, CBCL-ED; pre-74 vs. post-53, CBCL-ID; pre-76 vs. post-46, PSI; pre-96 vs. post-15, CAPI; pre-74 vs. post-56; follow-up: pre, mid, and post; 5 and 16 months |
| Multisystemic Therapy; Henggeler et al. (1999) | Yes; social ecological model | $n = 113$, ages 10–17, M/F | R; 2 groups; MST; CG | GSI-BSI, PEI, CBCL, FACES III, school attendance, FFS; ANOVA post hoc comparisons; frequency tables; effect size not mentioned | Daily support, crisis plan, focus family strengths and community resources | Structured supervision, coded tapes, treatment manual | GSI-BSI, PEI, CBCL-ED; $F = 3.99$, $p < .021$, CBCL-ID; $F = 4.13$, $p < .017$; FACES III $F = 3.28$, $p < .039$, School attendance = 5.72, $p < .018$, FFS; $F = 7.72$, $p < .006$; follow-up: baseline, 1 week, 2 weeks, and 4 months |

(Continued)

**Table 4.2** (Continued)

| Intervention and Referenced Study | Literature Review Yes or No, Theory or Model | Sample Size Age or Gender | Design or Sampling Method | Measures or Data Analysis, Effect Size | Focus of Treatment | Treatment Fidelity | Results and Follow-up |
|---|---|---|---|---|---|---|---|
| Multidimensional Treatment Foster Care; Chamberlain and Reid (1998) | Yes; developmental model | $n = 79$; ages 10–17, males | R; 2 groups; MTFC; CG | OYA, EBC; ANOVA hierarchal multiple regression; effect size not mentioned | FP trained in CBT, individual or family therapy, problem solving, social perspective, non-aggressive methods of self-expression FP participated | Supervision, daily contact with parents; videotaped treatment manual | OYA: fewer runaways (MTFC, 30.5% vs. CG, 57.8%) EBC; criminal referral rates decreased in MTFC group, $F(1, 77) = 3.93$, $p = .003$; follow-up: 1 year preplacement and post-placement |
| Holding Therapy; Myeroff, Mertlich, and Gross (1999) | Yes; attachment theory | $n = 23$, ages 4–14, M/F | NR, 2 groups, HT, CG | CBCL; two-tailed $t$ tests; effect size not mentioned | Cognitive restructuring, psychodramatic reenactments, inner child metaphor, therapeutic holding | Procedure manual | CBCL; Aggression scores: pre and post HT; $t = 4.26$, $df = 10$, $p < .002$, CG, $t = .58$, $df = 8$, $p = .5$, CBCL; delinquency scores: pre, post, HT; $t = 2.37$, $df = 10$, $p < .04$, CG, $t = 20$, $df = 8$, $p = .85$; no follow-up |
| Fostering Individualized Assistance Program; Clark and Prange (1994) | Yes; family preservation, wraparound | $n = 132$, ages 7–12, M/F | R, 2 groups, FIAP, SP | CBCL, YSR; MANOVA, ANOVA, chi-square; effect size not mentioned | Support, life-domain planning, strength assessment, stabilize placement, improve EBD | Supervision, independent reliability checks on 20% of data collected | Lower pathology CBCL-ID; $p < .05$; CBCL-ED; $p < .05$, YSR; F(8, 98) = 14.75, $p < .01$; follow-up: 4 and 18 months |

NOTE: BDI = Battelle Developmental Inventory; CAPI = Child Abuse Potential Inventory; CBCL = Child Behavior Checklist; CBT = Cognitive Behavioral Therapy ; C-GAS = Children's Global Assessment Scale; CSPS = Cognitive Social Problem-Solving; CG = control group; CT = child training; DPICS = Dyadic Parent-Child Interaction Coding System; EBC = Elliot Behavior Checklist; EBD = emotional and behavior disorders; ECBI = Eyeberg Child Behavior Inventory ; ED = externalizing disorders; EOW = Expressive One-Word Picture Vocabulary Test; ESP = Early Screening Profile; FFS = Family Friends and Self, FACES III = Family Adaptability and Cohesion Scale-III;FCC = Foster Care Clinic; FIAP = Fostering Individualized Assistance Program; FP = foster parents; GSI-BSI = The Global Severity Index of the Brief Symptom Inventory; HH = Hand in Hand; HT = Holding Therapy; ID = internalizing disorders; M/F = male and female; MTFC = Multidimensional Treatment Foster Care; MST=Multisystemic Therapy; $n$ = sample size; NCM = Negative Conflict Management; NR = nonrandom assignment; OYA = Oregon Youth Authority; PCIT = Parent-Child Interaction Therapy; PLACE = playfulness, love, acceptance, curiosity, and empathy; PMT = Parent Management Training; PPVT = Peabody Picture Vocabulary Test; PSI = Parenting Stress Index; PT = parent training; R = random assignment; RADQ = Reactive Attachment Disorder Questionnaire; SP = Standard Practice; TRF = Teacher Rating Form; VABS = Vineland Adaptive Behavior Scales; WLC = wait list control; YSR = Youth Self Report.

**Table 4.3**   Characteristics of Studies Focusing on Preventive Interventions

| Intervention and Referenced Study | Literature Review Yes or No, Theory or Model | Sample Size Age or Gender | Design or Sampling Method | Measures or Data Analysis, Effect Size | Focus of Treatment | Treatment Fidelity | Results and Follow-up |
|---|---|---|---|---|---|---|---|
| Enhanced Home Based Crisis Intervention (HBLC+); Evans et al. (2003) | Yes; family preservation model | $n = 238$, ages 5–18, M/F | R, 3 groups, HBCL, HBLC+, CCM | CDF, SAF, PHCSC, FACES II, BESR, CBCL; ANOVA frequency checks; effect size reported | Family centered, parent support group, counselor respite, maintain crisis in natural environment vs. hospitalization, bicultural advocate | Training by consultants | PHCS; $F(1, 144) = 16.98$, $p < .01$, $d = .25$, FACES II; HBLC vs. CCM, $F(1, 450) = 4.17$, $p < .05$, $d = .43$, HBLC+ vs. CCM, $F(1, 450) = 8.32$, $p < .01$, $d = .43$, BESR; no report, HBCL vs. CCM; $F(1, 458) = 7.11$, $p < .01$, $d = .48$; HBCL+ vs. CCM, $F(1, 458) = 8.79$, $p < .01$, $d = .43$; follow-up: baseline, discharge, and 6 months |
| Respite Care; Cowen and Reed 2002 | Yes, ecological theory | $n = 148$, ages 1 week, M/F | NR, 1 group, RC | PIF, PSI, descriptive statistics, t tests, logistic regression, effect size not mentioned | Developmental stimulation, social activities to improve self-esteem, self-confidence, and coping with stress | Not mentioned | PIF; parent domain scales, $t = 3.55$, df = 86, $p = .000$, child domain scales, $t = 2.2$, df = 86, $p = .02$, PSI (total stress); $t = 3.27$, df = 86, $p = .00016$; no follow-up |
| Empowerment Zone; Nabors, Proescher, and DeSilva (2001) | Yes, prevention model | $n = 53$, ages 5–11, M/F | NR, 1 group, EZ | TPCF, EZSS, HMCDS, t tests repeated measures, effect size not mentioned | Conflict resolution problem solving, parent training, anger management, healthy eating, physical and dental hygiene | Not mentioned | TPCF; $F = 4.12$, $p < .05$, EZSS; 87% liked activities, HMCDS; $F = 5.65$, $p < .024$; no follow-up |

*(Continued)*

**Table 4.3** (Continued)

| Intervention and Referenced Study | Literature Review Yes or No, Theory or Model | Sample Size Age or Gender | Design or Sampling Method | Measures or Data Analysis, Effect Size | Focus of Treatment | Treatment Fidelity | Results and Follow-up |
|---|---|---|---|---|---|---|---|
| Intensive Intervention; Zeanah, Larrieu, Heller, and Scott (2001) | Yes, multi-disciplinary approach | $n = 331$, ages birth to 4, M/F | NR, 2 groups, IG, CG | Length of time in care; permanent plan outcomes; maltreatment recidivism; MANOVA frequency tables; effect size not mentioned | Assessment of caregivers, court-ordered case plan, therapy, attachment issues, medication | Not mentioned | No significant differences in length of time in FCE, termination of parental rights increased, return of children to birth family decreased |
| Early Intervention Foster Care; Fisher, Gunnar, Chamberlain, and Reid (2000) | Yes, developmental theory, medical model | $n = 30$, ages 3–5, M/F | NR, 3 groups, EIFC, RFC, CC | ECI, salivary cortisol, PDR, CCIIF, ANOVA, MANOVA, post hoc analysis, effect size not mentioned | FP training with consistent non-abusive discipline parenting, close monitoring, therapeutic relationship between FP and FC, biological indicators of stress | FP training daily phone contact; home visits; 24-hour, on-call crisis intervention | ECI; $F = 21.7$, $p < .001$ salivary cortisol; over-all decrease in EFIC group, PDR; $F = 3.24$, $p < .08$, CCIIF; $F = 18.01$, $p < .001$; follow-up: 2 weeks after placement and 12 weeks |
| ENHANCE; O'Hara, Church, and Blatt 1998 | Yes, developmental theory | $n = 52$, ages birth to 18, M/F | NR, 1 group | DDST-II, ELM-2, HOME, INFANIB; descriptive statistics; effect size not mentioned | Developmental screening and treatment by home visiting by CNS, parent education, early intervention | Not mentioned | DDST-II; 65% passed, 35% failed, ELM; 92% passed, 8% failed HOME; 100% FCE adequate, INFANIB; 88% of FC less than 6 months had abnormalities, 33% of FC longer than 6 months had abnormalities |

| Intervention and Referenced Study | Literature Review Yes or No, Theory or Model | Sample Size Age or Gender | Design or Sampling Method | Measures or Data Analysis, Effect Size | Focus of Treatment | Treatment Fidelity | Results and Follow-up |
|---|---|---|---|---|---|---|---|
| Partner's Intervention; Webster-Stratton (1998) | Yes, developmental theory | $n = 394$, HeadStart mothers and 4-year-olds, M/F | R, 2 groups, partners control | OSCL, DDI, DPICS, CSCCPH-SC, ECBI, TRF; MANOVA; effect size not mentioned | Parent training to strengthen parent competence, teacher training | Training, treatment manual, videotaped session checklists | OSCL; $F_{(6, 377)} = 3.94$, $p < .01$; DDI; $F_{(12, 271)} = 3.98$, $p < .001$; DPICS; $F_{(14, 249)} = 2.86$, $p < .01$; CSCCPH; $F_{(6, 357)} = 4.46$, $p < .001$, CSCCPC; $F_{(2, 369)} = 4.08$, $p < .05$, ECBI; $F_{(12, 244)} = 1.98$, $p < .05$, TRF; $F_{(2, 373)} = 5.38$, $p < .01$; follow-up: 12 and 18 months |
| Intensive Preservation Service; Gillespie, Byrne, and Workman 1995 | Yes, family preservation, crisis intervention theory | $n = 42$, ages birth to 17, M/F | NR, 1 group, FPS | Reunification with birth parents, service provision, family characteristics and foster care; chi-square frequency tables; effect size not mentioned | Problems related to separation | Not mentioned | Overall, 79% children were reunited, most critical problem solved by IFPS; $p < .0070$, teen parent predicted remaining in FH; $p < .0155$, social worker contact with foster family prior to project; $p < .0058$; no follow-up |
| Prenatal and Childhood Nurse Visitation; Olds, Henderson, and Tatelbaum (1995) | Yes; family preservation, systems of care | $n = 400$, pregnant women | R, 4 groups, TX 1, TX 2, TX 3, TX 4 | CBHI, SBLFM, hospital records, CPS records; logistic linear model; effect size not mentioned | Improve outcomes of pregnancy qualities of parental care giving, maternal life course development | Not mentioned | CBHI; $p = .03$, SBLFM; no significant differences, hospital records; 84% fewer visits by PECNHV group, CPS; no significant differences; follow-up: CBHI; baseline, 34 months, 36 months, 46 months, and 48 months; 25 and 50 months of age; CPS records; birth to 4 SBLFM; 36 and 48 months |

*(Continued)*

**Table 4.3** (Continued)

| Intervention and Referenced Study | Literature Review or Theory or Model | Sample Size Age or Gender | Design or Sampling Method | Measures or Data Analysis, Effect Size | Focus of Treatment | Treatment Fidelity | Results and Follow-up |
|---|---|---|---|---|---|---|---|
| Prenatal and Childhood Nurse Visitation; Olds, Henderson, and Tatelbaum (1995) | Yes; family preservation; systems of care | $n = 400$, pregnant women | R, 4 groups, TX 1, TX 2, TX 3, TX 4 | CBHI, SBLFM, hospital records, CPS records; logistic linear model; effect size not mentioned | Improve outcomes of pregnancy, qualities of parental care giving, maternal life course development | Not mentioned | CBHI; $p = .03$, SBLFM; no significant differences, hospital records; 84% fewer visits by PECNHV group, CPS; no significant differences; follow-up: CBHI; baseline, 34 months, 36 months, 46 months, and 48 months; 25 and 50 months of age; CPS records; birth to 4 SBLFM; 36 and 48 months |

NOTE: BESR = Bureau of Evaluation and Services Research; CBCL = Child Behavior Checklist; CBHI = Caldwell and Bradley Home Inventory; CC = community control; CCIIF = Child Caregiver Interview Impressions Form; CCM = Crisis Case Management; CDF = Client Description Form; CG = control group; CNS = Clinical Nurse Specialist; CPS = Child Protective Service; CSCCPH-PC = Child Social Competence and Conduct Problems at Home, and at School; ECI = Early Childhood Inventory; DDI = Daily Discipline Interview; DDST-II = Denver Developmental Screening Test; DPICS = Dyadic Parent-Child Interaction Coding System; ECBI = Eye berg Child Behavior Inventory; EZ = Empowerment Zone; EZSS = Empowerment Zone Survey for Students; FACES II = Family Adaptability and Cohesion Scales II; FC = Foster child; FACES II = Family Adaptability and Cohesion Scales II; FH = foster home ; FP = foster parent; HBCI = Home Based Crisis Intervention; HBCI+ = Enhanced Home Based Crisis Intervention; HMCD = How My Child Is Doing Survey; HOME = Home Observation for Measurement of the Environment; IFPS = Intensive Family Preservation Service; IG = intervention group; INFANIB = Infant Neurological International Battery; M/F = male and female; n = sample size; NR = nonrandom assignment; OSCL = Oregon Social Learning Center; PDR = Parent Daily Report; PECNHV = Prenatal and Early Childhood Nurse Home Visitation; PIF = Parent Information Form; PHCSCS = Piers-Harris Children's Self-Concept Scale; PSI = Parenting Stress Inventory; R = random assignment; RC = Respite care; RFC = regular foster care; SAF = Supplemental Assessment Form; SBLFM = Stanford-Binet FormL-M;TPCF = Teacher Perception of Children's Functioning; TRF = Teacher Report Form; TX = treatment group.

articles containing the terms *foster care* or *foster children* were also included in the review if one of the terms was mentioned in the article as a part of the sample population but was not the main focus of the intervention.

Because foster children are at risk for developing a myriad of developmental, physical, and psychological problems, many therapeutic interventions involved multiple systems of care, and the programs were multifaceted. The wraparound process was found to be used by communities to prevent ineffective out-of-home placements. The term *wraparound* is a term to describe a philosophy and general approach that tailors the services to the specific individual needs of children and families (Myaard, Crawford, Jackson, & Alessi, 2000). Many studies involved the use of multiple community-based services.

# Empirical Literature of Interventions

## Focusing on Treatment

The following nine interventions were found to be specific to treatment and focused on specific problem behaviors: Multisystemic Therapy (Henggeler et al., 1999), Parent-Child Interaction Therapy (Borrego, Urquiza, Rasmussen, & Zebell, 1999), Dina Dinosaur (Webster-Stratton & Reid, 2003), Dyadic Developmental Psychotherapy (Becker-Weidman, 2004), Fostering Individualized Assistance Program (Clark & Prange, 1994), Hand in Hand (Whitemore, F ord, & S ack, 2003), Multidimensional Foster Care (Chamberlain & Reid, 1998), Holding Therapy (Myeroff, Mertlich, & Gross, 1999), and Foster Care Clinic (Horowitz, Owens, & Simms, 2000). Although aspects of some of these interventions were preventive, the intervention focused more on treating specific problem behaviors. The interventions and referenced studies are described in Table 4.2.

## Focusing on Prevention

Preventive interventions aim to counteract risk factors and reinforce protective factors to disrupt processes that contribute to human dysfunction (Coie et al., 1993). The goal is to prevent problem behaviors from developing. Several of the preventive interventions examined provide strategies by designing multiple intervention components to address multiple risk factors. The following interventions were found to address the needs of children with risk factors: Empowerment Zone (Nabors, Proescher, & DeSilva, 2001), Intensive Family Preservation Services (Gillespie, Byrne, & Workman, 1995), Early Intervention Foster Care

(Fisher et al., 2000), Respite Care (Cowen & Reed, 2002), Partner's Intervention (Webster-Stratton,1998), Excellence in Health Care to Abused and Neglected Children (ENHANCE; O'Hara, Church, & Blatt, 1998), Enhanced Home-Based Crisis Intervention (Evans et al., 2003), Prenatal and Early Childhood Home Visitation (Olds, Henderson, & Tatelbaum, 1995), and Preventive Intervention (Zeanah, Larrieu, Heller, & Scott, 2001). The interventions that focus on prevention are outlined in Table 4.3.

# Synthesis of Empirical Literature of Interventions in Tables 4.2 and 4.3

## Referenced Studies

Of the 18 studies reviewed, 9 were found to focus on treatment of specific behaviors that at-risk or foster children experience (see Table 4.3). Preventive intervention studies consisted of the remaining 9 (see Table 4.2). Interventions and their corresponding studies that targeted only foster children consisted of 6 studies. The remainder mentioned foster care in the article but were not specific to foster children. Several of the interventions were community- and family-based programs involving comprehensive, multidisciplinary approaches. This may be an attempt to address all the multiple components necessary for treating the at-risk child in the context of home, school, and peer relations. Many studies involved parent training, child training, case management, individual and family therapy, and developmental and medical screenings. A focus on family strengths was a repetitive theme throughout the evaluation of the interventions.

Five of the 18 referenced studies treated one or two specific problems such as Holding Therapy (Myeroff et al., 1999) and Dyadic Developmental Psychotherapy (Becker-Weidman, 2004) treating attachment disorders, Dina Dinosaur (Webster-Stratton & Reid, 2003) focusing on school success and peer interactions, Prenatal and Early Childhood Nurse Home Visitation (Olds et al., 1995) focusing on prenatal care for pregnant mothers until their children reach the age of 2, and a home-based intervention titled ENHANCE (O'Hara et al., 1998) that addresses the utility of developmental screening.

Three of the interventions used treatment foster care as an overall milieu that involves engaging the foster parent as the therapeutic agent (Chamberlain & Reid, 1998; Fisher et al., 2000; Whitemore et al., 2003). The Foster Care Clinic (Horowitz et al., 2000), Prenatal and Early Childhood Nurse Home Visitation (Olds et al., 1995), and ENHANCE (O'Hara et al., 1998) are three interventions that involved developmental screening along with medical and mental health screening. Four interventions focused on the prevention of out-of-home placement (Borrego et al., 1999; Evans et al., 2003; Gillespie et al., 1995; Olds et al., 1995). Three interventions involved home visits by nurses (Evans et al., 2003; O'Hara et al., 1998; Olds et al., 1995). Three interventions included the biological parents of the foster children as a part of the intervention (Fisher et al., 2000; Gillespie et al., 1995; Zeanah et al., 2001). Home visits were used by many of the intensive interventions that involved 8 of the 18 interventions (Chamberlain & Reid, 1998; Clark & Prange, 1994; Evans et al., 2003; Fisher et al., 2000; Gillespie et al., 1995; Henggeler et al., 1999; O'Hara, 1998; Olds et al., 1995).

## Literature Review or Theory

All the referenced studies included a literature review in the article and linked the review to the problem prior to describing the interventions. Theories of orientation varied by each article but centered on family preservation (Clark & Prange, 1994; Evans et al., 2003; Gillespie et al., 1995; Olds et al., 1995; Whitemore et al., 2003), developmental theory (Chamberlain & Reid, 1998; Fischer et al., 2000; O'Hara et al., 1998; Webster-Stratton, 1998; Webster-Stratton & Reid, 2003), and ecological theory (Cowen & Reed, 2002; Henggeler et al., 1999). Two intervention studies identified using a multidisciplinary approach (Horowitz et al., 2000; Zeanah et al., 2001). Two intervention studies focused primarily on attachment theory as the basic orientation of the intervention (Becker-Weidman, 2004; Myeroff et al., 1999). Social learning theory was described in one study as guiding the orientation of the intervention (Borrego et al., 1999). The Empowerment Zone (Nabors et al., 2001) did not mention a theoretical base but emphasized prevention as an important element of their intervention.

## Sample, Age, and Gender

The number of participants in the samples varied widely (range = 1–400, $M = 134.4$). Of the 18 studies reported (i.e., 9 interventions focusing on treatment, 9 focusing on prevention), 50% of the sample sizes can be categorized as relatively large (range = 100–400). The remaining 9 studies had sample sizes of fewer than 100 (range = 1–97). For the most part, convenience samples of children's families or foster children were obtained from local agencies.

One study involved pregnant, at-risk mothers, and another study included Head Start mothers and their 3-year-old children (Borrego et al., 1999; Olds et al., 1995). The age of all participants in the 18 studies varied from birth to 17 years, which provided a wide variety of therapeutic interventions at different developmental stages.

Six of the 18 studies involved a combination of young children and adolescents (Becker-Weidman, 2004; Chamberlain & Reid, 1998; Evans et al., 2003; Gillespie et al., 1995; Henggeler et al., 1999; Myeroff et al., 1998). Two studies focused only on infants (Horowitz et al., 2000; O'Hara et al.,

1998) and 1 on pregnant women at risk (Olds et al., 1994), and 4 used only preschool children (Fisher et al., 2000; Webster-Stratton & Reid, 2003; Whitemore et al., 2003; Zeanah et al., 2001). One study focused on children from 1 week to 7 years old (Cowen & Reed, 2002). Parent-Child Interaction Therapy was a single case study with a mother and her 3-year-old child (Borrego et al., 1999). Gender for the most part was evenly dispersed for most studies, with the exception of Multidimensional Treatment Foster Care (Chamberlain & Reid, 1998) and Parent-Child Interaction Therapy (Borrego et al., 1999), which used samples of only males.

All the studies were conducted in the United States. This contributed to a diverse sample including differing ethnic groups depending on the agency, geographical location, and nature of the intervention. Because of attrition and other factors, sample size decreased with the progression of time.

# Design or Sampling Method

Seven out of the 18 studies employed experimental designs with random assignment to treatment condition (Chamberlain & Reid, 1998; Clark & Prange, 1994; Evans et al., 2003; Henggeler et al., 1999; Olds et al., 1995; Webster-Stratton, 1998; Webster-Stratton & Reid, 2003). Six studies used treatment-only designs (Becker-Weidman, 2004; Cowen & Reed, 2002; Gillespie et al., 1995; Nabors et al., 2001; O'Hara et al., 1998; Whitemore et al., 2003). The remainder did not randomly assign study participants into treatment and control groups (Fisher et al., 2000; Horowitz et al., 2000; Myeroff et al., 1999; Zeanah et al., 2001). One single case study involving a mother and her 3-year-old son was included in the review (Borrego et al., 1999).

## Measures, Data Analysis, and Effect Size

### Measures

In all, 83% of the investigated studies used standardized measures to evaluate the effectiveness of their intervention. Standardized measures may take the form of traditional question and answer scales and checklists. Standardized instruments have procedures for administration and objective scoring criteria and guides for the interpretation of scores. The Child Behavior Checklist (CBCL) was used in nine studies and has been well standardized and has excellent reliability (test-retest correlation = .93, interparent correlation = .76, Cronbach's $\alpha$ = .96 (Wamboldt, Wamboldt, & Gavin, 2001). Family instruments, such as Home Observation of Measurement of Environment (O'Hara et al., 1998), Family Adaptability and Cohesion Scales (FACES II; Henggeler et al., 1999), and the Caldwell Bradley Home Inventory (Olds et al., 1995), were also utilized.

The prevention intervention (Zeanah et al., 2001) focus of treatment was preventive and used naturalistic observation with structured and unstructured interviews. Length of time in care, permanent plan outcomes, and maltreatment recidivism were the variables measured (Zeanah et al., 2001). The Intensive Family Preservation Service (Gillespie et al., 1995), in which the focus was reunification of foster children with their birth family, used measures that included family characteristics, service provision variables, and foster care variables to measure the effectiveness of their intervention.

The outcome measures varied because of the complexity of the interventions. Developmental screening instruments, social measures, hospital records, state agency records, teacher reports, and neurological measures were also used. Dyadic Developmental Therapy (Becker-Weidman, 2004) used the Reactive Attachment Disorder Questionnaire, which measures the symptoms of reactive attachment disorder.

Seven out of the 18 studies reported psychometric properties (e.g., validity and reliability) of the instruments in their description of measures in their studies (Cowen & Reed, 2002; Evans et al., 2003; Fisher et al., 2000; Horowitz et al., 2000; Myeroff et al., 1999; O'Hara et al., 1998; Webster-Stratton, 1998).

## Data Analysis

All but one of the studies used inferential statistics, testing differences in a dependent variable associated with various conditions of an experiment. ENHANCE (O'Hara et al., 1998) used descriptive statistics based on results of developmental screening of children in foster care. The data analysis used in each study varied to a degree depending on sample size, hypothesis, and problem. Eight out of 18 studies utilized analysis of variance to analyze data (Chamberlain & Reid, 1998; Clark & Prange, 1994; Evans et al., 2003; Fisher et al., 2000; Henggeler et al., 1999; Webster-Stratton, 1998; Webster-Stratton & Reid, 2003; Whitemore et al., 2003).

## Effect Size

Two recent studies mentioned effect size in their results (Evans et al., 2003; Webster-Stratton & Reid, 2003). Cohen (1992) contends that this statistical measure of power should be included in all method sections of data analysis, and there are ample accessible resources for estimating sample size in research planning using power analysis. The Webster-Stratton and Reid (2003) study reported in the form of effect size results for an overall analysis of statistical power (see Table 4.3). It also included Cohen's indexes and conventional values for operationally defining small, medium, and large effects. Their average results indicated moderate to large effect sizes (range $d = .25–.89$, $M = .79$). The other study was a home-based crisis intervention (Evans et al., 2003) and also reported the results of the effect size for each variable measured. They reported the effect size to be small to moderate (range $d = .25–.48$, $M = .40$).

## Focus on Treatment

The focus of treatment is designed to treat children, foster children, or families regarding specific behaviors or problems. The focus of the treatment is outlined in Table 4.2. The treatment foci were on specific problem behaviors such as attachment, abuse or neglect, and emotional and behavioral problems. Parent training, support, case management, therapy, cognitive restructuring, social reinforcements, and community resources are mentioned in several studies. In attachment disordered foster children, affective attunement and psychodramatic enactments are the focus of both treatments (Becker-Weidman, 2004; Myeroff et al., 1999). Dyadic Developmental Psychotherapy utilized PLACE, which is an acronym for playfulness, love, acceptance, curiosity, and empathy. The focus of school-based interventions was on emotional literacy, problem solving, school rules and success, friendship, and communication (Nabors et al., 2001; Webster-Stratton & Reid, 2003). Medical, developmental, and psychological screenings involved the treatment utilized by the Foster Care Clinic (Horowitz et al., 2000).

## Focus of Prevention

Nine of the 18 studies were preventive interventions. Their overall purpose is to prevent emotional, behavioral, and developmental problems in foster children and also to prevent out-of-home placement. These interventions target risk factors in children and families. The Partner's Intervention goal is to strengthen protective factors for children (Webster-Stratton, 1998). Intensive caregiver assessment is a focus of prevention in 3 studies (O'Hara et al., 1998; Olds et al., 1995; Zeanah et al., 2001). Other preventive procedures included improving the qualities of parenting (Fisher et al., 2000; Nabors et al., 2001; O'Hara et al., 1998; Olds et al., 1995; Webster-Stratton, 1998). Psychoeducation of health issues was addressed by Empowerment Zone (Nabors et al., 2001), which addressed healthy eating and physical and dental hygiene, and by Prenatal and Early Childhood Nurse Home Visitation (Olds et al., 1995), which focused on improving outcomes of pregnancy.

Many of the components of the preventive interventions involved education, training, socializing, and support. One study utilized teacher training (Webster-Stratton, 1998). Enhanced Home-Based Intervention (HBCL+) included a bicultural advocate who established a parent support group and provided individualized parent support and advocacy (Evans et al., 2003).

## Treatment Integrity

According to Waltz, Addis, Koerner, and Jacobson (1993), manipulation checks are a part of good scientific research. They should be used in psychotherapy trials to confirm that therapists followed the treatment manuals and performed therapy competently. Adherence to these manuals and explicating treatment modalities depend on a number of measures. Techniques are unique to each intervention and require specific training, including documentation of adherence to manuals and protocol of treatment (Waltz et al., 1993).

Only 6 of the 18 studies included treatment integrity in their article (Borrego et al., 1999; Chamberlain & Reid, 1998; Clark & Prange, 1994; Henggeler et al., 1999; Webster-Stratton, 1998; Webster-Stratton & Reid, 2003).

In all, 66% used a treatment manual to explicate treatment. Treatment integrity was maintained in the form of coded audio or videotapes, standardized adherence measures, treatment checklists, session protocols, reliability checks, and structured supervision. Although training was mentioned in several studies, it was not included in the overall evaluation as treatment integrity if training was not routinely checked for consistent delivery of services.

## Results and Follow-Up

Effectiveness of intervention treatment resulted in all but two interventions reporting significance of treatments effects (Horowitz et al., 2000; Zeanah et al., 2001). In the preventive intervention (Zeanah et al., 2001) outcomes for children in foster care were measured (see Table 4.3). Results indicated more children were freed for adoption and fewer were returned to their abusive birth families. This preventive intervention led to changes in the permanency plan outcomes made by judicial and child welfare systems. Termination of parental rights increased, and the return of children decreased. As a result of children not returning home, maternal maltreatment decreased in the intervention group (Zeanah et al., 2001).

Findings in the Foster Care Clinic (Horowitz et al., 2000) indicated that there were no significant differences between the two groups existing in medical, educational, developmental, or mental health problems identified by foster mothers. However, children in the intervention group were more likely to be identified with developmental (56.5% vs. 8.6%) and mental health problems (37.1% vs. 13.8%) by providers than were children in the comparison group. The authors concluded that community providers identify medical and educational needs of young children entering foster care but fail to recognize their developmental or mental health needs (Horowitz et al., 2000). Parent-Child Interaction Therapy (Borrego et al., 1999) revealed promising results with a decrease in externalizing and internalizing disorders, along with parenting stress (see Table 4.3). Enhanced Home-Based Crisis

Intervention (Evans et al., 2003) had a large sample size, effective effect sizes, and random assignment to three groups but no control group. Results indicated significant differences in HBCL+ versus other treatment groups, with a moderate effect size ($d = .43$, $p < .01$) in both FACES II and CBCL. Respite Care (Cowen & Reed, 2002) indicated significant differences in treatment effects and had a large sample size but did not have a control group. Partner's Intervention (Webster-Stratton, 1998) had a large sample size, random sampling to treatment, and control groups and reported significant results in all domains. The authors also included treatment protocol, along with comprehensive training, in their article. Prenatal and Home Visitation by Nurses (Olds et al.,1995) found that participation in early intervention was associated with a 79% reduction in state-verified cases of child abuse and neglect among mothers who were poor and unmarried.

In all, 12 out of the 18 studies used a follow-up. The authors of the Foster Care Clinic (Horowitz et al., 2000) reported that their follow-up rates were excellent, with 92% of the intervention group and 95% of the comparison group followed up at 6 months and 90% and 93% followed up at 12 months, respectively. The authors of the Prenatal and Early Childhood Home Visitation (Oldset al., 1995), Hand in Hand (Whitemore et al., 2003), and Preventive Intervention (Zeanah et al., 2001) followed their children for 4 years.

# Methodological Strengths and Weaknesses

In review of the findings of the 18 referenced studies, many methodological strengths and weaknesses emerged. Many interventions indicated positive findings but lacked other methodological rigor such as large sample size, random sampling, and treatment fidelity. Because of ethical concerns regarding employing a control group in treatment and preventive modalities, many effective interventions were limited to single treatment effects.

The researchers testing the Early Intervention Foster Care utilized a community comparison group along with an intervention group and regular foster care services. This community comparison revealed results consistent with findings that show that foster children lag behind their normal counterparts developmentally. Nonrandom assignment to Early Intervention Foster Care and RFC groups and small sample size limited the ability to generalize the results.

In the Partner's Intervention (Webster-Stratton, 1998), authors reported significant findings as a result of treatment, with follow-up at 12 and 18 months. In reporting their limitations, the authors noted that the control group was not actually a true control group. The families in the Head Start centers still obtained regular Head Start support services. Another limitation was that the results may not generalize to low-income families because only 50% of families in that geographical area are offered a placement in Head Start (Webster-Stratton, 1998).

In the intervention Hand in Hand (Whitemore et al., 2003), researchers reported that their results were also limited by no control group. They reported that an absence of a suitable control group and the loss of one third of their participants from the follow-up limited generalizability of their positive findings of day treatment with proctor care. Henggeler and colleagues (1999) reported that their sample was economically disadvantaged, and positive outcomes could not be generalizable to more advantaged populations.

Limitations of several studies included the developmental changes of children over time, recidivism rates, and children changing foster placements. Other limitations included lack of follow-up (Becker-Weidman, 2004; Cowen & Reed, 2002; Gillespie et al., 1995; Myeroff et al., 1999; Nabors et al., 2001; O'Hara et al., 1998), small sample size ($N > 40$; Becker-Weidman, 2004; Borrego et al., 1999; Fisher et al., 2000; Gillespie et al., 1995; Myeroff et al., 1999), and nonrandom assignments (Becker-Weidman, 2004; Cowen & Reed, 2002; Fisher et al., 2000; Gillespie et al., 1995; Horowitz et al., 2000; Myeroff et al., 1999; Nabors et al., 2001; O'Hara et al., 1998; Whitemore et al., 2003; Zeanah et al., 2001).

Methodological strengths of interventions include the variety of modalities reviewed that included multidisciplinary approaches such as interventions involving therapists, social workers, psychiatrists, and behavioral specialists. Half of the interventions reviewed involved large samples, and 40% were randomly assigned to two or more groups. There were two recent studies where the effect size was reported (Evans et al., 2003; Webster-Stratton & Reid, 2003). Literature reviews were included in all 18 studies with detailed descriptions of interventions. Six studies included treatment integrity protocols (Borrego et al., 1999; Chamberlain & Reid, 1998; Clark & Prange, 1994; Henggeler et al., 1999; Webster-Stratton, 1998; Webster-Stratton & Reid, 2003). In all, 88% of the studies used standardized measures. The Enhanced Home-Based Crisis Intervention (Evans et al., 2003) included a bilingual, bicultural advocate to assist with supporting the family.

# Treatment Classification

Many of the researched interventions in this review have been proven effective with use with children and have been conducted with numerous studies in various settings (e.g., school, home, foster care, institutions). Other interventions have had one or two studies but are considered useful with children. Using the classification system devised by Saunders et al. (2004), interventions were categorized according to their effectiveness at the time of this writing. Therefore, the system is used as a tool to disseminate the progress and empirical characteristics of specific interventions. Using a precise guideline, this classification system provided a clear, criteria-based system to classify interventions according to their theoretical, clinical, and empirical support. Classification is coded between 1 and 6. The lower score indicates a well-supported, efficacious treatment (see Table 4.1). The interventions were researched and classified according to the classification system.

Six of the interventions had been tested extensively with multiple studies to prove their effectiveness (Dina Dinosaur, Multidimensional Treatment Foster Care, Multisystemic Therapy, Parent-Child Interaction Therapy, Partner's Intervention, and Prenatal and Early Childhood Home Visitation; see Table 4.4). These interventions are currently being utilized in various settings around the country. Three interventions were found to be in Category 2, which indicated a supported and probably efficacious treatment with fewer studies conducted but extensively utilized with children (Early Intervention Foster Care, Intensive Intervention, and Respite Care). The remaining nine interventions are considered supported and acceptable according to the criteria provided by this classification system (Dyadic Developmental Psychotherapy, Empowerment Zone, ENHANCE, Enhanced Home-Based Crisis Intervention, Foster Care Clinic, Fostering Individualized Assistance

**Table 4.4**  Classification of Therapeutic Interventions

| Intervention | Classification |
|---|---|
| Dyadic Developmental Psychotherapy | Category 3 |
| Hand in Hand | Category 3 |
| Dina Dinosaur | Category 1 |
| Foster Care Clinic | Category 3 |
| Parent-Child Interaction Therapy | Category 1 |
| Multisystemic Therapy | Category 1 |
| Multidimensional Treatment Foster Care | Category 1 |
| Holding Therapy | Category 3 |
| Fostering Individualized Assistance Program | Category 3 |
| Enhanced Home-Based Crisis Intervention | Category 3 |
| Respite Care | Category 2 |
| Partners Intervention | Category 1 |
| Empowerment Zone | Category 3 |
| Intensive Intervention | Category 2 |
| Early Intervention Foster Care | Category 2 |
| ENHANCE | Category 3 |
| Intensive Preservation Service | Category 3 |
| Prenatal and Childhood Nurse Visitation | Category 1 |

NOTE: Category 1: Well-supported, efficacious treatment; Category 2: Supported and probably efficacious; Category 3: Supported and acceptable; Category 4: Promising and acceptable; Category 5: Novel and experimental; Category 6: Concerning treatment.

Program, Hand in Hand, Holding Therapy, and Intensive Preservation Service). Many of these interventions are being utilized in specific geographical areas where the researcher conducted the study.

Gaps were found in the current literature regarding the lack of specific interventions utilized with foster children. Only six interventions were found to be exclusive to foster children. Although the literature recognized behavioral problems such as externalizing and internalizing disorders, attachment issues, stigmatization, foster family dynamics, and other issues specific to foster children were sparse in the literature. The uniqueness of the foster family structure was not integrated within any interventions reviewed. Although numerous articles focused on the needs and deficits of foster children, effective interventions were limited to accessibility and family resources.

Attachment interventions were limited to two studies (Becker-Weidman, 2004; Myeroff et al., 1999). Considering the consequences of foster children dealing with attachment issues prompts the question, "Why are there no specific interventions for foster children being separated from their caregivers?" Intervention research continues to ignore the risk for attachment problems that concern foster children early in placement. Knowledge and awareness of attachment issues and their effects on foster children may be necessary for them to be considered in therapeutic interventions for foster children. Psychotherapy concerning loss of these relationships in combination with other factors bringing them into care may need to be addressed to resolve conflicts for necessary personality formation.

In an attempt to find additional promising interventions for foster children, interventions targeting children with multiple risk factors were also explored. Only 6 out of the 18 articles actually contained *foster children* in the title (Clark & Prange, 1994; Fisher et al., 2000; Gillespie et al., 1995; Horowitz et al., 2000; O'Hara et al., 1998; Zeanah et al., 2001). Considering that there are more than 500,000 children in foster care, it appears that there are deficits in our mental health system in providing evidenced-based interventions specifically for foster children.

# Discussion and Applications to Social Work Practice

Mental health professionals need to be knowledgeable about the foster family structure to appropriately serve foster children and their families. The foster family structure is unique and requires a mental health professional to examine the family organization through a different lens. Also, the developmental implications of normative childhood growth and development and foster family dynamics need special consideration. Werner and Smith (1982) contended that an understanding of development is essential if therapists are to correctly discriminate normal from abnormal behavior in children. This developmental perspective is multidimensional and includes biological, cognitive, social, emotional, moral, and vocational domains (Werner & Smith, 1982).

Despite the considerable challenges posed by research with children in foster care, more research is needed. Because children are the primary clients of the child welfare system, we need to include their perspective as important informants in developing interventions designed for their welfare. In a recent qualitative and quantitative study assessing the needs of foster children, one child complained that mental health professionals were described as inaccessible and irrelevant to foster children's needs. In addition, they complained about already being stigmatized for being in care and were concerned that a label of mental illness might stigmatize them further (Blower, Addo, Hodgson, Lamington, & Towlson, 2004).

Increasing emphasis should be placed on studying early protective and risk factors that appear common to many disorders. Preventive interventions provide potential precursors of dysfunction of health (Coie et al., 1993).

It has been well documented that intervening early in placement is essential in treating foster children (Clyman, Harden, & Little, 2002; Dozier et al., 2002; Stormont, 2002; Weil, 1998). With the increasing number of foster children entering the system, effective, evidence-based, therapeutic interventions are needed to treat this vulnerable population of children.

# References

Ainsworth, M. D. S. (1982). Attachment: Retrospect and prospect. In C. M. Parkes & J. Steven-Hinde (Eds.), *The place of attachment in human behavior* (pp. 3–30). New York: Basic Books.

Ainsworth, M. D. S. (1989). Attachments beyond infancy. *American Psychologist, 44*, 709–716.

American Academy of Pediatrics, Committee on Early Childhood, Adoption, and Dependent Care. (2001). Developmental issues for young children in foster care. *Pediatrics, 106*, 1145–1152.

Barbell, K., & Freundlich, M. (2001). *Foster care today.* Washington, DC: Casey Family Programs.

Becker-Weidman, A. (2004). *Dyadic developmental psychotherapy: An effective treatment for children with trauma-attachment disorders.* Retrieved May 10, 2005, from http://www.Center4familyDevelop.com.

Blower, A., Addo, A., Hodgson, J., Lamington, L., & Towlson, K. (2004). Mental health of "looked after" children: A needs assessment. *Clinical Child Psychology and Psychiatry, 1*, 1359–1045.

Borrego, J., Urquiza, A. J., Rasmussen, R. A., & Zebell, N. (1999). Parent-child interaction therapy with a family at high risk for physical abuse. *Child Maltreatment, 4*, 331–342.

Bowlby, J. (1969). *Attachment and loss* (Vol. 1). New York: Basic Books.

Carter, B., & McGoldrick, M. (1999). *The expanded family life cycle: Individual, family, and social perspective.* Boston: Allyn & Bacon.

Chamberlain, P., & Reid, J. B. (1998). Comparison of two community alternatives to incarceration for chronic juvenile offenders. *Journal of Consulting and Clinical Psychology, 66,* 624–633.

Chamberlain, S., Moreland, S., & Reid, K. (1992). Enhanced services and stipends for foster parents: Effects on retention rates and outcomes for children. *Child Welfare, 71,* 387–401.

Chernoff, R., Combs-Orme, T., Risley-Curiss, C., & Heisler, A. (1994). Assessing the health status of children entering foster care. *Pediatrics, 93,* 594–601.

Clark, H. B., & Prange, M. E. (1994). Improving adjustment outcomes for foster children with emotional and behavioral disorders: Early findings from a controlled study on individualized services. *Journal of Emotional and Behavioral Disorders, 2,* 207–219.

Clausen, J., Laudsverk, J., Ganger, W., Chadwick, D., & Litronwnik, A. (1998). Mental health problems of children in foster care. *Journal of Child and Family Studies, 7,* 283–296.

Clyman, R. B., Harden, B. J., & Little, C. (2002). Assessment, intervention, and research with infants in out-of-home care. *Infant Mental Health Journal, 23,* 435–453.

Cohen, J. (1992). A power primer. *Psychological Bulletin, 112,* 155–159.

Coie, J. D., Watt, N. F., West, S. G., Hawkins, J. D., Aarnow, J. J., Markman, H. J., et al. (1993). The science of prevention: A conceptual framework and some directions for a national research program. *American Psychologist, 48,* 1013–1022.

Cowen, P. S., & Reed, D. R. (2002). Effects of respite care for children with developmental disabilities: Evaluation of an intervention for at risk families. *Public Health Nursing, 19,* 272–283.

Dale, G., Kendall, J. C., & Sheehan, L. (1999). Screening young foster children for post-traumatic stress disorder and responding to their needs for treatment. *APSAC Advisor, 12,* 6–9.

dosReis, S., Zito, J. M., & Safer, D. J. (2001). Mental health services for youths in foster care and disabled youths. *American Journal of Public Health, 91,* 1094–1099.

Dozier, M., Higley, E., Albus, K. E., & Nutter, A. (2002). Intervening with foster infants' caregivers: Targeting three critical needs. *Infant Mental Health Journal, 23,* 541–554.

Evans, M. E., Boothroyd, R. A., Armstrong, M. I., Greenbaum, P. E., Brown, E. C., & Kupperinger, A. D. (2003). An experimental study of the effectiveness of intensive in-home crisis services for children and their families: Program outcomes. *Journal of Emotional and Behavioral Disorders, 11,* 93–104.

Fanshel, D., Finch, S. J., & Grundy, J. E. (1989). Modes of exit from foster care and adjustment at the time of departure of children with unstable life histories. *Child Welfare, 68,* 391–402.

Fisher, P. A., Gunnar, M. R., Chamberlain, P., & Reid, J. B. (2000). Preventive intervention for maltreated preschool children: Impact on children's behavior, neuroendocrine activity, and foster parent functioning. *Journal of the American Academy of Child and Adolescent Psychiatry, 39,* 1356–1364.

Gardner, H. (1996). The concept of family: Perceptions of children in family foster care. *Child Welfare, 75,* 161–183.

Garwood, M. M., & Close, W. (2001). Identifying the psychological needs of foster children. *Child Psychiatry and Human Development, 32,* 125–135.

George, R., & Wulczyn, F. (1999). Placement experiences of the youngest foster care population: Findings from a multistate foster care data archive. *Zero to Three, 19*(3), 8–13.

Gillespie, J. M., Byrne, B., & Workman, L. J. (1995). An intensive reunification program for children in foster care. *Child and Adolescent Social Work, 12,* 213–228.

Haury, C. S. (2000). The changing American family: A reevaluation of the rights of foster parents when biological parental rights have been terminated. *Georgia Law Review, 35,* 313–344.

Henggeler, S. W., Rowland, M. D., Randall, J., Ward, D. M., Pickeral, S. G., Cunningham, P. B., et al. (1999). Home-based multisystemic therapy as an alternative to hospitalization of youths in psychiatric crisis: Clinical outcomes. *Journal of the American Academy of Child and Adolescent Psychiatry, 38,* 1331–1347.

Hoagwood, K., & Olin, S. S. (2002). The NIMH blueprint for change report: Research priorities in child and adolescent mental health. *Journal of the Academy of Child and Adolescent Psychiatry, 41,* 760–770.

Horowitz, S. M., Owens, P., & Simms, M. D. (2000). Specialized assessments for children in foster care. *Pediatrics, 106,* 59–66.

Horowitz, S. M., Simms, M. D., & Farrington, R. (1994). Impact of developmental problems on young children's exit from foster care. *Developmental and Behavioral Pediatrics, 15,* 105–110.

James, B. (1994). *Handbook for treatment of attachment trauma problems in children.* New York: Lexington Books.

LeDoux, J. E. (1996). *The emotional brain: The mysterious underpinning of emotional life.* New York: Simon & Schuster.

Lee, R. E., & Lynch, M. T. (1998). Combating foster care drift: An ecosystemic treatment model for neglect cases. *Contemporary Family Therapy, 20,* 351–370.

Lee, R. E., & Stacks, A. M. (2004). In whose arms? The case for relational therapy in supervised visitation in foster care. *Journal of Family Psychotherapy, 15*(4), 1–14.

Lee, R. E., & Whiting, J. B. (Eds.). (2007). Introduction: The culture and environment of foster care. In R. E. Lee & J. B. Whiting (Eds.), *Foster Care Therapist Handbook: Relational Approaches to the Children and Their Families.* Washington, DC: Child Welfare League of America.

Lieberman, A. F., & Zeanah, C. H. (1995). Disorders of attachment in infancy. *Child and Adolescent Psychiatric Clinics of North America, 4,* 571–587.

McIntyre, A., & Keesler, T. (1998). Psychological disorders among foster children. *Journal of Clinical and Child Psychology, 15,* 297–303.

Myaard, M. J., Crawford, C., Jackson, M., & Alessi, G. (2000). Applying behavior analysis within the wraparound process: A multiple baseline study. *Journal of Emotional and Behavioral Disorders, 8,* 216–224.

Myeroff, R., Mertlich, G., & Gross, J. (1999). Comparative effectiveness of holding therapy with aggressive children. *Child Psychiatry and Human Development, 29,* 303–313.

Naastrom, K., & Koch, S. M. (1996, April). *Addressing the needs of children in out-of-home care.* Paper presented at the 28th annual meeting of the National Association of School Psychologists, Atlanta, GA.

Nabors, L., Proescher, E., & DeSilva, M. (2001). School-based mental health prevention activities for homeless and at-risk youth. *Child and Youth Forum, 30*(1), 3–18.

National Commission on Family Foster Care. (1991). *A blueprint for fostering infants, children and youths in the 1990s.* Washington, DC: Child Welfare League of America.

Noble, L. S. (1997). The face of foster care. *Educational Leadership,54,* 26–28.

O'Hara, M. T., Church, C. C., & Blatt, S. D. (1998). Home-based developmental screening of children in foster care. *Pediatric Nursing, 24,* 113–118.

Olds, D. L., Henderson, C. R., & Tatelbaum, R. (1995). Prevention of intellectual impairment in children of women who smoke cigarettes during pregnancy. *Pediatrics, 93,* 228–233.

Perry, B. D., Conrad, D. J., Dobson, C., Schick, S., & Ryan, D. (2000). *The children's crisis center model: A proactive multidimensional child and family assessment process.* Houston, Texas: The Child Trauma Academy.

Perry, B. D., Pollard, R. A., Blakley, T. L., & Vigilante, D. (1995). Childhood trauma, the neurobiology of adaption, and "use-dependent" development of the brain: How "states" become "traits." *Infant Mental Health Journal, 16,* 271–291.

Pilowsky, D. (1995). Psychopathology among children in foster care. *Psychiatric Services, 46,* 906–910.

Roman, N. P., & Wolfe, P. B. (1997). The relationship between foster care and homelessness. *Public Welfare, 55,* 4–9.

Rosenfeld, A. A., Pilowsky, D. J., Fine, P., Thorpe, M., Fein, E., Simms, M. O., et al. (1997). Foster care: An update. *Journal of American Academy of Child and Adolescent Psychiatry, 36,* 448–457.

Rothman, J., & Thomas, E. J. (1994). *Intervention research: Design and development for human service.* New York: Haworth.

Saunders, B., Berliner, L., & Hanson, R. (2004, April 26). *Child physical and sexual abuse: Guidelines for treatments* (Rev. Rep.). Retrieved September 8, 2005, from http://www.musc.edu/cvc/ guide1.htm.

Stein, E. (1997). Teacher's assessment of children in foster care. *Development Disabilities Bulletin, 25,* 1–17.

Stone, N., & Stone, S. F. (1983). The prediction of successful foster placement. *Social Casework, 64,* 11–19.

Stormont, M. (2002). Eternalizing behavior problems in young children: Contributing factors and early intervention. *Psychology in the Schools, 39,* 127–138.

Stovall, K. C., & Dozier, M. (2000). The development of attachment in new relationships: A single subject analysis for ten foster infants. *Development and Psychopathology, 12,* 133–156.

Sumner-Mayer, K. (2007). An integrative approach involving the biological and foster family systems. In R. E. Lee & J. B. Whiting (Eds.), *Foster Care Therapist Handbook: Relational Approaches to the Children and Their Families.* Washington, DC: Child Welfare League of America.

Tyrell, C., & Dozier, M. (1999). Foster parents' understanding of children's problematic behavior strategies: The need for therapeutic responsiveness. *Adoption Quarterly, 2,* 49–64.

U.S. Department of Health and Human Services, National Clearinghouse on Child Abuse Neglect Information. (2001). *Child maltreatment 1999: Reports from the states to the National Clearinghouse on Child Abuse and Neglect.* Washington, DC: U.S. Government Printing Office.

U.S. General Accounting Office. (1994). *Foster care: Parental drug abuse has alarming impact on young children* (GAO/HEHS-94–89). Washington, DC: Author.

U.S. House of Representatives. (2000). *2000 green book: Overview of entitlement programs.* Washington, DC: U.S. Government Printing Office.

Waltz, J., Addis, M. E., Koerner, K., & Jacobson, N. J. (1993). Testing the integrity of a psychotherapy protocol assessment of adherence and competence. *Journal of Consulting and Clinical Psychology, 61,* 620–630.

Webster-Stratton, C. (1998). Preventing conduct problems in Head Start children: Strengthening parenting competencies. *Journal of Consulting and Clinical Psychology, 66,* 715–730.

Webster-Stratton, C., & Reid, M. J. (2003). Treating conduct problems and strengthening social emotional competence in young children: The Dina Dinosaur Treatment Program. *Journal of Emotional and Behavioral Disorders, 11,* 13–27.

Weil, T. P. (1998). Children at risk: Outcome and cost measures needed. *Child Psychiatry and Human Development, 30,* 3–13.

Werner, E. E., & Smith, R. S. (1982). *Vulnerable but invincible: A longitudinal study of resilient children and youth.* New York: Adams, Banniater, Cox.

Whitemore, E., Ford, M., & Sack, W. H. (2003). Effectiveness of day treatment with proctor care for young children: A four-year follow-up. *Journal of Community Psychology, 31,* 459–468.

Williams, S. C., Fanolis, V., & Schamess, G. (2002). Adapting the Pynoos school based group therapy model for use with foster children: Theoretical and process considerations. *Journal of Child and Adolescent Group Therapy, 11,* 57–76.

Wilson, S. (2001). Attachment disorders: Review and current status. *The Journal of Psychology, 135,* 37–51.

Zeanah, C. H., Larrieu, J. A., Heller, S. S., Valliere, J. A., Hinshaw- Fuselier, S., Aoki, Y., & Drilling, M. (2001). Evaluation of a preventive intervention for maltreated infants and toddlers in foster care. *American Academy of Child and Adolescent Psychiatry, 40,* 214–221.

# Children and Families

## *Important Practice Points*

### Chapter 1

- In general, parent training programs are a useful option for addressing situations when a child is at risk for being physically abused or neglected by a parent. Parent training programs appear to foster more "child-friendly" beliefs. Parent programs that are more behaviorally based are more successful. However, there is little empirical evidence about the long-term effects of parent training programs.

- Information on child development and the importance of child socialization are areas where parents cannot be assumed to have knowledge. Thus, inclusion of this information is a critical component of parent training.

- Negative affect acts as a moderating factor on abuse outcomes. Findings suggest that parents' emotional well-being was strengthened through parent training. Specific emotional states such as anger or stress can be blunted by increased confidence of parenting roles.

### Chapter 2

- Small to medium effect sizes were found for parental involvement interventions for attention deficit hyperactivity disorder (ADHD). These studies were predicated on the principles of cognitive-behavioral treatment. It is important to note that the magnitude of effects of using stimulant medication on ADHD symptoms is medium to large.

- Child social functioning (i.e., social competence), a typical problem experienced by children with ADHD, did not appear to respond well to parent treatment.

- Analysis of moderator variables indicated that the older the child, the greater the positive effects derived from parent-involvement intervention.

Children residing in single-parent homes did not fare as well as children from two-parent homes.

## Chapter 3

• Several family-based interventions have demonstrated efficacy in treating multiproblem youth with substance use problems, including multidimensional family treatment and functional family treatment. These effects yielded large reductions in substance use. It is also important to point out that better executed treatments also yield greater retention and engagement.

• There are typically barriers to effective implementation of treatments in real-world settings. With respect to the present synthesis, these would include intensive therapist training and the associated costs and time.

## Chapter 4

• This synthesis underscores the need for social work practitioners who provide mental health services to be knowledgeable about the complexity of the foster care system. Effective system navigation is likely to enhance ease and execution of evidence-based treatments. This is particularly the case in the foster care system, where the family structure is somewhat different and there is a relative lack of empirically tested interventions.

• Foster care children are often stigmatized and face many barriers to a successful transition to adulthood. The typical supports are often nonexistent for foster children, and this implies that early screening and treatment referral are critical.

# PART II

## At-Risk Youth

### *Overview and Key Questions*

Substance abuse, delinquency, and suicide are three problem behaviors that often punctuate the period of adolescence. For example, the initiation of substance use and delinquent acts typically occurs during this developmental period. The earlier these behaviors begin (e.g., age 12), the more likely future social functioning is jeopardized. Although it is relatively normal for adolescents to experiment with alcohol and drugs or engage in minor delinquent acts, some youth are chronically involved in these acts. This is critical because successful transitions to adulthood are affected by these behaviors. As these syntheses demonstrate, there exists a wide variety of treatments designed to intervene in these behaviors.

In this section, Sandra Jo Wilson, Mark W. Lipsey, and Haluk Soydan examine whether mainstream programs designed to address juvenile delinquency are less effective for minority youth than majority youth. This is an important topic, given the overrepresentation of minorities in the criminal justice system. Next, Mark J. Macgowan tackles the problem of youth suicide by providing a systematic review of psychosocial treatments. Although there exists a relative dearth of high-quality studies designed to intervene with adolescent substance abusers, Michael G. Vaughn and Matthew O. Howard synthesize what is known based on controlled evaluations. Finally, William R. Nugent, Mona Williams, and Mark S. Umbreit meta-analyze results from studies that have examined the impact that participating in victim offender mediation programs has on future delinquent behavior.

As you read these selections, consider the following questions:

1. Based on the Wilson, Lipsey, and Soydan chapter, what are the implications of their research with respect to culturally competent practice in the juvenile justice system?

2. How can effective treatments for youth suicide be better implemented in systems of care?

3. What interventions would you recommend for adolescent substance abuse, and why?

4. What are the social work practice implications regarding victim-offender mediation programs with respect to at-risk youth?

# Are Mainstream Programs for Juvenile Delinquency Less Effective With Minority Youth Than Majority Youth?

## A Meta-Analysis of Outcomes Research

*Sandra Jo Wilson, Mark W. Lipsey, and Haluk Soydan*

5

The mission of the social work profession includes work with marginalized, needy, and economically disadvantaged groups and individuals in society. This often entails services for immigrant and ethnically diverse populations.

In the early decades of its development in the United States, the social work profession was called upon to assist newly arrived immigrants, especially in urban and densely populated areas (Addams, 1895; Soydan, 1999). Generations later, the clientele for social work continues to be characterized by ethnic diversity, as well as a multiplicity of languages, religions, and value systems. In other parts of the world, particularly in Europe, social work faces similar circumstances as migration has made populations more diverse (Williams, Soydan, & Johnson, 1998).

Ethnic diversity, in particular, has presented major challenges to social work practice. When people of different ethnic groups are assumed to have different needs or to respond differently to services, the methods for serving those groups become a matter of debate. At issue is whether clients of

Originally published in *Research on Social Work Practice* 2003; 13; 3. DOI: 10.1177/1049731502238754 The online version of this article can be found at: http://rsw.sagepub.com/cgi/content/abstract/13/1/3

ethnic minority groups should be treated with the same methods, interventions, and programs as the majority population of a particular country. Especially in the United States, the necessity of tailoring social work practice to meet the special needs of ethnically diverse populations has been much discussed (Soydan, Jergeby, Olsson, & Harms-Ringdal, 1999). Such concerns have resulted in various social work practice models for serving ethnic populations, for example, Cultural Awareness (Green, 1995), the Process Stage Approach in Minority Treatment (Lum, 1996), and Ethnic-Sensitive Social Work Practice (Devore & Schlesinger, 1996). These approaches are usually presented as generic models for ethnic minorities that are appropriate to different types of social work services, such as family counseling, group counseling, behavior contracting, interpersonal skills training, drug treatment programs, and the like.

However, the need for, and effectiveness of, ethnically tailored social work approaches have been vigorously debated in social work research and practice (Soydan et al., 1999; de Anda, 1997). The nature of the controversy is illustrated by the papers in the volume *Controversial Issues in Multiculturalism,* edited by de Anda (1997). The questions raised there include whether the emphasis on multicultural practice has resulted in more effective and appropriate services for ethnic minority clients, whether programs and service delivery systems should be culture-specific in their design, whether the therapeutic process is more effective if the client and the helping professional are of the same ethnic/cultural group, and whether ethnic agencies can more effectively serve ethnic communities than mainstream agencies. Debating whether the emphasis on multicultural practice has resulted in more effective and appropriate services for ethnic minority clients, for instance, John Longres wrote,

> Dr. Brown argues that multicultural practice has brought about more effective and appropriate services. I argue that it has not. . . . In the first place, Dr. Brown is largely talking about appropriateness, not effectiveness. She offers anecdotal evidence to demonstrate that her students, her colleagues, and apparently their clients seem to be satisfied with the counseling they are receiving. This anecdotal evidence hardly stands up to rigorous evaluation and so has to be taken for what it is, the opinion of an educator. Even if her evidence were more rigorously represented, Dr. Brown supplies no evidence of effectiveness: the clients and their helping professionals may feel good, but do the clients behave differently, and have their lives been changed for the better? The evidence suggests that as a collective, people of color are treading water; their lives have not been improved by the growth of a new multicultural sensitivity, however more appropriate it may appear to be. (de Anda, 1997, pp. 18–19)

As this comment indicates, arguments about this issue are seldom based on well-founded empirical knowledge. When relevant evidence is consulted, the results are often surprising. For example, empirical research related to one specific social work intervention, foster care for children who are maltreated or whose parents are unable to care for them, demonstrates that differences between ethnic groups in the outcome of mainstream programs, if they occur at all, do not necessarily favor majority groups. Using data on death rates, Barth and Blackwell (1998) showed that White and Hispanic children in foster care have higher rates of death than their counterparts in the general population, but the death rates for African American foster children are no worse than those for the African American children in the general population. On the other hand, Jonson-Reid and Barth (2000) found that the risk of incarceration following foster care was greater for African American youth than for Hispanic or White youth, even when gender, age at first placement, and characteristics of placement history were controlled.

Although the effectiveness of services in producing positive outcomes for the specific problems to which they are addressed is not the only important consideration in social work practice, it is certainly a critical one. Where such outcomes are concerned, the question of whether culturally tailored or mainstream social work practice is more effective for minority youth is an empirical one. Unfortunately, at present we lack a solid body of research on this issue, and where we do have some empirical findings, as in the foster care example above, the results do not always point in the same direction.

The present study was undertaken to assemble otherwise scattered research results about the effectiveness of service programs for minority juvenile delinquents relative to White majority delinquents. It uses the techniques of meta-analysis to address the question of whether mainstream interventions that are not culturally tailored for minority youth have positive outcomes for subsequent antisocial behavior. In addition, those outcomes are compared with the intervention effects for White majority samples to find out if there are any differences in the responsiveness of minority and majority youth to mainstream juvenile delinquency services.

# Meta-Analysis

Meta-analysis is a technique for recording and analyzing the statistical results of a collection of empirical research studies. Central to meta-analysis is the effect size statistic, which represents the quantitative findings of each study in a standardized way that permits comparison across studies. For the intervention studies of interest here, the effect size statistic (ES) is the standardized mean difference (Cohen, 1988; Lipsey & Wilson, 2001), defined as the difference between the treatment and control group means on an outcome variable divided by their pooled standard deviation. This effect size statistic indexes the outcomes for the treatment group relative to the control group in standard deviation units. Thus, ES = .50 indicates that the outcome for the treatment group was more favorable than that for the control group by an amount equivalent to half a standard deviation on the respective outcome measure. For binary outcomes (e.g., arrested/not arrested), the mean difference effect size was derived using Cohen's arcsine transformation for proportion values (Lipsey & Wilson, 2001). If a study assesses the effects of an intervention on more than one outcome, say, reoffending and social adjustment, that study would generate two effect sizes, one for each outcome.

The effect size is not the only piece of information recorded about each study that contributes to a meta-analysis. Studies of juvenile delinquency programs involve youth from a variety of different age groups, ethnicities, risk levels, and so forth and use different procedures and methods to evaluate program effectiveness. Of course, the interventions themselves also differ across studies. Thus, in addition to the effect sizes, a meta-analytic database includes detailed information about each study's methods, participants, treatments, and other such descriptive characteristics that may be relevant for understanding the results. Analysis of the coded information from a collection of studies can then investigate relationships between various characteristics of the studies and the effect sizes those studies produce. In addition, statistical techniques can be used to control for many of the sources of error and natural differences between studies so that better estimates of the effects of intervention can be derived (Cooper & Hedges, 1994; Hedges & Olkin, 1985).

The studies included in the meta-analysis presented here are drawn from a database of nearly 500 studies on the effects of intervention with juvenile delinquents (Lipsey, 1992, 1995; Lipsey & Wilson, 1998). This larger synthesis of research results has shown that intervention for juvenile offenders is generally effective at reducing recidivism (Lipsey, 1995), even among serious, violent, or chronic juvenile offenders (Lipsey & Wilson, 1998). However, the results of these analyses have also shown that there is considerable variability in effectiveness across different research studies and that this variability is related to the research methods used, participant characteristics, and format and nature of the treatment. The analysis reported below uses this extensive database to address the relative effects of service programs for minority versus majority juvenile offenders.

# Method

The database from which the studies for this meta-analysis are drawn includes empirical research on the effects of juvenile delinquency programs conducted between 1950 and 1996, both published and unpublished (Lipsey, 1992; Lipsey & Wilson, 1998). Trained personnel coded over 150 items for each study that describe the methods and procedures, participant samples, treatment and program characteristics, effect sizes, and other important information. Interrater reliability for the coding of effect sizes was .93, and interrater agreement was generally above 80% for items describing study characteristics. For the present analysis, the studies that allowed comparison of the effectiveness of delinquency programs for minority versus majority youth were selected from this database. Specifically, the 141 studies with participant samples comprised at least 60% minority youth, and the 164 studies with at least 60% White participants were selected. The mean percentage of minority youth in the studies selected to represent intervention with ethnic minorities was 82%, and the mean percentage of White youth in the comparison studies was about 80%. Among the minority samples, most were predominately African American, but Hispanic youth and, in much smaller numbers, other minority youth were also represented (see Table 5.1).

As with all studies in the full database, the selected studies met the following criteria:

- The youth in the study sample were identified as delinquent or displaying antisocial behavior; or, if the youth were not explicitly described as delinquent or antisocial, the study included delinquency or antisocial behavior among its primary outcome variables.
- The youth in treatment were between the ages of 12 and 21 and resided in the United States, Canada, Great Britain, New Zealand, or Australia.
- The research design was an experimental or quasi-experimental comparison of at least one treatment and one control/comparison group.

The selected studies reported intervention effects on a variety of outcome variables. The primary outcome of interest was subsequent delinquent behavior, most commonly measured by police contacts or arrests. Many studies also assessed other outcome variables that we have grouped into broad conceptual domains. Each of these domains covers a variety of specific individual variables; thus results presented for effects in these domains should be interpreted only as broad summaries. The domains we identified include the following outcome constructs. The number of studies contributing outcomes in each category is shown in parentheses.

- Academic achievement: grades and other measures of achievement in various academic subjects ($n = 34$)
- Attitude change: attitudes about delinquency or toward school, work, or community ($n = 57$)
- Behavior problems: nonaggressive behavior problems, such as acting out, disruptiveness, and hyperactivity ($n = 23$)
- Employment status: getting or keeping a job, number of jobs held, and the like ($n = 28$)
- Family functioning: measures of family relations, parental discipline, family stress, and the like ($n = 15$)
- Internalizing problems: withdrawal, shyness, anxiety, and other similar problems ($n = 23$)
- Peer relations: relations with peers, interpersonal skills, and social adjustment ($n = 31$)
- Psychological adjustment: locus of control, personality adjustment, and the like ($n = 36$)

**Table 5.1**    Characteristics of the 305 Studies Used in the Meta-Analysis

| Variable | N | %[a] | Variable | N | % |
|---|---|---|---|---|---|
| General study characteristics | | | Percentage of sample with prior offenses | | |
| Publication year | | | | | |
| 1950–1969 | 43 | 14 | None | 7 | 2 |
| 1970–1979 | 119 | 39 | Some (< 50%) | 56 | 19 |
| 1980–1989 | 116 | 38 | Most (≥ 50%) | 43 | 14 |
| 1990–1996 | 21 | 7 | All | 143 | 47 |
| Missing | 6 | 2 | Some, cannot estimate % | 38 | 12 |
| | | | Missing | 18 | 6 |
| Type of publication | | | | | |
| Technical report | 156 | 51 | Heterogeneity of treatment sample | | |
| Journal article, chapter | 93 | 31 | | | |
| Dissertation | 30 | 10 | Low | 107 | 35 |
| Book | 24 | 8 | Moderate | 132 | 43 |
| Conference paper | 2 | < 1 | High | 66 | 22 |
| Country in which study was conducted | | | Source of participants for treatment | | |
| United States | 280 | 92 | Volunteers | 18 | 6 |
| United Kingdom | 14 | 5 | Referred by parents/friends | 1 | < 1 |
| Canada | 9 | 3 | Referred by non-juvenile | | |
| Other English-speaking country | 2 | < 1 | justice (JJ) agency | 19 | 6 |
| | | | JJ referral (voluntary) | 91 | 30 |
| Characteristics of juveniles in treatment | | | JJ referral (mandatory) | 142 | 47 |
| Gender mix | | | Multiple sources | 12 | 4 |
| | | | Solicited by researcher | 18 | 6 |
| No males | 9 | 3 | Missing | 4 | 1 |
| Some males (< 50%) | 16 | 5 | | | |
| Mostly males (≥ 50%) | 144 | 47 | Treatment characteristics | | |
| All males | 136 | 45 | Program age | | |
| | | | Relatively new | 187 | 61 |
| Mean age at time of treatment | | | Established (2+ years) | 113 | 37 |
| < 12.9 | 14 | 5 | Defunct | 1 | < 1 |
| 13.0–13.9 | 27 | 9 | Missing | 4 | 1 |
| 15.0–15.9 | 56 | 18 | | | |
| 16.0–16.9 | 67 | 22 | Program sponsorship | | |
| 17.0–17.9 | 38 | 12 | | | |
| 18.0–18.9 | 11 | 4 | Research project | 85 | 28 |
| 19.0 | 27 | 9 | Private agency | 29 | 10 |
| Missing | 11 | 4 | Public agency, non-JJ | 54 | 18 |
| | | | Public agency, JJ | 132 | 43 |
| Predominant ethnicity (> 60%) | | | Missing | 5 | 2 |
| African American | 80 | 26 | | | |
| Hispanic | 19 | 6 | Duration of treatment (weeks) | | |
| Other (Asian, American Indian) | 8 | 3 | | | |
| Mixed (minority > 60%) | 34 | 11 | 1–10 | 48 | 16 |
| White | 164 | 54 | 11–20 | 81 | 26 |
| | | | 21–30 | 47 | 15 |
| Delinquency level | 31–40 | 66 | 31–40 | 66 | 22 |
| Predelinquent | 89 | 29 | 41–50 | 13 | 4 |
| Delinquent | 137 | 45 | 51 and up | 50 | 17 |
| Institutionalized | 79 | 26 | | | |

| Variable | N | %[a] | Variable | N | % |
|---|---|---|---|---|---|
| Frequency of treatment event | | | Private | 80 | 26 |
| Continuous | 57 | 19 | Mixed | 43 | 14 |
| Daily | 55 | 18 | Other | 20 | 7 |
| 2–4 times/week | 31 | 10 | | | |
| 1–2 times/week | 90 | 30 | Treatment type | | |
| Less than weekly | 24 | 8 | Multimodal programs | | |
| Missing | 48 | 16 | Institutional | 16 | 5 |
| | | | Non-institutional | 22 | 7 |
| Implementation problems | | | Casework, service brokage | 31 | 10 |
| Yes | 124 | 41 | Counseling, noninstitutional | 42 | 14 |
| Possible | 67 | 22 | Behavioral congnitive-behavioral | 14 | 5 |
| No | 114 | 38 | Employment related | 26 | 9 |
| | | | Wilderness/challenge | 9 | 3 |
| General study characteristics | | | Academic services | 25 | 8 |
| Publication year | | | Interpersonal skills | 6 | 2 |
| 1950–1969 | 43 | 14 | Vocational | 9 | 3 |
| 1970–1979 | 119 | 39 | Probation and variations | 21 | 7 |
| 1980–1989 | 116 | 38 | Other | 43 | 14 |
| 1990–1996 | 21 | 7 | | | |
| Missing | 6 | 2 | Method characteristics | | |
| | | | What control group receives | | |
| Rated amount of meaningful contact | | | Recevies nothing | 51 | 17 |
| 1 (Trivial) | 4 | 1 | Minimal contact | 19 | 6 |
| 2 | 41 | 13 | School, treatment as usual | 18 | 6 |
| 3 | 40 | 13 | Usual probation services | 72 | 24 |
| 4 (Moderate) | 67 | 22 | Usual institutional treatment | 84 | 28 |
| 5 | 69 | 23 | Other treatment as usual | 49 | 16 |
| 6 | 61 | 20 | Placebo | 12 | 4 |
| 7 (Substatial) | 23 | 8 | | | |
| | | | Role of evaluator | | |
| Who delivers treatment? | | | Delivered treatment | 13 | 4 |
| JJ personnel | 91 | 30 | Planned or supervised treatment | 88 | 29 |
| School personnel | 14 | 5 | Influential, no direct role | 52 | 17 |
| Public mental health presonnel | 20 | 7 | Independent of treatment | 137 | 45 |
| Private mental health presonnel | 44 | 14 | Missing | 15 | 5 |
| Non–mental health counselors | 66 | 22 | | | |
| Laypersons | 47 | 15 | Method of group assignment | | |
| Researcher | 6 | 2 | Random | 141 | 46 |
| Other | 6 | 2 | Matching | 80 | 26 |
| Missing | 11 | 4 | Other nonrandom | 84 | 28 |
| | | | | | |
| Primary treatment format | | | Blinding in data collection | | |
| Juvenile alone | 8 | 3 | No | 233 | 76 |
| Juvenile and provider | 81 | 27 | Yes | 72 | 24 |
| Juvenile group | 147 | 48 | | | |
| Juvenile and family | 19 | 6 | Sample size | | |
| Mixed | 41 | 13 | Up to 49 | 57 | 19 |
| Other | 9 | 3 | 50–99 | 65 | 21 |
| | | | 100–199 | 84 | 28 |
| Treatment site | | | 200–299 | 34 | 11 |
| Public, JJ | 98 | 32 | 300–399 | 16 | 5 |
| Public, non-JJ site | 64 | 21 | 400 and up | 49 | 16 |

a. Percentages may not add up to 100 because of rounding

- School participation: tardiness, truancy, and dropping out ($n = 56$)
- Self-esteem: measures of self-esteem or self-concept ($n = 27$)

# Characteristics of the
# Delinquency Treatment Studies

Table 5.1 presents a summary of the 305 studies that comprise the database for this meta-analysis. The characteristics of these studies were generally similar to those for the entire database from which they were drawn. In addition, the characteristics of the studies with minority samples were not appreciably different from those with predominantly White samples. Some of the general features of the studies are as follows:

- The majority of studies was conducted in the United States. Most studies were published subsequent to 1970, with the most common form of publication being technical reports.
- The juvenile samples were largely male, with most of the youth age 15 or older. The predominant ethnic classification among minority samples was African American, with smaller portions of mixed and predominantly Hispanic samples.
- Most of the studies involved youth who were delinquent or institutionalized, and, for most of the samples, all or the majority of the juveniles had prior offense histories.
- In nearly half of the studies, the treatment was delivered to a group of juveniles (rather than individually), and about one third of the programs were delivered by juvenile justice personnel.
- The most frequent intervention strategies were institutional and non-institutional counseling and casework or service brokerage–type services, although many other types of service programs were represented.

Nearly half of the studies used random assignment to place youth in treatment or comparison groups. In most of the studies, the youth in the comparison groups received usual or customary services, typically probation or institutionalization.

In addition to the descriptive information already coded on the selected studies, the original reports for those studies using minority samples were examined for statements relating to cultural tailoring of the interventions. We found one report indicating such tailoring (Wooldredge, Hartman, Latessa, & Holmes, 1994) and excluded it from our analyses. Thirteen of the 141 studies with minority youth mentioned using minority service providers with minority delinquents, but the services provided in these cases were not specifically culturally tailored. By all available indications, therefore, the interventions provided to the minority youth, like those provided to the White youth in the comparison studies, were predominantly mainstream services without any special tailoring to the ethnic or cultural characteristics of the juveniles receiving those services.

## _____ Effectiveness of Juvenile Delinquency Services

Figure 5.1 reports the mean effect size with its 95% confidence interval for each of the major intervention outcome constructs for minority and White samples. Hedges's (1981) small sample correction was applied to each effect size, and all computations with effect sizes were weighted by the inverse sampling variance to reflect the greater stability of estimates based on larger samples (Hedges & Olkin, 1985; Lipsey & Wilson, 2001; Shadish & Haddock, 1994).

For minority youth, the weighted mean effect size for delinquency outcomes across all treatment modalities was .11; for majority youth, the corresponding effect size value was .17. Both these values were statistically significant, as evidenced by confidence intervals that do not include zero.

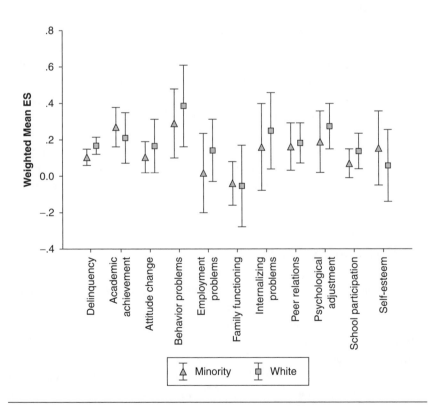

**Figure 5.1**     Weighted Mean Posttest Effect Sizes for Minority and White Youth
for Each Outcome Construct

Though the mean effect size for White youth was somewhat larger than that for minority youth, this difference was not statistically significant (as shown by the overlapping confidence intervals for Whites and minorities). To illustrate in more intuitive form what these effect size values mean, Cohen's (1988) arcsine transformation was used to convert them to percentage differences in recidivism rates. If the approximate rate of recidivism for delinquents in control groups is set at 50% (which is very close to the actual rate in the database), the mean effect size of .11 for minority youth is then equivalent to about a 5 percentage-point differential, that is, a 45% reoffense rate for treated juveniles compared to 50% for those in the control groups. The mean effect size of .17 for majority youth translates into a 42% reoffense rate for treated juveniles, that is, an 8 percentage-point decrease from that for untreated juveniles.

For the other outcome constructs, mean effect sizes for both minority and White juveniles were greater than zero for all outcome categories except family functioning, although not all were statistically significant (confidence intervals for self-esteem and employment status overlapped zero for both groups, and those for internalizing problems and school participation overlapped for the minority samples). Thus, the mainstream interventions represented in these studies, on average, had positive effects on both subsequent delinquency and a number of other important outcomes. Of greatest relevance for present purposes, however, were the differences between the minority and White samples on the various outcome constructs. Although the mean effect sizes for White samples were greater than those for minority samples on 7 of the 10 nondelinquency outcome categories, none of the differences in either direction was statistically significant, as evidenced by the highly overlapping confidence intervals. Thus, without exception, across all the outcome domains represented in these intervention studies, there were no significant differences between the overall effects of mainstream intervention services on predominantly minority treatment groups and those on predominantly White treatment groups.

# A Closer Look at Differential Effects on Delinquency Outcomes

The overall mean effect size values in Figure 5.1 give a general affirmative answer to the question of whether mainstream delinquency interventions without special tailoring are as effective for ethnic minority youth as for White youth. However, there is great variability around the mean effects shown there. For the central delinquency outcomes, there was about three times as much effect size variability across studies as would be expected if all the interventions produced the same effect with associated sampling error (the $Q$-statistic testing effect size heterogeneity was $Q_{305} = 991.5$, $p < .01$). Differences in delinquency outcomes observed across studies could be due to any of a number of factors, including between-study differences in method and procedure, participant characteristics, amount of treatment, and, of course, type of treatment. Indeed, the results of any one study are jointly determined by the nature of the treatments and participants in the study and the methods used to study them. It is, therefore, informative to investigate the study characteristics associated with larger or smaller effect sizes and, if necessary, to statistically control their influence on the comparison of intervention effects for minority and majority youth. The resulting comparison helps ensure that any difference, or lack of difference, found between the delinquency effect sizes for minority and majority youth represents comparable intervention circumstances and is not simply the result of a different mix of treatments, methods, and the like being used with the different ethnic groups.

The first possible source of effect size variability we examined for delinquency outcomes was differences across studies in methods and procedures. If two researchers use different methods to conduct their studies and those differences influence the findings, it is difficult to tell whether those findings reflect the effectiveness of the interventions or the influence of the methods used to study them. Thus, methodological differences across studies are nuisance variables that could influence the observed outcomes of intervention differently for minority and majority youth. We therefore sought to identify the methodological characteristics that were related to the observed effect sizes in the studies and statistically control them. We also included several more general nuisance variables in this analysis; for instance, type of publication, which is associated with effect size because of the greater tendency for large effects to be formally published (Dickersin, 1997). For the purposes of this analysis, the studies using minority and majority samples were combined. Once influential between-study differences in method were identified and controlled, intervention effects for minority and majority samples were again compared to determine if any difference appeared.

To investigate the relationship between the methodological characteristics of the studies and the delinquency outcomes observed in those studies, we performed an inverse-variance weighted random effects multiple regression analysis using the delinquency effect sizes for all 305 studies as the dependent variable (Hedges & Olkin, 1985). Next, the regression model was used to predict the overall mean effect size for each study with the method-related independent variables held constant (i.e., assigned the mean value for all studies). This predicted value was added to the residual for each effect size to generate a set of adjusted effect sizes that estimate the effects we would expect if all studies used similar methods.

This regression analysis showed that the delinquency effect sizes were significantly related to certain aspects of the study methods used. The model was significant ($Q_5 = 36.53$, $p < .01$) and about 10% of the variability in delinquency effect sizes was accounted for by the study methods used. The following method-related variables demonstrated the largest relationships with effect size in this analysis.

## Pretreatment Equivalence of
## Experimental and Control Groups

Studies in which treatment and control groups were similar prior to treatment (indicated by random assignment to conditions, no pretest statistical differences between groups, and coder ratings of high similarity between treatment and control groups) produced smaller effect sizes than those in which treatment and control groups were not similar.

*Type of publication.* Unpublished technical reports tended to produce smaller effect sizes than published journal articles, books, and dissertations.

*Role of evaluator.* Studies in which the evaluator assumed only a research role tended to produce smaller effect sizes. That is, evaluators who were not involved in the design, planning, or delivery of treatment tended to be associated with smaller treatment effects.

*Type of treatment received by control participants.* Studies in which control participants received more services as part of "treatment as usual" control groups (e.g., institutionalization vs. no treatment or probation) resulted in smaller effect sizes.

*Blinding in data collection.* Studies in which those collecting outcome data were blind to the group status of participants produced larger effect sizes than those in which data collectors were not blind.

With the effect sizes adjusted for differences between studies on the variables identified as influential in this multiple regression analysis, we then sought to identify the treatment and participant characteristics most strongly related to observed effect sizes. This was accomplished with a second weighted random effects multiple regression analysis that used the method-adjusted effect sizes generated by the procedure described above as the dependent variable. The independent variables for this analysis were organized into four clusters of study characteristics that were entered into the regression hierarchically. The first cluster included such participant characteristics as age, gender, heterogeneity of the sample, delinquency level, and proportion with prior offenses. Note that ethnicity was not included in this analysis because we did not want to control it statistically but, rather, examine it directly at a later stage.

The remaining three clusters involved treatment characteristics. One cluster included general treatment characteristics, including the age of the program, source of participants, and program sponsorship. Another encompassed treatment dose, including implementation quality, treatment duration, treatment frequency per week, total hours of contact, and coder ratings of the intensity and meaningfulness of treatment. The final cluster represented treatment delivery personnel, format of treatment sessions, and treatment site.

The overall model was statistically significant, indicating that the array of study predictors in the model accounted for a significant proportion of the variance between effect sizes ($Q_{21} = 41.20$, $p < .01$). Nearly 15% of the variance among effect sizes was related to the clusters of study characteristics in the model. Of the four clusters of predictor variables, the participant cluster was the largest factor in the model, indicating that the treatment effects varied according to the characteristics of the juveniles in treatment. The individual variables in this cluster that were most influential are discussed below. The cluster relating to treatment dose was the next most important in the model, with more treatment and fewer implementation problems associated with larger effect sizes. The cluster including the variables describing treatment format and the one involving general program characteristics did not make statistically significant contributions to the overall model.

The next step was to identify the individual participant and treatment variables from the influential clusters that had the strongest relationships to effect size. This was done by dropping in a stepwise fashion the variables that made the smallest contributions to the overall model. The final reduced regression model included five variables (Table 5.2). As the results in Table 5.2 show, two variables relating to the characteristics of the juveniles in the study samples had strong, independent relationships with treatment effect: the participants' delinquency level and the proportion of the juvenile sample with prior delinquent offenses. Participant samples in which all of the juveniles had prior offense records tended to produce larger effect sizes than studies in which fewer participants (or none) had priors. In addition, samples with youth identified as delinquent but not institutionalized tended to show larger effects than those in which the youth were predelinquent (minor offenses but not adjudicated) or already institutionalized. This

Table 5.2    Weighted Mixed Effects Multiple Regression: Reduced Model

| Variable | β | B | P |
|---|---|---|---|
| Participant characteristics | | | |
| Delinquents (vs. institutionalized and noninstitutionalized) | .1434 | .0946 | .012 |
| Prior offenses | .1262 | .0807 | .035 |
| Treatment characteristics | | | |
| Implementation quality | .1604 | .0578 | .004 |
| Amount of meaningful contact | .1330 | .0273 | .018 |
| Treatment delivered by juvenile justice personnel | −.1321 | −.0918 | .025 |
| Regression constant | | −.1322 | |
| Overall model | $Q(5) = 31.01$, $p < .01$ | | |
| Residual | $Q(299) = 289.58$, ns | | |

$R^2 = .10$
$N = 305$

pattern is not surprising given that predelinquent samples have little delinquent involvement to begin with and thus less room to reduce their involvement as a result of effective treatment. Institutionalized youth, on the other hand, are the most serious offenders and may have problems that are less amenable to the effects of treatment.

Two variables related to treatment dose also showed strong, independent relationships with effect size. Treatments rated by coders as more meaningful in terms of their likelihood of engaging the juvenile were associated with larger effect sizes than those rated as less meaningful. Also, when difficulties in treatment implementation were reported (e.g., not all juveniles received treatment, or treatment delivery was not complete), smaller treatment effects were found, as would be expected. The final variable in the reduced model indicated that interventions delivered by juvenile justice personnel were not as effective as those delivered by mental health personnel and non–mental health counselors.

As in the previous regression analysis with methodological variables, the reduced model representing the key participant- and treatment-related variables was used to statistically control for differences between studies on those variables. This was done by using the regression equation to "predict" the effect size value expected when the respective participant and treatment variables were given values equal to their means across all studies. This predicted value was then added to the residual for each effect size to create new effect size values that estimated the effect sizes that would result if all studies were equivalent on the independent variables represented in the regression model.

# Minority–Majority Differences With Influential Study Characteristics Controlled

With the most influential study characteristics identified, the relative effects of intervention for minority versus majority samples could be examined while controlling for any differences associated with those study characteristics. The first regression analysis described above produced a set of *method-adjusted* effect sizes for which key methodological differences between studies were held constant. The reduced model from the second regression analysis (Table 5.2) then generated another set of effect sizes from the method-adjusted set for which the influential sample and treatment characteristics were also held constant. This second set of effect sizes, which we will call *equated* effect sizes, statistically controls for all the between-study differences identified by either regression analysis as having a significant relationship to observed effect size values. This level of statistical control permits comparison between studies of minority youth and those of majority youth with increased confidence that any differences in intervention effects, or lack thereof, reflect the role of ethnicity and not other influential study characteristics that happen to be unevenly distributed across the two sets of studies.

Of course, different types of intervention may have different effects, so as a further control, we compared method-adjusted and equated effect sizes separately within each major intervention category. The observed, method-adjusted, and equated effect size means and confidence intervals for minority and majority youth receiving each of the most common types of intervention are shown in Figures 5.2 and 5.3. Figure 5.2 shows counseling-type programs in institutional and noninstitutional settings. The services in these programs include group and individual counseling, milieu therapy, guided group interaction, family counseling, reality therapy, and the like. Figure 5.3 shows casework and service brokerage–type programs, academic services such as tutoring and special classes, and probation with such juvenile justice enhancements as intensive supervision, restitution, and juvenile justice system education.

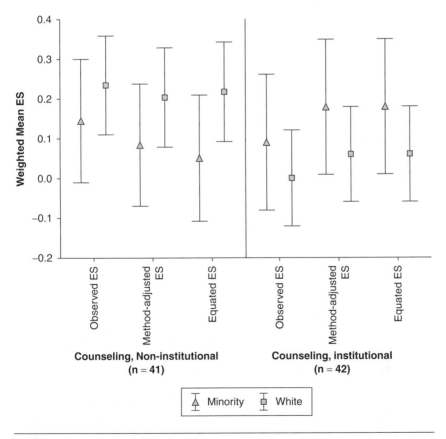

Figure 5.2     Mean Observed and Statistically Adjusted Effect Sizes for Minority and White Youth for Two Types of Counseling Services

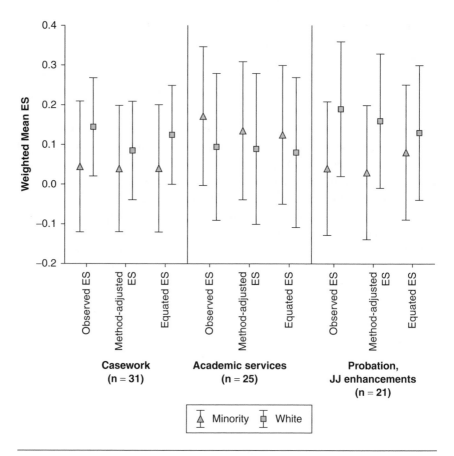

**Figure 5.3**    Mean Observed and Statistically Adjusted Effect Sizes for Minority
                  and White Youth for Select Program Types

There are advantages and disadvantages associated with each of the
three forms of effect size means shown in Figures 5.2 and 5.3. The observed
means represent the findings of the individual studies as they were originally reported. However, their values are influenced by the various method,
participant, and treatment characteristics discussed above, and those characteristics may not be uniform across studies with minority and majority
youth. The method-adjusted effect sizes statistically control for between-
study differences in method and procedure and thus give the best comparison of the effects actually produced by the treatments that were delivered
in the various studies.

However, there may be important differences in the participant characteristics (e.g., delinquency level), treatment implementation and amount,
personnel, and so forth between the interventions provided to the minority
and majority youth in these studies that would yield different effects irrespective of ethnicity. The equated effect sizes simulate a situation in which

key methodological, participant, and treatment characteristics are the same for minority and majority youth and thus permit direct comparison. But they represent configurations of method, participant, and treatment characteristics that, to some degree, were not actually provided to the youth in these studies.

With these considerations in mind, it is most appropriate to examine the three types of effect sizes together with attention to any patterns that may illuminate the differences or similarities between delinquency outcomes for minority and majority youth. The most strikingly consistent result in Figures 5.2 and 5.3 is the similarity of the delinquency effects for minority and majority youth across all the treatment types and all forms of the effect size. The overlapping confidence intervals for each pair of means show that the difference between the minority and majority means was not statistically significant for any comparison. Moreover, the pattern of nonsignificant differences does not strongly favor either group. The effect size means for minority youth are somewhat lower than those for majority youth when the interventions are noninstitutional counseling, casework, or enhanced probation services, but they are higher for academic services and counseling in institutional settings.

# Effects for Minority and Majority
## Youth Receiving the Same Interventions

The results presented thus far indicate that mainstream treatments without cultural tailoring are as effective for minority youth as they are for majority youth. However, these results are all based on comparisons of different sets of studies, some using samples of minority youth and some using majority youth. Although the use of statistical controls reduces the influence of differences between the sets of studies on characteristics that are irrelevant to the issue of differential effects for minority and majority youth, the possibility remains that other differences that were not controlled still distort the comparisons. The most direct comparison of the effects of delinquency intervention programs for minority versus majority youth comes from studies with both minority and majority participants that report effects separately for each group. Such studies would compare the outcomes for ethnic groups who received the same interventions that were evaluated under the same conditions with the same methods.

Relatively few studies in our database broke out and reported results separately for youth of different ethnicities. Figure 5.4 compares the mean effect sizes for each pair of ethnic groups from those studies that did compare outcomes for those groups. Thus, within each pair of effect size means, the youth in the respective ethnic groups participated side by side in the same treatment programs and research studies. Though the numbers are small, the results shown in Figure 5.4 are completely consistent with those

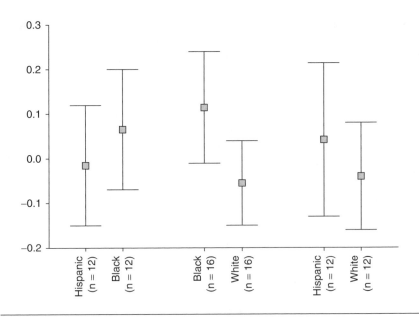

**Figure 5.4**    Differences in Mean Delinquency Effect Sizes for Minority and
Majority Groups in Breakout Samples

from the other analyses reported above. None of the effect size differences between ethnic groups was statistically significant, and the nonsignificant trends in those differences were in the direction of larger effects for minority youth than White youth. The limited data that permit direct comparison, therefore, also fail to support the view that the effects of mainstream programs for delinquency favor majority youth and are less effective with minorities.

## Discussion and Applications to Practice

The analyses reported above provide no evidence that mainstream delinquency intervention programs yield poorer outcomes for minority youth than for White youth despite their general lack of cultural tailoring for minority clientele. A large, representative selection of intervention studies showed no significant differences between minority and White samples in any outcome domain, including effects on delinquency, academic achievement, behavior problems, self-esteem, employment status, peer relations, internalizing problems, attitudes, school participation, family functioning, and psychological adjustment. Additional analysis of delinquent reoffending, the major target outcome for these programs, further supported the initial finding of no difference in effects for minority versus White youth. In particular, introducing a range of statistical controls for methodological and substantive differences among the studies into the analysis did not appreciably alter the results. Moreover, direct comparison of outcomes for minority and White youth receiving the same treatments in the same studies using the same methods and measures also showed no differences.

A more interesting, and more definitive, analysis would involve a three-way comparison of the effects of culturally tailored programs for minority youth with the effects of mainstream programs on both minority and White youth. However, too few controlled studies of the outcomes of culturally tailored programs for minorities have been conducted and reported to permit such analysis. The database from which the studies for the meta-analysis presented here were drawn was developed through vigorous search for all qualifying published and unpublished studies conducted between 1950 and 1996, and we believe it provides very good coverage of the extant research for that period. When we examined each of these studies for indications of culturally tailored interventions, however, we found only one (Wooldredge et al., 1994) of the nearly 500 available that clearly involved such tailoring. The effect size for this study was .03, indicating that treatment group youth were not better off than control group youth after participating in culturally tailored treatment. Another 13 reported using minority personnel to provide services to minority youth but gave no indication that the nature of the service itself was otherwise adjusted on the basis of cultural considerations for those youth. The recidivism effect size for the programs with minority service providers was .13. Even if these latter cases are counted as minimal instances of cultural tailoring, there are too few studies to permit an adequate comparison of their outcomes with those of comparable mainstream programs for comparable minority youth. Furthermore, the results of these few studies do not suggest that tailoring by matching the cultural characteristics of juveniles and providers produces better results than mainstream programming. Increased recent interest in culturally sensitive intervention programs may generate enough outcome research to support such comparison in the near future.

It should be noted that the mean effect sizes found for both minority and White youth in this meta-analysis are relatively modest. As Figure 5.1 indicates, there was no outcome domain for which the mean for either group exceeded .40, and most were in the range of .20 and below. The critical delinquency outcomes, in particular, showed a mean effect size of .11 for minority youth and .17 for White youth. By comparison with these values, the mean effect size for over 300 meta-analyses of the outcomes of psychological, educational, and behavioral interventions found by Lipsey and Wilson (1993) was .50.

One possible interpretation of the results presented in this study, therefore, is that the mainstream delinquency intervention programs reviewed are not generally successful in producing positive outcomes. Thus, the lack of any significant differences between the outcomes for minority and White youth demonstrates not that these programs are equally effective for minorities as Whites despite their lack of cultural tailoring but that they are equally ineffective for both groups of youth. The similarity in the outcomes of mainstream programs for minorities and Whites is only interesting if they have meaningful positive effects on both groups. If the programs do not work, no defensible case could be made for applying them to minority youth no matter how similar the results were to those for White youth.

For several reasons, we do not think the above interpretation of the results is correct. First, numerically small values of the standardized mean difference effect size statistic do not necessarily indicate that the practical significance of the effects is small. The mean effect sizes for the key delinquency reoffense outcomes, for instance, translate into 5–8 percentage-point decreases from a 50% recidivism baseline among control groups. This difference, therefore, represents a 10%–16% reduction in the number of juveniles reoffending, which is far from trivial even though one could hope for more.

And, indeed, larger effects on delinquency are represented in the mean effect sizes found. The distributions of effect sizes for minority and White youth summarized by the respective mean values have relatively large variance. That is, the mean values average over a wide range of delinquency effects, some much smaller than the mean but many that are much larger. In other analyses, we have shown that the effects produced by the high-end delinquency interventions are considerable, ranging as high as 40% reductions in recidivism (Lipsey, 1995; Lipsey & Wilson, 1998). One implication of this state of affairs is that the mean effect size is not an especially good summary of the full effect size distribution. Another implication, however, is that the statistically nonsignificant overall difference between the mean for minority youth and that for White youth encompasses the full range of effects, including those of unquestionable practical significance. This can be seen most clearly in Figures 5.2 and 5.3 where the confidence intervals around the mean effect sizes for different types of interventions are very broad, ranging upward to twice or three times the mean value, as well as downward an equivalent amount.

Overall, therefore, we believe the most defensible interpretation of the available research is that mainstream treatments for juvenile delinquents are generally effective and no less effective for ethnic minority youth than White youth. We must emphasize, however, that this does not mean that issues of cultural sensitivity are unimportant to such programs when minority youth are served. It could well be that the effects of programs with cultural tailoring would be larger than those of programs without even though those without do not have differential effects for minority and White youth. The evidence reviewed here only shows that cultural tailoring is not necessary for the programs to have positive outcomes and that the absence of such tailoring does not diminish the effects for minorities relative to Whites. As noted earlier, there are not yet sufficient outcome studies for programs with cultural tailoring to determine if they yield larger effects than comparable programs without such tailoring. In addition, all of the studies included here involved indigenous minority youth, rather than recent immigrants. Thus, our results do not speak to the particular needs of recent immigrant populations or the effectiveness of mainstream intervention for delinquent youth who are newly arrived.

Moreover, even if the major outcomes of mainstream programs for minority youth are comparable to those with White youth, there may be other benefits to culturally sensitive programming. It may well be that the likelihood of participation, the acceptance of the program plan, the ultimate satisfaction with the program experience, and other such factors not commonly measured in outcome studies are less positive for minority youth in mainstream programs than majority youth. This may be especially so for recent immigrant youth. Moreover, if such differences occur, programs especially tailored to specific ethnic groups may well alleviate them. What the evidence reviewed here indicates is only that such tailoring cannot be justified on the grounds that, without it, the programs are ineffective or not as effective as for majority youth. In addition, it is worth noting that in the course of developing culturally sensitive programs, some care must be taken to ensure that such tailoring does not reduce the effectiveness of the mainstream programs that are adapted. Ultimately, we must implement and evaluate a sufficient number and range of culturally tailored programs for delinquent youth to permit a direct assessment of their outcomes and how they compare with those of mainstream programs.

# References

Addams, J. (1895). *Hull-House maps and papers. A presentation of nationalities and wages in a congested district of Chicago, together with comments and essays on problems growing out of the social conditions.* New York: Thomas Y. Crowell.

Barth, R. P., & Blackwell, D. L. (1998). Death rates among California's foster care and former foster care populations. *Children and Youth Services Review, 20,* 577–604.

Cohen, J. (1988). *Statistical power analysis for the behavioral sciences* (2nd ed.). Hillsdale, NJ: Lawrence Erlbaum.

Cooper, H., & Hedges, L. V. (Eds.). (1994). *The handbook of research synthesis.* New York: Russell Sage.

de Anda, D. (Ed.). (1997). *Controversial issues in multiculturalism.* Boston: Allyn & Bacon.

Devore, W., & Schlesinger, E. G. (1996). *Ethnic-sensitive social work practice.* Boston: Allyn & Bacon.

Dickersin, K. (1997). How important is publication bias? A synthesis of available data. *AIDS Education and Prevention, 9,* 15–21.

Green, J. W. (1995). *Cultural awareness in the human services. A multiethnic approach.* Boston: Allyn & Bacon.

Hedges, L. V. (1981). Distribution theory for Glass's estimator of effect size and related estimators. *Journal of Educational Statistics, 6,* 107–128.

Hedges, L. V., & Olkin, I. (1985). *Statistical methods for meta-analysis*. New York: Academic Press.

Jonson-Reid, M., & Barth, R. P. (2000). From placement to prison: The path to adolescent incarceration from child welfare supervised foster or group care. *Children and Youth Services Review, 22,* 493–516.

Lipsey, M. W. (1992). Juvenile delinquency treatment: A meta-analytic inquiry into the variability of effects. In T. D. Cook, H. Cooper, D. S. Cordray, H. Hartmann, L. V. Hedges, R. J. Light, T. A. Louis, & F. Mosteller (Eds.), *Meta-analysis for explanation: A casebook* (pp. 83–127). New York: Russell Sage.

Lipsey, M. W. (1995). What do we learn from 400 research studies on the effectiveness of treatment with juvenile delinquents? In J. McGuire (Ed.), *What works? Reducing reoffending: Guidelines from research and practice* (pp. 63–78). New York: John Wiley.

Lipsey, M. W., & Wilson, D. B. (1993). The efficacy of psychological, educational, and behavioral treatment: Confirmation from meta-analysis. *American Psychologist, 48,* 1181–1209.

Lipsey, M. W., & Wilson, D. B. (1998). Effective intervention for serious juvenile offenders: A synthesis of research. In R. Loeber & D. P. Farrington (Eds.), *Serious and violent juvenile offenders: Risk factors and successful interventions* (pp. 313–345). Thousand Oaks, CA: Sage Publications.

Lipsey, M. W., & Wilson, D. B. (2001). *Practical meta-analysis* (Applied Social Research Methods Series, Vol. 49). Thousand Oaks, CA: Sage Publications.

Lum, D. (1996). *Social work practice and people of color. A process stage approach*. Monterey, CA: Brooks/Cole.

Shadish, W. R., & Haddock, C. K. (1994). Combining estimates of effect size. In H. Cooper & L. V. Hedges (Eds.), *The handbook of research synthesis* (pp. 261–281). New York: Russell Sage.

Soydan, H. (1999). *The history of ideas in social work*. Birmingham, AL: Venture Press.

Soydan, H., Jergeby, U., Olsson, E., & Harms-Ringdal, M. (1999). *Socialt arbete med etniska minoriteter. En litteraturöversikt* [Social work with ethnic minorities. A literature review]. Stockholm: Liber.

Williams, C., Soydan, H., & Johnson, M. R. D. (Eds.). (1998). *Social work and minorities: European perspectives*. London, UK: Routledge.

Wooldredge, J., Hartman, J., Latessa, E., & Holmes, S. (1994). Effectiveness of culturally specific community treatment for African American juvenile felons. *Crime & Delinquency, 40,* 589–598.

# 6

# Psychosocial Treatment of Youth Suicide

## A Systematic Review of the Research

*Mark J. Macgowan*

Youth suicide is a serious problem in the United States. Suicide is the second leading cause of death among 12- to 17-year-olds (National Center for Injury Prevention and Control, 2002). Suicide rates are highest among older adolescents, ages 15 to 17 years old. Among this age group, the rates have steadily declined since 1994 (National Center for Injury Prevention and Control, 2002). Researchers attribute the decline to a reduction in rates of alcohol and other drug abuse and to an increase in the use of prescribed antidepressants (American Academy of Child and Adolescent Psychiatry, 2001). Fewer younger adolescents ages 12 to 14 years die by suicide. However, their suicide rates have remained generally level since 1994 (National Center for Injury Prevention and Control, 2002), in contrast with the rates for older adolescents.

Concerns about the mortality rate among the young have led to increased monitoring of suicide morbidity (i.e., ideation and attempts) among young people. An important national source for morbidity data is the biennial Youth Risk Behavior Surveillance System (YRBSS). Since 1991, the YRBSS has included data on the prevalence of health risk behavior, including suicide ideation and attempts among high school students. The 2001 YRBSS revealed that 19% of students had seriously considered attempting suicide during the previous 12 months (Centers for Disease Control and Prevention, 2002). More than 14% (14.8%) of students had made a specific plan to attempt suicide during the 12 months preceding the survey. More than 8% (8.8%) of students had attempted suicide at least once during the 12 months preceding the survey. More than 2% (2.6%) of students had made a suicide

Originally published in *Research on Social Work Practice* 2004; 14; 147. DOI: 10.1177/
1049731503257889 The online version of this article can be found at: http://rsw.sagepub.com/
cgi/content/abstract/14/3/147

attempt in the 12 months before the survey resulting in treatment by a doctor or nurse. Trend data from 1991 to 2001 suggest significant declines in suicide ideation and plans to attempt suicide (Centers for Disease Control and Prevention, 2002). However, the number of students reporting suicide attempts or suicide attempts with injuries significantly increased from 1991 to 2001 (Centers for Disease Control and Prevention, 2003).

Yet despite the data suggesting that youth suicide is a significant public health concern, comparably little research has been done on how to treat suicidality among youth. Although there are many review papers and descriptions of interventions and treatment strategies (e.g., Holman, 1997; Jobes, 1995; Lum, Smith, & Ferris, 2002; Morrison, 1987; Rittner & Smyth, 1999; Trautman,1995; Wodarski & Harris, 1987), there are few experimental and quasi-experimental evaluations of suicide intervention strategies. More than a decade ago, the report of the Secretary's Task Force on Youth Suicide concluded that "there are no treatment studies—psychotherapeutic, behavioral, or psychopharmacologic—which show that a clearly defined treatment approach is superior to no treatment or to some other treatment" (Alcohol Drug Abuse and Mental Health Administration, 1989, p. 253). Since that time, a number of studies have tested the efficacy of psychosocial treatments for youth suicide. Although still relatively few, these studies form a sufficient body to provide a critical review.

This article provides a systematic review of psychosocial (i.e., nonpharmacological) interventions for youth suicidality. This review uses the general term *suicidality* to include attempted suicide, self-harm, suicide plans, and suicidal ideation. The more specific term *suicidal behavior* includes suicides, attempted suicides, and self-harm behaviors. This article focuses on interventions involving exclusive samples of youth younger than 18 years of age. Additionally, the review focuses on interventions, defined as those "intended to prevent an outcome or to alter the course of an existing condition" (U.S. Department of Health and Human Services, 2001, p. 201). Reflecting the irregular use of the terms in the literature, *treatment* and *intervention* are used interchangeably in this article. As a systematic review, this article first outlines the methods involved in both selecting and evaluating the research. The research is then summarized and critically reviewed. The evidence base for psychosocial interventions for youth suicidality is presented, and a foundation is laid on which future intervention research may be built. Specific applications of these findings for social work practice are presented.

# Method

## Selection Criteria

Studies selected for this review must have met certain criteria. First, only nonpharmacological treatments were included. In one or two cases, researchers indicated that medication may have been used, but it was not the primary treatment. Second, studies must have included samples consisting exclusively of adolescents (i.e., 10 to 17 years old). Third, studies must have included outcomes directly related to suicidality, such as suicide ideation or suicide attempts. Most studies also assessed other outcomes, such as treatment retention. Treatment adherence has been identified as an especially challenging area in treating adolescent suicidality (Piacentini, Rotheram-Borus, Gillis et al., 1995; Spirito, Plummer, Gispert, & Levy, 1992; Trautman, Stewart, & Morishima, 1993) and was an outcome also included in this review.

To find the research reviewed in this study, several sources were searched, including the Campbell Collaboration's Social, Psychological, Educational and Criminological Trials Register, the abstracts of Cochrane Reviews, PsycINFO, PubMed, and Social Work Abstracts. Search parameters were broad and used wildcards. The search included the terms *suicid\** or *self-harm* coupled with any of the following: *youth* or *adolescen\**. Additionally, the terms *treat\** or *intervent\** were used. Review articles were also scanned (e.g., American Academy of Child and Adolescent Psychiatry, 2001; Hawton et al., 1998; King & Knox, 2000; Rudd, 2000b; Stewart, Manion, & Davidson, 2002). All available dates were included up to the present (December 2002).

## Rating Criteria

The literature was examined in a systematic manner to answer the following three questions: (a) What is the treatment research? (b) What is the level of empirical support for the treatment of adolescent suicidality? and (c) Is treatment successful? To answer the first question, each study was described in the narrative of this article describing the treatment, samples, and methodology. To answer the second question, each intervention was evaluated according to standards for empirically supported therapies, defined as "treatments shown to be efficacious in controlled research with a delineated population" (Chambless & Hollon, 1998, p. 7). This review used criteria developed by American Psychological Association's Division 12 Task Force (Chambless et al., 1996, 1998), which defined well-established and probably efficacious treatments. As none of the studies reviewed used single-case designs, only the criteria for group designs were used. According to these criteria, well-established treatments

1. have at least two good between-group design experiments demonstrating efficacy in at least one of the following ways: (a) superior (statistically significantly so) to placebo or to another treatment or (b) equivalent to an already established treatment in experiments with adequate statistical power (about 30 per group),

2. must be conducted with treatment manuals,

3. must specify the characteristics of the client samples, and

4. must have demonstrated effects by at least two different investigators or investigating teams.

The criteria for probably efficacious treatments should include the following:

1. two experiments showing the treatment is superior (statistically significantly so) to a waiting-list control group or

2. one or more experiments meeting the well-established treatment criteria 1a or 1b, 2, and 3 but not 4.

Where a study failed to provide sufficient information to make a determination, a negative response was applied.

To assess each study's success in reducing suicidality, this study used Rudd's (2000a, 2000b) schema to systematically classify treatment outcomes and treatment success. The primary outcome of interest in this review was suicidal behavior (e.g., suicide attempts or instrumental behaviors with or without injuries), considered a direct marker of suicidality (Rudd, 2000a, 2000b). However, there are also indirect markers of suicidality, such as symptoms (e.g., suicidal thoughts or hopelessness), skills (e.g., problem solving or emotional regulation), or traits (e.g., personality disorders, social support, or introversion) (Rudd, 2000a, 2000b). In this review, treatment compliance was included as a direct marker of suicidality.

In studies that aggregated suicide attempts with suicide ideation, the author reviewed the markers and determined in which category they should be placed. Unless it was clear in the study that a majority of the outcomes were direct, they were categorized as indirect.

Additionally, Rudd (2000b) distinguished direct treatment success from indirect treatment success. Direct treatment success was defined as "characterized by a significant reduction in subsequent attempts and instrumental behaviors" (Rudd, 2000b, p. 63), and indirect treatment success was defined as "a significant change in symptom measures, skills, and maladaptive personality traits" (Rudd, 2000b, p. 63). Rudd also proposed that success can be further classified as short term or enduring, with 12 months as the line of demarcation.

Using this multifaceted methodology, the following sections provide a systematic review of the intervention research on youth suicidality followed by a discussion of the findings and methodologies of the research and applications to social work practice.

# Results

The broad search of the electronic databases and other sources initially yielded several hundred citations. However, when these were examined for relevance using the strict criteria previously noted, 10 studies were identified. This section describes each study, summarizes the commonalities across studies, and then applies the criteria previously noted in determining the level of empirical support and whether the intervention was successful in reducing suicidality.

## Descriptive Review of the Intervention Research

Cotgrove, Zirinsky, Black, and Weston (1995) examined the effects of an individualized intervention involving a sample of youth ($n = 105$) discharged from a hospital following a suicide attempt. Researchers randomly assigned youth either to standard treatment that included a token (green card) allowing immediate readmission to the hospital ($n = 47$) or to standard treatment only ($n = 58$). The authors believed that the token approach would be helpful by allowing youth a means by which they could communicate their distress to others in a way that would be taken seriously and that would provide them an escape from distress without resorting to self-harm. The results showed that the treatment group had a lower suicide attempt rate (3% or 6% versus 7% or 12%), but the rate was not statistically different from that of the control group, likely due to the low base rate.

In discussing the clinical significance of this finding, the authors reported that the suicide attempt repeat rate among those in the control group (12%) corresponded with other figures cited in the literature. The authors calculated that the use of a simple token scheme would reduce the suicide attempt rate from 135 to less than 70 per annum. Thus, whereas the findings between groups were not significantly different, the authors noted that the effectiveness of the approach in reducing suicide attempts was significant.

The study's strengths included using an experimental design and the clinically significant finding of reduced suicide attempts in the treatment group. A limitation was the lack of comparisons at pretest to determine equivalence between groups. Additionally, it was unclear what was included in the usual services condition.

Greenfield, Larson, Hechtman, Rousseau, and Platt (2002) tested the effects of a rapid-response outpatient model in reducing suicidality and use of hospitalization among a sample of suicidal youth released from an emergency department of a pediatric hospital. The rapid-response treatment model involved a team consisting of a part-time psychiatrist and a psychiatric nurse who delivered outpatient care immediately after assessment in the emergency department. The team met with the youth and his or her family to further assess the circumstances of the crisis and to evaluate the youth's support system. As described by the authors, treatment consisted of "reframing any misconceptions, maladaptive behaviors, and communication patterns that contributed to the patient's or the family's stresses. Medication was used when appropriate, and community resources were used when available" (Greenfield et al., 2002, pp. 1575–1576).

Youth were assigned to either the rapid-response program ($n = 158$) or to a control group ($n = 28$). The control condition consisted of either hospitalization, following the client as an outpatient, or referral to community resources. Assignment was based on which team of psychiatrists was present when the youth came to the emergency department (each condition included its own team of psychiatrists). To ensure there were no essential differences between conditions, the researchers used a system that included a prearranged, on-call schedule "balanced in terms of total duration, times of the day (morning, afternoon, evening, or night), days of the week (including weekends), weeks of the month, and months of the year during both study years" (Greenfield et al., 2002, p. 1575). Statistical analyses revealed that the experimental and control groups were not different with respect to a range of demographic (e.g., age, sex, language, marital status of parents, and annual family income) and clinical variables (e.g., suicidal thoughts, suicide attempts, depression, alcohol use, and illegal drug use). Thus, whereas the researchers did not use strict random assignment, there was a high likelihood of comparability between conditions.

At 2 and 6 months after the initial assessment, suicidality-related hospitalization rates and levels of suicidality were compared. Youth in the treatment group had significantly fewer hospitalizations than did those in the control group at 6 months. No between-group differences were observed in changes in levels of suicidality or in overall functioning during the follow-up period. The authors concluded that a rapid-response outpatient follow-up resulted in a lower hospitalization rate than those who did not and similar increases in level of functioning and decreases in levels of suicidality.

Although the findings suggest that outpatient treatment was a successful alternative to hospitalization, limitations of the study are that the article provided little information about the outpatient treatment model and that the control group may have contained elements of the treatment model. Thus, the specific effects of the rapid response model were unclear.

Brent and colleagues (1997) examined the effects of three different treatments in reducing depression and suicidality (ideation or attempts) among 107 clinically referred, depressed adolescents. The first condition ($n = 37$) consisted of individual cognitive behavior therapy (CBT) adapted from Beck's (1979) CBT. The treatment was adapted for adolescents by socializing youth to the treatment model, using concrete examples, exploring autonomy and trust, highlighting cognitive distortions and affective shifts that occur during sessions, and developing problem solving, affect regulation, and social skills (Brent & Poling, 1997). The second condition ($n = 35$)

consisted of systemic behavior family therapy that combined functional family therapy (Alexander & Parsons, 1982) and problem solving (Robin & Foster, 1989). The third condition ($n = 35$) was nondirective supportive therapy consisting of the provision of support, affect clarification, and active listening. All conditions also received family psychoeducation about affective illness and its treatment. During 3 to 4 months of treatment, all three conditions reduced suicidal ideation, but cognitive therapy was more effective at reducing major depression than were the other treatments.

The study included important controls, such as manualized treatments, fidelity measures, and intent-to-treat analyses (inclusion of all eligible clients without regard to compliance with protocol). One limitation was that the study did not separate suicide ideation from suicide attempts, so it was not clear how these two outcomes were differentially affected.

Dialectical behavior therapy (DBT), a type of cognitive-behavioral therapy, is a theory-based treatment originally developed for chronically suicidal adult women, including those with borderline personality disorder (BPD) (Linehan, Armstrong, Suarez, Allmon, & Heard, 1991). DBT is based on Linehan's biosocial theory that views problematic behavior (e.g., BPD and suicidality) as emerging from biological-emotional vulnerability and an invalidating environment (Miller, Rathus, Linehan, Wertzler, & Leigh, 1997). The therapy views suicidal behaviors as "having important affect-regulating properties as well as servicing to elicit helping behaviors from an otherwise invalidating environment" (Miller et al., 1997, p. 79). Studies involving adults with BPD (e.g., Linehan et al., 1991) indicate that this treatment is promising. DBT was adapted for adolescents by incorporating family members in the multifamily skills training group and by shortening treatment from 1 year to 12 weeks. The efficacy of DBT in reducing adolescent suicidality has been examined in one empirical study.

The study (Rathus & Miller, 2002) involved a total sample of 111 in a quasi-experimental design. A total of 29 mostly female (93%) adolescents with suicidality and BPD were assigned to the outpatient treatment condition consisting of DBT, which was manualized. DBT treatment consisted of 12 weeks of twice-weekly individual sessions and multifamily skills training group sessions. Additionally, each individual session was structured to address specific targets in descending order of importance as follows: life-threatening behaviors, therapy-interfering behaviors, quality-of-life interfering behaviors, and increasing behavioral skills. The group sessions consisted of four modules: mindfulness, interpersonal effectiveness, emotional regulation, and distress tolerance.

A total of 82 youth were assigned to a comparison group that received treatment as usual (TAU), consisting of 12 weeks of twice-weekly individual and family sessions. The individual sessions consisted of short-term psychodynamic or supportive therapy, and the family sessions used a family systems approach, helping the family resolve acute conflicts, and provided psychoeducation about youth depression.

At the end of treatment, youth in the BPD group had significantly fewer within-treatment psychiatric hospitalizations and a significantly higher rate of treatment completion than did the TAU group. The researchers reported no significant differences in the number of suicide attempts during treatment, likely due to low base rates. However, fewer youth in the DBT group attempted suicide than those in the TAU group (1 versus 7, respectively). Additionally, youth in the DBT condition had significantly fewer psychiatric hospitalizations and completed significantly more weeks of treatment than did those in the TAU group. Among youth within the DBT condition, the researchers reported significant reductions from pretest to posttest in suicidal ideation, general psychiatric symptoms, and symptoms of borderline personality. The researchers concluded that DBT was a promising treatment for suicidal youth with BPD.

The study was strong in providing a manualized intervention with adherence protocols, using established measures, and including a diverse sample that included 67.5% Hispanics/Latinos and 17.1% African Americans. However, the lack of randomization and limiting the analyses to only posttest comparisons limited the study's findings.

Harrington and colleagues (Harrington et al., 1998; Kerfoot, Harrington, & Dyer, 1995) examined the effects of a home-based intervention that included problem solving and communication. The study (Harrington et al., 1998) involved 162 adolescents who had deliberately poisoned themselves and who were randomly assigned to routine care plus the home-based family intervention ($n = 85$) or to routine individual services ($n = 77$). The intervention consisted of an assessment session and four home visits by master's-level social workers who directed family communication and problem-solving sessions. Routine services consisted of visits to the clinic by the youth and their families, who received "a diverse range of interventions, including sessions with psychiatrists and with psychiatric nurses" (Harrington et al., 1998, p. 513) but not home-based family interventions. Outcomes were assessed at 2- and 6-month posttests.

At posttests, there were no significant differences in suicidal ideation and hopelessness between the intervention and control groups. However, subgroup analyses revealed that youth without major depression in the family intervention had significantly lower suicidal ideation than did the control group at posttests. The researchers noted that the clinical significance of this finding was limited; the ideation scores of nondepressed youth were lower than those of the depressed youth, and nondepressed youth are generally at relatively low risk for subsequent problems (Pfeffer et al., 1993). A subsequent study by Harrington and colleagues (2000) examined whether the efficacy of the family intervention among those without major depression was the result of mediating variables such as an improvement in family functioning. The results showed that improvements among those who were nondepressed were not related to family functioning. The researchers concluded that a brief five-session family intervention may not be sufficient to reduce suicidal thinking among depressed youth.

This study used rigorous methodology, including randomization, a man-ualized treatment, intent-to-treat analyses, statistical controls for covari-ates, and blinding researchers to treatment condition. Rotheram-Borus and colleagues (Rotheram-Borus et al., 1996; Rotheram-Borus, Piacentini, Cantwell, Belin, & Song, 2000) completed two studies of a family inter-vention delivered in an emergency room (ER) after a suicide attempt. The sample consisted of 140 female adolescents, mostly Latina (88%). The studies intended to determine the effects of the intervention on suicidality and on treatment adherence. The specialized ER care condition included training workshops for ER staff, a videotaped presentation for families about the dangers of ignoring suicide attempts and the potential benefits of treatment, an on-call family therapist, and one structured family therapy session while in the ER ($n = 65$). The comparison group received standard ER care ($n = 75$), which consisted of an evaluation by a pediatrician to address medical concerns and an assessment by a psychiatrist to determine the need for psychiatric hospitalization. If hospitalization was not needed, the adolescents and their families were referred to outpatient treatment. Both groups also received a six-session manualized cognitive-behavioral aftercare treatment called Successful Negotiation Acting Positively (SNAP) (Piacentini, Rotheram- Borus, & Cantwell, 1995).

In the first study, Rotheram-Borus and colleagues (1996) examined the immediate effects of the specialized ER intervention on suicidal ideation and other variables and on adherence to SNAP aftercare treatment. The results indicated that participants receiving the specialized program were significantly less depressed and had less suicidal ideation than those receiv-ing standard ER care. Additionally, those in the specialized program were significantly more likely to attend the SNAP program than those receiving standard ER care.

In the second study (Rotheram-Borus et al., 2000), the long-term (18-month) effects of the family intervention were examined along with an eval-uation of suicide reattempts. At posttest, rates of suicide reattempts and suicidal reideation were lower than expected and similar across conditions. There were fewer suicide reattempts in the treatment group (6 in specialized care versus 11 in standard care), but the base rates were too low and samples sizes were too small to permit meaningful comparisons. The authors did not expect ideation to improve as "feeling suicidal was normative and a signal for taking behavioral actions to stop progression to suicidal acts" (Rotheram-Borus et al., 2000, p. 1091). The program resulted in significant improve-ments in maternal emotional distress and family cohesion among families with children who were symptomatic. The program also contributed to greater attendance and completion rates of the SNAP therapy among youth in the intervention group than among those in the comparison condition.

These studies by Rotheram-Borus and colleagues (1996, 2000) were valuable because they included mostly Latinas. The research designs were limited by lacking randomization, but the authors attempted to minimize the internal validity problems by examining pretest differences to assess comparability, reporting no significant differences. The other challenge was the small number of suicide attempters involved in the study, which did not permit statistical comparisons between groups.

Gutstein and Rudd (1990) tested the effects of a family-involved outpatient intervention called the Systemic Crisis Intervention Program. Unlike the other family interventions, this one involved components intended to restructure the youth's family and social networks. Treatment consisted of several stages. Within a day of an initial contact, two crisis staff members undertook a 3-hour evaluation. Following this contact, the family was prepared for the subsequent crisis gatherings. During this preparatory stage, the youth's extended family members were invited to the gatherings, and a process called multiple advocacy was invoked in which a team of therapists became involved by advocating the needs of family members. The next stage consisted of the crisis gatherings that involved two 4-hour meetings involving the nuclear and extended family and team members. As described by the authors, "The express purpose of these gatherings was to foster a process of reconciliation among family members that could be used to prevent future extreme reactions to stresses and developmental milestones" (Gutstein & Rudd, 1990, p. 268). This crisis treatment typically lasted 2 to 6 weeks, often followed by a referral for ongoing family and group therapy. Occasionally, brief hospitalization was used to manage crises.

In testing the effects of the intervention, the authors used a single-group, pretest-posttest design involving 47 youth who had either made a recent suicide attempt ($n = 21$) or voiced serious threats of suicide ($n = 26$). During the 18-month follow-up, the authors reported that only two of the youth had attempted suicide, with no attempts during treatment. The authors also reported significant declines in the severity of the presenting problem and significant improvements in adaptive behavior (e.g., school, family, and interpersonal functioning) and family and marital functioning during 12 months of follow-up. Hospital or residential care use in the year before and after treatment significantly declined; in the year before, 10 youth were institutionalized; only one was institutionalized the year after treatment. Thus, the intervention appeared to have a substantial impact on both the direct and the indirect markers of suicidality. However, without controls or a comparison group, the specific cause of the change was unclear.

Deykin, Hsieh, Joshi, and McNamarra (1986) examined the effects of an intervention that included a community-based component that did not require direct family involvement. In a two-group, nonrandomized study, the researchers examined the effects of the intervention program for youth admitted to a hospital for suicidal behavior (i.e., attempts, gestures, or life-threatening events such as potential lethal injuries due to youth's acts of omission or commission) or serious suicidal ideation. The program consisted of the following two elements: a prevention-based education curriculum targeted for human service workers and high school student peer leaders and direct service to suicidal adolescents. The education component included eight day-long conferences or workshops designed to increase participants' knowledge of suicidal behavior and to inform them of relevant community resources. The direct service component was community based, used an aggressive outreach, and attempted to achieve the following objectives: provide emotional, social, and physical support to the youth; ensure follow-up with postdischarge care; advocate for the youth with family and community resources; provide liaison between the youth and the hospital and between the hospital and community resources; explore and maximize social supports to the youth; and facilitate attainment of social and/or financial resources for the youth and their families. To achieve these objectives, the intervention had a loose structure in that youth were not required to adhere to appointments, there was no requirement on the length of the service, and parents were not required to be involved. As the authors noted, "This practice constituted a departure from the traditional youth mental heath services, which usually require active parental participation and personal commitment to the treatment process" (p. 90). The comparison condition included TAU consisting of standard medical care and referral as needed.

The authors reported that after controlling for pretest differences in suicidal history and race, those in the intervention group ($n = 172$) had the same risk of study-eligible rehospitalization as did the comparison condition ($n = 147$) within 2 years of the intervention program. However, the intervention group was significantly more compliant with medical recommendations such as referrals to medical clinics or keeping appointments. The authors also reported that the prevention component helped to increase identification and referral for youth with suicide ideation.

The findings from this study were limited in that there was no evidence that the intervention reduced repeated suicidal, life-threatening behavior. Additionally, due to the limited research design and loose structure of the intervention, it was unclear what part of the treatment package contributed to change. However, the study is notable because it is the only one in this review that included a majority (57%) of African American youth in the treatment condition.

Group work has often been recommended to reduce youth suicidality (Aronson & Scheidlinger, 1995; Rittner & Smyth, 1999; Ross & Motto, 1984), but few studies have tested its efficacy. In a randomized clinical trial involving youth who had deliberately harmed themselves within the past year, group therapy and routine care ($n = 32$) were compared with routine care alone ($n = 31$) (Wood, Trainor, Rothwell, Moore, & Harrington, 2001). The group approach was "developmental group psychotherapy" and included elements of problem solving, cognitive-behavioral therapy, dialectical behavioral therapy, and psychodynamic group psychotherapy. The stages of treatment included an initial assessment phase followed by six "acute" group sessions covering the following risk-based topics: relationships, school problems, family problems, anger management, depression and self-harm, and hopelessness. Following the acute phase, youth attended "long-term" weekly group sessions emphasizing group process until they felt ready to leave, which included a median of eight group sessions during 6 months of the trial. According to the authors, routine care was monitored with a resource use questionnaire and consisted of a number of interventions, such as family sessions, nonspecific counseling with the adolescent, and psychotropic medication, if indicated.

Using intent-to-treat analyses, the results at the 7-month interview were that youth who participated in group therapy were less likely to have repeated deliberate self-harm on two or more occasions than were those in routine care. The group treatment had a powerful effect on the risk of a second episode of self-harm, with a risk reduction of 26%. They were also less likely to need routine care, had better school attendance, and had a lower rate of behavioral problems than did youth who had received routine care. The group treatment did not reduce depression or suicidal thinking, a finding consistent with other research (Linehan et al., 1991; Rotheram-Borus et al., 2000). The authors also reported a dosage effect: Adolescents who attended more sessions of group therapy were less likely to repeat deliberate self-harm. In contrast, more sessions of routine care resulted in more incidents of self-harm.

## Summary of the Studies' Treatment and Methodological Variables

The research studies can be summarized in terms of treatment variables and methodological rigor. Different theoretical approaches were used, but the modal type of treatment was a form of CBT (Brent et al., 1997; Harrington et al., 1998; Rathus & Miller, 2002; Rotheram-Borus et al., 2000; Wood et al., 2001). Some of the components of CBT in these studies include monitoring and modification of automatic thoughts, assumptions, and beliefs and acquisition of problem solving, communication, affect regulation, and social skills. All but one (Cotgrove et al., 1995) of the interventions were short-term, defined as 6 months or less (Rudd, 2000b).

One study emphasized working only with the youth in treatment (Cotgrove et al., 1995), but most involved the youth's families and/or others. Several studies included group methods, but only one study used it as the primary method (Wood et al., 2001).

With respect to the samples, most of the studies included a substantial majority of girls (average of 86.5% across the studies), with none including a majority of boys. Of those that documented the racial and ethnic composition of the samples, three involved mostly European Americans (average of 72.3%) (Brent, 1997; Greenfield et al., 2002; Gutstein & Rudd, 1990). Another three included a majority of Hispanics or Latinos (average of 80.7%; Rathus & Miller, 2002; Rotheram-Borus et al., 1996, 2000). Only one study included a sample of mostly African Americans (57% in the treatment group; Deykin et al., 1986).

With respect to methodology, half of the studies used an experimental design (Brent et al., 1997; Cotgrove et al., 1995; Greenfield et al., 2002; Harrington et al., 1998; Wood et al., 2001). Except for a couple of studies (Cotgrove et al., 1995; Greenfield et al., 2002), the research added one or more of the following controls: manualized treatments with fidelity monitors, researchers blind to treatment condition, and intent-to-treat analyses. Five studies used a quasi-experiment design involving nonrandomization or single-group designs (Deykin et al., 1986; Gutstein & Rudd, 1990; Rathus & Miller, 2002; Rotheram-Borus et al., 1996, 2000).

## Evaluation of the Level of Empirical Support of the Interventions

Table 6.1 examines the efficacy of the treatments using the criteria cited by Chambless and colleagues (1998) as previously noted. No studies included a well-established treatment largely due to the criterion that requires two randomly controlled clinical trials involving two different investigator teams. Two treatments that met the criteria for probably efficacious were developmental group psychotherapy (Wood et al., 2001) and family communication and problem solving (Harrington et al., 2000). However, the findings were limited. The group intervention had significantly better reductions in self-harm than did the comparison groups but not depression or suicidal thinking, with power to detect only large differences. The family intervention was effective in reducing suicidal ideation but only among those without major depression. None of the other treatments was superior to the control or comparison conditions.

## Evaluation of the Direct and Indirect Treatment Success of the Interventions

Table 6.2 presents each study's outcomes using Rudd's (2000a, 2000b) schema and reports whether treatment was directly or indirectly successful in significantly reducing suicidality. Of the six studies that assessed suicide attempts or deliberate self-harm, only two (Gutstein & Rudd, 1990; Wood et al., 2001) reported successful outcomes, with one reporting outcomes enduring for 1 year (Gutstein & Rudd, 1990). Both also had short-term and/or long-term effects on most of the indirect markers of suicidality.

For the studies that included indirect markers of suicidality, such as suicide ideation or threats of suicide, most reported successes (Brent et al., 1997; Greenfield et al., 2002; Gutstein & Rudd, 1990; Rathus & Miller, 2002; Rotheram-Borus et al., 1996). In four cases, there were findings that indicated no changes. The family-based intervention (Harrington et al., 1998) reduced suicide ideation among a subgroup without major depression but had no success in reducing ideation among those with major

**Table 6.1**    Level of Empirical Support for Treatments for Adolescent Suicidality

| Treatment (study) | Level of Support | |
| --- | --- | --- |
| | Well-Established Treatment | Probably Efficacious Treatment |
| Cognitive-behavior therapy (individual), systemic behavior family therapy, and individual nondirective supportive therapy (Brent et al., 1997) | No | No |
| Developmental group psychotherapy (includes problem solving, cognitive behavioral, dialectical behavior therapy, and psychodynamic group psychotherapy) (Wood, Trainor, Rothwell, Moore, & Harrington, 2001) | No | Yes[a] |
| Dialectical behavior therapy (Rathus & Miller, 2002) | No | No |
| Direct services to the adolescent and community education (Deykin, Hsieh, Joshi, & McNamarra, 1986) | No | No |
| Family and social network support (Gutstein & Rudd, 1990) | No | No |
| Family communication and problem solving (Harrington et al., 1998) | No | Yes[b] |
| Family education in the emergency room (ER), single session family therapy, training workshop for ER staff (Rotheram-Borus et al., 1996), and 6 sessions of cognitive-behavioral therapy (Rotheram-Borus, Piacentini, Cantwell, Belin, & Song, 2000) | No | No |
| Rapid response outpatient treatment in the emergency department: reframing misconceptions, maladaptive behaviors, and communication patterns; medication when appropriate, and community resources when available (Greenfield, Larson, Hechtman, Rousseau, & Platt, 2002) | No | No |
| Token for immediate rehospitalization plus usual services (Cotgrove, Zirinsky, Black, & Weston, 1995) | No | No |

NOTE: The well-established and probably efficacious treatment criteria used in this table were developed by the American Psychological Association's Division 12 Task Force (Chambless et al., 1998). Well-established treatment should include 1 = at least two good between-group design experiments demonstrating efficacy in at least one of the following ways: (a) superior (statistically significantly so) to placebo or to another treatment or (b) equivalent to an already established treatment in experiments with adequate statistical power (about 30 per group); 2 = used a treatment manual; 3 = characteristics of the client samples clearly specified; and 4 = two different investigators or investigating teams. The criteria for probably efficacious treatment should include (a) two experiments showing the treatment is superior (statistically significantly so) to a waiting-list control group or (b) one or more experiments meeting the well-established treatment criteria 1a or 1b, 2, and 3 but not 4.

a. Statistically significant difference between groups on self-harm but not depression or suicidal thinking, with power to detect only large differences.

b. Statistically significant difference between groups on suicidal ideation for those without major depression.

**Table 6.2**   Treatment Outcomes and Treatment Success of Empirical Research Involving Suicidal Youth Using Rudd's (2000a, 2000b) Schema

| Study | Intervention | Was Treatment Successful? | | Outcome Markers of Suicidality (short-term or long-term effects) | |
|---|---|---|---|---|---|
| | | Direct | Indirect | Direct | Indirect |
| Brent et al. (1997) | T1: Individual cognitive behavior therapy (CBT) T2: Systemic behavior family therapy T3: Nondirective supportive therapy | —[a] | Suicidality (attempt or ideation with a plan), a major depression, functional impairment | —[a] | Yes: suicidality and functional impairment (all conditions); major depression (CBT condition); short term |
| Cotgrove, Zirinsky, Black, and Weston (1995) | TAU and a token allowing immediate readmission to hospital | Suicide attempts | — | No[b] | — |
| Deykin, Hsieh, Joshi, and McNamarra (1986) | Direct services to youth and community education | Study-eligible admissions (suicide attempts, gestures, life-threatening events, and suicide ideation)[c] | Treatment adherence | No[d] | Yes (short term) |
| Greenfield, Larson, Hechtman, Rousseau, and Platt (2002) | Rapid-response outpatient treatment | — | Suicidality, suicide-related hospitalizations, global functioning | — | Yes: hospitalizations (short-term) No: suicidality and global functioning |
| Gutstein and Rudd (1990) | Systemic crisis intervention | Suicide attempts | Suicide threats, problem severity and adaptive behavior, institutional use, family and marital functioning | Yes (short and long term) | Yes (short and long term) |

*(Continued)*

**Table 6.2** (Continued)

| Study | Intervention | Was Treatment Successful? | | Outcome Markers of Suicidality (short-term or long-term effects) | |
|---|---|---|---|---|---|
| | | Direct | Indirect | Direct | Indirect |
| Harrington et al. (1998) | TAU and five-session home-based intervention | — | Suicide ideation, hopelessness, family functioning; social problem solving, stress, satisfaction with treatment, treatment expectancies | — | Yes: ideation (among subgroup without major depression); satisfaction with treatment (parents), short term<br><br>No: ideation (among those with major depression), hopelessness, and family functioning |
| Rathus and Miller (2002) | Dialectical behavior therapy | Suicide attempts | Suicide ideation, depression, psychiatric hospital admissions, treatment completion, life problems, BPD symptoms, general psychiatric symptoms | No[f] | Yes for all indirect markers (short term) |
| Rotheram-Borus et al. (1996) | Specialized ER care | — | Suicide ideation, youth and maternal depression, treatment adherence, maternal emotional distress, maternal psychopathology, family adaptability, and cohesion | — | Yes: ideation, youth and maternal depression, youth adherence to aftercare treatment, maternal psychopathology, family adaptability, and cohesion (short term)<br><br>No: maternal treatment adherence |

*(Continued)*

**Table 6.2** (Continued)

| Study | Intervention | Was Treatment Successful? | | Outcome Markers of Suicidality (short-term or long-term effects) | |
|---|---|---|---|---|---|
| | | Direct | Indirect | Direct | Indirect |
| Rotheram-Borus et al. (2000) | Specialized ER care and six sessions of successful negotiation acting positively aftercare | Suicide attempts | Suicide ideation, youth and maternal depression, treatment adherence, maternal emotional distress, family cohesion | No[g] | Yes: youth and maternal depression, maternal emotional distress, youth treatment attendance (long term); No: suicide ideation, maternal treatment adherence, and family cohesion |
| Wood, Trainor, Rothwell, Moore, and Harrington (2001) | Group therapy and TAU | DSH (e.g., self-poisoning and self-cutting) | Depression, suicide ideation, use of routine care, school attendance, and behavioral problems | Yes: DSH (short term) | Yes: use of routine care, behavioral problems (short term); No: depression and suicide ideation |

NOTE: This table uses Rudd's (2000a, 2000b) schema to classify treatment outcomes and treatment success. Direct outcome markers are suicidal behavior (e.g., suicide attempts or instrumental behaviors with or without injuries). Indirect outcome markers include symptoms (e.g., suicidal thoughts and hopelessness), skills (e.g., problem solving and emotional regulation), traits (e.g., personality disorders, social support, and introversion), or treatment compliance. Direct treatment success is defined as "a significant reduction in subsequent attempts and instrumental behaviors" (Rudd, 2000b, p. 63). Indirect treatment success is defined as "a significant change in symptom measures, skills, and maladaptive personality traits" (Rudd, 2000b, p. 63). Long-term success lasts for 12 or more months. BPD = borderline personality disorder; T = treatment (i.e., T1, T3, T3 = three different treatments); DSH = deliberate self-harm; TAU = treatment as usual; CBT = cognitive behavior therapy; DBT = dialectical behavior therapy.

a. This study used a measure that lumped suicide attempts with suicide ideation.

b. The treatment group had three further suicide attempts in the next year compared with seven in the control group (the difference, however, did not achieve statistical difference).

c. These outcomes are classified as direct markers as they were mostly behaviors (except ideation).

d. The treatment group had a reduction of study-eligible admissions, but it was not significant.

e. This outcome is classified as an indirect marker as suicidality was measured on an ordinal scale ranging from 1 (no suicidal behavior) to 5 (serious suicide attempts) (Pfeffer, 1986).

f. Fewer youth in the DBT group attempted suicide than in the TAU group (1 versus 7, respectively), but the differences between groups were not statistically significant due to the low base rate.

g. There were fewer suicide reattempts in the treatment group (6 versus 11 in the comparison group), but statistical comparisons were not done due to low base rates.

depression or in reducing hopelessness and family functioning. Wood and colleagues' (2001) study successfully reduced self-harm, behavioral problems, and increased use of routine care but failed to significantly decrease depression or suicide ideation. Another intervention (Rotheram-Borus et al., 1996) showed improvements in most of the indirect markers of suicidality but did not increase mothers' adherence to treatment. The other study by Rotheram-Borus and colleagues (2000) decreased depression and maternal emotional distress but did not decrease suicide ideation.

All studies that included the assessment of treatment adherence were successful, to some degree, in increasing treatment retention. The studies by Rotheram-Borus and colleagues (1996, 2000) increased youth adherence to aftercare treatment but had no effect on maternal treatment adherence.

# Discussion and Applications to Social Work Practice

A total of 10 studies were reviewed, half of which were published in the past 5 years. From the findings reported in Table 6.1, no studies included interventions that could be defined as well established, and only two of the interventions were probably efficacious but had limitations. In examining Table 6.2, we found that only two interventions reduced suicide attempts or deliberate self-harm, and most interventions reduced the indirect markers of suicidality. This section examines the features of the interventions that were probably efficacious and that had direct and indirect treatment success, explores the methodological problems of the research, offers recommendations for improvement, and concludes with applications for social work practice.

## Features of the Interventions That Reduced Suicide Attempts or Deliberate Self-Harm

Only two studies that assessed suicide attempts and deliberate self-harm (Gutstein & Rudd, 1990; Wood et al., 2001) reported successful outcomes (see Table 6.2). One common feature of these interventions was that both were short-term interventions in outpatient settings. Both involved family members; one was primarily a group intervention, and the other used a systemic intervention involving family and important others. The samples in these studies involved mostly female European Americans.

When examining the studies that reported reductions in suicide attempts (although not statistically significant in terms of reductions or in comparison with comparison groups), several observations may be made. First, three of the four used short-term treatment (Deykin & Buka, 1994; Rathus & Miller, 2002; Rotheram-Borus et al., 2000). Second, although one worked primarily with the individual (Cotgrove et al., 1995), most involved the family. The modal type of treatment used was a form of CBT (Rathus & Miller, 2002; Rotheram-Borus et al., 2000).

Thus, all studies noted changes, some significantly better than pretest and/or significantly better than the comparison group. However, because of the lack of rigorous designs, it was unclear what specifically caused change in most of the studies.

## Features of the Interventions That Reduced the Indirect Markers of Suicidality

Of the eight studies that intended to reduce suicide ideation or suicide threats, five reported unqualified success (Brent et al., 1997; Greenfield et al., 2002; Gutstein & Rudd, 1990; Rathus & Miller, 2002; Rotheram-Borus et al., 1996) (see Table 6.2). What were the common features of these interventions that helped to reduce suicide ideation? All were short term. In addition, three of the five (Brent et al., 1997; Rathus & Miller, 2002; Rotheram-Borus et al., 2000) included some element of CBT and included family involvement.

All studies that included the assessment of treatment adherence were successful in increasing treatment retention among youth. One of the common features of these interventions was that they were short term. All involved a majority of Latinas (Rathus & Miller, 2002; Rotheram-Borus et al., 1996, 2000) or African Americans (Deykin et al., 1986) and involved families. Although there was not a common theoretical model, CBT elements were used in two of the studies (Rathus & Miller, 2002; Rotheram-Borus et al., 2000).

## Features of the Promising Interventions

Although the review found no studies that were well established and only two that were probably efficacious (with limitations), the most promising interventions and common elements of the promising interventions may be summarized. The findings from other research will be integrated to help provide an agenda for future research and practice. These interventions and features are offered tentatively, as they are based on promising and not efficacious research.

1. Developmental group psychotherapy was significantly superior to the comparison group in reducing self-harm (with power to detect only large differences) (Wood et al., 2001). This finding is consistent with other studies that have found that group work with cognitive-behavioral elements works well with adolescents with depression (Petrocelli, 2002).

2. Family communication and problem solving were more likely to reduce suicide ideation than were the comparison conditions but only among a sample without major depression (Harrington et al., 1998).

3. Family interventions did not reduce suicidality among youth with major depression (Brent et al., 1997; Harrington et al., 1998). The researchers speculated that the family treatments may have delayed effects considering the larger numbers of people involved and the lack of direct focus on the depressed, suicidal adolescent. Harrington and colleagues (1998) concluded that a brief five-session family intervention may not be sufficient to reduce suicidal thinking among depressed youth.

4. Short-term, outpatient treatments were effective in reducing suicide attempts or deliberate self-harm among suicide attempters (Gutstein & Rudd, 1990; Wood et al., 2001).

5. Outpatient treatment was an effective alternative to hospitalization in two studies (Cotgrove et al., 1995; Greenfield et al., 2002). Other reviewers have noted that high-risk suicidal clients can be safely treated on an outpatient basis if acute hospitalization is available and accessible (Rudd, 2000b).

6. CBT and problem solving were included in many of the interventions that reduced the direct and indirect markers of suicidality. CBT has also been effective in reducing suicide risk behaviors (Eggert, Thompson, Herting, & Nicholas, 1994; Eggert, Thompson, Randell, & Pike, 2002) and depression (Michael & Crowley, 2002; Reinecke, Ryan, & DuBois, 1998) among youth. Studies involving adults have shown the efficacy of problem solving and CBT, with problem solving as a core intervention in reducing depression, hopelessness, and suicidal behavior (Hawton et al., 1998; Rudd, 2000b; Townsend et al., 2001).

7. DBT (Rathus & Miller, 2002) was helpful in reducing a number of indirect markers of suicidality among youth with both suicidality and BPD. The finding is congruent with the evidence involving adult women with BPD (e.g., Hawton et al., 1998; Linehan et al., 1991).

8. Short-term interventions that involved families increased youths' compliance with treatment recommendations (Deykin et al., 1986; Rathus & Miller, 2002; Rotheram-Borus et al., 1996, 2000). Retention and compliance are often problems in treating youth who have attempted suicide (Piacentini, Rotheram-Borus, Gillis, et al., 1995; Trautman et al., 1993), and treatment follow-through appears to be protective (King & Knox, 2000). Compliance with treatment is particularly important for youth released from psychiatric hospital ERs. Researchers have found significantly more suicide reattempts among youth released from psychiatric hospital ERs than among those released from general hospitals (Spirito et al., 1992).

These advancements in our understanding of what works in reducing suicidality should be incorporated and tested in future research. Such research, however, must be aware of the limitations of the body of the research and offer improvements in methodology.

## Methodological Challenges and Recommendations

Most of the findings previously noted are based on research with mixed empirical strength. The research that has been done can form a basis for further research that is more rigorous. Some specific ways in which future studies can improve include increasing the internal validity (to answer "What reduces suicidality?") and external validity (to answer "What reduces suicidality for whom?") of the studies.

Strengthening the internal validity of the research will substantially help determine what reduces suicidality. Two areas that need attention are the research designs and protocols related to defining and monitoring the treatment conditions. In the case of research designs, only half of the studies used randomization. The number of experimental designs is a substantial improvement from 10 years ago, but more are needed to bring suicidality research to the point where there are well-established treatments.

Another internal validity problem relates to protocols related to defining and monitoring the treatment conditions. Due to the ethical problem of denying treatment to suicidal clients, most designs include treatment comparison conditions. However, with the use of two treatments, several challenges emerge such as defining and controlling the delivery of the treatments. In many cases, treatments are hard to classify because in some cases, there are multiple components, or the authors include little detail about the treatments. Determining what treatment or intervention has been used in empirically supported treatment is complex and difficult:

> We find no guidelines in the [American Psychological Association] Task Force [on Promotion and Dissemination of Psychological Procedures] documents for deciding when two different versions of a treatment program should and should not be considered the same treatment. As an additional complication, investigators frequently describe their tested treatment as based "partly" or "largely" on a treatment development by another investigator. (Weisz & Hawley, 1998, p. 210)

As an effort to increase treatment fidelity, manuals are often used. Treatment manuals (or their logical equivalent) have been considered an important criterion in establishing empirically supported treatments (Chambless et al., 1998; Chambless & Hollon, 1998). Among the studies reviewed in this article, none shared a common treatment manual but rather shared only elements of several treatment approaches or theories. Many of the studies included a treatment manual and fidelity to treatment monitors. Several did not, and it was unclear in these studies about what type and dosage of treatment were received and how the primary treatment was different from the comparison conditions (e.g., Deykin et al., 1986; Greenfield et al., 2002). Thus, in addition to reporting using a treatment manual, researchers should also provide specific details on the length and content of manuals used (Weisz & Hawley, 1998).

Another concern relates to the comparison condition itself. Researchers have argued that the most effective design uses a comparison condition because they not only control for processes independent of treatment and common to all treatments but may also involve tests between competing specific mechanisms. . . . Moreover, such comparisons can provide explicit information regarding the relative benefits of competing interventions. For this reason, treatments that are found to be superior to other rival alternative interventions are more highly valued still. (Chambless & Hollon, 1998, p. 8)

However, with so few treatment alternatives, researchers are left with few options. One commonly used option is the TAU condition. However, a common problem with this condition is that it is often inadequately described (Spirito, Stanton, Donaldson, & Boergers, 2002). This was a problem in some of the studies reviewed (e.g., Cotgrove et al., 1995; Deykin et al., 1986; Greenfield et al., 2002). An improvement in future research is to adequately describe the TAU condition (e.g., setting of treatment and frequency and duration of sessions) and intervention techniques (e.g., active therapist behaviors used during contacts with clients) (Spirito et al., 2002).

A challenge to external validity was the size and type of samples. A major limitation of most of the studies reviewed, particularly the ones assessing suicide attempts, was small sample sizes, which limited the statistical power of the findings. Larger samples are needed in studies examining the effects of treatment on suicide attempts. Wood and colleagues (2001) projected that a sample size of 25 was needed for each condition to detect large treatment effects on the repetition of deliberate self-harm. Future studies need to include larger sample sizes with sufficient power to detect differences.

Another limitation related to external validity was the lack of studies involving American Indian and/or Alaska Native youth. The suicide rate for Native Americans and/or Alaska Natives is more than double that of European Americans and is the highest in the United States (National Center for Injury Prevention and Control, 2002). Additionally, only one study included a substantial number of African Americans (Deykin et al., 1986). More research with diverse samples would expand our understanding of how treatment is effective with different racial/ethnic groups.

## Applications to Social Work Practice

Social workers have been well represented in the literature on youth suicidality (e.g., de Anda & Smith, 1993; Morrison, 1987; Proctor & Groze, 1994; Queralt, 1993; Rittner & Smyth, 1999; Sykes, 1986; Zayas, Kaplan, Turner, Romano, & Gonzalez-Ramos, 2000) and were involved in service delivery in two of the studies reviewed (Deykin et al., 1986; Harrington et al., 1998). Additionally, considering the high numbers of youth with suicidality in community samples (cf. the YRBSS data previously noted), social workers employed in youth services are very likely to be involved with suicidal clients. Social work practitioners may apply the findings from this review in several ways.

First, social workers should use the best supported treatments in their practice. Although much of what is done in practice has yet to be empirically tested, social workers should be aware of the research to maintain congruity with the best available evidence. This article reviewed 10 studies with findings that are promising. The studies provided details of the interventions or provided ways in which manuals may be obtained so that social workers may replicate the promising interventions or elements of the promising interventions in practice. The research base is currently thin and can only partly inform social work practice, but social workers should remain attuned to the literature for new findings and incorporate them into practice.

Second, social workers may add to the research, which can be accomplished in two ways. No studies have yet used a single-subject design. However, aggregated single-subject designs ($n > 9$) that demonstrate efficacy are acceptable evidence in determining the empirical support of treatments (Chambless et al., 1998). Whereas most social work practitioners may not be able to mount group-level designs, graduate-level professional social workers have the knowledge to undertake multiple small sample studies of the efficacy of their interventions. There are excellent resources available (Bloom, Fischer, & Orme, 2003; Nugent, Sieppert, & Hudson, 2001), and social work practitioners could partner with faculty in local schools of social work for further technical assistance. Good single-subject design studies are critically needed, are readily publishable, and would expand the limited knowledge base about what can help reduce suicidality among youth.

Another way that social workers can expand the evidence base is to include suicide-related outcome markers in research in areas closely linked with suicidality. For example, depression, violence, and substance abuse are important risk factors for suicidality (Macgowan, 2004). Outcome research in these areas should include measures of suicidality. Examples of measures with good psychometric properties (Goldston, 2000; Range & Knott, 1997) include the Beck Scale for Suicide Ideation (Beck & Steer, 1991), the Suicide Ideation Questionnaire (Reynolds, 1988), and the Lethality of Suicide Attempt Rating Scale (Smith, Conroy, & Ehler, 1984). It is possible—and perhaps likely—that the mechanisms that reduce these problems might also reduce suicidality. This information would be important in not only expanding the number of interventions that reduce suicidality but also understanding what reduces the often co-occurring problems of depression, alcohol and other drug problems, violence, and suicidality.

In summary, this study systematically reviewed 10 suicide intervention studies involving adolescents. Only two studies were found that used treatments that were more effective than controls in reducing some form of suicidality that may be classified as probably efficacious. However, these studies had circumscribed findings in that one had power to detect only large differences and the other reduced deliberate self-harm but not suicide ideation or depression. No treatments were classified as well established. Using other criteria to assess whether each study's treatment was successful in reducing suicidality (whether the study included a comparison condition), we found that most were successful. Some reductions were statistically significant, but others were not due to low base rates. The elements that characterized promising interventions should be replicated or incorporated into future research. Methodological limitations affected many of the studies reviewed. Only half of the studies used randomized designs, and most were affected by small sample sizes, resulting in too little power to detect differences between groups. Additionally, there was no research involving Native Americans and/or Alaska Natives, who have the highest rates of suicide among youth.

In conclusion, suicide among adolescents is a serious public health problem. The number of controlled studies has increased in the past 10 years, and studies have emerged that reduce suicidality. The number of promising interventions is limited but is growing and offers hope in reducing youth suicide.

# References

Alcohol Drug Abuse and Mental Health Administration. (1989). *Report of the Secretary's Task Force on youth suicide: Volume 3. Prevention and intervention in youth suicide.* Washington, DC: Government Printing Office.

Alexander, J., & Parsons, B. V. (1982). *Functional family therapy.* Pacific Grove, CA: Brooks/Cole.

American Academy of Child and Adolescent Psychiatry. (2001). Practice parameter for the assessment and treatment of children and adolescents with suicidal behavior. *Journal of the American Academy of Child and Adolescent Psychiatry, 40*(Suppl. 7), 24S–51S.

Aronson, S., & Scheidlinger, S. (1995). Group treatment of suicidal adolescents. In J. K. Zimmerman & G. M. Asnis (Eds.), *Treatment approaches with suicidal adolescents* (pp. 189–202). New York: John Wiley.

Beck, A. T. (1979). *Cognitive therapy of depression.* New York: Guilford.

Beck, A. T., & Steer, R. (1991). *Manual for the Beck Scale for Suicidal Ideation.* San Antonio, TX: Psychological Corporation.

Bloom, M., Fischer, J., & Orme, J. G. (2003). *Evaluating practice: Guidelines for the accountable professional* (4th ed.). Boston: Allyn & Bacon.

Brent, D. A. (1997). The aftercare of adolescents with deliberate self-harm. *Journal of Child Psychology and Psychiatry, 38,* 277–286.

Brent, D. A., Holder, D., Kolko, D., Birmaher, B., Baugher, M., Roth, C., et al. (1997). A clinical psychotherapy trial for adolescent depression comparing cognitive, family, and supportive therapy. *Archives of General Psychiatry, 54,* 877–885.

Brent, D. A., & Poling, K. (1997). *Cognitive therapy treatment manual for depressed and suicidal youth.* Pittsburgh, PA: University of Pittsburgh, Services for Teens at Risk.

Centers for Disease Control and Prevention. (2002). Youth risk behavior surveillance—United States, 2001. *Morbidity and Mortality Weekly Report, 51*(SS04), 1–64.

Centers for Disease Control and Prevention. (2003). Youth Risk Behavior Surveillance System: Online analysis of Youth Risk Behavior Survey results. Retrieved June 2, 2003, from http:// www.cdc.gov/nccdphp/dash/yrbs/2001/ youth01online.htm.

Chambless, D. L., Baker, M. J., Baucom, D. H., Beutler, L. E., Calhoun, K. S., Crits-Christoph, P., et al. (1998). Update on empirically validated therapies: Vol. 2. *Clinical Psychologist, 51,* 3–16.

Chambless, D. L., & Hollon, S. D. (1998). Defining empirically supported therapies. *Journal of Consulting and Clinical Psychology, 66,* 7–18.

Chambless, D. L., Sanderson, W. C., Shoham, V., Johnson, S. B., Pope, K. S., Crits-Christoph, P., et al. (1996). An update on empirically validated therapies. *Clinical Psychologist, 49*(2), 5–18.

Cotgrove, A. J., Zirinsky, L., Black, D., & Weston, D. (1995). Secondary prevention of attempted suicide in adolescence. *Journal of Adolescence, 18,* 569–577.

de Anda, D., & Smith, M. A. (1993). Difference among adolescent, young adult, and adult callers of suicide help lines. *Social Work, 38,* 421–428.

Deykin, E. Y., & Buka, S. L. (1994). Suicidal ideation and attempts among chemically dependent adolescents. *American Journal of Public Health, 84,* 634–639.

Deykin, E. Y., Hsieh, C. C., Joshi, N., & McNamarra, J. J. (1986). Adolescent suicidal and self-destructive behavior: Results of an intervention study. *Journal of Adolescent Health Care, 7,* 88–95.

Eggert, L. L., Thompson, E. A., Herting, J. R., & Nicholas, L. J. (1994). Prevention research program: Reconnecting at-risk youth. *Issues in Mental Health Nursing, 15,* 107–135.

Eggert, L. L., Thompson, E. A., Randell, B. P., & Pike, K. C. (2002). Preliminary effects of brief school-based prevention approaches for reducing youth suicide-risk behaviors, depression, and drug involvement. *Journal of Child and Adolescent Psychiatric Nursing, 15*(2), 48–64.

Goldston, D. B. (2000). *Assessment of suicidal behaviors and risk among children and adolescents.* Bethesda, MD: National Institute of Mental Health.

Greenfield, B., Larson, C., Hechtman, L., Rousseau, C., & Platt, R. (2002). A rapid-response outpatient model for reducing hospitalization rates among suicidal adolescents. *Psychiatric Services, 53,* 1574–1579.

Gutstein, S. E., & Rudd, M. D. (1990). An outpatient treatment alternative for suicidal youth. *Journal of Adolescence, 13,* 265–277.

Harrington, R., Kerfoot, M., Dyer, E., McNiven, F., Gill, J., Harrington, V., et al. (1998). Randomized trial of a home-based family intervention for children who have deliberately poisoned themselves. *Journal of the American Academy of Child and Adolescent Psychiatry, 37,* 512–518.

Harrington, R., Kerfoot, M., Dyer, E., McNiven, F., Gill, J., Harrington, V., et al. (2000). Deliberate self-poisoning in adolescence: Why does a brief family intervention work in some cases and not others? *Journal of Adolescence, 23,* 13–20.

Hawton, K., Arensman, E., Townsend, E., Bremner, S., Feldman, E., Goldney, R., et al. (1998). Deliberate self-harm: Systematic review of efficacy of psychosocial and pharmacological treatments in preventing repetition. *British Medical Journal, 317,* 441–447.

Holman, W. (1997). "Who would find you?": A question for working with suicidal children and adolescents. *Child and Adolescent Social Work Journal, 14,* 129–137.

Jobes, D. A. (1995). Psychodynamic treatment of adolescent suicide attempters. In J. K. Zimmerman & G. M. Asnis (Eds.), *Treatment approaches with suicidal adolescents* (pp. 137–154). New York: John Wiley.

Kerfoot, M., Harrington, R., & Dyer, E. (1995). Brief home-based intervention with young suicide attempters and their families. *Journal of Adolescence, 18,* 557–568.

King, C. A., & Knox, M. (2000). Recognition and treatment of suicidal youth: Broadening our research agenda. In T. Joiner & M. D. Rudd (Eds.), *Suicide science: Expanding the boundaries* (pp. 251–269). Norwell, MA: Kluwer Academic.

Linehan, M. M., Armstrong, H. E., Suarez, A., Allmon, D., & Heard, H. L. (1991). Cognitive-behavioral treatment of chronically parasuicidal borderline patients. *Archives of General Psychiatry, 48,* 1060–1064.

Lum, W., Smith, J., & Ferris, J. (2002). Youth suicide intervention using the Satir model. *Contemporary Family Therapy, 24,* 139–159.

Macgowan, M. J. (2004). Suicidal behaviors among youth. In M. Fraser (Ed.), *Risk and resilience in childhood* (2nd ed.). Washington, DC: National Association of Social Workers Press.

Michael, K. D., & Crowley, S. L. (2002). How effective are treatments for child and adolescent depression? A meta-analytic review. *Clinical Psychology Review, 22,* 247–269.

Miller, A. L., Rathus, J. H., Linehan, M. M., Wertzler, S., & Leigh, E. (1997). Dialectical behavior therapy adapted for suicidal adolescents. *Journal of Practical Psychiatry and Behavioral Health, 3,* 78–86.

Morrison, J. (1987). Youth suicide: An intervention strategy. *Social Work, 32,* 536–537.

National Center for Injury Prevention and Control. (2002). Customized leading cause of death report, year 2000, all races, both sexes. Retrieved February 15, 2003, from http://webapp.cdc.gov/sasweb/ ncipc/leadcaus.html.

Nugent, W. R., Sieppert, J. D., & Hudson, W. W. (2001). *Practice evaluation for the 21st century.* Pacific Grove, CA.: Brooks/Cole.

Petrocelli, J. V. (2002). Effectiveness of group cognitive-behavioral therapy for general symptomatology: A meta-analysis. *Journal of Specialists in Group Work, 27,* 92–115.

Pfeffer, C. R. (1986). *The suicidal child.* New York: Guilford.

Pfeffer, C. R., Klerman, G. L., Hurt, S. W., Kakuma, T., Peskin, J. R., Siefker, C. A. (1993). Suicidal children grow up: Rates and psychosocial risk factors for suicide attempts during follow-up. *Journal of the American Academy of Child and Adolescent Psychiatry, 32,* 106–113.

Piacentini, J., Rotheram-Borus, M. J., & Cantwell, C. (1995). Brief cognitive-behavioral family therapy for suicidal adolescents. In L. VandeCreek, S. Knapp, & T. L. Jackson (Eds.), *Innovations in clinical practice: A source book* (Vol. 14, pp. 151–168). Sarasota, FL: Professional Resource Press.

Piacentini, J., Rotheram-Borus, M. J., Gillis, J. R., Graae, F., Trautman, P., & Cantwell, C., et al. (1995). Demographic predictors of treatment attendance among adolescent suicide attempters. *Journal of Consulting and Clinical Psychology, 63,* 469–473.

Proctor, C. D., & Groze, V. K. (1994). Risk factors for suicide among gay, lesbian, and bisexual youths. *Social Work, 39,* 504–513.

Queralt, M. (1993). Psychosocial risk factors associated with a small community of Latino adolescent attempters. *Social Work in Education, 15,* 91–103.

Range, L. M., & Knott, E. C. (1997). Twenty suicide assessment instruments: Evaluation and recommendations. *Death Studies, 21,* 25–58.

Rathus, J. H., & Miller, A. L. (2002). Dialectical behavior therapy adapted for suicidal adolescents. *Suicide & Life-Threatening Behavior, 32,* 146–157.

Reinecke, M. A., Ryan, N. E., & DuBois, D. L. (1998). Cognitive-behavioral therapy of depression and depressive symptoms during adolescence: A review and meta-analysis. *Journal of the American Academy of Child and Adolescent Psychiatry, 37,* 26–34.

Reynolds, W. M. (1988). *Suicidal ideation questionnaire, professional manual.* Odessa, FL: Psychological Assessment Resources.

Rittner, B., & Smyth, N. J. (1999). Time-limited cognitive-behavioral group interventions with suicidal adolescents. *Social Work With Groups, 22*(2–3), 55–75.

Robin, A. L., & Foster, S. L. (1989). *Negotiating parent-adolescent conflict: A behavioral-family systems approach.* New York: Guilford.

Ross, C. P., & Motto, J. A. (1984). Group counseling for suicidal adolescents. In H. S. Sudak, A. B. Ford, & N. B. Rushforth (Eds.), *Suicide in the young* (pp. 367–392). Boston: John Wright.

Rotheram-Borus, M. J., Piacentini, J., Cantwell, C., Belin, T. R., & Song, J. (2000). The 18-month impact of an emergency room intervention for adolescent female suicide attempters. *Journal of Consulting and Clinical Psychology, 68,* 1081–1093.

Rotheram-Borus, M. J., Piacentini, J., Van Rossem, R., Graae, F., Cantwell, C., Castro-Blanco, D., et al. (1996). Enhancing treatment adherence with a specialized emergency room program for adolescent suicide attempters. *Journal of the American Academy of Child and Adolescent Psychiatry, 35,* 654–663.

Rudd, M. D. (2000a). A conceptual scheme for assessing treatment outcome in suicidality. In T. Joiner & M. D. Rudd (Eds.), *Suicide science: Expanding the boundaries* (pp. 271–278). Norwell, MA: Kluwer Academic.

Rudd, M. D. (2000b). Integrating science into the practice of clinical suicidology: A review of the psychotherapy literature and a research agenda for the future. In R. Maris, S. Cannetto, J. Macintosh, & M. Silverman (Eds.), *Review of suicidology* (pp. 47–83). New York: Guilford.

Smith, K., Conroy, R., & Ehler, B. (1984). Lethality of Suicide Attempt Rating Scale. *Suicide and Life-Threatening Behavior, 14,* 214–242.

Spirito, A., Plummer, B., Gispert, M., & Levy, S. (1992). Adolescent suicide attempts: Outcomes at follow-up. *American Journal of Orthopsychiatry, 62,* 464–468.

Spirito, A., Stanton, C., Donaldson, D., & Boergers, J. (2002). Treatment-as-usual for adolescent suicide attempters: Implications for the choice of comparison groups in psychotherapy research. *Journal of Clinical Child Psychology, 31,* 41–47.

Stewart, S. E., Manion, I. G., & Davidson, S. (2002). Emergency management of the adolescent suicide attempter: A review of the literature. *The Journal of Adolescent Health, 30*(5), 312–325.

Sykes, D. (1986). Adolescent stress and suicide: Intervention and prevention for schools. *School Social Work Journal, 11,* 10–15.

Townsend, E., Hawton, K., Altman, D. G., Arensman, E., Gunnell, D., Hazell, P., et al. (2001). The efficacy of problem-solving treatments after deliberate self-harm: Meta-analysis of randomized controlled trials with respect to depression, hopelessness and improvement in problems. *Psychological Medicine, 31,* 979–988.

Trautman, P. D. (1995). Cognitive behavior therapy of adolescent suicide attempters. In J. K. Zimmerman & G. M. Asnis (Eds.), *Treatment approaches with suicidal adolescents* (pp. 155–173). New York: John Wiley.

Trautman, P. D., Stewart, N., & Morishima, A. (1993). Are adolescent suicide attempters noncompliant with outpatient care? *Journal of the American Academy of Child and Adolescent Psychiatry, 32,* 89–94.

U.S. Department of Health and Human Services. (2001). *National strategy for suicide prevention: Goals and objectives for action.* Rockville, MD: Author.

Weisz, J. R., & Hawley, K. M. (1998). Finding, evaluating, refining, and applying empirically supported treatments for children and adolescents. *Journal of Clinical Child Psychology, 27,* 206–216.

Wodarski, J., & Harris, P. (1987). Adolescent suicide: A review of influences and the means for prevention. *Social Work, 32,* 477–484.

Wood, A., Trainor, G., Rothwell, J., Moore, A., & Harrington, R. (2001). Randomized trial of group therapy for repeated deliberate self-harm in adolescents. *Journal of the American Academy of Child and Adolescent Psychiatry, 40,* 1246–1253.

Zayas, L. H., Kaplan, C., Turner, S., Romano, K., & Gonzalez-Ramos, G. (2000). Understanding suicide attempts by adolescent Hispanic females. *Social Work, 45,* 53–63.

# 7

# Adolescent Substance Abuse Treatment

## A Synthesis of Controlled Evaluations

*Michael G. Vaughn and Matthew O. Howard*

Widespread concerns persist within the U.S. regarding the prevalence and consequences of adolescent substance abuse. In addition to age-old drugs like alcohol, marijuana, and cocaine, "new" drugs and related problems continually emerge, such as "club drugs" like ecstasy and Gamma-Hydroxy-Butyrate (GHB). Rates of adolescent drug use fluctuate significantly over time. For example, National Household Survey on Drug Abuse (NHSDA) trend data, administered yearly and based on responses from 12- to 17-year-olds about whether they have ever used an illicit drug, reveal peak usage in 1979 (31.8%), declining to a low point in 1993 (16.4%); followed by an upsurge again in 2001 (28.4%) (NHSDA, 2002). Monitoring The Future study findings indicate that in the late 1970s nearly 40% of high school seniors had used an illicit drug in the past month, a rate which declined by the early 1990s, only to rise again to a level of approximately 25% in 2001 (Johnston, O'Malley, & Bachman, 2002). Further, national data on the number of drug-related emergency room episodes show alarming increases from 1978 (323,100) to 2001 (639,484) (Drug Abuse Warning Network, 2001).

Several interrelated issues are germane to the study of adolescent substance use and abuse. Distinctions need to be made between individuals who use drugs and those who abuse or become dependent on them. This is because most adolescents who use drugs do not escalate into abuse or dependence (Newcomb, 1995). For example, in a large community sample of 3,072 adolescents, Young and colleagues (2002) found that although drug experimentation was common, a much smaller percentage of older adolescents met criteria for substance dependence. Early initiation of illicit

Originally published in *Research on Social Work Practice* 2004; 14; 325. DOI: 10.1177/1049731504265834 The online version of this article can be found at: http://rsw.sagepub.com/cgi/content/abstract/14/5/325

drug use is associated with an increased risk for a constellation of problem behaviors (Perkonigg, Lieb, Hofler, Schuster, Sonntag, & Wittchen, 1999). Also, etiological research is showing an emergence of positive findings related to individual-level characteristics (e.g., genetic, physiological, and personality traits) and family variables (Weinberg, Rahdert, Colliver, & Glantz, 1998).

Previous narrative reviews have identified a number of promising interventions designed to treat adolescent substance abusers (Deas & Thomas, 2001; Waldron, 1997; Williams & Chang, 2000). These reviews, however, did not synthesize the subject matter in any quantifiable way. The conceptual bases of these interventions vary widely. Although there are disparate theoretical models guiding these interventions, the primary difference lies in the scope of each intervention's target level. For example, behavioral therapy and 12-step programs primarily focus attention at the level of the individual. Conversely, multisystemic therapy targets individual, family, and community level factors that influence substance abuse. The predominant conceptual basis for many of these interventions is drawn from human ecology, the essential proposition being that individuals are embedded in a web of relationships across various levels of interaction (i.e., self, peers, family, community) that influence their behavioral trajectory along the life-course (Bronfenbrenner, 1999).

Given the multitude of interventions in this area coupled with the growing consensus that treatment protocols should be rooted in scientific research, three primary research questions drive the present inquiry: (1) Which interventions are most effective in reducing substance use and abuse among adolescents? (2) What is the comparative methodological quality of studies in the adolescent substance abuse treatment domain? and (3) How effective are particular interventions in light of research design strength? Answers to these questions represent a preliminary step toward a path of employing evidence-based treatments for adolescents in multiple settings as well as identifying promising interventions that can be replicated in future research.

# Methods

## Study Selection

Controlled evaluations were selected according to the following eligibility criteria:

(a) no evaluations of interventions targeting adults were included unless studies of mixed groups of adults and adolescents could allow specific determinations as to the effectiveness of treatment outcomes for adolescent subjects, (b) investigations utilizing pharmacological therapies were included only if drugs were administered as part of an integrated treatment protocol combining medications with one or more psychosocial interventions,

(c) substance use treatment outcomes (as opposed to compliance, safety, other problem behaviors, or prevention-only outcomes) were examined, (d) studies included a drug or alcohol use outcome measure, (e) studies were controlled evaluations (i.e., comparison group that included a control group, wait-list control, or contrasting treatment group as part of the design) published in English.

## Literature Search

The search objective was to identify all controlled evaluations of substance abuse treatments for adolescent clients for a fifteen-year time span (between 1988 and 2003). This time frame was selected because experimental designs for adolescent substance abusers were not readily available before this period; also, this period of time parallels the rise in evidence-based treatment approaches in allied health professions. Databases systematically searched included *MEDLINE* (1988–March, 2003), *PsycINFO* (1988–March, 2003), *Social Science Abstracts* (1988–March, 2003), *Criminal Justice Abstracts* (1996–March, 2003), the Cochrane Library of Systematic Reviews and Controlled Trials Register, the C2 registries of the Campbell Collaboration Library, and a National Library of Medicine computerized bibliographic search. Numerous alcohol and drug treatment Web sites were also searched. Manual searches of the reference sections of identified studies, other relevant articles, reference sections of recent pertinent book titles, and government documents were also conducted. Keyword searches included the following descriptors entered singularly and in Boolean format with "and" or "or": "Adolescent," "Drug Abuse," "Drug Dependence," "Substance Abuse," "Substance Use Disorders," "Psychosocial Interventions," "Psychosocial Treatments," "Youth," "Behavioral Interventions," "Behavioral Treatments," "Psychotherapy," "Randomized Controlled Trials," and "Controlled Clinical Trials." Total search results incorporating the above-mentioned keywords yielded a total of 3,012 citations. Following search descriptor refinements, duplicate citation removal, and step-by-step screening and filtering of articles vis-à-vis inclusion criteria, 32 publications remained. Full-text articles were retrieved and reexamined for relevance and final study selection. Findings from 15 investigations published between 1989 and 2002 in 18 journal articles constituted the final study sample.

## Coding Procedures

Study characteristics such as citation information, methodological attributes, outcome variable information, measures, key findings, intervention description, as well as other pertinent information, were recorded by both authors onto an intervention coding form. Following this initial coding procedure, information was double-coded for all of the articles. An interrater reliability of .96 showed minimal coding error. Further, the first author reviewed all coding forms for accuracy and completeness, and for rare cases of discrepant codes for study variables, study authors met and achieved consensus via discussion.

## Analysis of Methodological Quality

Each study was rated with regard to methodological characteristics using an adapted version of the Methodological Quality Rating Scale (MQRS). This scale was developed by Miller, Brown, Simpson, Handmaker, Bien, Luckie, Montgomery, Hester, & Tonigan (1995) and the Mesa Grande project evaluating alcohol dependence treatment outcome studies (Miller, Andrews, Wilbourne, & Bennett, 1998; Miller & Wilbourne, 2002) and has been used in other systematic reviews (Vaughn & Howard, 2003) and meta-analyses (Apodaca & Miller, 2003). Table 7.1 displays the thirteen dimensions of methodological quality assessed by the MQRS. Each study was evaluated across 13 methodological attributes. The maximum number of points a study could garner ranged from 1 (extremely poor quality) to 16 (exceptionally high quality). Interrater agreement of the 13 MQRS dimensions was assessed across the entire sample of 15 studies; only 9 of 195 ratings of the two raters differed, yielding an interrater agreement of 95%.

## Effect Size Calculation

For intervention studies with sufficient statistical information, we calculated the effect size, $d$ (Cohen, 1988). For treatment/comparison design studies, the effect size was calculated as the difference between the intervention group's mean posttest score and the comparison group's mean posttest score divided by the pooled standard deviation. When the researchers reported only a $t$- or $F$-statistic, we estimated the effect size by applying the formulas derived by Rosenthal and colleagues (Rosenthal, 1991; Rosenthal & Rosnow, 1984):

$$d = \frac{2t}{\sqrt{df}}$$

$$d = \frac{2\sqrt{F}}{\sqrt{df(error)}}$$

When only a chi-square test was available, a correlation measure of the effect size, $r$, was estimated by applying a formula developed by Rosenthal (1991):

$$r = \phi = \sqrt{\frac{x^2(1)}{N}}$$

**Table 7.1**       Methodological Quality Ratings Scale

| Methodological Attributes | Points Assessed |
|---|---|
| A. Study design: | 1 = Single group pretest posttest. |
| | 2 = Quasi-experimental (nonequivalent control). |
| | 3 = Randomization with control group. |
| B. Replicability: | 0 = Procedures contain insufficient detail. |
| | 1 = Procedures contain sufficient detail. |
| C. Baseline: | 0 = No baseline scores, characteristics, or measures reported. |
| | 1 = Baseline scores, characteristics, or measures reported. |
| D. Quality control: | 0 = No standardization specified. |
| | 1 = Intervention standardization by manual, procedures, specific training, etc. |
| E. Follow-up length: | 0 = Less than 6 months. |
| | 1 = 6 to 11 months. |
| | 2 = 12 months or longer. |
| F. Dosage: | 0 = No discussion of dosage or % of treatment received. |
| | 1 = Dosage, % treatment enumerated and accounted for. |
| G. Collaterals: | 0 = No collateral verification. |
| | 1 = Collaterals interviewed. |
| H. Objective verification: | 0 = No objective verification. |
| | 1 = Verification of records (paper records, blood, materials, etc.). |
| I. Dropouts/ attrition: | 0 = Dropouts neither discussed nor accounted for. |
| | 1 = Dropouts enumerated and discussed. |
| J. Statistical power: | 0 = Inadequate power due to sample size/dropouts. |
| | 1 = Adequate power with adequate sample size. |
| K. Independent: | 0 = Follow-up nonblind, unspecified. |
| | 1 = Follow-up of interventions treatment-blind. |
| L. Analyses: | 0 = No statistical analyses or clearly inappropriate analyses. |
| | 1 = Appropriate statistical analyses (group differences, characteristics comparable). |
| M. Multisite: | 0 = Single site or comparison of differing intervention. |
| | 1 = Parallel replications at two or more sites. |

NOTE: Adapted from Miller et al. (1995). Scores could range from 0 (*low*) to 16 (*high*).

Then, *r* was converted to *d* as follows:

$$d = \frac{r}{\sqrt{1 - r^2}}$$

These various methods allowed different interventions to be compared against one another and facilitated comparisons across studies using standardized quantitative values. Effect size magnitude was categorized as small (.20), medium (.50), and large (.80) as suggested by Cohen (1988).

## Intervention Classification Scheme

Interventions were classified relative to their methodological rigor and strength of outcome into one of five categories: (A) Evidence of clinically meaningful effect (ES > .20) with at least one year follow-up or replication and using relatively strong designs; (B) Evidence of clinically meaningful effect (ES > .20) with relatively strong designs and < one year follow-up and no replication; (C) Evidence of negligible or undesired effect with less strong designs; (D) Evidence of negligible or undesired effect with relatively strong designs; (I) Evidence of indeterminate effect, mixed or incomplete findings. Given the lack of objective classification of methodological quality ratings, the relative strength of study designs was based on a median split (i.e., garnering 1–8 MQRS points could be considered less strong methodologically and 9–16 MQRS points as relatively strong methodologically).

# Results

Study characteristics and synthesis results across studies are presented in Table 7.3 for the 15 evaluations appearing in 18 published articles involving both comparison and control groups of adolescents treated for substance abuse ($n = 1,928$). Beneficial effect sizes for substance use reduction outcome variables appear as a negative value (-). Beneficial effect sizes for abstinence-related outcomes are reflected in positive values.

*Intervention targets.* Clearly, the family is a critical area of intervention focus, as ten out of twenty-four (42%) treatments examined targeted this point of change. Group treatments were represented by six (25%) interventions. Five (21%) interventions focused treatment explicitly on individual factors. Remaining treatments were of a mixed component design not clearly targeting the individual, group, or family. There was a notable absence of pharmacological treatments, which contrasts with the adult treatment literature that is increasingly employing medications, such as opioid antagonists, for substance use disorders (Vaughn & Howard, 2004; Volpicelli, Pettinati, McClellan, & O'Brien, 2001).

*Methodological quality of identified reports.* Table 7.2 presents the methodological characteristics of the studies reviewed. Overall, methodological quality was high as exemplified by 13 studies (86.7%) utilizing randomization with a control group. Further, 14 studies (93.3%) provided detail judged sufficient to allow for replication. Baseline scores, characteristics,

**Table 7.2**    Methodological Quality Characteristics of Studies of Adolescent Substance Abuse
Treatments (n = 15)

| Methodological Criteria | N | % |
|---|---|---|
| 1. Quasi-experimental (nonequivalent control group). | 2 | 13.3 |
| 2. Randomization with control group. | 13 | 86.7 |
| 3. Procedures contain sufficient detail for replication. | 14 | 93.3 |
| 4. Baseline scores, characteristics, or measures reported. | 13 | 86.7 |
| 5. Intervention standardization by manual, procedures, specific training, etc. | 15 | 100.0 |
| 6. Follow-up less than 6 months. | 7 | 46.7 |
| 7. Follow-up 6 to 11 months. | 3 | 20.0 |
| 8. Follow-up 12 months or longer. | 5 | 33.3 |
| 9. Dosage, % treatment enumerated and accounted for. | 15 | 100.0 |
| 10. Collaterals interviewed. | 9 | 60.0 |
| 11. Verification of records (paper records, blood, materials, etc.). | 11 | 73.3 |
| 12. Dropouts enumerated and discussed. | 15 | 100.0 |
| 13. Adequate power with adequate sample size. | 12 | 80.0 |
| 14. Follow-up nonblind, unspecified. | 11 | 73.3 |
| 15. Follow-up of interventions treatment-blind. | 4 | 26.7 |
| 16. Appropriate statistical analyses. | 13 | 86.7 |
| 17. Single-site or comparison of differing interventions. | 13 | 86.7 |
| 18. Parallel replications at two or more sites. | 2 | 13.3 |

and/or measures were reported in 13 studies (86.7%). All 15 studies employed intervention standardization procedures, enumerated and accounted for treatment dosages, and discussed and enumerated dropouts. Collateral contacts were utilized to validate subject self-reports in nine studies (60.0%). Objective verification of records (urinalysis, arrest records) occurred in 11 studies (73.3%). The majority of studies (86.7%) employed appropriate statistical analyses. Finally, two studies were multi-site trials.

*MQRS scores, interventions, outcome variables and measures.* As previously mentioned, MQRS scores were generally impressive. The range of scores across the 15 studies ranged between 8 (Sealock, Gottfredson, & Gallagher, 1997) and 15 (Liddle et al., 2001). The mean score across studies was 12.0 (*SD* = 1.9). The majority of the 24 interventions evaluated in these studies focused treatment at the family level. These interventions typically spanned 8–16 weeks. However, several were longer in duration. As shown in Table 7.4, the primary outcome of interest in this review was substance use reduction. This outcome could be and often was expressed as alcohol use, months of abstinence, drug use, "hard" drug use, "soft" drug use, and marijuana use. In terms of outcome measures, self-report instruments were predominant. Collateral reports (typically parental), urinalysis, and arrest records were also employed

*Samples.* Table 7.3 displays sample data for each study. Sample sizes ranged from 22 to 426 (*M* = 128.5, *SD* = 103.8). Eight of 15 studies (53.0%) had sample sizes of > 100. In terms of gender, treatment samples were largely male. Participants typically ranged from 14 to 21 with most samples having a modal age of 15. Although overall samples had a preponderance of Caucasians, African-Americans were well represented. Latinos, though not represented to any significant degree across studies, were the entire focus of one investigation (Santisteban et al., 2003). Seven of 15 studies were of juvenile offenders, probationers, or court-referred youth. Most studies reported that samples were from lower socioeconomic status populations.

*Outcome Findings.* Table 7.3 presents the outcome findings for interventions by study. Overall, many of the treatments reduced substance use and increased abstinence rates. Treatment gains occurring immediately following treatment were often not maintained at follow-up. Posttreatment effect sizes ranged from an increase in substance use of .51 (medium non-beneficial effect) (McGillicuddy, Rychtarik, Duquette, & Morsheimer, 2001) for coping skills training to a substantial reduction in substance use of 1.25 (large) for behavioral therapy (Azrin, Donohue, Besalel, Kogan, Acierno, 1994). At follow-up, effect sizes ranged from .39 (medium non-beneficial effect) (Waldron, Slesnick, Brody, Turner, & Peterson, 2001) for cognitive behavioral treatment, to large reductions in substance use for both cognitive-behavioral group treatment (Kaminer & Burleson, 1999) and multidimensional family therapy of −.87 and −.86 respectively.

*Classification of interventions.* Table 7.4 displays the 24 interventions grouped by the evidence criteria previously described. Two interventions, multidimensional family therapy and Cognitive-Behavioral Group Treatment, had the highest support ("A" rating). Seven interventions attained a ("B" rating): behavioral therapy, multisystemic therapy, combined cognitive-behavioral therapy and functional family therapy, family systems therapy, functional family therapy, combined Botvin life-skills with additive programs, and psycho-educational therapy. Interventions in the ("C" rating) category were supportive group counseling, interactional group treatment, aftercare services, and residential treatment services. Four interventions (individual counseling, family education, adolescent group treatment, and individual cognitive-behavioral treatment) received a ("D" rating). At this stage, study findings indicate that some interventions do not possess a high level of empirical support ("D" category) or perhaps have not been given enough of an opportunity to be effective owing to design features ("C" category), or the data are not present to make a clear judgment ("I" category).

**Table 7.3**    Characteristics and Outcome Findings of Adolescent Substance Abuse Treatment Studies

| | Study | MQRS | Intervention Type & Duration | Sample | Outcome Variable & Measure | Effect Size — Posttest | Effect Size — Follow-Up | Key Findings |
|---|---|---|---|---|---|---|---|---|
| 1. | Azrin, Donohue, Besalel, Kogan, & Acierno (1994) | 11 | Behavioral therapy (BT; 6 months) or supportive group (SG) counseling (6 months) | 26 adolescents: mean age = 16.0, 77% male, 23% female, 81% White, 19% African American and Hispanic. | Months of abstinence (SR, CR, U), days of drug use per month (SR, CR, U), alcohol use (SR, CR, U) | BT v. SG: d = −1.25; BT v. SG: d = −1.02; BT v. SG: d = −.96 | No follow-up data reported | Reduction of illegal drug use by behavioral program was superior compared to supportive counseling. |
| 2. | Friedman (1989) | 13 | Family therapy (FT) method (24 weeks) or parent group (PG) method (24 weeks) | 135 adolescents: mean age = 17.9, 60% male, 40% female, predominantly White. | Drug severity index score (SR) | | FT v. PG: d = 0 | Both groups saw a 50% reduction on drug severity index score (mean value). No differences between groups. |
| 3. | Friedman, Terras, & Glassman (2002) | 10 | Botvin Life Skills Training (BLST) and Prothrow-Stith Anti-Violence Program (PS) and Values Clarification (VC; 4 weeks) or basic residential treatment (not specified) | 201 court-adjudicated youths: mean age = 15.5, 100% males, predominantly African American, low SES. | Drug use (SR), alcohol use (SR) | Unable to compute or estimate effect sizes at post due to limited data. | BLST, PS, & VC v. BRT: d = −.36; BLST, PS, & VC v. BRT: d = −.18 | Dosage and process analysis point to BLST for lowering drug use; however, impossible to eliminate effects of simultaneous modalities. Treatment group had significant reduction in drug use (not alcohol) vs. comparison group. |
| 4. | Henggeler et al. (1991) | 10 | Site 1: Multisystemic therapy (MST; 16 weeks) or individual counseling (IC; not specified) | 144 juvenile offenders: mean age = 14.4, 67% male, 33% female, 70% White, 30% African American, low SES. | Substance-related offenses (A) | MST v. IC: d = −.18 | No follow-up data reported | Youths in the MST condition experienced significant reduction in alcohol use and marijuana use relative to comparison condition. Follow-up on substance-related offense yielded small reduction. |
| | | | Site 2: Multisystemic therapy (MST; 16 weeks) or usual services (US; not specified) | 47 juvenile offenders: mean age = 15.1, 72% male, 74% African American, 26% White, low SES. | Soft drug use—alcohol and marijuana (SR) | MST v. US: d = −.64 | No follow-up data reported | |

*(Continued)*

**Table 7.3** (Continued)

| Study | MQRS | Intervention Type & Duration | Sample | Outcome Variable & Measure | Effect Size Posttest | Effect Size Follow-Up | Key Findings |
|---|---|---|---|---|---|---|---|
| 5a. & 5b. | Henggeler, Clingempeel, Brondino, & Pickrel (2002); Henggeler, Pickrel, & Brondino (1999) | 13 | Multisystemic therapy (MST; 18 weeks) or usual community services (US; not specified). | 118 juvenile offenders: mean age = 15.7, 79% male, 50% African American, 47% White, 3% Other, low SES. | Alcohol/marijuana use (SR; post & follow-up), cocaine and other drug use (SR; post & follow-up), abstinence from marijuana (U; follow-up) | MST v. US: $d = -.38$; MST v. US: Insufficient data; MST v. US: $d = -.09$ | MST v. US: $d = -.03$ MST v. US: $d = .24$ | MST decreased self-report use of marijuana and other drugs at posttreatment. These changes were not maintained at 6-month follow-up. Four-year follow-up by urinalysis showed significant differences between groups with MST being superior for marijuana abstinence; small reductions in cocaine use and self-reported marijuana use. |
| 6. | Joanning, Quinn, Thomas, & Mullen (1992) | 11 | Family systems therapy (FST; 12 weeks) or adolescent group therapy (AGT; 12 weeks) or family drug education (FDE; biweekly for 6 sessions). | 89 adolescents: mean age = 15.4, predominantly White and Mexican American, low SES. | Drug use—abstinence (SR, CR, U) | FST v. AGT: $d = .46$; FST v. FDE: $d = .41$; AGT v. FDE: $d = -.14$ | No follow-up data reported | Posttest results showed all three therapies led to greater numbers of nonuse with FST having the most impact. Negligible differences between AGT and FDE. |
| 7a. & 7b. | Kaminer & Burleson (1999); Kaminer, Burleson, Blitz, Sussmann, & Rounsaville (1998) | 14 | Cognitive-behavioral group treatment (CBGT; 12 weeks) or interactional group treatment (IGT; 12 weeks). | 32 adolescents: mean age = 15.8, predominantly White and male. | Substance use (SR, U), severity of substance use (SR U), alcohol use (SR; follow-up), drug use (SR; follow-up) | CBGT v. IGT: $d = -.81$; CBGT v. IGT: $d = -.62$ | CBGT v. IGT: $d = -.87$; CBGT v. IGT: $d = -.62$ | Adolescents assigned to CBGT demonstrated a large reduction in severity of substance use compared to IGT at 3 months. At 15 months both therapies showed positive impacts with CBGT superior. Very small follow-up sample size. |

| | Study | MQRS | Intervention Type & Duration | Sample | Outcome Variable & Measure | Effect Size Posttest | Effect Size Follow-Up | Key Findings |
|---|---|---|---|---|---|---|---|---|
| 8. | Kaminer, Burleson, & Goldberger (2002) | 12 | Cognitive-behavioral coping skills group therapy (CBGT; 8 weeks) or psycho-education therapy (PET; 8 weeks). | 88 adolescents: mean age = 15.4, 90% White, 42% female. | Alcohol use problems (SR, U), substance abuse problems (SR, U) | CBGT (with coping) v. PET: d = −.15; CBGT (with coping) v. PET: d = −.42 | CBGT (with coping) v. PET: d = −.57; CBGT (with coping) v. PET: d = 0 | Both conditions demonstrated substance use reduction at 3- and 9-month follow-up. CBGT condition superior to PET at all points except 9-month follow-up. |
| 9. | Lewis, Piercy, Sprenkle, & Trepper, (1990) | 12 | Purdue brief family therapy (12 weeks) or training in parenting skills (12 weeks) | 84 adolescents (51.2% juvenile offenders): mean age = 16, 81% male, 96% White, 3% African American. | No drug use (SR, U), soft drug use (SR, U), hard drug use (SR, U) | Insufficient data to calculate effect sizes at 3-month posttest. | No follow-up data reported. | Both therapies appeared to be effective from pretest to posttest. However, Purdue brief family therapy reduced drug use for a larger proportion of adolescents. |
| 10. | Liddle et al. (2001) | 15 | Multidimensional family therapy (MDFT; 16 weeks) or adolescent group therapy (AGT; 14 to 16 weeks) or multifamily educational intervention (MEI; 16 weeks) | 97 adolescents (61% juvenile offenders): mean age = 15.9, 80% male, 51% White, 18% African American, 15% Hispanic, 6% Asian, 10% Other, low SES. | Drug use—combined alcohol and marijuana (SR, CR, U) | MDFT v. AGT: d = −.77; MDFT v. MEI: d = −.58; AGT v. MEI: d = .02 | MDFT v. AGT: d = −.25; MDFT v. MEI: d = −.86; AGT v. MEI: d = −.57 | Improvement attained with all three treatments. MDFT was superior overall at posttreatment and 1-year follow-up on combined drug use outcome (reduction). |
| 11. | McGillicuddy, Rychtarik, Duquette, & Morsheimer (2001) | 11 | Coping skills training (CST; 8 weeks) or delayed treatment conditions (DTC; 8 weeks) | 22 adolescents: mean age = 16, 72% male, 28% female, predominantly White. | Alcohol use days (CR), drinks per drinking day (CR), marijuana use days (SR, CR) | CST v. DTC: d = .16; CST v. DTC: d = .51; CST v. DTC: d = −.60 | No follow-up data reported. | Results suggest improvements in parental coping skills may lead to reductions in marijuana use. However, increases in alcohol-related outcomes versus delayed treatment condition. |

*(Continued)*

**Table 7.3** (Continued)

| Study | MQRS | Intervention Type & Duration | Sample | Outcome Variable & Measure | Effect Size Posttest | Effect Size Follow-Up | Key Findings |
|---|---|---|---|---|---|---|---|
| 12. Santisteban et al. (2003) | 11 | Brief strategic family therapy (BSFT; 4 to 20 weeks) or general group treatment (GGT; 6 to 16 weeks) | 126 adolescents (school referred for behavior problems); mean age = 15.6, 100% Hispanic. | Alcohol use (SR, U), marijuana use (SR, U) | BSFT v. GGT: d = .58; BSFT v. GGT: d = −.21 | No follow-up data reported | Adolescents enrolled in BSFT showed reductions in substance use from pre to post. However, for alcohol use GGT superior at treatment termination. High dropout rates for both conditions. |
| 13. Sealock, Gottfredson, & Gallagher (1997) | 8 | Residential Treatment Program (6 to 8 weeks) and After Care Program (44 weeks) or probation and usual services | 426 juvenile offenders: primarily male and non-White. | Drug use (SR, U, A) | AA, SG v. P: d = −.21 | AA, SG, & AC v. P & US: d = .19 | Modest reductions during residential treatment. However, these were not maintained during after care services. |
| 14. Waldron, Slesnick, Brody, Turner, & Peterson (2001) | 13 | Individual cognitive-behavioral therapy (CBT; 8 to 12 weeks) or individual cognitive-behavioral therapy and functional family therapy (FFT; 8 to 12 weeks) or FFT (8 to 12 weeks) or group counseling (GC; 8 to 12 weeks) | 114 adolescents (majority court-adjudicated youth): mean age = 15.6, 80% male, 20% female, 38% White, 7% Native American, 47% Hispanic, 8% Other, low SES. | % days marijuana used (SR, CR, U) | CBT v. CBT & FFT: d = .37; CBT v. FFT: d = .79; CBT v. GC: d = −.10; CBT & FFT v. FFT: d = .41; CBT & FFT v. GC: d = −.49; FFT v. GC: d = −.99 | CBT v. CBT & FFT: d = .39; CBT v. FFT: d = .28; CBT v. GC: d = .24; CBT & FFT v. FFT: d = −.09; CBT & FFT v. GC: d = −.14; FFT v. GC: d = −.04 | Three of the four intervention packages demonstrated reductions in percentage of days of marijuana use (CBT alone was not effective at posttreatment and follow-up). At 4- month posttreatment FFT alone was superior to other interventions. At 7-month follow-up, however, the combined CBT and FFT intervention was slightly more effective than FFT alone. |
| 15. Winters, Stinchfield, Orland, Weller, & Latimer (2000) | 14 | Minnesota Model 12-Step Program (MM; 4 to 6 weeks) or delayed treatment condition (6 weeks) | 179 adolescents: 60% between the ages 16 and 21 years; 56% male, largely White (85%). | Alcohol and drug; abstinence (SR, CR, U), lapses (SR, CR U), relapses (SR, CR, U) | Insufficient data to calculate effect sizes | Insufficient data to calculate effect sizes | MM 12-Step Program appeared to be superior to nontreatment group and delayed treatment group at 1-year follow-up. |

NOTE: BRT = basic residential treatment; MQRS = Methodological Quality Rating Scale; SR = self-report; CR = collateral report; U = urinalysis; A = arrest records. MQRS score $M = 12.0$ ($SD = 1.9$).

**Table 7.4**       Evidence Summary (ES) of Interventions for Adolescent Substance Abuse Treatment

A.   Evidence of clinically meaningful effect (ES > .20) with at least 1-year follow-up or replication and using relatively strong designs.
Multidimensional family therapy (MDFT)
Cognitive-behavioral group treatment (CBGT)

B.   Evidence of clinically meaningful effect (ES > .20) with relatively strong designs and less than 1-year follow-up and no replication.
Behavioral therapy (BT)
Combined cognitive-behavioral therapy and functional family therapy (CBT & FFT)
Family systems therapy (FST)
Functional family therapy (FFT)[a]
Multisystemic treatment (MST)[a]
Combined Botvin life-skills training (BLST), Prothrow-Stith Anti-Violence Program (PSAV), and Values Clarification Program (VC)
Psycho-educational therapy (PET)

C.   Evidence of negligible or undesired effect with less strong designs.
Supportive group counseling (SG)
Interactional group treatment (IGT)
Aftercare services (AS)
Residential treatment services with multiple and variable components (RST)

D.   Evidence of negligible or undesired effect with relatively strong designs.
Individual counseling (IC)
Family education (FE; multidimensional educational intervention [MEI])
Adolescent group treatment (AGT)
Individual cognitive-behavioral treatment (CBT)

I.   Evidence of indeterminate effect, mixed or incomplete findings.
Parent group method (PG)
Minnesota Model 12-Step Program (MM)[b]
Coping skills training (CST)
Brief strategic family therapy (BSFT)
General group treatment (GGT)
Purdue brief family therapy (PBFT)[b]
Training in parenting skills (TIPS)[b]

NOTE: MQRS = Methodological Quality Rating Scale.
One to 8 points on MQRS = *less strong design*; 9 to 16 points on
MQRS = *relatively strong design*
a. Shown to be effective in other studies with reducing adolescent violence and problem behavior.
b. Insufficient data available to calculate effect sizes.

# Discussion and Implications
# for Social Work Practice

Studies of adolescent substance abuse treatment suggest that several interventions are effective in reducing substance use. For example, multidimensional family therapy is capable of producing and maintaining significant treatment gains for up to a year. Several other interventions also are supported to a substantial degree by current empirical evidence. Further, these intervention studies were of relatively good quality methodologically. Most of the studies reviewed were randomized controlled trials employing standardized protocols. Although there exists a range of effective and promising treatments, many interventions were found to be either ineffective or of uncertain efficacy. As such, interventions listed under the "C," "D," and "I" categories on Table 7.4 cannot yet be recommended for clinical applications, particularly in light of alternative interventions more strongly supported by available empirical evidence. Also, it should be emphasized that these conclusions are tentative. The presence of weak effect sizes does not mean that an intervention did not contribute *any* beneficial or harmful effects to individual participants. Yet, given the existence of more effective alternatives and the ethical responsibility to provide the best treatments available, their deployment may be ill advised at this time. Because many of the effective treatments are family-centered and target a range of factors that influence adolescent chemical use behavior, social work practitioners should find these treatments appealing.

The conclusions reached are to some extent limited by the modest number of controlled evaluations of adolescent substance abuse treatments. By comparison, there are over 300 controlled evaluations of alcohol dependence treatments in the adult literature (Miller & Wilbourne, 2002). Additional limitations include the possibility that we did not identify all published studies of adolescent substance abuse treatments. Although comprehensive search methods were employed in this review, it is possible that some published evaluations meeting inclusion criteria were not identified. In addition, some potential methodological criteria were not a part of the Methodological Quality Rating Scale employed. This procedure, however, does represent a reasonable assessment of study quality that attempts to move beyond simple descriptions. In addition, 7 of 15 studies reviewed included samples of juvenile offender or court-referred youth. As such, this observation reduces the potential generalizability of these findings to adolescents evidencing substance abuse problems who are not offenders. Although there is a strong relationship between drug use and crime, using illegal substances in itself is a criminal offense. Therefore, it is not surprising that many studies of adolescents with substance use problems are drawn from this population.

In the future, more controlled evaluations are needed that assess adolescent substance abuse treatment outcomes across longer periods of time. Additional studies of youth with co-occurring disorders who take medications would also be useful. Further, specific analyses of heavy substance abusing youth and substance dependent youth are critical. As substance abuse and dependence is a costly problem that tends to begin early and become chronic, it is paramount that policymakers and practitioners utilize those interventions with the greatest scientific support. Finally, it should be noted that there was a relative lack of contribution from social work researchers with most interventions developed by psychiatrists and clinical psychologists. Given that social workers frequently encounter adolescents with substance abuse problems, greater social work research involvement in the adolescent substance abuse treatment domain may prove beneficial to the profession and the clients they serve.

# References

References marked with an asterisk indicate studies included in the meta-analysis.

*Azrin, N. H., Donohue, B., Besalel, V. A., Kogan, E. S., & Acierno, R. (1994). Youth drug abuse treatment: A controlled outcome study. *Journal of Child & Adolescent Substance Abuse, 3,* 1–17.

Apodaca, T. R., & Miller, W. R. (2003). A meta-analysis of the effectiveness of bibliotherapy for alcohol problems. *Journal of Clinical Psychology, 59,* 289–304.

Bronfenbrenner, U. (1999). Environments in developmental perspective: Theoretical and operational models. In S. L. Friedman & T. D. Wach (Eds.), *Measuring environment across the life span* (pp. 3–28). Washington, DC: American Psychological Association.

Cohen, J. (1988). *Statistical power for the behavioral sciences* (2nd ed.). Hillsdale, NJ: Lawrence Erlbaum Associates.

Deas, D., & Thomas, S. E. (2001). An overview of controlled studies of adolescent substance abuse treatment. *The American Journal on Addictions, 10,* 178–189.

Drug Abuse Warning Network. (2001). *Emergency department drug mentions for selected drug groups, total drug mentions, and total drug episodes: 1978 to 2001.* 2001 DAWN ED Report. Rockville, MD: DHHS.

*Friedman, A. S. (1989). Family therapy vs. parent groups: Effects on adolescent drug abusers. *The American Journal of Family Therapy, 17,* 335–347.

*Friedman, A. S., Terras, A., & Glassman, K. (2002). Multimodel substance use intervention program for male delinquents. *Journal of Child & Adolescent Substance Abuse, 11,* 43–65.

Glass, G. G., McGaw, B., & Smith, M. L. (1981). *Meta-analysis in social research.* Beverly Hills, CA: Sage Publications.

*Henggeler, S. W., Borduin, C. M., Melton, G. B., Mann, B. J., Smith, L. A., Hall, J. A., et al. (1991). Effects of Multisystemic therapy on drug use and abuse in serious juvenile offenders: A progress report from two outcome studies. *Family Dynamics Addiction Quarterly, 1,* 40–51.

*Henggeler, S. W., Pickrel, S. G., & Brondino, M. J. (1999). Multisystemic treatment of substance-abusing and dependent delinquents: Outcomes, treatment fidelity, and transportability. *Mental Health Services Research, 1,* 171–184.

*Henggeler, S. W., Clingempeel, G. W, Brondino, M. J., & Pickrel, S. G. (2002). Four-year follow-up of multisystemic therapy with substance-abusing and substance-dependent juvenile offenders. *Journal of the American Academy of Child & Adolescent Psychiatry, 41,* 868–874.

*Joanning, H., Quinn, W., Thomas, F., & Mullen, R. (1992). Treating adolescent drug abuse: A comparison of family systems therapy, group therapy, and family drug education. *Journal of Marital and Family Therapy, 18*, 345–356.

Johnston, L. D., O'Malley, P. M., & Bachman, J. G. (2002). *Monitoring the Future. National results on adolescent drug use; Overview of key findings, 2001.* Rockville, MD: National Institute on Drug Abuse, DHHS.

*Kaminer, Y., Burleson, J. A., Blitz, C., Sussman, J., & Rounsaville, B. J. (1998). Psychotherapies for adolescent substance abusers: A pilot study. *The Journal of Nervous and Mental Disease, 186*, 684–690.

*Kaminer, Y., & Burleson, J. A. (1999). Psychotherapies for adolescent substance abusers: 15-month follow-up of a pilot study. *The American Journal on Addictions, 8*, 114–119.

*Kaminer, Y., Burleson, J. A., & Goldberger, R. (2002). Cognitive-behavioral coping skills and psychoeducation therapies for adolescent substance abuse. *The Journal of Nervous and Mental Disease, 190*, 737–745.

*Lewis, R. A., Piercy, F. P., Sprenkle, D. H., & Trepper, T. S. (1990). Family-based interventions for helping drug-abusing adolescents. *Journal of Adolescent Research, 5*, 82–95.

*Liddle, H. A., Dakof, G. A., Parker, K., Diamond, S. Barrett, K., & Tejeda, M. (2001). Multidimensional family therapy for adolescent drug abuse: Results of a randomized clinical trial. *American Journal of Drug and Alcohol Abuse, 27*, 651–688.

*McGillicuddy, N. B., Rychtarik, R. G., Duquette, J. A., & Morsheimer, E. T. (2001). Development of a skill training program for parents of substance-abusing adolescents. *Journal of Substance Abuse Treatment, 20*, 59–68.

Miller, W. R., Andrews, N. R., Wilbourne, P., & Bennett, M. E. (1998). A wealth of alternatives: Effective treatments for alcohol problems. In W. R. Miller & N. Heather (Eds.), *Treating addictive behaviors: Processes of change* (2nd ed., pp. 203–216). New York: Plenum Press.

Miller, W. R., Brown, J. M., Simpson, T. L., Handmaker, N. S., Bien, T. H., Luckie, L. H., et al. (1995). What works? A methodological analysis of the alcohol treatment outcome literature. In R. K. Hester & W.R. Miller (Eds.), *Handbook of alcoholism treatment approaches: Effective alternatives* (2nd ed., pp. 12–44). Boston: Allyn & Bacon.

Miller, W. R., & Wilbourne, P. L. (2002). Mesa grande: A methodological analysis of clinical trials of treatment for alcohol use disorders. *Addiction, 97*, 265–277.

National Household Survey on Drug Abuse. (2002). *Results from the 2001 national household survey on drug abuse: Volume I. Summary of national findings.* Rockville, MD: DHHS.

Newcomb, M. D. (1995). Identifying high risk youth: Prevalence and patterns of adolescent drug abuse. In E. Rahdert, & D. Czerkowicz (Eds.). *Adolescent drug abuse: Clinical assessment and therapeutic interventions (NIDA research monograph 156).* Rockville, MD: U.S. DHHS.

Perkonigg, A., Lieb, R., Hofler, M., Schuster, P., Sonntag, H., & Wittchen, H. U. (1999). Patterns of cannabis use, abuse and dependence over time: Incidence, progression and stability in a sample of 1,228 adolescents. *Addiction, 94*, 1663–1678.

Rosenthal, R. (1991). *Meta-analytic procedures for social research.* Thousand Oaks, CA: Sage Publications.

Rosenthal, R., & Rosnow, R. L. (1984). *Essentials of behavioral research*. Thousand Oaks, CA: Sage Publications.

*Santisteban, D. A., Coatsworth, J. D., Perez-Vidal, A., Kurtines, W. M., Schwartz, S. J., LaPierriere, A., & Szapocznik, J. (2003). Efficacy of brief strategic family therapy in modifying Hispanic adolescent behavior problems and substance use. *Journal of Family Psychology, 17*, 121–133.

*Sealock, M. D., Gottfredson, D. C., & Gallagher, C. A. (1997). Drug treatment for juvenile offenders: Some good and bad news. *Journal of Research in Crime and Delinquency, 34*, 210–236.

Vaughn, M. G., & Howard, M. O. (2004). Integrated psychosocial and opioid antagonist treatment for alcohol dependence: A systematic review of controlled evaluations. *Social Work Research, 28*, 41–53.

Volpicelli, J. R., Pettinati, H. M., McLellan, A. T., & O'Brien, C. P. (2001). *Combining medication and psychosocial treatments for addictions: The BRENDA approach*. New York: Guilford.

Waldron, H. B. (1997). Adolescent substance abuse and family therapy outcome. *Advances in Clinical Child Psychiatry, 19*, 199–234.

*Waldron, H. B., Slesnick, N., Brody, J. L., Turner, C. W., & Peterson, T. R. (2001). Treatment outcomes for adolescent substance abuse at 4- and 7-month assessments. *Journal of Consulting and Clinical Psychology, 69*, 802–813.

Weinberg, N. Z., Rahdert, E, Colliver, J. D., & Glantz, M. D. (1998). Adolescent substance abuse: A review of the past 10 years. *Journal of the American Academy of Child and Adolescent Psychiatry, 37*(3), 252–261.

Williams, R. J., & Chang, S. Y. (2000). A comprehensive and comparative review of adolescent substance abuse treatment outcome. *Clinical Psychology: Science and Practice, 7*, 138–166.

*Winters, K. C., Stinchfield, R. D., Orland, E., Weller, C., & Latimer, W. W. (2000). The effectiveness of the Minnesota model approach in the treatment of adolescent drug abusers. *Addiction, 95*, 601–612.

Young, S. E., Corley, R. P., Stallings, M. C., Rhee, S. H., Crowley, T. J., & Hewitt, J. K. (2002). Substance use, abuse, and dependence in adolescence: Prevalence, symptom profiles, and correlates. *Drug and Alcohol Dependence, 68*, 309–322.

# Participation in Victim-Offender Mediation and the Prevalence of Subsequent Delinquent Behavior

8

## A Meta-Analysis

*William R. Nugent, Mona Williams, and Mark S. Umbreit*

R ecent times have seen the re-emergence of an ancient philosophy of justice referred to as "restorative justice." In this philosophy a crime is
viewed as an offense against a victim, and the emphasis is on resolving conflict, repairing harm to the victim, holding the offender accountable to the
victim, and returning things as much as possible to the way they were before
the offense occurred. The emphasis on punishment seen in the retributive
justice model, the philosophy on which the current justice system in the
United States is based, is replaced with an emphasis on personal accountability to the victim and a recognition of the harm done by the offender to
the victim (Galaway, 1988; Umbreit, 2001; Zehr, 1990).

Victim-offender mediation (VOM) is the oldest and most widely practiced expression of restorative justice (Umbreit, 2001; Zehr, 1990). VOM
programs most commonly involve the victims and perpetrators of juvenile
property offenses and minor assaults, though there have been efforts to
broaden the scope of VOM to include adult offenders and serious violent
crimes (Flaten, 1996; Umbreit, 1994a). A recent survey found more than

Originally published in *Research on Social Work Practice* 2004; 14; 408. DOI: 10.1177/
1049731504265831 The online version of this article can be found at: http://rsw.sagepub.com/
cgi/content/abstract/14/6/408

300 VOM (also referred to as victim-offender reconciliation, or VORP) programs in the United States and more than 1,000 in Europe. In about 80% of VOM programs the mediator (usually a trained volunteer) meets initially with the victim(s) and the offender separately. Following these separate sessions, which help prepare the victim(s) and offender for subsequent dialogue, there is a mediation session that is the heart of VOM. The goal of the mediation is to create an environment that allows the parties to engage in a dialogue in which emotional and informational needs are met and in which a plan for the offender "to make things right," as much as possible, is developed (Umbreit, 2001; Umbreit & Greenwood, 1999).

The development of empirically supported programs is a high priority in social work. A number of studies have compared the reoffense rates of VOM participants with those of nonparticipants (Umbreit, Coates, & Vos, 2001). A meta-analysis of this research could help shed light on the relationship between VOM participation and subsequent delinquent behavior. This article reports the results of a meta-analysis (Lipsey & Wilson, 2001) of the research on VOM participation and recidivism and focuses on three meta-analytic questions: (a) are the "VOM effects"—defined as the ratio of the odds of VOM participants reoffending to the odds of nonparticipants reoffending—homogeneous? and if not, (b) what univariate and multivariate relationships appear to exist between explanatory variables and magnitude of VOM effects? and finally, (c) within the best available group formation methodological base, does VOM participation appear to be associated with a lower likelihood of reoffense?

A major concern about meta-analysis is the so-called apples-and-oranges problem, a phrase referring to concerns about comparing studies of widely varying methodological quality. Two methods were used to address this problem. In the first, methodological characteristics of the included studies were used as explanatory variables so that the relationship between VOM effects and methodological quality were a matter of empirical investigation. In the second, studies with group formation methodology in the upper quintile in terms of methodological quality were included in a separate meta-analysis (Lipsey & Wilson, 2001).

# Method

## Inclusion Criteria

To be included in this meta-analysis a study had to have (a) focused exclusively on juveniles; (b) investigated the relationship between participation in VOM and the prevalence of subsequent delinquent behavior; and (c) employed a VOM group and at least one comparison group of juveniles who had not participated in VOM. These inclusion criteria allowed a focus on what the extant research tells us about the differences in prevalence of delinquent behavior between juveniles who participated in VOM and those who did not.

## Selection of Studies

An extensive search was conducted for studies that met the inclusion criteria (Lipsey & Wilson, 2001). The search included a comprehensive exploration of electronic databases, of the World Wide Web, of reference lists and bibliographies, as well as person-to-person contacts with restorative justice researchers. This search identified 19 studies, 15 of which met the inclusion criteria. Four studies were not included because they did not use a non-VOM comparison group and/or included adults in their sample (Carr, 1998; Dignan, 1990; Roberts, 1998; Wynne, 1996). The final sample included 15 studies conducted at 19 sites that focused on 19 VOM programs, involving a total of 9,307 juveniles (includes the following studies that were not cited in the text: Carr & Nelson, 2000; Cosden, Casas, & Wolfe, 1999; Dick, 1999; Hitao, 1999; Lee, 1999; Nugent, Umbreit, & Williams-Hayes, 2003; Roy, 1993; Stone, 2000; Stone, Helms, & Edgeworth, 1998; URSA Institute, 1993). These studies included six published in books and/or peer-reviewed journals, one unpublished master's thesis, and eight program evaluations.

## Outcome Measure

The effect size of focus was the "VOM effect," defined as the ratio of the odds of VOM participants reoffending to the odds of nonparticipants reoffending.

## Definitions of Reoffense

*Reoffense* was defined in the Umbreit (1994b; Umbreit & Coates, 1993), Nugent & Paddock (1996), and Wiinamaki (1997) studies as any subsequent offense for which a youth was adjudicated guilty. Similarly, in the Schneider (1990) study, a reoffense was any subsequent offense that was neither dismissed for lack of evidence nor led to exoneration of the juvenile. In contrast, reoffense was defined more broadly in the remaining studies as any official contact with a law enforcement agency, as any subsequent court contact, or as any record of a rearrest.

## Explanatory and Moderating Variables

One important and plausible explanation for differences in reoffense rates between VOM and non-VOM participants was the creation of initially nonequivalent groups. An important goal in the meta-analysis was to represent methodological differences in the ways VOM and non-VOM groups were formed and to use this information to identify the best available studies in terms of group formation methodology. To this end, 12 dichotomously scored items (see Table 8.1) were created, each indicating the presence/absence of a methodological feature (such as random assignment, and so on) related to the creation of initially equivalent groups, and each study (and the evaluation done at each site) was rated using these items. Total scores on this Group Formation Methodology Scale could range from 0 to 12, with higher scores indicative of studies more likely to have created initially equivalent groups, and vice versa.

Two raters independently rated the group formation methodology (GFM) used at each site, using this scale. The mean item score by item score interrater agreement was 91.7% (range 75% to 100%). Generalizability theory (or G-theory) methods were used to estimate a generalizability coefficient for generalizing from the means of the two raters' averaged item ratings to the means that would be obtained by having all raters in a universe of raters rate each site using all items in a universe of group formation methodology items (Brennan, 1983). The resulting coefficient was .92. Consistent with G-theory, in the analyses below the mean scores across the averaged (across the two raters) item scores for each site were used as the GFM scores, producing scores ranging from 0 to 1, with higher scores indicative of better quality GFM, and vice versa. These scores were used as an independent variable in analyses and to identify sites with GFM scores in the top quintile (i.e., top 20%).

Four other variables were used to represent methodological factors. Duration of follow-up was defined as the duration in months that youths were monitored for reoffense. Longer follow-up periods may be associated with larger reoffense rates and with smaller VOM effects (Niemeyer & Shichor, 1996). The type of sample was a dichotomous variable that indicated whether the sample of juveniles comprised only property offenders (type of sample = 0) or property and violent offenders (type of sample = 1). A second dichotomous sampling variable was titled "all VOM referrals" and was scored 1 for those studies in which the sample of juveniles was all VOM referrals, and 0 otherwise. In some studies, all involved juveniles had been selected for VOM participation by juvenile court and/or VOM program staff, and the non-VOM group comprised those referred juveniles who did not participate, potentially producing a biased sample. A dichotomous variable was used to identify the definition of reoffense (0 = narrow definition, 1 = broader definition) because the definition used might affect the reoffense rates observed at a study site. The broader definitions used in some of the studies may have led to larger observed reoffense rates than the more narrow definitions, used in the Nugent and Paddock, Wiinamaki, Umbreit, and Schneider studies, because more juveniles may be charged with offenses than are ultimately adjudicated guilty.

One variable, symbolized by the Greek letter $\delta$ and defined as the non-VOM group's percentage of violent offenders minus the VOM group's percentage, represented an outcome of the GFM used at a study site. Efforts were made to reconstruct the between-group differences in percentage of violent offenders at each study site. This variable could not be reconstructed for two of the studies (13% of studies; 10.5% of sites). Following Gibson (1999), expectation maximization (EM) procedures were used to estimate these missing values, and a dummy variable (0 = study/site had no missing value, 1 = study/site had missing value) used to indicate missing data on this variable. Univariate and multivariate analyses gave no evidence of a relationship between missing data on $\delta$ and magnitude of VOM effects.

There were two nonmethodological explanatory variables. A dichotomous variable was used to identify the population of the county served by the VOM program (0 = population less than or equal to 100,000, 1 = population greater than 100,000). Juveniles in counties with larger populations may be at greater risk of reoffense because of greater access to peer groups and other environmental factors related to delinquent activity. Finally, a dichotomous variable (1 = published in peer-reviewed source, 0 = otherwise) was used to represent publication status of a study because it has been found that effect sizes in studies published in peer-reviewed journals can be different than those found in non-peer-reviewed sources (Lipsey & Wilson, 2001).

## Data Analysis Methods

Correlational, binomial, and V-known hierarchical generalized linear model (HGLM) techniques (Raudenbush, Bryk, Cheong, & Congdon, 2000) were used to analyze effect sizes across sites. The binomial HGLM model is reminiscent of logistic regression and allowed the simultaneous estimation of two equations to explain variation in outcomes: one for the magnitude of VOM effects and one for the magnitude of non-VOM groups' reoffense rates. Given the minimum sample size requirements for each equation of this type, as well as the principal focus on explaining variation in VOM effects, only the equation for modeling VOM effects was developed and results reported. However, the fully multivariate nature of estimation in the HGLM approach did take into account the relationship between VOM effects and non-VOM groups' reoffense rates (Bryk & Raudenbush, 1992; Raudenbush et al., 2000).

## Analytic Strategies

A fully unconditional HGLM binomial model (i.e., one with no predictors) for predicting VOM effects was fitted and a test of homogeneity conducted. If this test suggested heterogeneity, then a stepwise variable entry approach was used. The variable with the largest statistically significant chi-square statistic was placed into the model, then remaining variables added individually to this single variable model to determine the next variable with the largest statistically significant chi-square. The new variable with the largest statistically significant chi-square value was then added to the model, and this procedure continued until all significant variation in VOM effects was explained or until there w ere n o remaining statistically significant explanatory variables.

A second strategy involved the simultaneous entry of all explanatory variables into a HGLM binomial model. This allowed the testing of each explanatory variable while controlling for all the other explanatory variables. A final approach assessed the relationship between VOM participation and subsequent delinquent behavior within the best available group formation methodology. The study sites that had GFM scores in the top quintile were used to represent VOM effects from extant studies with the most rigorous GFM and separate analyses conducted (Lipsey & Wilson, 2001).

## Misspecification Tests

The possibility existed that the HGLM models for explaining variation in VOM effects created using the above methods would have biased parameter estimates because they would, by design, have no predictors for non-VOM groups' reoffense rates. Given the fully multivariate nature of HGLM procedures, the misspecification of the equation for non-VOM groups' reoffense rates may bias parameter estimates in the equation for explaining VOM effects (Bryk & Raudenbush, 1992). Because of this possibility, the sensitivity of the model for VOM effects to the possible misspecification of the equation for non-VOM groups' reoffense rates was assessed using procedures described by Bryk & Raudenbush (1992).

# Results

## Sample Sizes and Sample Characteristics

The 15 studies, and 19 sites, gave a combined sample of 9,307 juveniles. The characteristics of the samples in each of these studies were discussed in the cited studies, and these descriptions are not repeated here. Figure 8.1 shows the effect sizes, represented as the natural log of the ratio of the odds of VOM participants reoffending to the odds of nonparticipants reoffending (Lipsey & Wilson, 2001), along with approximate 95% confidence intervals.

A negative effect size represents the outcome in which VOM participants reoffended at lower rates than nonparticipants, and 95% confidence intervals that fail to touch the horizontal axis indicate statistically significant outcomes. Also shown in this figure are the GFM scores (shown as the numbers by each effect size and associated confidence interval) for the GFM used in the study conducted at each of the included sites.

## GFM Scores

The mean GFM score was .34 (*SD* = .27; range 0 to 1.0). The mean GFM score for top quintile sites was .64 (median = .59), with a range from .5 to 1.0 (*SD* = .2).

Within this group of top quintile studies, 5 of 6 (83.3%) used the narrow definition of reoffense; 5 of 6 (83.3%) appeared in peer-reviewed sources; 4 of 6 (66.7%) used samples containing only property offenders; 4 of 6 (66.7%) studied VOM programs serving counties with a population less than 100,000; and 3 of 6 (50%) used samples containing only VOM-referred juveniles. The mean duration of follow-up was 18.8 months (range 12 to 35); the mean VOM percentage of reoffenders minus non-VOM percentage was –8.4 (*SD* = 5.4; range –15 to –1.2), whereas the mean percentage of reoffenders in the non-VOM groups was 39.2 (*SD* = 12.0; range 31.3 to 63.4).

In contrast, the mean GFM score in the lower 80% of GFM scores was .21 (*SD* = .18), with a range from 0 to .46. Within this group of studies with GFM scores in the lower 80%, 10 of 13 (76.9%) used the broader definition of reoffense; 5 of 13 (38.5%) appeared in peer-reviewed sources; 3 of 13 (23.1%) used samples containing only property offenders; 1 of 13 (7.7%) studied VOM programs serving counties with a population fewer than 100,000; and 4 of 13 (30.8%) used samples containing only VOM-referred juveniles. The mean duration of follow-up was 13.8 months (range 6 to 24); the mean VOM percentage of reoffenders minus non-VOM percentage was –7.4 (*SD* = 15.7; range –32.2 to +25.3), whereas the mean percentage of reoffenders in the non-VOM groups was 29.3 (*SD* = 9.3; range 18.5 to 43.2).

**Table 8.1**        Items on Group Formation Methodology Scale

| | |
|---|---|
| Item 1. | Juveniles randomly assigned to groups. |
| Items 2 to 10. | Youths in VOM and non-VOM groups were matched via (a) random assignment, (b) direct matching by researchers, or (c) statistical tests revealing that the two groups were equivalent in terms of the following variables within limits of sampling variability: age, gender, ethnicity, number of prior offenses, type of original offense, severity of prior offenses, family type, number of years of formal education, and number of siblings in family. |
| Item 11. | Youths were placed into the non-VOM group in an unbiased manner. |
| Item 12. | Youths were placed into the VOM group in an unbiased manner. |

NOTE: VOM = victim-offender mediation.

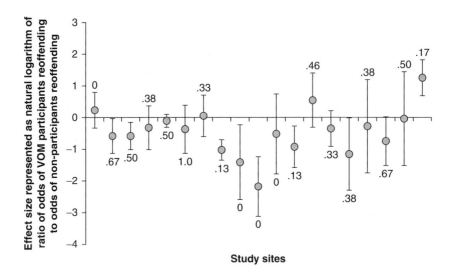

**Figure 8.1**     Graphic representation of VOM effects by site, with VOM effect defined as the natural logarithm of the ratio of the odds of VOM participants reoffending to the odds of nonparticipants reoffending. A negative VOM effect indicates that VOM participants reoffended at a lower rate than did nonparticipants. Vertical bars indicate approximate 95% confidence intervals for effect sizes. Number by each effect size and confidence interval is the GFM score for the group formation methodology used at the study site.

**Table 8.2**     Correlations Between VOM Effects, Non-VOM Groups' Reoffense Rates, and Explanatory Variables

|         | Effect | Time | δ    | Def   | Size | Sample | All VOM | Score | Missing | Pub  |
|---------|--------|------|------|-------|------|--------|---------|-------|---------|------|
| Time    | .03    |      |      |       |      |        |         |       |         |      |
| δ       | −.77*  | .16  |      |       |      |        |         |       |         |      |
| Def     | .07    | .13  | −.05 |       |      |        |         |       |         |      |
| Size    | .26    | .32  | −.06 | .46*  |      |        |         |       |         |      |
| Sample  | −.09   | .21  | −.06 | .23   | .53* |        |         |       |         |      |
| All VOM | −.21   | −.09 | .01  | .17   | −.38 | −.19   |         |       |         |      |
| Score   | .15    | .26  | <.01 | −.70* | −.28 | −.35   | −.40    |       |         |      |
| Missing | −.15   | −.02 | .08  | .29   | .20  | −.09   | .44     | −.36  |         |      |
| Pub     | .10    | .12  | −.01 | −.81* | −.33 | −.29   | −.04    | .55*  | −.36    |      |
| Non-VOM | −.52*  | .36  | .41  | −.04  | −.18 | .16    | .05     | .33   | .01     | −.15 |

NOTE: VOM = victim-offender mediation; effect = VOM effect size; time = duration of follow-up; δ = difference between non-VOM and VOM groups in percentage of violent offenders; def = definition of reoffense; size = population of county served by VOM program; sample = type of sample; all VOM = all VOM referrals in sample; score = score on Group Formation Methodology (GFM) Scale; missing = missing data on δ; pub = publication status of study; non-VOM = reoffense rate in non-VOM group.

* indicates correlation statistically significant at .05 level (two-tailed)

## Bivariate Correlations

The correlations between VOM effect size, represented as VOM percentage of reoffenders minus non-VOM percentage, and explanatory variables (and non-VOM groups' reoffense proportions) are shown in Table 8.2. The only statistically significant correlation between VOM effects and an explanatory variable was that with $\delta$, $r = -.77$; $t(17) = -4.98$, $p < .001$.

## Relationship Between VOM Effect Variance and GFM Scores

A graphic plot of VOM effects versus the ranking of GFM scores suggested that variability in VOM effects decreased as the GFM increased in rigor (see Figure 8.2). The variance of VOM effects (defined as the natural log of the odds ratio) for sites with GFM scores in the lower 50% of GFM scores was .896, and for sites with GFM scores in the upper 50%, .232, a statistically significant difference, $F(10,9) = 3.86$, $p < .025$. A V-known HGLM analysis was conducted in which the dispersion of VOM effects, represented by

$$d_j = \ln(s_j) + \frac{1}{2(n_j - 1)}$$

(where $d_j$ is the dispersion estimate of VOM effect sizes for quintile $j$, $s_j$ is the estimated standard deviation of VOM effect sizes in quintile $j$, and $n_j$ is the number of effect sizes in quintile $j$), was predicted from quintile of GFM scores (see Bryk & Raudenbush, 1992; Raudenbush et al., 2000). The results of this analysis were also indicative of decreasing variability in VOM effect sizes as quintile ranking of GFM score increased, $\chi^2(1) = 6.55$, $p < .015$. These results suggested that studies that used more methodologically sound group formation procedures led to results with lower across-study variability in VOM effects.

## Results for HGLM Binomial Model for All Data

*Stepwise entry results.* The results of fitting an unconditional HGLM binomial model to the data from all sites strongly suggested significant heterogeneity of VOM effects, estimated VOM effect parameter variance = .40, $\chi^2(18) = 97.5$, $p < .001$ (Bryk & Raudenbush, 1992). The first variable to enter into the VOM effect equation from the stepwise analysis was $\delta$, $\chi^2(1) = 28.0$, $p < .0001$. Duration of follow-up was the next variable found to be a statistically significant predictor of VOM effects after controlling for

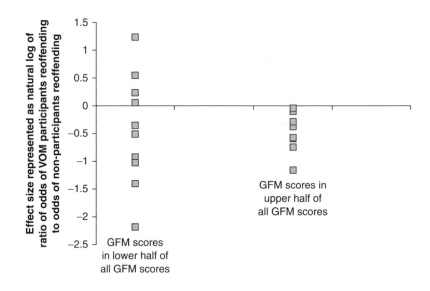

**Figure 8.2**    Graphic representation of dispersion of VOM effects, with VOM effect defined as the natural logarithm of the ratio of the odds of VOM participants reoffending to the odds of nonparticipants reoffending, as a function of which one half of the distribution of GFM scores a study site's GFM score was in.

$\delta$, $\chi^2(1) = 4.24$, $p < .04$, and this variable accounted for all of the remaining significant variation in VOM effects, estimated residual VOM effect variance = .04, $\chi^2(16) = 25.3$, $p > .05$.

The results of the misspecification tests suggested that the standard errors for $\delta$ and duration of follow-up may have been slightly underestimated when the VOM effect equation was estimated without any predictors in the equation for non-VOM groups' reoffense rates, and ameliorative strategies described by Bryk and Raudenbush (1992) led to results differing minimally from those described immediately above. These results suggested that when groups were matched in terms of percentages of violent offenders (i.e., $\delta = 0$), the study results would show that the odds of a VOM participant reoffending at 6 months post–court involvement would be approximately .54 as great as the odds of nonparticipants reoffending; .60 as great at 12 months; .68 as great at 18 months; .77 as great at 24 months; and .87 as great at 30 months post–court involvement. These results were consistent with Niemeyer & Shichor's (1996) speculation that VOM effects may decrease in magnitude across time.

*Simultaneous entry results.* The results from the HGLM model that contained all explanatory variables was statistically significant, $\chi^2(9) = 44.8$, $p < .00001$. Three variables were statistically significant predictors of VOM effect size, controlling for all other explanatory variables: $\delta$, $\chi^2(1) = 7.2$,

$p < .01$; definition of reoffense, $\chi^2(1) = 5.4$, $p < .02$; and GFM scores, $\chi^2(1) =$ 14.6, $p < .001$. Although the results of the misspecification analysis suggested that standard errors for $\delta$, duration of follow-up, and GFM scores may have been underestimated when no predictors were in the HGLM equation for non-VOM groups' reoffense rates, the results using ameliorative strategies suggested by Bryk and Raudenbush (1992) were consistent with the foregoing. The results of this analysis implied that, when $\delta = 0$ and the GFM score approached a level putting it in the upper quintile of the top quintile of currently available VOM research GFM scores (i.e., a GFM score of .87 or greater), the expected odds of VOM participants reoffending would be approximately .73 as great as the odds of nonparticipants reoffending when the narrow definition of reoffense was used. None of the sites with GFM scores in the upper quintile of the top quintile of GFM scores used the broader definition of reoffense, so no estimate of the expected odds ratio obtained in a study with this level of GFM can be made without the risks inherent in extrapolating beyond the range of joint observations (Neter, Wasserman, & Kutner, 1983). However, the results of this analysis implied that, when $\delta = 0$ and the GFM score approached a level putting it in the lower quintile of the top quintile of currently available VOM research GFM scores, the expected odds of VOM participants reoffending were about the same (.95) as the odds of nonparticipants reoffending.

*Synthesis of results.* The stepwise and simultaneous entry strategies suggested four possible explanatory variables for explaining VOM effects: $\delta$, duration of follow-up, definition of reoffense, and GFM scores. The results of analytic strategies identified $\delta$ as a predictor of VOM effects; however, the two analytic strategies disagreed on which of the other three explanatory variables were related to VOM effects. A second simultaneous HGLM binomial analysis was conducted in an effort to resolve the inconsistency in results between the two analytic approaches. In this simultaneous analysis, $\delta$, duration of follow-up, definition of reoffense, and GFM scores were entered simultaneously into the HGLM binomial model. The results suggested that $\delta$, $\chi^2(1) = 20.8$, $p < .0001$; definition of reoffense, $\chi^2(1) = 4.6$, $p < .05$; and GFM scores, $\chi^2(1) = 6.7$, $p < .01$, were statistically significant predictors of VOM effects, whereas duration of follow-up was not, $\chi^2(1) = .17$, $p > .50$. The results of a weighted least squares regression in which duration of follow-up was predicted from definition of reoffense and GFM scores showed that the multiple correlation between duration of follow-up and the combination of definition of reoffense and GFM scores was about .82, $F(2,16) = 16.0$, $p < .001$, results suggesting that in the stepwise analysis, duration of follow-up served as a proxy variable for the definition of reoffense–GFM score combination. A specific test of the six variables left out of the model that contained $\delta$, definition of reoffense, and GFM scores produced statistically nonsignificant results, $\chi^2(6) = 7.76$, $p > .25$. These results all converged to suggest that $\delta$, definition of reoffense, and GFM scores were most likely the explanatory variables that predicted VOM effects across the included studies, and that the relationship between duration of follow-up and VOM effects found in the stepwise analysis was a result of substantial collinearity between duration of follow-up and the combination of definition of reoffense and GFM scores.

## Results for Binomial Model for Sites With GFM Scores in Upper Quintile

The results of fitting an unconditional HGLM binomial model to the data from the sites with GFM scores in the top quintile suggested homogeneity of VOM effect parameter variance, estimated VOM effect variance = .06, $\chi^2(5) = 10.4$, $p > .05$. These results implied that, within this context of best available evidence in terms of GFM, the odds of VOM participants reoffending were about .70 as great as the odds of nonparticipants reoffending (approximate 95% confidence interval .52 to .94).

## Results From Alternate Analysis

Weighted least squares regression methods, described by Lipsey and Wilson (2001) were also used to analyze the VOM effect sizes. The results, not reported here because of space limitations, were consistent with those discussed above. This consistency provided some evidence that the foregoing results were not artifacts of a single data analysis method.

# Discussion and Application to Social Work Practice

The most significant limitation in this meta-analysis is the small number of included studies, a limitation implying that the results may be sensitive to the addition of only a small number of new studies. One particular limitation was the inclusion of only one randomized experiment, a limitation affecting the ability of the meta-analysis to provide results from the strongest possible GFM base. Another limitation concerns the possibility that studies meeting the inclusion criteria were missed in the literature search and not included. Although the search was comprehensive and there is no evidence that studies meeting the inclusion criteria were missed, the possibility nonetheless exists that studies were missed whose inclusion would have altered the results. Another limitation concerns the missing variables problem. This meta-analysis was a correlational study and, as such, vulnerable to the omission of explanatory variables that, had they been included in analyses, might have led to different results. These limitations all converge to suggest that the results be interpreted cautiously, provisionally, and tentatively.

Within this context of limitations, the results strongly suggested that the answer to the first research question was that VOM effects were not homogeneous and that variability in VOM effects was related to GFM. Specifically, results suggested that the variability in outcomes across studies decreased as the quality of GFM increased. The results also suggested that the answer to the second research question was that GFM, δ, and definition of reoffense may be factors related to significant variation in VOM effects. Finally, the results suggested that the answer to the third meta-analytic question was that, based on the best available GFM, there is indeed evidence that VOM participation is associated with a lower likelihood of reoffense. Results suggested that VOM participants may be as much as 30% less likely to reoffend as nonparticipants. These results clearly support continued research on the relationship between VOM participation and subsequent delinquent behavior.

The results suggested that the magnitude of VOM effects depended on not only group formation methodology but also on how reoffense was defined. The broader definition of reoffense used in some of the included studies implied a domain of events and activities that bring youths to the attention of law enforcement officers. This broad class of events and youth behaviors likely includes not only new delinquent behavior but also any of a number of events and situations not specifically related to new delinquent activity, such as being a known delinquent in an environment where a crime has occurred. A youth could easily come to the attention of law enforcement because he or she is a known delinquent and yet not have committed a new delinquent act subsequent to previous court involvement.

In contrast, the more narrow definition of reoffense implies a universe of indicators that includes not only events and behaviors that bring youths to the attention of law enforcement officials but also juvenile court activities the goals of which are, presumably, to validate accusations that a youth has engaged in a delinquent act. To the extent the juvenile court procedures accurately identify youths who have, and have not, committed delinquent acts, the more narrow definition of reoffense would appear to create a conceptual net more appropriate for identifying those who have engaged in delinquent behavior subsequent to VOM participation.

These considerations, if correct, imply that the above results suggested that (a) VOM participation may be associated with lower reoffense rates than nonparticipation and that (b) VOM participation may not be associated with a lower likelihood of new contacts with law enforcement agencies among youths who have a history of delinquent behavior. These speculations represent avenues for further future research on the relationship between VOM participation and subsequent delinquent behavior.

An interesting finding of this meta-analysis was that the explanatory variables identified as statistically significant predictors of VOM effects depended on the analytic strategy employed. The stepwise entry strategy led to findings somewhat different from those obtained when the simultaneous entry approach was used. This could be due to the fact that among the included studies, duration of follow-up was related to the combination of definition of reoffense and GFM score. Clearly, δ was an important predictor because it appeared as a statistically significant predictor regardless of the analytic strategy used. The chi-square statistic for duration of follow-up was statistically nonsignificant in the HGLM model that included all explanatory variables, as well as in the analysis in which duration of follow-up, δ, definition of reoffense, and GFM scores were simultaneously included in a HGLM binomial model, findings suggesting that definition of reoffense and GFM scores may have been the variables related to VOM effects. However, the reader should interpret the findings related to duration of follow-up, and to definition of reoffense and GFM scores, cautiously and in part as heuristic guides for future research.

The results of the analyses of the VOM effects from sites with GFM scores in the upper quintile of all GFM scores provide an estimate of the magnitude of VOM effects within the context of the best GFM that currently exists in the research literature. These results suggested that the odds of VOM participants reoffending may be .70 as great as the odds of nonparticipants reoffending. Thus, the results tentatively suggested a relationship between VOM participation and reduced delinquent activity. None of the above results provided any evidence that VOM participation was associated with an increase in delinquent behavior. This should be good news to anyone concerned that participation in restorative justice programs, such as VOM, may not be harsh enough on offenders and therefore lead to increases in delinquent activity. The findings of this meta-analysis, together with the findings from research on outcomes for victims who participate in VOM programs (see Umbreit et al., 2001) lend considerable support to the efforts of social workers to develop and work within VOM programs. Social workers in juvenile justice settings can use these findings to support the development of VOM programs, to advocate for juvenile justice policies that emphasize restorative justice approaches, and to use the VOM process to serve the victims of and perpetrators of juvenile delinquent behavior. There have been calls for harsher treatment of juvenile offenders, with the promise that a "just desserts" philosophy will deter delinquent activities. Research has suggested that this notion is in error (Risler, Sweatman, & Nackerud, 1998), and the results of this meta-analysis suggest that restorative justice approaches may hold great promise for the development of juvenile justice practices that lead to more positive outcomes for juvenile offenders and for the general public, as well as for victims.

# References

Brennan, R. (1983). *Elements of generalizability theory.* Iowa City, IA: ACT.
Bryk, A., & Raudenbush, S. (1992). *Hierarchical linear models.* Newbury Park, CA: Sage Publications.

Carr, C. (1998). *VORS evaluation report*. Los Angeles County, CA.

Carr, C., & Nelson, P. (2000). *Centinela Valley's victim offender restitution services*. Los Angeles: Centinela Valley Victim Offender Restitution Services.

Cosden, M., Casas, M., & Wolfe, M. (1999). *Evaluation of Santa Barbara's restorative justice project*. Santa Barbara, CA: University of California, Counseling, Clinical, and School Psychology Program.

Dick, E. (1999). *Victim offender reconciliation program of Mendocino County*. Mendocino, CA: VORP of Mendocino, California..

Dignan, J. (1990). *Repairing the damage: An evaluation of an experimental adult reparation scheme in Kettering, Northamptonshire*. Sheffield, UK: University of Sheffield, Centre for Criminological Legal Research, Faculty of Law.

Flaten, C. (1996). Victim offender mediation: Application with serious offenses committed by juvenile. In B. Galaway & J. Hudson (Eds.), *Restorative justice: International perspectives* (pp. 387–402). Monroe, New York: Library Research Associates Incorporated.

Galaway, B. (1988). Crime victim and offender mediation as a social work strategy. *Social Service Review, 62*, 668–683.

Gibson, M. (1999). Treatment of missing data at the second level of hierarchical linear models. *Dissertation Abstracts International, Section A: Humanities and Social Sciences, 60*(11-A), 3901. (AAI9949501)

Hitao, G. (1999). *Measures of program participation and success for the Redwood Empire Conflict Resolution Services Victim Offender Reconciliation Program*. Santa Rosa, CA: Data Trends.

Lee, S. (1999). *Victim offender mediation program evaluation*. San Jose, CA: Community Crime Prevention Associates.

Lipsey, M., & Wilson, D. (2001). *Practical meta-analysis*. Thousand Oaks, CA: Sage Publications.

Neter, J., Wasserman, W., & Kutner, M. (1983). *Applied linear regression models*. Homewood, IL: Richard D. Irwin.

Niemeyer, M., & Shichor, D. (1996). A preliminary study of a large victim offender reconciliation program. *Federal Probation, 60*(3), 30–34.

Nugent, W., & Paddock, J. (1996). Evaluating the effects of a victim-offender reconciliation program on reoffense. *Research on Social Work Practice, 6*(2), 155–178.

Nugent, W., Umbreit, M., & Williams-Hayes, M. (2003). The relationship between participation in victim offender mediation and the prevalence and severity of subsequent delinquent behavior. *Utah Law Review, 2003*(1), 137–166.

Raudenbush, S., Bryk, A., Cheong, Y., & Congdon, R. (2000). *HLM 5: Hierarchical linear and nonlinear models*. Lincolnwood, IL: Scientific Software.

Risler, E., Sweatman, T., & Nackerud, L. (1998). Evaluating the Georgia legislative waiver's effectiveness in deterring juvenile crime. *Research on Social Work Practice, 8*(6), 657–667.

Roberts, L. (1998). *Victim-offender mediation: An evaluation of the Pima County juvenile court center's victim offender mediation program (VOMP)*. Langley, Canada: Frasier Area Community Justice Initiatives.

Roy, S. (1993). Two types of juvenile restitution programs in two midwestern counties: A comparative study. *Federal Probation, 57*, 48–53.

Schichor, D., Sechrest, D., & Matthew, R. (2000). *Victim offender mediation in Orange County, California*. Santa Ana, CA: Institute for Conflict Management, St. Vincent de Paul Center for Community Reconciliation.

Schneider, A. (1990). *Deterrence and juvenile crime: Results from a national policy experiment.* New York: Springer-Verlag.

Stone, K. (2000). *An evaluation of recidivism rates for resolutions northwest's victim-offender mediation program.* Unpublished master's thesis, Portland State University, Portland, Oregon.

Stone, S., Helms, W., & Edgeworth, P. (1998). *Cobb County juvenile court mediation program evaluation.* Cobb County, GA: Juvenile Court Mediation Program.

Umbreit, M. (1994a). Mediating homicide cases: A journey of the heart through dialogue and mutual aid. *Victim-Offender Mediation, 5,* 1–4.

Umbreit, M. S. (1994b). *Victim meets offender: The impact of restorative justice and mediation.* Monsey, NY: Criminal Justice Press.

Umbreit, M. (2001). *The handbook of victim offender mediation.* San Francisco: Jossey-Bass.

Umbreit, M. S., & Coates, R. B. (1993). Cross-site analysis of victim-offender mediation in four states. *Crime & Delinquency, 39*(4), 565–585.

Umbreit, M., Coates, R. B., & Vos, B. (2001). The impact of victim-offender mediation: Two decades of research. *Federal Probation, 65*(3), 29–35.

Umbreit, M. S., & Greenwood, J. (1999). National survey of victim-offender mediation programs in the United States. *Mediation Quarterly, 16*(3), 235–251.

URSA Institute. (1993). *Final evaluation report: Community involvement in mediation of first and second time juvenile offenders project of the community board project of San Francisco.* Washington, DC: U.S. Department of Justice.

Wiinamaki, L. A. (1997). *Victim-offender reconciliation programs: Juvenile property offender recidivism and severity of reoffense in three Tennessee counties.* Unpublished doctoral dissertation, University of Tennessee, Knoxville.

Wynne, J. (1996). Leeds mediation and reparation service: Ten years' experience with victim-offender mediation. In B. Galaway & J. Hudson (Eds.), *Restorative justice: International perspectives* (pp. 445–461). Monsey, NY: Criminal Justice Press.

Zehr, H. (1990). *Changing lenses: A new focus for crime and justice.* Scottsdale, PA: Herald.

# At-Risk Youth

*Important Practice Points*

**Chapter 5**

- Mainstream treatments for juvenile delinquents are generally effective; however, the effects vary across programs. These programs are no less effective for minority youth than for White youth.

- This synthesis of programs indicates that cultural tailoring of programs is not necessary to achieve positive effects for minority youth being served. However, this does not imply that cultural sensitivity is unimportant and should not be a feature of services. There are not enough studies using standardized cultural tailoring to demonstrate whether or not this would produce larger effects for minority youth.

**Chapter 6**

- Ten studies were reviewed. None of the treatments could be characterized as "well-established," and thus considerable care needs to be taken in terms of their employment. Two studies were seen as possessing a likelihood of efficacy. Some intervention reduced the indirect markers of suicide.

- In terms of treatments that reduced suicide attempts and deliberate self-harm, a common theme is that these interventions were short-term and involved a family member in an outpatient setting. This was also true of treatments that reduced the indirect markers of suicide.

- Treatment manuals are obtainable, and this is often helpful in beginning to understand the systematic nature of standardized treatments.

**Chapter 7**

- This synthesis of treatments for adolescent substance abusers reveals that there are many types of interventions being used. Several interventions are effective in reducing substance use. For example, multidimensional family therapy is capable of producing and maintaining significant treatment gains for up to a year.

• Effect sizes greater than .20 have been attained by many treatments. It is important to understand, however, that there is often substantial degradation in treatment effect over time. Small effects can be important, particularly if the treatment can be used on a large scale.

• Because many of the effective treatments are family-centered and target a range of factors that influence adolescent chemical use behavior, social work practitioners should find the multidimensional nature of these treatments appealing. Because many of these treatments are standardized and manual based, their execution requires a high degree of fidelity.

## Chapter 8

• There was variability in the effects of victim-offender mediation programs. However, this was related to group formation methods. Overall, there is empirical evidence that participation in victim-offender mediation is associated with a decreased likelihood of reoffending.

• Results also show that participation in victim-offender mediation was not associated with any increases in delinquent offending.

• Restorative justice is an appealing alternative to punitive-retribution approaches to justice. It may also be less costly. Social work practitioners may find that advocating for well-executed victim-offender mediation programs is worthwhile.

# PART III

## Mental Health
## and Well-Being

*Overview and Key Questions*

Mental health disorders are pervasive. They are common both nationally and internationally. In fact, a recent study conducted by the World Health Organization (WHO) has demonstrated that the total disease burden from mental health disorders has been underestimated. Its estimates have concluded that mental health disorders account for a greater burden than all forms of cancer. Mental health disorders are varied and involve both chronic conditions and short-term episodes. These disorders interfere with daily functioning, such as education and employment, and therefore exact a heavy toll on families. It is critical not only to identify evidence-based treatments but also to develop more efficient and effective service delivery systems. Moreover, increased scientific information on special populations whom social workers frequently encounter is pressing. In Chapter 9, Marian L. Dumaine uses meta-analysis to examine intervention effects for persons with both severe mental illness and substance abuse. As social work practitioners regularly interact with persons with co-occurring disorders, sorting the wheat from the chaff in this area is critical. Following this, in Chapter 10, Sarah E. Bledsoe and Nancy K. Grote provide preliminary results of a quantitative synthesis for treating depression during pregnancy and the postpartum period. Leopoldo J. Cabassa and Marissa C. Hansen present findings from their systematic review of treatments for depression for Latino adults in primary care. Next, in Chapter 12, Edmon W. Tucker and Miriam Potocky-Tripodi execute a systematic review of the extant literature on changing heterosexuals' attitudes toward homosexuals. Finding useful methods that can be diffused into practice in order to mitigate the deleterious effects of discrimination based on sexual orientation is badly needed. The last chapter by David R. Hodge is a meta-analysis focused on prayer for the benefit of others (i.e., intercessory prayer). Although empirical science has yet to demonstrate the positive benefits of intercessory prayer, Hodge correctly points out that this practice is important to evaluate, given the historical and ongoing use of intercessory prayer as a therapeutic intervention.

As you read these selections, consider the following questions:

1. When considering the various populations affected by depressive disorders, to what extent are there treatment principles that are applicable across various groups?

2. What are some of the methodological limitations and practice barriers to widespread dissemination of programs to counteract the antigay attitudes of some heterosexuals?

3. What are some of the ethical considerations surrounding the evaluation of intercessory prayer?

# Meta-Analysis of Interventions With Co-Occurring Disorders of Severe Mental Illness and Substance Abuse

*9*

## Implications for Social Work Practice

*Marian L. Dumaine*

o-occurring disorders of severe mental illness and substance abuse (dual diagnosis) are a major mental health problem in this country, affecting 28% to 61% of the 4.6 million chronically mentally ill (U.S. Department of Health and Human Services, Substance Abuse and Mental Health Services Administration, 1995; Warner, Taylor, Wright, & Sloat, 1994). There are multiple issues to recognize in providing treatment to those who are dually diagnosed. First is the issue of prevalence. The Epidemiologic Catchment Area study data indicate that the likelihood of having a diagnosis of substance abuse is 4.6 times higher for those with schizophrenia and 6.6 times higher for those with bipolar disorder as compared with the rest of the general population (Regier et al., 1990). In addition, 47% of individuals with schizophrenia and 61% of individuals with a bipolar disorder have or have had an alcohol or illicit drug use disorder during their lifetime. The Epidemiologic Catchment Area study predates the availability of crack cocaine, suggesting that the prevalence is underestimated if this drug is factored in. Co-occurring disorders of this type are reported in 45% of emergency room patients and have, in fact, become so prevalent among the mentally ill that substance use is assumed (Mueser, Yarnold, & Bellack, 1992; Sullivan & Maloney, 1992). It is estimated

Originally published in Research on Social Work Practice 2003; 13; 142. DOI: 10.1177/ 1049731502250403 The online version of this article can be found at: http://rsw.sagepub.com/ cgi/content/abstract/13/2/142 that co-occurring disorders account for between one fourth and one half of the more than $148 billion spent by taxpayers for mental health care each year (Flynn, 1994; *Testimony on NIMH's FY 1998 Budget,* 1997), primarily through a significantly greater use of psychiatric inpatient and emergency services (Bartels, Drake, & Wallach, 1995).

Second, there is a greater likelihood that dually diagnosed clients experience more severe psychosocial stressors in their environment. Many are homeless (Center for Substance Abuse Treatment in Woody, 1996), evidence a greater potential for violence and self-injury, and find themselves in the criminal justice system where they receive less intense and fewer services (Drake, McLaughlin, Pepper, & Minkoff, 1991; Kivlahan, Heiman, Wright, Mundt, & Shupe, 1991). Furthermore, these clients have an increased risk of HIV infection, medical illness, and early mortality (Teague, Drake, & Ackerson, 1995), and more problems obtaining meals, managing money, and maintaining stable housing (Cuffel, Heithoff, & Lawson, 1993).

Third, managed care policies and financial cutbacks to programs threaten the existing and limited supports available for these clients (Weil, 1991). The number of state and county mental health hospital beds has declined dramatically by 84%, from more than half a million in 1955 to less than 100,000, leaving providers "bewildered, overtaxed, and struggling to find solutions" for these individuals, who often receive no treatment at all (Beaulieu & Flanders, 2000, p. 428).

Fourth, lack of accessible treatments and the fragmentation of services continue to exist. The dually diagnosed must access, negotiate, and secure services from two different and sometimes contradictory systems of care: mental health and substance abuse (Hoffman, DiRito, & McGill, 1993). Coordination of care between the two service systems with separate funding streams and treatment philosophies has been difficult, and many gaps remain (Burnam et al., 1995).

Finally, treatment interventions have generally not been effective with this population, who are often in crisis, unable to meet their basic needs, caught in a revolving door from hospital to community agency or residence to the street (Drake et al., 1998; Ridgely, 1991). In fact, a diagnosis of a co-occurring disorder has been found to be the greatest predictor of subsequent hospitalizations and the best indicator of missed-appointment rates (Ford, Snowden, & Walser, 1991), reinforcing the view of treatment of the dually diagnosed as "mission impossible" (Roberts, Shaner, Eckman, Tucker, & Vaccaro, 1992, p. 55).

In summary, the dually diagnosed present a major treatment challenge, whether at home, in the hospital or institution, or the community (Cuffel et al., 1993). Because this is a serious, persistent, and growing problem, there is a need to understand which treatments are beneficial in reducing the problems and maintaining those persons with a dual diagnosis in community-based systems of care.

Three prior systematic reviews of treatment interventions with this population were located. Drake et al. (1998) reviewed 36 studies of integrated treatment models. Mercer-McFadden, Drake, Brown, and Fox (1997) reviewed 13 community service projects funded by the National Institute of Mental Health (NIMH). Mueser and Noonday (1996) examined 11 studies of group treatment with the dually diagnosed. None, however, used a quantitative meta-analysis to identify and evaluate the strengths of the relationships between study characteristics and treatment outcomes or focused specifically on the role of the social worker.

The purpose of this study is to address three research questions: What client characteristics are correlated significantly with treatment intervention effectiveness? What practitioner characteristics are significantly correlated with treatment intervention effectiveness? What types of interventions are most effective? Suggestions for social work practice with the dually diagnosed are presented, based on both the quantitative analysis and treatment issues underscored in the selected studies.

## Method

The first step toward determining the most effective interventions with the dually diagnosed consisted of a literature search of studies published between 1990 and 1999. A search of the following computerized databases was conducted: Psychlit, Dissertation Abstracts, and Sociofile. In addition, a search was conducted by the National Clearinghouse for Alcohol and Drug Information. Keywords used were dual diagnosis, comorbidity, substance abuse mental illness, and co-occurring disorders.

The four inclusion criteria for study selection were (a) a psychosocial intervention was provided; (b) the clients were dually diagnosed, that is, individuals diagnosed with schizophrenia, schizoaffective disorder, bipolar I or major depression, and substance abuse; (c) a control or comparison group was used; and (d) quantitative outcomes were reported. Fifteen experimental or quasi-experimental studies were found to meet these conditions. A list of the studies selected and a summary of selected client and intervention characteristics to be studied in this meta-analysis are presented in Table 9.1.

The meta-analysis consisted of three steps. First, a content analysis was conducted to provide frequency counts for relevant client, practitioner, intervention, and methodology characteristics. Second, effect sizes were determined for each study intervention. Finally, effect sizes were correlated with the characteristics from Step 1 to determine which characteristics were associated with treatment effectiveness.

Seven of the studies in this meta-analysis did not report statistics that could be transformed into an estimate of effect size. Therefore, the results were coded using the conventional values of effect size: small (0.20), medium (0.50), and large (0.80) (Glass, McGaw, & Smith, 1981). The addition of two smaller effect sizes was needed to represent a lower level of improvement (0.10) and no improvement (0.00) of the dually diagnosed, because modifications to conventional effect size values are recommended to tailor data extraction to the characteristics of the client population (Welkowitz, Ewen, & Cohen, 1982).

Effect size was determined by examining the substantive significance of the intervention outcome. The criterion used to determine values was the degree of posttreatment stabilization and improvement in the experimental group's quality of life or functional status. Quality of life was defined as positive changes in clients associated with the intervention. Functional status was defined as an increased ability to maintain oneself in the community. Abstinence or the reduction of substance abuse did not affect the coding category classification. Each value was defined as follows: No improvement equals 0.00, or the treatment outcome was associated with no change in the experimental group's quality of life or functional status; very small equals 0.10, or treatment outcome was associated with little effect on the experimental group's quality of life or functional status; small equals 0.20, or treatment efficacy was limited to the study; medium equals 0.50, or less homelessness, more stable housing, less psychiatric hospital or institutional use, or if homeless, a reduction in antisocial behavior; and large equals 0.80, or less homelessness, more stable housing, less psychiatric hospital or institutional use, employment, and continued involvement in comprehensive, integrated services. The results of these studies were independently coded by a Ph.D. licensed clinical social worker and an MSW social work research assistant. The interrater reliability was 0.82; however, the effect sizes of the Ph.D. social worker were lower, and these more conservative statistics were chosen for data analysis in this study.

## Coding Scheme

The studies were coded for relevant client, practitioner, intervention, and methodology characteristics as follows.

*Client characteristics.* Each study was coded to determine the percentage of the total experimental subjects diagnosed with thought disorder (including schizoaffective disorder), mood disorder (major depression and bipolar I), and other mental illness. The following demographic categories were coded to reflect percents reported: age, gender, ethnicity (Caucasian, African American, and Hispanic), marital status, and residential status (homeless, group living, family, or independent). Education was coded as 1 if most subjects had not completed high school, 2 if most subjects had completed high school, and 3 if most subjects had post–high school training. The percentages of clients reported in the studies as veterans, unemployed, involuntary, and with a known legal history were noted. In addition, alcohol, marijuana, cocaine, polydrug, and combined alcohol and drug use were coded. The experimental dual diagnosis group was used whenever possible for these calculations, except in four instances when only combined characteristics of the experimental and control or comparison group

**Table 9.1** Summary of Dual Diagnosis Research Study Characteristics

| | Alfs and McClellan (1992) | Blankertz and Cnaan (1992) | Bond et al. (1991) | Burnam et al. (1995) | Drake et al. (1998) | Drake et al. (1997) | Durell et al. (1993) | Hellerstein et al. (1995) |
|---|---|---|---|---|---|---|---|---|
| **Client characteristics[a]** | | | | | | | | |
| **Mean percentage** | | | | | | | | |
| Age | — | 33.10 | 31.50 | 37.00 | 34.00 | 36.20 | 34.80 | 31.90 |
| Gender | | | | | | | | |
|   Male | — | 64.00 | 79.00 | 84.00 | 74.00 | 36.00 | 56.00 | 77.00 |
|   Female | — | 36.00 | 21.00 | 16.00 | 26.00 | 64.00 | 44.00 | 23.00 |
| Ethnicity | | | | | | | | |
|   Caucasian | — | 40.00 | 67.00 | 58.00 | 96.00 | 10.00 | 70.00 | 25.00 |
|   Black | — | 48.00 | 33.00 | 28.00 | — | 89.00 | 30.00 | 43.00 |
|   Hispanic | — | 12.00 | — | 14.00 | — | — | — | 32.00 |
| Marital status | | | | | | | | |
|   Unmarried/single | — | 85.00 | 97.00 | 94.00 | 85.00 | 98.00 | — | — |
| Residential status | | | | | | | | |
|   Homeless | — | 100.00 | — | 100.00 | 96.00 | 100.00 | — | — |
| Diagnosis | | | | | | | | |
|   Thought disorder | — | 78.00 | 70.00 | 45.00 | 75.00 | 50.00 | 89.00 | — |
|   Mood disorder | — | 16.00 | — | 55.00 | 24.00 | 47.00 | 7.00 | — |
|   Other mental illness | — | 6.00 | — | — | — | — | — | — |
| Substance abuse | | | | | | | | |
|   Alcohol | — | 66.00 | 61.00 | 79.00 | 73.00 | 55.00 | 16.00 | 92.00 |
|   Drug | — | — | 13.00 | 72.00 | 42.00 | — | — | — |
|   Polydrug | — | 57.00 | — | — | — | 61.00 | — | 66.00 |
| **Intervention characteristics** | | | | | | | | |
| **Number of clients** | | | | | | | | |
|   $E_1$ | 145.00 | 84.00 | 31.00 | 67.00 | 105.00 | 158.00 | 43.00 | 23.00 |
|   $E_2$ | — | 63.00 | 23.00 | 144.00 | — | — | — | — |
|   C | 126.00 | — | 43.00 | 65.00 | 98.00 | 59.00 | 41.00 | 24.00 |

(Continued)

**Table 9.1** (Continued)

| | Alfs and McClellan (1992) | Blankertz and Cnaan (1992) | Bond et al. (1991) | Burnam et al. (1995) | Drake et al. (1998) | Drake et al. (1997) | Durell et al. (1993) | Hellerstein et al. (1995) |
|---|---|---|---|---|---|---|---|---|
| Methodology treatment | Quasi | Quasi | Quasi | Exptl | Exptl | Quasi | Quasi | Exptl |
| E1 | DTSG | RTSG | ICMSG | RTSF | ICMSG | ICMSG | ICM | SCSG |
| E2 | — | RT | SCSG | DT | — | — | — | — |
| C | DT | — | SC | SC | SCSG | SC | ICM | SCSG |
| Duration of treatment | 6–8 wks | 5.5 mo. | 18 mo. | 9 mo. | 36 mo. | 18 mo. | 18 mo. | 8 mo. |
| Effect size | 0.20 | 0.50 | 0.10 | 0.10 | 0.20 | 0.50 | 0.20 | 0.00 |
| Client characteristics[a] | | | | | | | | |
| Mean percentage | | | | | | | | |
| Age | 33.40 | 33.30 | — | 31.00 | 39.00 | 33.40 | 35.80 | |
| Gender | | | | | | | | |
| Male | 74.00 | 67.00 | 75.00 | 73.00 | 50.00 | 100.00 | 100.00 | |
| Female | 26.00 | 33.00 | 25.00 | 27.00 | 50.00 | — | — | |
| Ethnicity | | | | | | | | |
| Caucasian | 23.00 | — | 70.00 | 33.00 | 47.00 | 18.00 | 33.00 | |
| Black | 77.00 | — | — | 67.00 | 47.00 | 60.00 | 50.00 | |
| Hispanic | — | — | — | — | 6.00 | 22.00 | 17.00 | |
| Marital status | | | | | | | | |
| Unmarried/single | 92.00 | — | — | — | — | 85.00 | — | |
| Residential status | | | | | | | | |
| Homeless | — | — | — | — | 100.00 | 58.00 | 92.00 | |
| Diagnosis | | | | | | | | |
| Thought disorder | 28.00 | 42.00 | 76.00 | 65.00 | — | 59.00 | 59.00 | |
| Mood disorder | 14.00 | 58.00 | — | 35.00 | — | 20.00 | 33.00 | |
| Other mental illness | — | — | — | — | — | — | — | |
| Substance abuse | | | | | | | | |
| Alcohol | 46.00 | 33.00 | 40.00 | 79.00 | — | 22.00 | 100.00 | |
| Drug | — | — | — | 14.00 | — | — | — | |
| Polydrug | — | 17.00 | 19.00 | — | — | — | — | |

| | Alfs and McClellan (1992) | Blankertz and Cnaan (1992) | Bond et al. (1991) | Burnam et al. (1995) | Drake et al. (1998) | Drake et al. (1997) | Durell et al. (1993) | Hellerstein et al. (1995) |
|---|---|---|---|---|---|---|---|---|
| Intervention characteristics | | | | | | | | |
| Number of clients | | | | | | | | |
| $E_1$ | 286.00 | 12.00 | 48.00 | 29.00 | 67.00 | 317.00 | 12.00 | |
| $E_2$ | — | — | 45.00 | — | — | 299.00 | — | |
| C | 141.00 | 16.00 | 39.00 | 25.00 | 47.00 | — | 12.00 | |
| Methodology treatment | Exptl | Quasi | Quasi | Exptl | Exptl | Exptl | Quasi | |
| $E_1$ | IP | IP | SCSG | ICMSG | ICM | RTSG | IP | |
| $E_2$ | — | — | SCSG | — | — | RT | — | |
| C | IP | IP | ICM | SC | ICM | — | IP | |
| Duration of treatment | 28 days | 2 mo. | 18 mo. | 12 mo. | 31 mo. | 12 mo. | 7 days | |
| Effect size | 0.10 | 0.00 | 0.50 | 0.00 | 0.50 | 0.10 | 0.20 | |

NOTE: Dashes = no data; E = experimental dually diagnosed group; C = comparison singly diagnosed group; Quasi = quasi-experimental design; Exptl = experimental design; DTSG = day treatment with specialized groups; RTSG = residential treatment with specialized groups; ICMSG = intensive case management with specialized groups; ICM = intensive case management; SCSG = standard care with specialized groups; IP = inpatient; RT = residential treatment; DT = day treatment; SC = standard care.

a. Client characteristics describes experimental group if reported separately, otherwise total dual diagnosis sample.

were given (Blankertz & Cnaan, 1992; Herman et al., 1997; Hellerstein, Rosenthal, & Miner, 1995; Ridgely & Jerrell, 1996).

*Practitioner characteristics.* Each study was coded to determine the ratio of practitioner to clients, as well as the extent of prior specialized training and experience. The presence of a social worker and substance abuse counselor also were coded to determine if the unique roles of these disciplines in treatment of the dually diagnosed were identified.

*Intervention characteristics.* The length and type of each treatment were coded, with the type of treatment ranked by settings from least to most restrictive, as follows: 1 = standard aftercare treatment, 2 = standard aftercare and outpatient psychoeducational groups, 3 = standard aftercare and intensive case management with no specialized outpatient psychoeducational groups, 4 = standard aftercare and intensive case management with specialized outpatient psychoeducational groups, 5 = standard aftercare and day treatment, 6 = nonintegrated residential treatment, 7 = integrated residential treatment with structured psychoeducational groups, and 8 = inpatient treatment. Furthermore, it was noted whether a psychosocial orientation was used in addition to the medical approach.

Standard aftercare treatment consists of regular (usually monthly) contact with a psychiatrist at a community mental health center for medication monitoring, as well as access to an assigned case manager for service coordination, linkage, and outreach. Outpatient psychoeducational groups entail regular (usually weekly) meetings with a group facilitator specifically tailored to address substance abuse among clients with severe mental illness through education, peer support, and skills training (Mueser & Noordsy, 1996). Intensive case management entails the use of multidisciplinary teams that directly and continuously provide comprehensive services to clients in their living environment (Test, 1992). Day treatment entails a minimum of 4 hours daily of supportive group treatment, mental health and substance abuse education, and behavioral skills training. Nonintegrated residential treatment consists of parallel mental health and substance abuse services, one on-site and the other off-site, to clients living in a supervised community setting, whereas integrated residential treatment consists of integrated on-site services. Inpatient treatment is defined as inpatient hospitalization on either a detoxification unit or a specialized unit for the treatment of mental illness or substance abuse.

*Outcome characteristics.* Several categories of outcome measures were coded in this analysis: 1 = compliance with treatment, including attendance and drop-out rates; 2 = rates of rehospitalization, psychiatric crises, use of hospital days, and length of community tenure; 3 = psychiatric symptomatology; 4 = severity of alcohol addiction or alcohol use; 5 = severity of drug addiction or drug use; 6 = substance abuse relapse; 7 = functioning level and employment; 8 = quality of life; 9 = housing stability; 10 = legal incidents; 11 = knowledge and motivation relative to dual diagnosis; and 12 = client satisfaction.

*Methodology characteristics.* Several aspects of the studies were categorized to assess the stringency of the research methodology: 1 = number of subjects in each treatment, control, or comparison group; 2 = type of research design; 3 = measurement reliability of the data sources; 4 = the use of corroborative data sources; 5 = number of standardized measures used; 6 = number of categories of outcomes reported; and 7 = attrition rate. The type of the research design was coded 1 if it was quasi-experimental and 2 if it was experimental. Measurement reliability ratings of the data sources were coded as 1 if no procedures to increase reliability were reported, 2 if one or two procedures were reported, and 3 if three or more were reported. It was noted if corroborative data sources of the treatment effects were used (i.e., structured interviews, record reviews, reports from significant others, and computerized records of interagency contacts). Finally, attrition was coded as 1 if it was high (> 40%) and unequal for both the experimental and control or comparison group or high for the experimental group only; 2 for high and equal; 3 for moderate (20%–40%) and unequal, or moderate for the single experimental group only; 4 for moderate and equal; 5 for low (< 20%) and unequal, or low for the experimental group only; and 6 for low and equal.

# Results

The selected characteristics of the 15 studies are summarized in Table 9.1. For each chosen characteristic reported as percentages (e.g., schizophrenia, Caucasian, etc.), the mean percentage and standard deviation of studies reporting on that characteristic are reported. For each chosen characteristic reported as means (e.g., age, length of treatment), the average mean and standard deviation are reported. For each chosen characteristic reported as a categorical variable (e.g., presence of a social worker), the percentage of studies reporting the presence of the chosen characteristic is reported. Finally, correlations of effect size and selected client, practitioner, and intervention characteristics are presented, as well as the effect size for each type of treatment.

*Client characteristics* (see Table 9.2). Sixty-four percent of the clients were diagnosed with a thought disorder and evidenced the characteristics of the young chronic population with major mental illness and substance abuse: male, single, unemployed, in their mid-30s ($M = 34.34$, $SD = 2.31$). Most of the studies (75%) reported that the clients had completed high school. Of the nine studies reporting residential status, most of the clients were either homeless (79%) or in a supervised group-living situation (11%). Prior legal charges were reported in four studies ($M = 0.40$, $SD = 0.16$), and involuntary status was reported in seven studies ($M = 0.10$, $SD = 0.18$). Themes of childhood maltreatment and abandonment were reported in their backgrounds, as well as parental mental health or substance abuse problems, especially among the homeless.

Substance use and abuse were defined differently in the studies and ranged from definitions based on client self-report, client records, reports by significant others, addiction severity scales, or a combination of these methods. Different substances of abuse were variably reported, with alcohol most frequently indicated. However, although pre-1995 studies within the sample reported the extensive use of alcohol and marijuana, the later studies (post-1995) reported greater use of cocaine and polysubstances.

*Practitioner characteristics* (see Table 9.2). Interventions were administered by mental health agencies and hospitals, all using both medical and psychosocial models. All studies reported multidisciplinary treatment teams, although the specific practitioner characteristics, composition, and experience of the psychiatrists, nurses, substance abuse counselors, and social workers were not extensively described. Case management was discussed, although it was not clear who was providing the case management. It was inferred from the studies that all practitioners had some prior related training, whereas some had extensive and specialized training (40%), but the specific training content was rarely reported. Practitioner professional qualifications and licensing were not reported. It was unclear if the social worker position was filled by an individual possessing undergraduate or graduate social work credentials or a license. Of the six studies reporting practitioner-to-client ratios, the average was 1 to 10.

*Intervention and outcome characteristics* (see Table 9.3). The treatments ranged from the least restrictive—standard aftercare—to the most restrictive—inpatient—with the former being used most often as the control group intervention. Six of the studies used a comparison group composed of singly diagnosed clients with the following interventions: Two studies used intensive case management, one used day treatment, and three used inpatient treatment. The other nine studies examined a total of 27 treatments with dually diagnosed clients only, either in experimental or control groups. The most frequent intervention in these nine studies was standard aftercare with psychoeducational groups, although the most frequent intervention with the control groups was standard aftercare.

The length of the treatment interventions ranged from 7 days to 3 years, with a mean of 12.69 months ($SD$ = 10.77). Inpatient treatment was short term ($M$ = 1.05 months), whereas the duration of the other treatments varied from 1.5 to 36 months. The outcomes of half of the treatment interventions were measured after a year or more of treatment. This lengthy reporting period was used because the dually diagnosed are severely impaired, needing medication and support for most of their lives; therefore, treatment effects might not have been immediately apparent.

The most frequent primary goals of the treatment interventions were attendance or compliance with treatment, reduction of psychiatric symptomatology or substance use, and improved functioning. Less attention was paid to quality of life, client satisfaction, and cost of services. Dropout before, during, and after treatment was pervasive.

**Table 9.2**        Frequency of Study Characteristics: Client and Practitioner

| Variable (number of studies reporting) | Mean Percentage[a] | Standard Deviation |
|---|---|---|
| Client characteristics | | |
| Diagnosis | | |
| Thought disorder (1) | 64 | 20 |
| Schizoaffective (5) | 33 | 23 |
| Mood disorder (10) | 31 | 18 |
| Major depression (5) | 17 | 12 |
| Bipolar (5) | 16 | 11 |
| Other diagnosis (4) | 20 | 24 |
| Ethnicity (13) | | |
| Caucasian (13) | 45 | 25 |
| African American (11) | 52 | 20 |
| Hispanic (6) | 17 | 9 |
| Age (13) (mean) | 34.34 | 2.31 |
| Marital status (7) | | |
| Unmarried | 91 | 5 |
| Gender (14) | | |
| Male | 72 | 17 |
| Employment status (6) | | |
| Unemployed | 95 | 4 |
| Education (8) Completed high school | 75[b] | |
| Residential status (9) | | |
| Homeless (6) | 79 | 37 |
| Structured or supervised residence (1) | 11 | 5 |
| Independent (2) | 8 | 3 |
| Legal status (8) | | |
| Involuntary (7) | 10 | 18 |
| Prior legal history (4) | 40 | 16 |
| Substance use (13) | | |
| Alcohol (13) | 59 | 26 |
| Cocaine (7) | 37 | 21 |
| Marijuana (6) | 33 | 28 |
| Polydrug (8) | 38 | 25 |
| Alcohol and drugs (5) | 54 | 8 |
| Practitioner characteristics | | |
| Discipline (15) | | |
| Presence of social worker | 80 | |
| Presence of substance abuse counselor | 80 | |
| Practitioner-to-client ratio (6) (mean ratio) | 1:10 | |
| Training (15) | | |
| Moderate | 60 | |
| Extensive or specialized | 40 | |

a. Mean percentage of characteristic in studies reporting characteristic.

b. Categorical variable; percentage of studies reporting chosen characteristic in studies reporting on the variable.

*Research methodology characteristics* (see Table 9.4). Six of the studies used an experimental design, whereas nine studies used a quasi-experimental design. Almost half of the studies (47%) used three or more procedures to increase measurement reliability, and 80% employed corroborative measures of the treatment effects. The mean number of standardized scales used was 3 (*SD* = 1.83), ranging from 0 to 6. The number of outcomes measured ranged from 2 to 10 (*M* = 5.5, *SD* = 2.20). The mean number of subjects was 95 (*SD* = 95), ranging from 12 to 317.

Attrition was high or unequal for the experimental versus the comparison group in more than half of the studies reporting on this variable, and it was often reported as the outcome variable "compliance."

**Table 9.3**     Frequency of Study Characteristics: Intervention Characteristics

| Variable (number of studies reporting) | Mean Percentage[a] |
|---|---|
| Type of treatment to singly diagnosed (6) | |
| Intensive case management and no specialized groups | 33 |
| Day treatment | 17 |
| Inpatient treatment | |
| Type of treatment to dually diagnosed (27[b]) | 50 |
| Standard aftercare | 15 |
| Outpatient psychoeducational groups/standard aftercare | 23 |
| Intensive case management and no specialized groups | 11 |
| Intensive case management with specialized groups | 15 |
| Day treatment | 7 |
| Nonintegrated residential treatment | 7 |
| Integrated residential treatment | 11 |
| Inpatient treatment | 11 |
| Length of treatment in months (15) (mean) | 12.69 (*SD* = 10.71) |
| Treatment goals (78[b]) | |
| Attendance/drop-out rates | 15 |
| Psychiatric symptomatology | 13 |
| Rehospitalization rates, psychiatric crises | 12 |
| Severity of alcohol addiction and use | 12 |
| Functioning level | 12 |
| Severity of drug addiction and use | 10 |
| Substance abuse relapse | 6 |
| Quality of life | 6 |
| Stable housing | 6 |
| Legal incidents | 5 |
| Knowledge and motivation | 1 |
| Client satisfaction | 1 |
| Costs | 1 |

a. Categorical variable; percentage of studies reporting chosen characteristic in studies reporting on the variable.

b. *N* > 15 due to multiple categories reported in some studies.

**Table 9.4**    Frequency of Study Characteristics: Methodology Characteristics

| Variable (number of studies reporting) | Mean Percentage[a] |
|---|---|
| Size of experimental group (15) (mean) | 95 (SD = 95) |
| Comparison group (15) | |
|    Dually diagnosed | 80 |
|    Singly diagnosed | 20 |
| Research design (15) | |
|    Experimental | 40 |
|    Quasi-experimental | 60 |
| Reliability of measures (15) | |
|    Low | 20 |
|    Medium | 33 |
|    High | 47 |
| Number of standard measures (15) (mean) | 3.1 (SD = 1.83) |
| Number of outcomes (15) (mean) | 5.5 (SD = 2.20) |
| Attrition (13) | |
|    High/unequal | 38 |
|    High/equal | 8 |
|    Moderate/unequal | 23 |
|    Low/equal | 31 |

a. Categorical variable; percentage of studies reporting chosen characteristic in studies reporting on the variable.

## Research Questions Results

*Client characteristics and treatment intervention effectiveness* (see Table 9.5). Of the client characteristics examined, age and unemployed were significantly positively correlated with effect size, whereas male and being Hispanic were significantly inversely correlated with effect size. A diagnosis of schizoaffective disorder was highly inversely correlated with effect size ($r = .87$), a result that approached statistical significance ($p = .054$). Other demographic characteristics were not significantly correlated with treatment effectiveness.

Although type of substance used was not statistically significantly correlated with effect size, it was noted in several studies that cocaine use was associated with more negative outcomes than alcohol use, and that it was often difficult to extricate clients from the drug peer group (Drake, Yovetich, Bebout, Harris, & McHugo, 1997; Meisler, Blankertz, Santos, & McKay, 1997). A distinction also was made in one study between substance-sensitive participants who needed to reduce use and benefited from psychoeducational groups and substance dependent participants who required the structured format of Alcoholics Anonymous/Narcotics Anonymous aimed at abstinence (Bond, McDonel, Miller, & Pensec, 1991).

**Table 9.5**      Correlations of Effect Size and Client Characteristics

| Variable (number of studies reporting) | Correlation |
|---|---|
| Diagnosis | |
| Thought disorder (13) | .09 |
| Schizoaffective disorder (5) | −.87 |
| Mood disorder (10) | −.10 |
| Bipolar (5) | −.37 |
| Major depression (5) | −.32 |
| Other diagnosis (4) | .36 |
| Substance abuse | |
| Alcohol use (13) | −.17 |
| Cocaine use (7) | .33 |
| Marijuana use (6) | −.21 |
| Drug and alcohol use (5) | −.19 |
| Polydrug use (8) | .04 |
| Other demographic and treatment characteristics | |
| Age (13) | .56* |
| Unmarried (7) | −.03 |
| Male (14) | −.56* |
| Homeless (7) | .45 |
| Unemployed (6) | .89* |

*$p < .05$.

*Practitioner characteristics and treatment effectiveness* (see Table 9.6). The specific composition and experience of the practitioners were inconsistently reported, and no statistically significant correlations were found between practitioner training or practitioner-to-client ratio and effect size.

*Intervention characteristics and treatment effectiveness* (see Table 9.7). The overall average effect size for the studies was low (0.22), ranging from 0 to 0.50. Intensive case management with no specialized outpatient psychoeducational groups received the highest average effect size (0.35), followed by standard aftercare with specialized outpatient psychoeducational groups (0.25), whereas inpatient treatment received the lowest (0.13). The low effect size assigned for inpatient treatment was related to the lack of substantive difference in outcome between inpatient integrated and nonintegrated treatment, as well as the short-term impact of the outcome measures reported (e.g., increased knowledge). No statistically significant correlation was found between length of treatment or treatment restrictiveness and effect size.

*Summary of quantitative results.* Most clients evidenced the characteristics of the young chronic population with major mental illness and substance abuse: male, single, unemployed, and ranging in age from 31 to 39 years. Increased use of cocaine and polysubstances was noted in later studies.

**Table 9.6**      Correlations of Effect Size: Practitioner and Intervention Characteristics

| Variable (number of studies reporting) | Correlation |
| --- | --- |
| Practitioner characteristics | |
| Staff training (15) | .37 |
| Ratio of staff to clients (6) | .10 |
| Intervention characteristics | |
| Restrictiveness of treatment (15) | −.23 |
| Length of treatment (15) | .35 |

Of all the characteristics examined (client, practitioner, and intervention), only some of the client characteristics were statistically correlated with effect size: age, male, Hispanic, and unemployed. The implications of the association of unemployment and Hispanic, both characteristics reported in six studies, with effect size are unclear and would require further study. The impact of gender on outcome is not known, although most clients were male (72%). Increasing age might be associated with improved coping skills, thereby influencing treatment outcome. It should be noted that if a more stringent statistical level (e.g., $p < .01$) was applied to the correlation results to correct for performing multiple correlations with the same data, none of the characteristics would reach statistical significance.

The average length of treatment was more than a year ($M = 12.69$), with most treatment interventions ranging from 2 months to 2 years. Treatment dropout was high. Effect sizes were highest for intensive case management and standard aftercare with specialized outpatient psychoeducational groups. In addition, specific assessment and treatment planning recommendations were underscored.

# Discussion and Applications to Social Work Practice

A content analysis of the studies was conducted to extract recommendations for assessment and treatment planning. Social work practice implications, based on the results of the quantitative analysis and specific recommendations identified in the studies, involve eight key intervention areas: outreach; engagement; assessment; goal setting; leverage, structure, and limit setting; linkage, coordination, and integration of treatment services; long-term continuity of care; and advocacy and resource development. Many of these intervention areas (outreach; linkage, coordination, and integration of treatment services; advocacy and resource development) are intrinsic to case management, the intervention associated with the greatest effect size (Solomon, 1992).

**Table 9.7**      Effect Sizes by Experimental Group Treatment Type

| Variable (number of studies reporting) | Effect Size |
|---|---|
| Experimental group treatment type (15) | |
|     Intensive case management with no specialized groups (2) | .35 |
|     Standard aftercare/outpatient psychoeducational groups (2) | .25 |
|     Integrated residential treatment (3) | .23 |
|     Intensive case management with specialized groups (4) | .20 |
|     Day treatment (1) | .20 |
|     Inpatient treatment (3) | .13 |

*Outreach.* Outreach is needed to engage the dually diagnosed in treatment, and it entails bringing services to clients in a variety of settings (Drake et al., 1997). Social workers need to provide services to the dually diagnosed while in crisis in hospitals and jails, on the streets, in self-help groups, health clinics, or with families. Extensive and consistent outreach is crucial upon discharge from inpatient and residential facilities.

*Engagement.* During the early stages of treatment, engagement is crucial to prevent dropout and serves as preparation for more formal interventions (Blankerz & Cnaan, 1992). Dually diagnosed clients need support and understanding and gradual persuasion to commit to reduced substance use through recovery rewards and instruction. Engagement might be facilitated by assertive case management (Drake et al., 1997). These findings are mirrored in even earlier research (Brown, Ridgely, Pepper, Levine, & Ryglewicz, 1989; Kline, Harris, Bebout, & Drake, 1991; Osher & Kofoed, 1989).

*Assessment.* The pervasiveness of substance use disorders in persons with severe mental illness was recognized by every study, as well as its deleterious effect on adjustment. Dually diagnosed clients often deny or minimize substance use, and treatment needs and responsiveness are related to type and frequency of substance used. Psychosocial assessments of individuals with mental illness should routinely include exploration of types and patterns of substance use.

One of the studies in this analysis offered the insight that the seeds of distress are sown early, meaning that many of the dually diagnosed were childhood victims of abuse and abandonment, and their parents often evidenced mental health and substance abuse problems (Rahav et al., 1995). Social workers should explore the role of early childhood experiences and parental influences in the present maladjustment. If these early childhood experiences are associated with an exacerbation of mental illness, substance abuse, and the capacity to parent effectively, the need for early childhood intervention is supported, as well as interventions to help clients overcome coping barriers related to earlier traumas and family stressors.

The majority of the dually diagnosed clients were men in their mid-30s, unemployed, unmarried, and living in structured or supervised residences.

During these midlife years, it is common for individuals to establish a vocation, commit to long-term relationships, and begin a family. The impact of the possible disparity between life goals and current reality for these individuals is unknown and should be included in assessment and treatment planning.

*Goal Setting.* Expectations for positive treatment outcomes need to be reframed to reflect a long-term perspective, with realistic short-term goals based on client stage of readiness, because treatment engagement is difficult, dropout is high, and many continue to evidence increased psychiatric crises and impaired functioning levels despite treatment. Total abstinence, particularly during the initial stages of treatment, is unrealistic (Blankertz & Cnaan, 1992; Burnam et al., 1995; Durell, Lechtenberg, Corse, & Frances, 1993; Lehman, Herron, Schwartz, & Myers, 1993; Meisler et al., 1997). Intervention strategies and goals should differ based on stage of readiness for treatment. For example, educational, persuasive, and nonconfrontational interventions are recommended for persons who are marginally connected to treatment and evidence low motivation levels (Meisler et al., 1997) during the first phase of entry to "boost participation" (Burnam et al., 1995. p. 130). Once engaged, social skills training, cognitive remediation, and assertive case management with behavioral contracts are indicated. Individuals in the recovery phase might be responsive to education about relapse prevention strategies and the development of support networks. Consequently, the goals change depending on treatment readiness—from awareness of impact of substance use, to reduction of substance use, and finally to possible abstinence (Lehman et al., 1993). Stage of treatment readiness might be assessed by a scale developed by McHugo, Drake, Burton, and Ackerson (1995), which uses a motivational hierarchy.

Long-term functioning goals reflecting a gradual stepwise progression over time are useful and permit differential comparisons among different levels of and across interventions. The adoption of a more global, holistic perspective that reflects magnitudes of change over time might constitute a strategy toward the interventions attaining clinical significance (Tripodi, 1990, as cited in Videka-Sherman & Reid, 1990, p. 287).

*Leverage, structure, and limit setting.* Leverage is useful in countering the clients' reluctance to become consistently involved in treatment (Blankertz & Cnaan, 1992). A clearly articulated contingency contract, delineating program expectations associated with the reward of financial assistance or other desired client needs or wants, might increase client compliance (Durell et al., 1993; Lehman et al., 1993). Leverage might consist of the agency functioning as co-payee, and avoidance of rescuing clients from the natural consequences of substance use. The social worker's decision not to rescue clients should be based on a studied consideration of the client's current circumstances and history, as well as the possible long-term aftereffects. The challenge is to simultaneously set limits and monitor treatment compliance, while providing nurturance based on individualized needs and presenting behaviors.

*Linkage, coordination, and integration of treatment services.* The dually diagnosed need assistance in locating, accessing, and using community resources (Herman et al., 1997; Lehman et al., 1993; Rahav et al., 1995).

In addition, these clients face obstacles transitioning to less restrictive programs because of the lack of community resources, particularly housing (Hoffman et al., 1993; Wilens, Saley, Renner, & O'Keefe, 1994). The scarcity of specialized residential facilities often results in discharges to unstructured settings, thereby perpetuating the cycle of crisis, intense treatment, and discharge.

Coordination of services between multiple service providers as well as family and informal support networks is needed. Clients whose services are nonintegrated must negotiate both the mental health and substance abuse systems, meet requirements for each system, and build their own support network in a piecemeal fashion. The dually diagnosed often experience difficulty securing assistance from each system simultaneously, because the qualifications for services from one system sometimes preclude receiving services from the other. In addition, these clients need a changing matrix of social services depending on their symptoms, resources, and psychosocial stressors. Coordination of services is needed to avoid "ping-pong therapy" (Ridgely, 1991, p. 30).

*Long-term continuity of care.* The positive correlation of effect size with age suggests that maturity or years of prior treatment might be an important factor in treatment effectiveness. If age reflects more years in treatment, an increased knowledge and acceptance of one's illness, or improved coping skills, it is possible that older clients are more receptive to treatment and that a long-term perspective about progress toward recovery should be adopted.

In fact, the need for consistent, coordinated care over a period of years rather than brief sequential interventions was frequently cited (Drake et al., 1997). The implication is that social workers might need to be involved with dually diagnosed clients long-term, adjusting interventions based on level of severity of both mental illness and substance abuse, as well as progress toward recovery.

Staff burnout is frequent (Blankertz & Cnaan, 1992), a trend that was also noted by earlier researchers (Brown et al., 1989) who found that social workers experience frustration, feelings of hopelessness, and possibly disgust when working with the dually diagnosed and when having to deal with multiple conflicting agency and organizational services. Furthermore, these clients frequently relapse, need many concrete services, and are often in crisis (Lehman et al., 1993). More effective staff training modules are needed that reflect an increased understanding of the dynamics related to dual diagnosis, and suggestions are needed for more promising treatment directions (Brown et al., 1989; Burnam et al., 1995). Additional alleviative measures include regularly allocating staff time for specialized training, the use of team responses, small caseloads, and a focus on strategies geared toward increasing motivation, morale, and enthusiasm (Jerrell & Ridgely, 1995).

*Advocacy and resource development.* Additional community resources, particularly community residential services, are needed to provide supports to the dually diagnosed (Blankertz & Cnaan, 1992; Burnam et al., 1995; Hoffman et al., 1993). Ongoing, active advocacy by social workers is needed to remove barriers related to limited funding and contradictory treatment philosophies of the mental health and substance abuse communities.

Mental health and substance abuse funding and service delivery systems should be integrated or their linkage facilitated to ensure that the dually diagnosed do not remain "system misfits" (Howland, 1993, p. 1134). More focused attention through long-range, coordinated efforts needs to be given to the problems of the dually diagnosed. Although these persons are often considered treatment failures, with high rates of noncompliance, frequent rehospitalizations, relapse, psychiatric symptomatology, and impaired functioning levels, they gradually respond positively to consistent outreach and engagement efforts. Suggested treatment interventions based on this meta-analysis are intensive case management and standard aftercare with specialized outpatient psychoeducational treatment groups.

Longitudinal studies are needed to examine the impact of psychosocial stressors on dual diagnosis. More specific treatment protocols, including outreach, leverage, structure, limit setting, and coordination of care, need to be developed and evaluated. Additional research is needed to compare the efficacy of different treatment approaches at different stages of readiness for treatment. Long-range follow-up studies are needed to assess factors associated with treatment engagement, improved functioning, and abstinence. Strategies for reducing worker burnout should be examined. Finally, the specific roles of the social worker in the treatment of the dually diagnosed need to be determined and assessed. Although the challenges of treating this population are great, a cumulative knowledge base founded on varied treatment experiences provides insights about effective social work interventions.

# Appendix

The following references indicate studies included in the meta-analysis: Alfs and McClellan (1992); Blankertz and Cnaan (1992); Burnam et al. (1995); Drake et al. (1998); Drake, Yovetich, Bebout, Harris, and McHugo (1997); Durell, Lechtenberg, Corse, and Frances (1993); Hellerstein, Rosenthal, and Miner (1995); Herman et al. (1997); Hoffman, DiRito, and McGill (1993); Jerrell and Ridgely (1995); Meisler, Blankertz, Santos, and McKay (1997); Rahav et al. (1995); Ridgely and Jerrell (1996); Wilens, Saley, Renner, and O'Keefe (1994).

# References

Alfs, D. S., & McClellan, T. A. (1992). Day hospital program for dual diagnosis patients in a VA medical center. *Hospital and Community Psychiatry, 43,* 241–244.

Bartels, S. J., Drake, R. E., & Wallach, M. A. (1995). Long-term course of substance use disorders among patients with severe mental illness. *Psychiatric Services, 46,* 248–251.

Beaulieu, G., & Flanders, T. (2000). Uncovering the elements of success: Working with co-occurring disorders in residential support programs. *International Journal of Psychosocial Rehabilitation, 4,* 428–432.

Blankertz, L. E., & Cnaan, R. A. (1992). Principles of care for dually diagnosed homeless persons: Findings from a demonstration project. *Research on Social Work Practice, 2,* 448–464.

Bond, G. R., McDonel, E. C., Miller, L. D., & Pensec, M. (1991). Assertive community treatment and reference groups: An evaluation of their effectiveness for young adults with serious mental illness and substance abuse problems. *Psychosocial Rehabilitation Journal, 15,* 31–43.

Brown, V. B., Ridgely, M. S., Pepper, B., Levine, I. S., & Ryglewicz, H. (1989). Dual crisis: Mental illness and substance abuse. *American Psychologist, 44,* 565–569.

Burnam, M. A., Morton, S. C., McGlynn, E. A., Petersen, L. P., Stecher, B. M., Hayes, C., & Vaccaro, J. V. (1995). An experimental evaluation of residential and nonresidential treatment for dually diagnosed homeless adults. *Journal of Addictive Diseases, 14*(4), 111–134.

Cuffel, B. J., Heithoff, K. A., & Lawson, W. (1993). Correlates of patterns of substance abuse among patients with schizophrenia. *Hospital and Community Psychiatry, 44,* 247–251.

Drake, R. E., McHugo, G. J., Clark, R. E., Teague, G. B., Xie, H., Miles, K., & Ackerson, T. H. (1998). Assertive community treatment for patients with co-occurring severe mental illness and substance use disorder. *American Journal of Orthopsychiatry, 68,* 201–215.

Drake, R. E., McLaughlin, P., Pepper, B., & Minkoff, K. (1991). Dual diagnosis of major mental illness and substance disorder: An overview. *New Directions for Mental Health Services, 50,* 3–11.

Drake, R. E., Yovetich, N. A., Bebout, R. R., Harris, M., & McHugo, G. J. (1997). Integrated treatment for dually diagnosed homeless adults. *The Journal of Nervous and Mental Disease, 185,* 298–305.

Durell, J., Lechtenberg, B., Corse, S., & Frances, R. J. (1993). Intensive case management of persons with chronic mental illness who abuse substances. *Hospital and Community Psychiatry, 44,* 415–428.

Flynn, L. (1994). Schizophrenia from a family point of view: A social and economic perspective. In N. C. Andreasen (Ed.), *Schizophrenia, from mind to molecule* (pp. 21–30). Washington, DC: American Psychiatric Press.

Ford, L., Snowden, L. R., & Walser, E. J. (1991). Outpatient mental health and the dual-diagnosis patient: Utilization of services and community adjustment. *Evaluation and Program Planning, 14,* 291–298.

Glass, G. G., McGaw, B., & Smith, M. L. (1981). *Meta-analysis in social research.* Beverly Hills, CA: Sage Publications.

Hellerstein, D. J., Rosenthal, R. N., & Miner, C. R. (1995). Prospective study of integrated outpatient treatment for substance-abusing schizophrenic patients. *American Journal on Addictions, 4,* 33–42.

Herman, S. E., BootsMiller, B., Jordan, L., Mowbray, C. T., Brown, W. G., Deiz, N., Bandla, H., Solomon, M., & Green, P. (1997). Immediate outcomes of substance use treatment within a state psychiatric hospital. *Journal of Mental Health Administration, 24,* 126–138.

Hoffman, G. W., DiRito, D. C., & McGill, E. C. (1993). Three-month follow-up of 28 dual diagnosis inpatients. *American Journal of Drug and Alcohol Abuse, 19,* 79–88.

Howland, R. H. (1993). Barriers to community treatment of patients with dual diagnosis. *Hospital and Community Psychiatry, 41,* 1134–1135.

Jerrell, J. M., & Ridgely, M. S. (1995). Comparative effectiveness of three approaches to serving people with severe mental illness and substance alcohol and other drug abuse disorders. *Journal of Nervous and Mental Disease, 183,* 566–576.

Kivlahan, D. R., Heiman, J. R., Wright, R. C., Mundt, J. W., & Shupe, J. A. (1991). Treatment cost and rehospitalization rate in schizophrenic outpatients with a history of substance abuse. *Hospital and Community Psychiatry, 42,* 609–614.

Kline, J., Harris, M., Bebout, R. R., & Drake, R. F. (1991). Contrasting integrated and linkage models of treatment for homeless, dually diagnosed adults. *New Directions for Mental Health Services, 50,* 95–106.

Lehman, A. F., Herron, J. D., Schwartz, R. P., & Myers, C. P. (1993). Rehabilitation for adults with severe mental illness and substance use disorders. *Journal of Nervous and Mental Disease, 181,* 86–90.

McHugo, G. J., Drake, R. E., Burton, H. L., & Ackerson, T. H. (1995). Scale for assessing the stage of substance abuse treatment in persons with severe mental illness. *Journal of Nervous and Mental Disease, 183,* 762–767.

Meisler, N., Blankertz, L., Santos, A. B., & McKay, C. (1997). Impact of assertive community treatment on homeless persons with co-occurring severe psychiatric substance use disorders. *Community Mental Health Journal, 33,* 113–122.

Mercer-McFadden, C., Drake, R. E., Brown, N. B., & Fox, R. S. (1997). The community support program demonstrations of services for young adults with severe mental illness and substance use disorders. *Psychiatric Rehabilitation Journal, 20,* 13–24.

Mueser, K. T., & Noordsy, D. L. (1996). Group treatment for dually diagnosed adults. *New Directions for Mental Health Services, 70,* 33–51.

Mueser, K. T., Yarnold, P. R., & Bellack, A. S. (1992). Diagnostic and demographic correlates of substance abuse in schizophrenia and major affective disorder. *Acta Psychiatrica Scandinavia, 85,* 48–55.

Osher, F. C., & Kofoed, L. L. (1989). Treatment of patients with psychiatric and psychoactive substance abuse disorders. *Hospital and Community Psychiatry, 40,* 1026–1030.

Rahav, M., Rivera, J. J., Nuttbrock, L., Ng-Mak, D., Sturz, E. L., Link, B. G., et al. (1995). Characteristics and treatment of homeless, mentally ill, chemical-abusing men. *Journal of Psychoactive Drugs, 27,* 93–103.

Regier, D. A., Farmer, M. E., Rae, D. S., Locke, B. Z., Keith, S. J., Judd, L. L., & Goodwin, F. K. (1990). Comorbidity of mental disorders with use. *Journal of the American Medical Association, 264,* 2511–2518.

Ridgely, M. S. (1991). Creating integrated programs for severely mentally ill persons with substance disorders. *New Directions for Mental Health Services, 50,* 29–41.

Ridgely, M. S., & Jerrell, J. M. (1996). Analysis of three interventions for substance abuse treatment of severely mentally ill people. *Community Mental Health Journal, 32,* 561–572.

Roberts, L., Shaner, A., Eckman, T. A., Tucker, D. E., & Vaccaro, J. V. (1992). Effectively treating stimulant-abusing schizophrenics: Mission impossible? *New Directions for Mental Health Services, 53,* 55–57.

Solomon, P. (1992). Efficacy of case management services for severely mentally disabled clients. *Community Mental Health Journal, 28,* 163–179.

Sullivan, W., & Maloney, P. (1992). Substance abuse and mental illness: Social work practice with dual diagnosis clients. *Arete, 17,* 1–15.

Teague, G. B., Drake, R. E., & Ackerson, T. H. (1995). Evaluating use of continuous treatment teams for persons with mental illness and substance abuse. *Psychiatric Services, 46,* 689–695.

Test, M. A. (1992). Training in community living. In R. P. Liberman (Ed.), *Handbook of psychiatric rehabilitation* (pp. 153–170). Boston: Allyn & Bacon.

*Testimony on NIMH's FY 1998 Budget: Hearing before the House Appropriations Committee, Subcommittee on Labor, Health, and Human Services, Education and Related Agencies,* 105th Cong. (1997, March 6) (testimony of Steven E. Hyman, director, National Institute of Mental Health).

U.S. Department of Health and Human Services, Substance Abuse and Mental Health Services Administration and National Institutes of Health. (1995). *Substance abuse and mental health statistics sourcebook* (DHHS Publication No. SMA 95–3064). Washington, DC: Government Printing Office.

Videka-Sherman, L., & Reid, W. J. (Eds.). (1990). *Advances in clinical social work research* (pp. 286–289). Silver Spring, MD: NASW Press.

Warner, R., Taylor, D., Wright, J., & Sloat, A. (1994). Substance use among the mentally ill: Prevalence, reasons for use, and effects on illness. *American Journal of Orthopsychiatry, 64,* 30–39.

Weil, T. P. (1991). Mental health services under a U.S. national health insurance plan. *Hospital and Community Psychiatry, 42,* 695–700.

Welkowitz, J., Ewen, R. B., & Cohen, J. (1982). *Introductory statistics for the behavioral sciences* (3rd ed.). New York: Academic Press.

Wilens, T. E., Saley, P., Renner, J. A., & O'Keefe, J. (1994). A public detoxification unit: Short-term efficacy of treatment. *American Journal on Addictions, 3,* 194–203.

Woody, G. (1996). The challenge of dual diagnosis. *Alcohol Health & Research World, 20*(2), 76–80.

# 10 Treating Depression During Pregnancy and the Postpartum

## A Preliminary Meta-Analysis

*Sarah E. Bledsoe and Nancy K. Grote*

Depression during pregnancy and the postpartum is a widespread, serious health problem for women and infants. Approximately 10% of women develop nonpsychotic maternal postpartum depression following delivery (Cooper, Campbell, Day, Kennerley, & Bond, 1988; Cooper, Murray, Wilson, & Romaniuk, 2003; Cox, Holden, & Sagovsky, 1993; O'Hara & Swain, 1996). A recent study of depression during pregnancy and the postpartum has documented that in a cohort of 1,400 women, 13.5% met criteria for major depression at 32 weeks of pregnancy and 9.1% met criteria at 8 weeks postpartum (Evans, Heron, Francomb, Oke, & Golding, 2001). Similar rates of major and minor depression were found in middle-income women and predominantly Latina women (Yonkers et al., 2001) during pregnancy: 9% to 10% (Gotlib, Whiffen, Wallace, & Mount, 1991; O'Hara, Neunaber, & Zeboski, 1984). Higher rates (26%), however, have been identified in low-income, urban, African American and Caucasian women (Hobfoll, Ritter, Lavin, Hulszier, & Cameron, 1995).

Nonpsychotic postpartum depression has harmful, lasting effects on infant and child well-being (Moore, Cohn, & Campbell, 2001; Murray & Cooper, 1997), on the mothers' and fathers' subsequent mental health (Areias, Kumar, Barros, & Figueiredo, 1996; Kumar & Robson, 1984), and on the quality of the couple's relationship (Campbell, Cohn, Flanagan, Popper, & Meyers, 1992; O'Hara, 1994). Additionally, depression during pregnancy has been demonstrated repeatedly to be the most powerful predictor of postpartum depression (O'Hara & Swain, 1996). Evidence also suggests that depression during pregnancy results in adverse outcomes for

Originally published in *Research on Social Work Practice* 2006; 16; 109. DOI: 10.1177/1049731505282202 The online version of this article can be found at: http://rsw.sagepub.com/cgi/content/abstract/16/2/109

mother and fetus or infant well-being. Higher levels of anxiety and stress are associated with maternal depression and predict dysregulation of hypothalamic-pituitary-adrenal axis in the fetus (Sandman et al., 1994), low birth weight, and prematurity (Wadwha, Sandman, Porto, Dunkel-Schetter, & Garite, 1993). Furthermore, infants of mothers depressed during pregnancy exhibit substandard neuromotor performance (Lundy et al., 1999) and dysregulation in behavior, physiology, and biochemistry (Field, 2000).

Although women are not more vulnerable to depression during pregnancy and the postpartum than at any other points across the life span (Gotlib, Whiffin, Mount, Milne, & Cordy, 1989; Kumar & Robinson, 1984; O'Hara, Zekoski, Philipps, & Wright, 1990), this period may be critical because of the risk posed to the fetus or infant as well as the mother and other family members. Furthermore, pregnant women may be unusually open to interventions directed at improving their own mental health before the birth of their child (Cowan & Cowan, 2000), and pregnancy is known to be an opportune time for suggesting health interventions (Institute of Medicine, 1996). It is imperative that doctors, clinicians, and social workers be provided with evidence regarding the treatment of depression during pregnancy and the postpartum on which to base best-practice decisions. Higher rates of depression during pregnancy and the postpartum among low-income, urban women may create a special relevance for social work practitioners. Treatment that reduces maternal depression may offer protective advantages, not only for the woman herself but also for the fetus, infant, and other family members (Kaplan, Bachorowski, Smoski, & Hudenko, 2002; Orr, James, & Prince, 2002; Sanderson et al., 2002; Susman, Trickett, Iannotti, Hollenbeck, & Zahn-Waxler, 1985; Zuravin, 1989).

The following interventions for nonpsychotic major depression are included in this review based on their use in treatment trials: (1) medication in combination with cognitive behavioral therapy (CBT); (2) medication; (3) group therapy with cognitive behavioral, educational, and transactional analysis components; (4) interpersonal psychotherapy (IPT); (5) CBT; (6) psychodynamic therapy; (7) counseling; and (8) educational interventions. IPT, used in four studies, is a time-limited, manualized treatment for depression focused on interpersonal problems related to the onset of the current episode of depression (Klerman, Weissman, Rounsaville, & Chevron, 1984). All four studies using this approach modified IPT to address the particular needs of women with major depression during pregnancy or postpartum (Grote, Swartz, Bledsoe, & Frank, 2004; O'Hara, Stuart, Gorman, & Wenzel, 2000; Spinelli, 1997; Spinelli & Endicott, 2003). CBT was used in three studies. CBT is a manualized form of psychotherapy focused on enhancing cognitive skills, evaluating and modifying dysfunctional thoughts, encouraging self-reinforcement, generating positive coping statements, developing problem-solving abilities, and improving social skills (Appleby, Warner, Whitton, & Faragher, 1997; Beck, Rush, Shaw, & Emery, 1979; Chabrol et al., 2002; Cooper et al., 2003; D'Zurilla, 1986). One study used a psychodynamic approach focused on the early attachment experiences, mother's representation of the infant, and the mother-infant relationship (Cooper et al., 2003; Cramer et al., 1990; Stern, 1995). Two studies provided counseling interventions where women were given an opportunity to raise any personal or infant-care concerns (Cooper et al., 2003; Holden, Sagovsky, & Cox, 1989). A group intervention with a cognitive behavioral component, an educational component and a transactional analysis component was employed by Lane, Roufeil, Williams, and Tweedie (2001). Two studies used educational interventions to address major depression during pregnancy and the postpartum. These interventions were tailored to the educational needs of pregnant and postpartum women and focused on topics such as parenting education and perinatal depression (Hayes, Muller, & Bradley, 2001; Spinelli, 2003). Two studies used antidepressant medications (fluoxetine and fluvoxamine) to treat postpartum depression (Appleby et al., 1997; Suri, Burt, Altshuler, Zuckerbrow-Miller, & Fair, 2001). One study included an intervention that combined medication with CBT (Appleby et al., 1997).

The primary aim of this review is to evaluate the effects of current treatment interventions for nonpsychotic major depression during pregnancy and the postpartum. A second aim is to compare the relative effect sizes of the different types of interventions for nonpsychotic major depression during pregnancy and the postpartum to determine which treatments appear to be most effective. A third and final aim is to evaluate the effect of the timing (during pregnancy or postpartum) of the interventions targeting nonpsychotic major depression. In examining and synthesizing the available evidence relevant to these specific aims, this review contributes to the literature available to social work practitioners and other professional clinicians working with pregnant or postpartum women who desire to make evidence-based, best-practice decisions.

# _____ Criteria for Considering Studies for This Review

## Types of Studies, Participants, Interventions, and Outcome Measures

All treatment trials that evaluated interventions directed at treating women with nonpsychotic major depression during pregnancy and the postpartum that used either a randomized controlled trial or a pretest, posttest (without comparison or control group) were sought for the purposes of this review. Because of the limited number of trials focusing on depression during pregnancy and postpartum the decision was made to include both randomized controlled trials and nonrandomized studies (but limited to those with a pretest, posttest design) in this meta-analysis. Only studies with participants who were women diagnosed with nonpsychotic major depression during pregnancy or the postpartum were selected for inclusion in this review. The review was further limited to studies using

interventions designed to treat nonpsychotic major depression during pregnancy or the postpartum. A standardized measure of depressive symptomatology was the main outcome measure.

# Search Strategy for Identification of Studies

Electronic searching, reference searching, and personal contact were used to
identify studies for inclusion in this review. Relevant treatment trials were identified by searching the following electronic databases using the following
terms: *depression, treatment* or *clinical trials* or *trials*, and *postpartum* or *pregnancy* or *postnatal*. Terms such as *interpersonal psychotherapy* or IPT, *education, cognitive behavioral* or CBT, *Group* (cognitive behavioral, educational,
and transactional analysis components), and *medication* were used to ensure
that additional trials were not overlooked. This search was also limited to
studies published in the past 15 years to increase relevance to current clinical
practice (Weissman & Sanderson, 2002). Four databases were used in electronic searching: Cochrane Central Register of Controlled Trials, MEDLINE,
Psychlit, and Social Work Abstracts. The reference lists of all papers selected
were inspected for further relevant studies. Additionally, personal contact
resulted in the inclusion of one article that has been recently published.

# Methods of the Review

## Selection of Studies

The entire search was performed by two reviewers. All studies were evaluated according to the above criteria. Studies not meeting the above criteria were discarded, and only those studies that met the criteria of being
treatment studies for nonpsychotic depression during pregnancy or the postpartum were retained. Authorship was not concealed at the point of data
collection.

## Quality Assessment

Studies were given a quality rating of high, medium, or low based on the
following criteria: presence of randomization, presence of a control group,
number of participants, and year of publication. The rating scale was
entered into the analysis as a grouping variable.

## Data Extraction and Management

All data were extracted by one reviewer. Studies that met the inclusion criteria regarding the targeted outcome (reduction of depressive symptomatology)

were reported as detailed in the *Type of Outcome* section. Reported analyses include only participants who completed the intervention. We report the attrition rate for each study in Appendix A. Although some studies provide follow-up data, follow-up data were not included in the meta-analysis.

*Comprehensive Meta-Analysis* software (Borenstein & Rothstein, 1999) was used to assess continuous outcome data with a 95% confidence interval. Data were reported as presented in the original studies with no exceptions. Analysis of interventions by type of treatment is also presented. Type of treatment data were retrieved from the published studies. Timing of intervention implementation is also presented. Studies were divided into two categories based on the reported start time of intervention: (a) pregnancy (for interventions implemented before the birth of the child) and (b) postpartum (for interventions implemented after the birth of the child). For more detail see Appendix A.

# Description of Studies

## Included, Excluded, and Ongoing Studies

Eleven studies describing 16 intervention trials met inclusion criteria for the review (see Appendix A for more details about the studies). Eight identified studies were excluded from the review (see Appendix B). Three studies were prevention studies, and all participants did not meet criteria for major depression at prevention implementation. One study did not focus specifically on women during pregnancy and the postpartum. Data reported specifically on women during pregnancy and the postpartum could not be separated from the study sample based on information in the study publication. Two studies did not focus on depression as the outcome measure. One study was excluded because the type of intervention—early, middle, or late-night sleep deprivation—was not easily compared to the interventions included in this analysis. One study was excluded because it had a sample size of one (see Appendix B). One ongoing study was identified. This study was a randomized, controlled treatment trial testing IPT in a low-income population of pregnant women. Because outcome data were not available at the time of this review, the study is not included. However, it has been identified for inclusion in future reviews.

## Interventions

All interventions were designed to treat nonpsychotic depression during pregnancy and the postpartum. The treatments are classified as follows for further analysis: IPT, CBT, psychodynamic therapy, counseling, educational, group therapy with cognitive behavioral, educational, and transactional analysis components, medication, and medication in combination with CBT.

## Outcome Scales

Depressive symptomatology was measured using one of the following standardardized inventories or standardized interviews (see Appendix A for the measures used in each study). Rating scales used to measure clinical outcomes are the Edinburgh Postnatal Depression Scale (EPDS; Cox, Holden, & Sagovsky, 1987), Hamilton Rating Scale for Depression (Hamilton, 1960), and Profile of Mood States (McNair, Lorr, & Droppleman, 1981). Because the EPDS was designed to differentiate the symptoms of depression from the somatic symptoms of pregnancy (Cox et al., 1987), we chose it as the primary outcome measure for the meta-analysis. For studies that did not include the EPDS as a measure of depressive symptomatology, we chose the Hamilton Rating Scale for Depression that was used in one study, and the Profile of Mood States, which was the only measure of depressive symptoms used in another study.

## Methodological Quality

A relatively simple method was used to determine the quality of studies. Studies were given a quality rating of high, medium, or low based on the following criteria: presence of randomization, presence of a control group, number of participants, and year of publication. Randomization in each of the trials was assessed using the following scale: 1 = *randomized*, 2 = *not randomized*. Studies were ranked on the presence or absence of a control group using the following scale: 1 = *control group present*, 2 = *no control group*. All studies falling into the second category used a pretest, posttest design to measure depressive symptomatology before and after intervention. Studies were ranked based on the number of participants using the following scale: 1 = *more than 30 participants*, 2 = *less than 30 participants*. Interventions of 30 or more scored more favorably because of the likelihood of greater generalization for trials including 30 or more participants. Studies were ranked based on year of publication using the following scale: 1 = *less than 10 years from date of publication*, 2 = *10 to 15 years from date of publication*. The cutoff for year of publication was chosen based on relevance to current clinical practice as there has been an increase in evidence for the efficacy of interventions in mental health based on controlled clinical trails in the past decade (Weissman & Sanderson, 2002).

Studies were given the following quality rankings based on the above criteria.

High: Appleby et al., 1997; Cooper et al., 2003; Hayes et al., 2001; O'Hara et al., 2000; and Spinelli et al., 2003.

Medium: Chabrol et al., 2002; Grote et al., 2004; Holden et al., 1989; Lane et al., 2001; and Spinelli, 1997.

Low: Suri et al., 2001.

# Results

The first objective of this review was to evaluate the effects of current evidence-based treatments for nonpsychotic major depression during pregnancy and the postpartum (see Table 10.1). Eleven studies provided 16 treatment trials with a total of 922 participants contributing to this analysis. The overall effect size of all interventions in the analysis was .673 (p < .001). Of the 16 interventions compared, 14 interventions from the 11 studies included in the review had a positive effect size. Of the 16 interventions, 8 had effect sizes between 1.193 and 4.718 (p < .020). Five had effect sizes between .434 and .955 (p < .047). None of the final 3 interventions (counseling— Cooper et al., 2003; educational—Hayes et al., 2001; intervention—CBT (Appleby et al., 1997) showed any significant effect size.

The second objective was to compare the relative effectiveness of treatments for nonpsychotic major depression during pregnancy and the postpartum. For this analysis, studies were grouped according to type of treatment intervention (see Table 10.2). From the 16 treatment trials, treatments were categorized into eight intervention types. Of the eight interventions types compared, four had positive effect sizes between 1.260 and 3.871 (*p* < .001). Of the 8 interventions types, three had effect sizes between .418 and .642 (*p* < .014). The final intervention type (educational) did not show any significant effect size. The results in Table 10.3 are shown by treatment intervention and ranked from highest to lowest by effect size.

The third objective was to evaluate the effect of the timing of the implementation (during pregnancy or postpartum) of interventions targeting nonpsychotic major depression (see Table 10.3). For this analysis, interventions were grouped according to the timing of the implementation of the intervention. Of the 16 interventions, 11 were implemented after diagnosis of nonpsychotic major depression in the postpartum period. For this group, N = 618 and effect size = .837, (*p* < .001). The remaining 5 interventions were implemented during pregnancy after the diagnosis of nonpsychotic major depression. For this group, N = 304 and effect size = .377 (*p* = .002). To determine whether inclusion of medication in postpartum interventions was responsible for the difference in effect size between interventions begun during pregnancy and those initiated postpartum, a second analysis was run. In this analysis, the 3 interventions using medication to treat depression postpartum were removed from the analysis. When treatments using medication were eliminated, the postpartum effect size decreased from .837 to .703, p <.001 (N = 256).

# Discussion and Applications
# to Research and Practice

According to Thomas Insel (2004), director of the National Institute of Mental Health, social workers are doing the majority of frontline work

**Table 10.1**     Meta-Analysis: All Interventions Ranked by Effect Size

| Study | Type of Intervention | Timing of Intervention | Number of Participants | Effect Size (−8 to 8) | p Value |
|---|---|---|---|---|---|
| Appleby, Warner, Whitton, and Faragher (1997) | Medication + CBT | Postpartum | 30 | 3.871 | < 0.001 |
| Appleby et al. (1997) | Medication | Postpartum | 33 | 4.781 | < 0.001 |
| Grote, Swartz, Bledsoe, and Frank (2004) | IPT-B | Pregnancy | 18 | 2.178 | < 0.001 |
| Chabrol et al. (2002) | CBT | Postpartum | 48 | 2.109 | < 0.001 |
| Lane, Roufeil, Williams, and Tweedie (2001) | Group[a] | Postpartum | 30 | 2.046 | < 0.001 |
| Spinelli (1997) | IPT | Pregnancy | 26 | 1.598 | < 0.001 |
| Suri, Burt, Altshuler, Zuckerbrow-Miller, and Fair (2001) | Medication | Postpartum | 12 | 1.473 | 0.020 |
| O'Hara, Stuart, Gorman, and Wenzel (2000) | IPT | Postpartum | 99 | 1.193 | < 0.001 |
| Spinelli and Endicott (2003) | IPT | Pregnancy | 38 | 0.955 | 0.005 |
| Holden, Sagovsky, and Cox (1989) | Counseling | Postpartum | 50 | 0.747 | 0.01 |
| Spinelli and Endicott (2003) | Education | Pregnancy | 34 | 0.693 | 0.047 |
| Cooper, Murray, Wilson, and Romanuik (2003) | Psychodynamic | Postpartum | 95 | 0.526 | 0.011 |
| Cooper et al. (2003) | CBT | Postpartum | 92 | .434 | 0.039 |
| Cooper et al. (2003) | Counseling | Postpartum | 97 | 0.259 | 0.202 |
| Hayes, Muller, and Bradley (2001) | Education | Pregnancy | 188 | 0.000 | 1.00 |
| Appleby et al. (1997) | CBT | Postpartum | 92 | −0.099 | 0.777 |
| Total | | | 922 | 0.673 | < 0.001 |

NOTE: CBT = cognitive behavioral therapy; IPT-B = brief interpersonal psychotherapy; IPT = interpersonal psychotherapy.

a. Group therapy with cognitive behavioral, educational, and transactional analysis components.

treating individuals with mental illnesses. According to a 1998 SAMSA report, the current psychotherapy workforce is dominated by social work consisting of 192,814 social workers, 73,014 psychologists, 33,486 psychiatrists, and 17,318 psychiatric nurses (Insel, 2004). Given this information, it seems

**Table 10.2**   Meta-Analysis: All Interventions Grouped by Intervention Type

| Type of Intervention | Number of Intervention Trials | Number of Participants | Effect Size | p Value |
|---|---|---|---|---|
| Medication + CBT | 1 | 30 | 3.871 | < .001 |
| Medication | 2 | 45 | 3.048 | < .001 |
| Group[a] | 1 | 30 | 2.046 | < .001 |
| IPT | 4 | 181 | 1.260 | < .001 |
| CBT | 3 | 172 | 0.642 | < .001 |
| Psychodynamic | 1 | 95 | 0.526 | .014 |
| Counseling | 2 | 147 | 0.418 | .014 |
| Educational | 2 | 222 | 0.100 | .457 |

NOTE: CBT = cognitive behavioral therapy; IPT = interpersonal psychotherapy.

a. Group therapy with cognitive behavioral, educational, and transactional analysis components.

**Table 10.3**   Meta-Analysis: All Interventions Grouped by Timing of Implementation of Intervention

| Timing of Intervention | Number of Intervention Trials | Number of Participants | Effect Size | p Value |
|---|---|---|---|---|
| Postpartum | | | | |
| Analysis 1 | 11 | 618 | .837 | < .001 |
| Analysis 2 | 8 | 256 | .703 | < .001 |
| Pregnancy | 5 | 304 | .377 | .002 |

necessary that social workers be informed regarding intervention evidence in the treatment of mental illnesses such as depression during pregnancy and postpartum, specifically in a population where medication may not be an option for treatment. Therefore, the findings of this review are specifically relevant to social workers.

With respect to the primary aim of this review, the results of the first analysis provide an overview of the effects of current treatments for nonpsychotic major depression during pregnancy and the postpartum included in this review. With the exception of CBT, there is a marked split between the individual treatment interventions when arranged hierarchically by effect size. Interventions using medication, medication in combination with CBT, IPT, and group therapy with cognitive behavioral, educational, and transactional analysis components had the largest effect sizes (> .95), whereas interventions using counseling, educational, and psy-chodynamic approaches had smaller effect sizes (< .75) or no effect. It is important to note that in this analysis, several of the evaluated treatment types (medication in combination with CBT, group therapy, and psychody-namic therapy) were represented by only one treatment intervention trial. The remaining interventions in this analysis were represented by two, three, or four trials. As research evolves in the treatment of major depression dur-ing pregnancy and the postpartum, additional, updated meta-analyses will be needed. Additionally, extraneous variables may be contributing to the effect sizes detected in the analyses.

Regarding the second aim of this review, when we grouped the treatment interventions by type of treatment to determine their relative effectiveness, the results are similar to those reported above. Medication in combination with CBT has the largest effect size (3.871, $p < .001$) followed by medica-tion alone (3.048, $p < .001$); group therapy with cognitive behavioral, edu-cational, and transactional analysis components (2.046, $p < .001$); and IPT (1.260, $p < .001$). The combined effect size of CBT, .642 ($p < .001$), is fol-lowed by psychodynamic therapy (.526, $p = .014$), counseling (.418, $p = .014$), and educational interventions (.100, $p = .457$).

With respect to those treatments with the largest effect sizes (medication and CBT, medication alone, group therapy with cognitive behavioral, edu-cational and transactional analysis components, and IPT), findings are sim-ilar to those of the National Institute of Mental Health Treatment of Depression Collaborative Research Program (NIMHTDCRP; Elkin et al., 1989) suggesting that the treatment of major depression in women during pregnancy and the postpartum and the treatment of depression at other times in the life cycle may be similar. There are two exceptions, however. The first is the large effect size (2.046, $p < .001$) found for the treatment inter-vention using group therapy with cognitive behavioral, educational, and transactional analysis components. Although the NIMHTDCRP did not examine the use of group treatment for depression, studies support the use of group therapy, especially in postnatal populations, because of its ability to address both psychosocial problems and cognitive behavioral deficits (Meager & Milgrom, 1996). In light of the results of the NIMHTDCRP sug-gesting the efficacy of medication, medication and psychotherapy (CBT or IPT), and CBT and IPT alone for the treatment of major depression, the fact that CBT had varied effect sizes in this analysis is surprising. Although this could suggest that CBT may not be as effective in the treatment of major depression during pregnancy and the postpartum, there is an alternate expla-nation. Because of the limited scope of this analysis, the reviewers were only able to examine one of the targeted outcomes for each included study. The reviewers chose to use the EPDS, if available, because this scale was designed to assess depressive symptomatology during pregnancy and the postpartum period (Cox et al., 1987). CBT is focused strongly on the cognitive symp-toms of depression (Beck et al., 1979). If the measurement of the targeted outcome had been a scale more sensitive to the cognitive symptoms of depression, such as the Beck Depression Inventory (Beck, Steer, & Garbin, 1988), the analysis might have yielded different results.

The third and final aim of this review was to evaluate the effect sizes of interventions based on the timing of implementation. Whereas those interventions implemented postpartum had a slightly larger effect size (.837, $p < .001$) than those implemented during pregnancy (.377, $p = .002$), this may be due to an alternative explanation. Medication interventions were implemented only during postpartum. When interventions using medication are omitted from analysis, the effect size of interventions implemented postpartum decreases (from .837 to .703, $p < .001$). This indicates that although part of the difference in timing effect size can be attributed to medication interventions (with large effect sizes) being used in the postpartum period and not during pregnancy, differences cannot be explained in their entirety. Further investigation is needed to examine these differences.

The scope of this review is limited by the fact that we did not assess all of the reliable and valid measures of depressive symptomatology that most of the reported treatment intervention studies used. Future research should conduct further meta-analyses using other available measures of depression.

The mixing of randomized and nonrandomized studies may be a limitation, but this is necessitated by the fact that currently, there are a limited number of adequate studies on depression during pregnancy and postpartum that can be selected. As the field develops, future meta-analyses on randomized and nonrandomized studies should be run separately. This review also includes treatment trials with small numbers of participants and meta-analyses are less robust with small trials. Thus, the results should be interpreted with caution. In addition, the overall quality of trials was variable. Publication bias is suggested by the paucity of negative or no effect trials found for this analysis.

However, it is possible that the small number of negative or no effect trials denotes the effectiveness of treatment interventions reported in the literature to date. Additional trials and larger numbers of participants in a future meta-analysis would be required to address these issues. Furthermore, the review was only able to rank the methodological quality of studies using a simple method. Additionally, reported results were limited to the main outcome, depressive symptomatology. Future studies should examine other important variables of interest such as occupational and social functioning, social support, and cost-effectiveness of interventions.

Nonpsychotic major depression during pregnancy and the postpartum is a widespread health threat to mothers, infants, and families. This review has described the effects of treatments for depression during pregnancy and has begun to identify those treatments that are most effective in this population. Although further research and analyses are needed to validate the results of this review, preliminary findings suggest that medication, alone or in combination with CBT; group therapy with cognitive behavioral, educational, and transactional analysis components; interpersonal therapy; and CBT produce the largest effect sizes in this population. However, doctors may be reluctant to prescribe medication during pregnancy and the postpartum (for mothers who choose to breastfeed) because absolute safety cannot be assured, although some selective serotonin reuptake inhibitors and other antidepressant medications have demonstrated relative safety during this period (Wisner, Gelenberg, Leonard, Zarin, & Frank, 1999). Additionally, many women may be unwilling to take medication during pregnancy and the postpartum (Oren et al., 2002). This situation creates an urgent need to develop other effective, non-pharmacological treatment alternatives to antidepressant medication. This review has begun the process of identifying these alternative treatments with findings supporting group therapy with cognitive behavioral, educational, and transactional analysis components; IPT; and CBT, respectively.

Although this review has attempted to evaluate the effects of current treatment interventions for nonpsychotic major depression during pregnancy and the postpartum, additional research is needed to validate the findings in this report. In light of the fact that medication—alone and in combination with CBT—was found to have the largest effect size, research should continue to address the safety of pharmacological treatment for major depression during pregnancy and the postpartum. Additional research is also needed to develop and improve existing non-pharmacological treatment of perinatal depression as many women prefer alternatives to medication for the treatment of major depression while pregnant and breastfeeding. Culturally relevant treatments should also be explored in research on depression during pregnancy and the postpartum as low-income and ethnic minority women have higher rates of depression during this point in the life cycle (Hobfoll et al., 1995).

**Appendix 10A**   Characteristics of Included Studies

| Study | Study Design | Participants | Interventions | Outcomes | Site | Timing | Study Quality |
|---|---|---|---|---|---|---|---|
| Appleby et al. (1997) | Randomized, controlled treatment trial | 87 women satisfying criteria for depressive illness 6 to 8 weeks postpartum completed the study; 30% attrition rate | Fluoxetine plus one counseling session (Medication), Placebo plus one counseling session (Control), Fluoxetine plus six sessions of CBT therapy (Medication + CBT), six sessions of CBT | Revised Clinical Interview Schedule, EPDS, and the Hamilton Rating Scale for Depression at 1, 4, and 12 weeks posttreatment | South Manchester | Postpartum | High |
| Chabrol et al. (2002) | Randomized, controlled treatment trial | 48 women meeting criteria for major depression at 4 to 6 weeks postpartum; 0% attrition rate | CBT for 5 to 8 weeks provided in the participant's home | EPDS, Hamilton Rating Scale for Depression, and Beck Depression Inventory posttreatment at 10 to 12 weeks postpartum | Toulouse and Narbonne, France | Postpartum | High |
| Cooper et al. (2003) | Randomized, controlled treatment trial | 193 women meeting criteria for postpartum depression in the early postpartum period completed the study; 17% attrition rate | Routine primary care (Control), nondirective counseling (Counseling), CBT, or psychodynamic therapy (Psychodynamic); counseling, CBT, and Psychodynamic interventions delivered weekly from 8 to 18 weeks postpartum in the participant's home | EPDS, Structured Clinical Interview for DSM-III-R immediately posttreatment at 4.5 postpartum and at 9, 18, and 60 months postpartum | Cambridge | Postpartum | High |

*(Continued)*

**Appendix 10A** (Continued)

| Study | Study Design | Participants | Interventions | Outcomes | Site | Timing | Study Quality |
|---|---|---|---|---|---|---|---|
| Grote et al. (2004) | Open trial treatment study using pretest and posttest design | 9 women meeting criteria of major and minor depression during pregnancy completed the study; 78% of women were African American or Latina, 22% were Caucasian; all women were financially disadvantaged | Brief Interpersonal Psychotherapy for Depression—8 weekly sessions of acute treatment during pregnancy, monthly maintenance sessions posttreatment up to 6 months postpartum delivered in clinic or by telephone | Diagnostic Interview Schedule, EPDS, Beck Depression Inventory, Hamilton Rating Scale for Depression, Beck Anxiety Inventory immediately following 8-session intervention and at 2 and 6 months postpartum | Pittsburgh, Pennsylvania | Pregnancy | Medium |
| Hayes et al. (2001) | Randomized, controlled treatment trial | 188 primaparous women meeting criteria for major depression during pregnancy completed the study; 8.7% attrition rate; 94% were Caucasian | Educational intervention (Education) from Week 28 to 36 of pregnancy; Delivered at antenatal clinic or in the participant's home | Profile of Mood States at 8 to 12 and 16 to 24 weeks postpartum | Townsville, Melbourne, and Adelaide, Australia | Pregnancy | High |
| Holden et al. (1989) | Randomized, controlled treatment trial | 50 women identified as depressed by screening at 6 weeks postpartum and by psychiatric interview at 13 weeks postpartum completed the study; 9 % attrition rate | Counseling for postnatal depression (Counseling) for 8 weeks in the participant's home | Goldberg's Standardized Psychiatric Interview and EPDS posttreatment | Edinburgh and Livingston | Postpartum | Medium |
| Lane et al. (2001) | Open treatment trial using a pretest and posttest design | 18 rural women diagnosed with postpartum depression at 13 weeks postpartum completed the study; 22% attrition rate | Group therapy with cognitive behavioral, educational, and transactional analysis components for postnatal depression (Group) for 10 weeks | EPDS posttreatment | New South Wales, Austrailia | Postpartum | Medium |

| Study | Study Design | Participants | Interventions | Outcomes | Site | Timing | Study Quality |
|---|---|---|---|---|---|---|---|
| O'Hara et al. (2000) | Randomized, controlled treatment trial | 99 postpartum women meeting DSM-IV criteria for major depression completed the study; 18% attrition rate | IPT for 12 weekly sessions | Hamilton Rating Scale for Depression, Structured Clinical Interview for DSM-IV Axis 1 Disorders, and Beck Depression Inventory at 4, 8, and 12 weeks in treatment | Polk, Johnson, Linn, and Scott Counties Iowa | Postpartum | High |
| Spinelli (1997) | Open treatment trial using a pretest and posttest design | 9 pregnant women who met DSM-III-R criteria for major depression; 31% attrition rate; 54% of participants were Latina, 15% were Black, and 31% were Caucasian | 16 weeks of IPT for antepartum depression | Structured Clinical Interview for DSM-IV Axis 1 Disorders, Clinical Global Impression, Hamilton Rating Scale for Depression, Beck Depression Inventory, and EPDS posttreatment | | Pregnancy | Medium |
| Spinelli et al. (2003) | Randomized, controlled, bilingual treatment trial | 38 pregnant women who met DSM-IV criteria for major depression; 24% attrition rate; 66% were Latina, 29% were Caucasian, and 5% were African American; 53% had total annual household incomes under $25,000 | IPT for antenatal depression, didactic parenting education (Education); 16 weekly sessions | Structured Clinical Interview for DSM-IV Axis 1 Disorders, Clinical Global Impression, Hamilton Rating Scale for Depression, Beck Depression Inventory, and EPDS posttreatment | New York City | Pregnancy | High |
| Suri et al. (2001) | Open treatment trial | 6 women diagnosed with major depression within 8 weeks postpartum completed the study; 17% attrition rate | Treatment with Fluvoxamine (50mg to start, titrated to 150mg by Week 2) for 8 weeks (Medication) | Hamilton Rating Scale for Depression and the EPDS weekly | Los Angeles, California | Postpartum | Low |

CBT = cognitive behavioral therapy; DSM-III-R = Diagnostic and Statistical Manual of Mental Disorders, 3rd edition, revised; DSM-IV = Diagnostic and Statistical Manual of Mental Disorders, 4th edition; IPT = interpersonal psychotherapy; EPDS = Edinburgh Postnatal Depression Scale.

**Appendix 10B**    Characteristics of Excluded Studies

| Study | Reason for Exclusion |
|---|---|
| Bosquet and Egeland (2001) | Study did not focus on depression as a main outcome |
| Lewis-Hall, Wilson, Tepner, and Koke (1997) | Study was not specifically focused on women during pregnancy and the postpartum; data on this subgroup could not be separated from the study sample |
| Morrell, Spiby, Stewart, Walters, and Morgan (2000) | Study did not focus on depression as a main outcome |
| Nahas et al. (1999) | N = 1 |
| Parry et al. (2000) | Intervention not comparable to interventions included in the analysis |
| Reid, Glazener, Murray, and Taylor (2002) | This was a prevention study, not a treatment study |
| Wisner et al. (2001) | This was a prevention study, not a treatment study |
| Zlotnick, Johnson, Miller, Pearlstein, and Howard (2001) | This was a prevention study, not a treatment study |

# References

References marked with an asterisk indicate studies included in the meta-analysis.

*Appleby, L., Warner, R., Whitton, A., & Faragher, B. (1997). A controlled study of fluoxetine and cognitive-behavioural counseling in the treatment of postnatal depression. *British Medical Journal, 314,* 932–936.

Areias, M., Kumar, R., Barros, H., & Figueiredo, E. (1996). Correlates of postnatal depression in mothers and fathers. *British Journal of Psychiatry, 169,* 36–41.

Beck, A. T., Rush, J. A., Shaw, B. F., & Emery, G. (1979). *Cognitive therapy for depression.* New York: Guilford.

Beck, A. T., Steer, R., & Garbin, M. (1988). Psychometric properties of the Beck Depression Inventory: Twenty-five years of evaluation. *Clinical Psychology Review, 8,* 77–100.

Borenstein, M., & Rothstein, H. (1999). *Comprehensive meta-analysis: A computer program for research synthesis.* Englewood, NJ: Biostat. Retrieved from www.MetaAnalysis.com.

Bosquet, M., & Egeland, B. (2001). Associations among maternal depressive symptomatology, state of mind and parent and child behaviors: Implications for attachment-based interventions. *Attachment & Human Development, 3,* 173–99.

Campbell, S. B., Cohn, J. F., Flanagan, C., Popper, S., & Meyers, T. (1992). Course and correlates of postpartum depression during the transition to parenthood. *Development and Psychopathology, 4,* 29–47.

*Chabrol, H., Teissedre, F., Saint-Jean, M., Teisseyre, N., Roge, B., & Mullet, E. (2002). Prevention and treatment of postpartum depression: A controlled randomized study on women at risk. *Psychological Medicine, 32,* 1039–1047.

Cooper, P. J., Campbell, E. A., Day, A., Kennerley, H., & Bond, A. (1988). Non-psychotic psychiatric disorder after childbirth: A prospective study of prevalence, incidence, course, and nature. *British Journal of Psychiatry, 152,* 799–806.

*Cooper, P. J., Murray, L., Wilson, A., & Romaniuk, H. (2003). Controlled trial of the short- and long-term effect of psychological treatment of post-partum depression. 1. Impact on maternal mood. *British Journal of Psychiatry, 182,* 412–419.

Cowan, C., & Cowan, P. (2000). *When partners become parents: The big life change for couples.* Mahwah, NJ: Lawrence Erlbaum.

Cox, J. L., Holden, J., & Sagovsky, R. (1987). Detection of postnatal depression: Development of the Edinburgh postnatal depression scale. *British Journal of Psychiatry, 198,* 213–220.

Cox, J. L., Murray, D., & Chapman, G. (1993). A controlled study of the onset, duration and prevalence of postnatal depression. *British Journal of Psychiatry, 163,* 27–31.

Cramer, B., Robert-Tissot, C., Stern, D., Serpa-Rusconi, S., De Muralt, G. B., Palacio-Espasa, F., et al. (1990). Outcome evaluation in brief mother-infant psychotherapy: A preliminary report. *Infant Mental Health Journal, 11,* 278–300.

D'Zurilla, T. J. (1986). *Problem-solving therapy: A social competence approach to clinical intervention.* New York: Springer.

Elkin, I., Shea, T., Watkins, J. T., Imber, S. D., Sotsky, S. M., Collins, J. F., et al. (1989). National Institute of Mental Health Treatment of Depression Collaborative Research Program: General effectiveness of treatments. *Archives of General Psychiatry, 46,* 971–982.

Evans, J., Heron, J., Francomb, H., Oke, S., & Golding, J. (2001). Cohort study of depressed mood during pregnancy and after childbirth. *British Medical Journal, 323,* 257–260.

Field, T. (2000). Infants of depressed mothers. In S. Johnson & A. Hayes (Eds.), *Stress, coping, and depression* (pp. 3–22). Mahwah, NJ: Lawrence Erlbaum.

Gotlib, I., Whiffen, V., Wallace, P., & Mount, J. (1991). Prospective investigation of postpartum depression: Factors involved in onset and recovery. *Journal of Abnormal Psychology, 100,* 122–132.

Gotlib, I. H., Wiffen, V. E., Mount, J. H., Milne, K., & Cordy, N. I. (1989). Prevalence rates and demographic characteristics associated with depression in pregnancy and the postpartum. *Journal of Consulting & Clinical Psychology, 57,* 269–274.

*Grote, N. K., Swartz, H. A., Bledsoe, S. E., & Frank, E. (2004). Treating depression in low-income pregnant patients: The role of brief interpersonal psychotherapy. *Research on Social Work Practice, 14,* 397–406.

Hamilton, M. (1960). A rating scale for depression. *Journal of Neurology, Neurosurgery and Psychiatry, 23,* 56–62.

*Hayes, B. A., Muller, R., & Bradley, B. S. (2001). Perinatal depression: A randomized controlled trial of an antenatal education intervention for primaparas. *Birth, 28,* 28–35.

Hobfoll, S., Ritter, C., Lavin, J., Hulszier, M., & Cameron, R. (1995). Depression prevalence and incidence among inner-city pregnant and postpartum women. *Journal of Consulting and Clinical Psychology, 63,* 445–453.

*Holden, J. M., Sagovsky, R., & Cox, J. L. (1989). Counseling in a general practice setting: Controlled study of health visitor intervention in treatment of postnatal depression. *British Medical Journal, 298,* 223–226.

Insel, T. (2004, January 16). *Science to service: Mental health care after the decade of the brain.* Presentation given at Society for Social Work Research Annual Conference, New Orleans, LA.

Institute of Medicine. (1996). *Fetal alcohol syndrome: Diagnosis, epidemiology, prevention, and treatment.* Washington, DC: National Academy Press.

Kaplan, P. S., Bachorowski, J., Smoski, M. J., & Hudenko, W. J. (2002). Infants of depressed mothers, although competent learners, fail to learn in response to their own mothers' infant-directed speech. *Psychological Science, 13,* 268–271.

Klerman, G. L., Weissman, M. M., Rounsaville, B. H., & Chevron, E. S. (1984). *Interpersonal psychotherapy for depression.* New York: Basic Books.

Kumar, R., & Robson, M. (1984). A prospective study of emotional disorders in childbearing women. *British Journal of Psychiatry, 144,* 35–47.

*Lane, B., Roufeil, L. M., Williams, S., & Tweedie, R. (2001). It's just different in the country: Postnatal depression and group therapy in a rural setting. *Social Work in Healthcare, 34,* 333–348.

Lewis-Hall, F. C., Wilson, M. G., Tepner, R. C., & Koke, S. C. (1997). Fluoxetine vs. tricyclic antidepressants in women with major depressive disorder. *Journal of Women's Health, 6,* 337–343.

Lundy, B., Jones, N., Field, T., Nearing, G., Davalos, M., Pietro, P. A., et al. (1999). Prenatal depression effects on neonates. *Infant Behavior and Development, 22,* 119–129.

McNair, D. M., Lorr, M., & Droppleman, L. (1981). *Manual: Profile of mood states.* San Diego, CA: Education and Industrial Testing Service.

Meager, I., & Milgrom, J. (1996). Group treatment for postpartum depression: A pilot study. *Australian and New Zealand Journal of Psychiatry, 30,* 852–860.

Moore, G., Cohn, J., & Campbell, S. (2001). Infant affective responses to mother's still face at 6 months differentially predict externalizing and internalizing behaviors at 18 months. *Developmental Psychology, 37,* 706–714.

Murray, L., & Cooper, P. (1997). The role of infant and maternal factors in postpartum depression, mother-infant interactions, and infant outcome. In L. Murray & P. J. Cooper (Eds.), *Postpartum depression and child development* (pp. 201–220). New York: Guilford.

Nahas, Z., Bohning, D. E., Molloy, M. A., Oustz, J. A., Risch, S. C., & George, M. S. (1999). Safety and feasibility of repetitive transcranial magnetic stimulation in the treatment of anxious depression in pregnancy: A case report. *Journal of Clinical Psychiatry, 60,* 50–52.

O'Hara, M. (1994). *Postpartum depression: Causes and consequences.* New York: Springer-Verlag.

O'Hara, M., Neunaber, D., & Zekoski, E. (1984). Prospective study of postpartum depression: Prevalence, course, and predictive factors. *Journal of Abnormal Psychology, 93,* 158–171.

O'Hara, M. H., & Swain, A. M. (1996). Rates and risks of postpartum depression— A meta-analysis. *International Review of Psychiatry, 8,* 37–54.

O'Hara, M. H., Zekoski, E. M., Philipps, L. H., & Wright, E. J. (1990). Controlled prospective study of postpartum mood disorders: Comparison of childbearing and nonchildbearing women. *Journal of Abnormal Psychology, 99,* 3–15.

*O'Hara, M. W., Stuart, S., Gorman, L. L., & Wenzel, A. (2000). Efficacy of interpersonal psychotherapy for postpartum depression. *Archives of General Psychiatry, 57,* 1039–1045.

Oren, D. A., Wisner, K. L., Spinelli, M., Epperson, C. N., Peindl, K. S., Terman, J. S., et al. (2002). An open trial of morning light therapy for treatment of antepartum depression. *American Journal of Psychiatry, 159,* 666–669.

Orr, S. T., James, S. A., & Prince, C. B. (2002). Maternal prenatal depressive symptoms and spontaneous preterm births among African American women in Baltimore, Maryland. *American Journal of Epidemiology, 156,* 797–802.

Parry, B. L., Curran, M. L., Stuenkel, C. A., Yokimozo, M., Tam, L., Powell, K. A., et al. (2000). Can critically timed sleep deprivation be useful in pregnancy and postpartum depression? *Journal of Affective Disorders, 60,* 201–212.

Reid, M., Glazener, C., Murray, G. D., & Taylor, G. S. (2002). A two-centered pragmatic randomized controlled trial of two interventions for postnatal support. *BJOG: An International Journal of Obstetrics & Gynecology, 109,* 1164–1170.

Sanderson, C. A., Cowden, B., Hall, D. M. B., Taylor, E. M., Carpenter, R. G., & Cox, J. L. (2002). Is postnatal depression a risk factor for sudden infant death? *British Journal of General Practice, 52,* 636–640.

Sandman, C., Wadhwa, P. D., Dunkel-Schetter, C., Chicz-Demet, A., Belman, J., Porto, et al. (1994). Psychobiological influence of stress and HPA regulation on the human fetus and birth outcomes. *Annals of the New York Academy of Sciences, 739,* 198–210.

*Spinelli, M. G. (1997). Interpersonal psychotherapy for depressed antepartum women: A pilot study. *American Journal of Psychiatry, 154,* 1028–1030.

*Spinelli, M. G., & Endicott, J. (2003). Controlled clinical trial of interpersonal psychotherapy versus parenting education program for depressed pregnant women. *American Journal of Psychiatry, 160,* 555–562.

Stern, D. (1995). *The motherhood constellation.* New York: Basic Books.

*Suri, R., Burt, V. K., Altshuler, L. L., Zuckerbrow-Miller, J., & Fair, L. (2001). Fluvoxamine for postpartum depression. *American Journal of Psychiatry, 10,* 1739–1740.

Susman, E. J., Trickett, P. K., Iannotti, R. J., Hollenbeck, B. E., & Zahn-Waxler, C. (1985). Child-rearing patterns in depressed, abusive, and normal mothers. *American Journal of Orthopsychiatry, 55,* 237–251.

Wadhwa, P. D., Sandman, C., Porto, M., Dunkel-Schetter, C., & Garite, T. (1993). The association between prenatal stress and infant birth weight and gestational age at birth: A prospective investigative investigation. *American Journal of Obstetrics and Gynecology, 169,* 858–865.

Weissman, M. M., & Sanderson, W. C. (2001). Promises and problems in modern psychotherapy: The need for increased training in evidence-based treatments. In M. Hager (Ed.), *Modern psychiatry: Challenges in educating health professionals to meet new needs* (pp. 132–165). New York: Josiah Macy, Jr., Foundation.

Wisner, K. L., Gelenberg, A. J., Leonard, H., Zarin, D., & Frank, E. (1999). Pharmacologic treatment of depression during pregnancy. *Journal of the American Medical Association, 282,* 1264–1269.

Wisner, K. L., Perel, J. M., Peindl, K. S., Hanusa, B. H., Findling, R. L., & Rapport, D. (2001). Prevention of recurrent postpartum depression: A randomized clinical trial. *Journal of Clinical Psychiatry, 62,* 82–86.

Yonkers, K., Ramin, S., Rush, J., Navarrete, C., Carmody, T., March, D., et al. (2001). Onset and persistence of postpartum depression in an inner-city maternal health clinic system. *American Journal of Psychiatry, 158,* 1856–1863.

Zlotnick, C., Johnson, S. L., Miller, I. W., Pearlstein, T., & Howard, M. (2001). Postpartum depression in women receiving public assistance: Pilot study of an interpersonal-therapy-oriented group intervention. *American Journal of Psychiatry, 158,* 638–640.

Zuravin, S. J. (1989). Severity of maternal depression and three types of mother-to-child aggression. *American Journal of Orthopsychiatry, 59,* 377–389.

# Systematic Review of Depression Treatments in Primary Care for Latino Adults

## 11

*Leopoldo J. Cabassa and Marissa C. Hansen*

Depression is a common and disabling disorder among Latino adults served in primary-care settings (Olfson et al., 2000). However, this diverse population faces considerable disparities in the recognition and treatment of major depression (Lewis-Fernández, Das, Alfonoso, Weissman, & Olfson, 2005). Compared to non-Latino Whites with similar mental health needs, Latinos have less access to mental health care and are less likely to receive guideline-congruent depression care (U.S. Department of Health and Human Services [USDHHS], 2001; Young, Klap, Sherbourne, & Wells, 2001). Moreover, Latinos are more likely to seek mental health services from the primary health care sector than from mental health specialists (Vega, Kolody, & Aguilar-Gaxiola, 2001; Wells, Klap, Koeke, & Sherbourne, 2001). This pattern of care seeking suggests that primary-care settings are an important source of mental health care for this underserved population (Cabassa, Zayas, & Hansen, 2006). Given the inequities in depression care faced by Latinos, the implementation of effective and sustainable depression treatments for Latinos in primary health care settings has been proposed as a strategy to reduce mental health care disparities (USDHHS, 2001).

Studies show pharmacological and/or psychosocial treatments (e.g., cognitive-behavioral therapy [CBT]) can be effectively used to treat depression in primary-care patients (e.g., Brown & Schulberg, 1995). Until recently, few randomized clinical trials testing the effectiveness of depression treatments have included adequate numbers of Latinos to evaluate the quality and outcomes of these treatments in this underserved population (USDHHS, 2001). This lack of empirical evidence poses a serious threat to the ecological validity of depression treatments and places this growing

Originally published in *Research on Social Work Practice* 2007; 17; 494. DOI: 10.1177/1049731506297058 The online version of this article can be found at: http://rsw.sagepub.com/cgi/content/abstract/17/4/494

minority population at considerable risk for receiving inadequate depression care (Bernal, Bonilla, & Bellido, 1995).

This article addresses this gap in knowledge by systematically reviewing recent published randomized clinical trials examining the effectiveness of depression treatments in primary care for Latino adults. Effectiveness trials evaluate the outcomes and responses of treatments delivered in real-world settings (Wells, 1999). These trials differ from efficacy studies in that they (a) are conducted in community settings employing usual providers to deliver the intervention, (b) draw a heterogeneous sample of patients who come from a variety of socioeconomic and ethnic backgrounds and often have different comorbidities, (c) compare two or more active treatments, and (d) examine an array of outcomes (e.g., functioning, quality of life, costs, cost-effectiveness) during longer periods (Lagomasino, Dwight-Johnson, & Simpson, 2005).

Evidence generated from effectiveness trials help clinicians and policy makers make informed decisions about how to deliver high-quality and cost-effective mental health care to different populations (Lagomasino et al., 2005). Results of effectiveness studies that test the adequacy and outcomes of depression treatments are essential for developing and implementing evidence-based practices aimed at improving the quality of depression care for Latinos.

The aims of this literature review are (a) to rate the methodological quality of studies, (b) to examine the cultural and linguistic adaptations used in these effectiveness studies, (c) to summarize and discuss studies' clinical outcomes and cost-effectiveness findings, and (d) to draw conclusions from this growing body of research for improving depression care among this diverse population.

# Method

## Selection of Studies

Studies were identified through electronic bibliographic databases, Web sites, and manual searches. Databases searched included MEDLINE, PsycINFO, Social Science Abstracts, and the Cochrane Database of Systematic Reviews. Web sites, such as the National Institute of Mental Health (www.nimh.nih.gov), ClinicalTrial.gov (www.clinicaltrial.gov), and the Agency for Healthcare Research and Quality (www.ahrq.gov), were searched. Manual searches of the reference sections of identified articles, pertinent published books, and government reports were also conducted. Keywords used to guide our search included the following: *effectiveness studies, randomized controlled trials, controlled clinical trials, major depression, depression, dysthymia, dysthymic disorder, depression treatment, psychosocial treatments, cognitive behavior therapy, interpersonal therapy, problem solving therapy, pharmacological treatments, antidepressant treatments, primary care, Latinos, Hispanics, Puerto Ricans, Cubans, Mexicans, Mexican Americans, Central Americans,* and *South Americans.*

Abstracts of 60 articles were retrieved and reviewed for relevance. Studies were chosen for review if they met the following criteria: (a) compared the effectiveness between one or more depression treatments and usual care in primary health care settings, (b) randomized patients and/or clinics to treatment conditions, (c) reported treatment effectiveness and/or cost-effectiveness findings for Latinos. Nine peer-reviewed articles published between 2003 and 2006 reporting findings from four randomized clinical trials met these criteria and were included in this review. Seven of the 9 articles reported treatment effectiveness findings from these trials. The other 2 articles included in this review reported cost-effectiveness findings.

## Analytical Strategies

An adapted version of Miller and colleagues' (1995) Methodological Quality Rating Scale (MQRS) was used to evaluate studies' methodological characteristics. This instrument assesses studies' methodological quality across 12 dimensions (e.g., study design, enumeration of baseline data, follow-up rate, analyses; see Table 11.1), and it has been used in previous systematic reviews of intervention studies (e.g., Burke, Arkowitz, & Menchola, 2003; Vaughn & Howard, 2004). One dimension was added to the scale to assess the absence or presence of cultural and/or linguistic adaptations of depression treatments for Latino patients. This added dimension enabled us to rate whether studies explicitly discussed strategies used to adapt depression treatments to the needs of Latino patients. Each study MQRS score could range from 0 (*poor quality*) to 17 (*high quality*).

The two authors, working independently, rated each of the 7 studies that reported effectiveness findings across the 13 dimensions of the MQRS. Of the 182 ratings (13 ratings per article × 7 articles × 2 raters) completed by the two raters, only 6 (3%) were in disagreement. In these cases, minor differences were identified by the two raters and were resolved through consensus. For example, the follow-up length of a particular study was rated by one rater to be 6 to 11 months, and 12 months or longer by the other rater. Both authors then met to resolve this disagreement by rereading the study in question and identifying the correct follow-up length, which in this case was 6 to 11 months. Last, a review form following Lipsey and Wilson's (2001) recommendations was used to systematically code study-level characteristics, such as study aims, designs, sampling and randomization strategy, intervention components and control groups, outcome measures, data analysis, findings, study limitations, and conclusions.

# Results

## Studies Characteristics

The trials reviewed included (a) Women Entering Care (Miranda, Chung, et al., 2003; Miranda et al., 2006), (b) the San Francisco General Hospital Depression Clinic trial (hereafter, the San Francisco Trial; Miranda, Azocar, Organista, Dweyer, & Areáne, 2003), (c) Partners in Care (PIC; Miranda, Duan, et al., 2003; Miranda, Schoenbaum, Sherbourne, Duan, & Wells, 2004; Wells et al., 2004), and (d) Improving Mood-Promoting Access to Collaborative Treatment (IMPACT; Areán et al., 2005). An overview of the 7 articles presenting effectiveness findings from these 4 trials is shown in Table 11.2. The other 2 articles included in this review reported cost-effectiveness evaluations of the Women Entering Care (Revicki et al., 2005) and PIC (Schoenbaum, Miranda, Sherbourne, Duan, & Wells, 2004) trials. Women Entering Care was the only trial to recruit from county health and welfare services. The rest of the trials were conducted in primary health care clinics within different health care organizations (e.g., private group practices, health maintenance organizations). Women Entering Care and the San Francisco trials included patients who were uninsured. The remaining studies recruited patients with private or public insurances.

## Studies Methodological Characteristics and Ratings

The total QRS score for each study ranged from 13 to 16, with a mean of 14 ($SD = 1.1$). Three of the four trials randomized individuals into different treatment conditions. In contrast, PIC used a group-level randomized controlled trial design in which 46 primary-care clinics from six managed-care organizations were divided into clusters of group practices and then randomized into usual care or one of two quality improvement (QI) programs (QI-therapy and QI-medication). QI sites received study materials, staff training, and limited support during the implementation of the trials. The goal of the QI programs was to train staff and provide the necessary resources to improve depression care under naturalistic conditions. Throughout the PIC trial, patients and clinicians retained choice of treatment, and it was optional for them to use intervention resources.

All studies provided sufficient detail to replicate the intervention, reported detailed baseline patient characteristics (e.g., gender, ethnicity/race, age, marital status, education, clinical status), and used annualized psychosocial depression treatments and/or guideline-congruent pharmacological treatment protocols. Follow-up periods ranged from 6 to 57 months, and follow-up rates ranged from 73% to 83%, with an average rate across studies of 80% ($SD = 4.01\%$). One study (the San Francisco Trial) used collateral information from medical chart abstractions to derive a chronic disease score, and case manager records were used to describe case-management services received during a 6-month period. The rest of the studies reported no use of collateral information (e.g., medical records, insurance claims, interviewing family members) to corroborate and/or supplement self-report measures and service use patterns. Objective verification of patients' depression and other mental health conditions was done in all studies through the use of structured diagnostic instruments, such as the World Health Organization Composite International Diagnostic Interview (Robins et al., 1988) and the Structured Clinical Interview (Spitzer, Williams, Gibbon, & First, 1990).

All studies enumerated dropout rates and used appropriate statistical analyses. Statistical procedures used to evaluate treatment outcomes for Latinos and other racial and ethnic groups included mixed-effects repeated-measure analysis, repeated-measure analysis of variance and covariance, multivariate regression, and logistic regression, among others. Follow-up measures were collected through a combination of mail surveys and blind telephone interviews in PIC, and the rest of the studies used blind personal or telephone interviews. The San Francisco Trial was the only single-site study; the rest were multisite studies. All studies, some in more detail than others, discussed cultural and/or linguistic adaptations to treatment programs

## Depression Treatment Programs

All trials used manualized, short-term psychotherapy and/or standardized medication-management protocols based on published depression treatment guidelines. CBT was delivered in individual or group sessions by trained clinical staff (licensed clinical psychologist or social worker) supervised by a licensed clinical psychologist with expertise in CBT. The manualized protocol ranged from 8 to 12 weeks of sessions, and patients' improvements were regularly assessed with standardized depression scales (e.g., Hamilton Depression Rating Scale). In the San Francisco trial, CBT was enhanced by adding a case-management program. The program was developed by licensed clinical social workers and was designed to help patients during a 6-month period to cope with psychosocial problems affecting their depression care.

The IMPACT trial used problem solving therapy adapted for primary care (PST-PC settings; Areán, Hagel, & Unützer, 1999), a brief psychotherapy derived from CBT, delivered within a collaborative care program (CC). Trained depression clinical specialists (nurses or clinical psychologists) delivered PST-PC and monitored depression symptoms with standardized instruments following the Agency for Health Care Policy and Research depression treatment guidelines.

Medication management based on depression treatment guidelines were used in 3 of the 4 trials. A stepped-care approach in which a trained clinician

**Table 11.1**    Adapted Methodological Rating Scale

| *Methodological Attributes* | *Points Awarded* |
|---|---|
| 1. Study Design | 1. Single group pretest-posttest<br>2. Quasi-experimental (nonequivalent control group/nonrandomization)<br>3. Randomization with control group |
| 2. Replicability | 0. Intervention or follow-up description insufficiently detailed<br>1. Procedures contain sufficient detail |
| 3. Baseline | 0. No baseline scores, client characteristics or measures reported<br>1. Baseline scores, client characteristics or measures reported |
| 4. Quality control | 0. No intervention standardized specified<br>1. Intervention standardized by manual, procedures, specific training and so forth |
| 5. Follow-up length | 0. Less than 6 months<br>1. 6–11 months<br>2. 12 months or longer |
| 6. Follow-up rate | 0. Less than 70% completion<br>1. 70% to 84.9% completion<br>2. 85% to 100% completion |
| 7. Collaterals | 0. No collateral verification of participant self-report<br>1. Collaterals interviewed |
| 8. Objective verification | 0. No objective verification of participant self-report<br>1. Verification of records (paper records, insurance claim, medical charts, diagnostic interviews) |
| 9. Dropouts | 0. No discussion or enumeration of dropouts or dropout excluded from analysis (no intent to treat analysis)<br>1. Intervention dropout enumerated |
| 10. Independent | 0. Follow-up conducted nonblind or by an unspecified method<br>1. Follow-up conducted by person blind to participants' treatment conditions |
| 11. Analyses | 0. No statistical analyses conducted or clearly inappropriate analyses<br>1. Appropriate statistical analyses |
| 12. Multisite | 0. Single site study<br>1. Parallel replication at two or more sites |
| 13. Cultural and linguistic adaptations to depression treatments | 0. Cultural and linguistic adaptations not reported or discussed.<br>1. Cultural and linguistic adaptation reported or discussed |

NOTE: Scores could range from 0 (low) to 17 (high). Adapted from Miller et al. (1995) and Vaughn and Howard (2003).

**Table 11.2** Overview of Effectiveness Studies of Latino Depression Treatments in Primary Care

| Author and Study | Intervention | Control Group | Sample | Outcome Measures | Follow-up | Quality Rating Scale Score |
|---|---|---|---|---|---|---|
| Miranda, Chung, et al. (2003), Women Entering Care[a] | Pharmacotherapy (e.g., paroxetine switched to bupropion, if lack response) or CBT | Referral to community care | 267, 6% White, 51% Latinas, 44% African Americans | Depressive symptoms (HDRS) Instrumental role functioning (Social Adjustment Scale) Social Functioning (Short-form 36-item Health Survey) | 6 months | 14 |
| Miranda, Azocar, Organista, Dwyer, and Areáne (2003), San Francisco Trial | CBT supplemented with case management | CBT alone | 199, 33% White, 39% Spanish-speaking Latinos/as, 25% African American, 4% Other | Severity of depressive symptoms (BDI) Social adjustment (SAS) | 6 months | 13 |
| Wells et al. (2004), PIC | Quality improvement programs (QI): QI-medication (antidepressants) or QI-therapy (CBT) | Usual care | 991 completed 57-month telephone follow-up, 61% Whites, 27% Latinos/as, 5% African Americans, 7% Other | Rates of probable major depression in previous 6 months (modified CIDI stem items) Mental health-related quality of life (MCS12) Primary care or mental health specialist visits Counseling or antidepressant medication in previous 6 months Unmet need: depressed and not receiving appropriate care | 57 months | 14 |
| Miranda, Duan, et al. (2003), PIC | QI: QI-medication (antidepressants) or QI-therapy (CBT) | Usual care | 938, 64% White, 27% Latinos/as, 6% African Americans, 3% Asian or Native Americans | Rates of probable major depression (modified CIDI stem items) Employment status Rates of receiving guideline-congruent depression care | 6 months | 13 |

*(Continued)*

**Table 11.2** (Continued)

| Author and Study | Intervention | Control Group | Sample | Outcome Measures | Follow-up | Quality Rating Scale Score |
|---|---|---|---|---|---|---|
| Miranda, Schoenbaum, Sherbourne, Duan, and Wells (2004), PIC | QI: QI-medication (antidepressants) or QI-therapy (CBT) | Usual care | 1,269, 61% White, 31% Latinos/as, 7% African Americans1[a] | Rate of receiving guideline-congruent depression care<br><br>Rates of probable major depression (modified CIDI stem items)<br><br>Employment status<br><br>Rate of receiving guideline-congruent depression care<br><br>Rates of probable major depression (modified CIDI stem items)<br><br>Employment status | 12 months | 14 |
| Areán et al. (2005), IMPACT[b] | Collaborative care (antidepressant or problem-solving therapy adapted for primary care, based on patients' preference) | Usual care[b] | 1,801, 77% White, 8% Latinos, 12% African Americans, 3% Other | Use of antidepressants medication or psychotherapy<br><br>Satisfaction with depression care<br><br>Depressive symptoms (HSCL-20)<br><br>Treatment response (50% or more decrease in HSCL)<br><br>Treatment remission (HSCL-20 score smaller than .05) Health-related functional impairment (SDS) | 12 months | 16 |
| Miranda et al. (2006), Women Entering Care | Pharmacotherapy (e.g., paroxetine switched to bupropion, if lack response) or CBT | Referral to community care | 267, 6% White, 51% Latinas, 44% African Americans | Depressive symptoms (HDRS)<br><br>Instrumental role functioning (Social Adjustment Scale)<br><br>Social Functioning | 12 months | 15 |

NOTE: CBT = cognitive-behavioral therapy; HDRS = Hamilton Depression Rating Scale; BDI = Beck Depression Inventory; PIC = Partners in Care; QI = Quality Improvement; CIDI = Composite International Diagnostic Interview; MCS12 = Mental Health Composite Score; HSCL-20 = Hopkins Symptoms Checklist-20; SDS = Sheehan Disability Scale.

a. Recruited exclusively women from Women, Infants, and Children food subsidy programs and Title X family planning clinics.

b. All Latinos in this study were English-speaking elders (60 years of age or older).

(e.g., nurse or psychologist) in consultation with a psychiatrist managed and monitored patients during the acute and maintenance phase of depression treatment was used in these trials. For instance, in the IMPACT study, the depression care specialist monitored depressive symptoms, side effects, and adherence every 2 weeks during the acute phase of treatment and then monitored patients through monthly contacts for 1 year after stabilization of depression. The DCS met weekly with a consulting psychiatrist to discuss cases and revised treatment plan. If after 4 to 6 weeks patients did not show improvements, either treatment was changed to another antidepressant or PST-PC was given. If the patient still did not improve, other treatments were considered (e.g., referral to specialty mental health).

Before starting treatment (psychotherapy or medication), all treatment programs included education meetings into their protocols. In these meetings, patients were educated about depression and its treatments with short educational videos, printed media (brochures, educational pamphlets), and/or discussions with their clinicians. For instance, in Women Entering Care, up to four education sessions could be scheduled to help participants with the decision to initiate treatment. Miranda, Chung, et al. (2003) reported that 96% of women attended a mean of 1.89 education sessions before beginning medications and 67% attended 2.37 education visits before beginning psychotherapy.

## Cultural and Linguistic Adaptations of Depression Programs

Cultural and linguistic adaptations used in the trials are presented in Table 11.3. The most common adaptations included employing bilingual and bicultural clinicians (e.g., social workers, nurse practitioners, psychologists) to deliver care, having educational and intervention materials available in English and Spanish, and including references to minority groups in educational materials (e.g., brochures, videos). All trials, aside from IMPACT, used a CBT protocol that was specifically developed and previously tested with low-income, Spanish- and English-speaking medical patients (Muñoz & Mendelson, 2005). Staff cultural sensitivity training that directly discussed cultural norms (e.g., *simpatia, respeto, marianismo*) believed to influence the treatment of Latinos was used in PIC and the San Francisco Trial. PIC also used minority investigators to provide consultations to treatment teams in the intervention sites and employed experts in mental health interventions for minorities to design all educational materials used in the trial.

## Treatment Outcomes

*Clinical outcomes and functioning.* Instruments used to measure clinical outcomes and functioning are listed in Table 11.2. Six-month outcomes

**Table 11.3**     Cultural and Linguistic Adaptations to Depression Treatment
                   Programs

| Trial | Cultural and Linguistic Adaptations |
| --- | --- |
| Women Entering Care | CBT manual was adapted from a 12-session protocol, developed and tested for low-income Spanish- and English-speaking medical patients. |
| | Bilingual providers treated all Spanish-speaking women. |
| | All written materials, including psychotherapy manuals, were available in Spanish. |
| | All psychotherapists and nurse practitioners had extensive experience working with low-income minority patients. |
| | Transportation and child care funds were provided to participants in the two intervention groups. |
| San Francisco Trial | CBT manual, developed and tested for low-income Spanish- and English-speaking medical patients, was used. |
| | Employing bilingual and bicultural providers. |
| | Having educational materials and interventions material available in Spanish. |
| | Staff training on how to show *respeto* and *simpatia* to patients and create warmer, more personalized interactions than were typical for English-speaking patients. |
| Partners in Care | CBT manual developed and tested for low-income Spanish- and English-speaking medical patients was used. |
| | Experts in mental health intervention for minority patients participated in the design of quality improvement educational materials. |
| | All educational and intervention materials were available in Spanish and English. Latino and African American providers were included in the depression education video. |
| | Bilingual and bicultural staff were used to treat minority patients. |
| | Minority investigators provided supervision to local experts throughout the intervention. All staff received cultural sensitivity training. |
| IMPACT | Few cultural adaptations were made to the treatment model. |
| | Written and video materials included references to older adults from varying ethnic groups. |
| | No linguistic adaptations were made because all participants were English speaking. |

NOTE: CBT = cognitive-behavioral therapy.

showed that CBT and antidepressants were superior to usual care in reducing the rates of patients with probable depression in PIC and lowering depression and improving functioning in the Women Entering Care trial. Miranda, Chung, et al. (2003) found that in the Women Entering Care trial medication was superior to CBT in lowering depressive symptoms and improving instrumental role functioning among their sample of low-income minority women. They partially attributed this finding to the fact that more women engaged in a sufficient duration of medication treatment than in CBT. Moreover, a higher proportion of women received appropriate care in the medication group compared to those in the CBT group (76% vs. 36%, respectively). Appropriate care in the medication group was defined as receiving at least 9 weeks of guideline-congruent medication treatment, whereas appropriate care for CBT was defined as receiving at least 6 CBT sessions.

Latinos' engagement into psychotherapy was improved in the San Francisco trial by adding supplemental case management to the CBT protocol. In this trial, Miranda, Azocar, et al. (2003) found that Spanish-speaking patients ($n = 77$) in the CBT with supplemental case-management groups reported significantly fewer depressive symptoms and improved functioning at 4 and 6 months compared to Spanish-speaking patients who only received CBT. This finding was not replicated with the English-speaking patients who participated in this trial. Miranda and colleagues concluded that their study provides initial evidence that supplementing CBT with case management may improve treatment retention and outcomes for Spanish-speaking patients.

Twelve-month outcomes from the Women Entering Care, PIC, and IMPACT trials point to sustained treatment gains for those receiving CBT, antidepressants, or PST-PC compared to those in usual care. In Women Entering Care, the CBT and medication groups were significantly better in lowering depressive symptoms than those who were in the community referral group at the 1-year follow-up. The superiority of medication over CBT in decreasing depressive symptoms and improving functioning observed at 6 months was maintained at 12 months. However, the remission rates at 12 months (defined as HDRS scores $\leq 7$ and a 50% change from baseline to 12 months) of the CBT (56.9%) and medication (50.9%) groups were not significantly different, and both were higher than those of the community referral group (37.1%).

The QI and CC programs from the PIC and IMPACT trials improved depression outcomes at 12 months for Latinos and African Americans compared to their counterparts in usual care. For example, in the IMPACT trial, Latinos and African Americans in the CC group had significantly better depression outcomes, higher rates of treatment response, and higher rates of remission than those in the usual care group (Areán et al., 2005). In PIC, the QI interventions significantly decreased the likelihood of probable depression for Latinos and African Americans but did not significantly improve their rates of employment, an indicator of functioning (Miranda, Duan, et al., 2003).

Sustained positive treatment effects for Latinos and African Americans at 57 months were reported for PIC. QI-therapy in particular was related to significantly lowering rates of probable depression rates and unmet needs for appropriate care and to improving health outcomes for African Americans and Latinos but had little effect for non-Latino Whites at the 57-month follow-up (Wells et al., 2004).

*Access to guideline-congruent care.* In Women Entering Care, PIC, and IMPACT, the interventions programs compared to usual care increased Latinos' access to guideline-congruent depression care. Miranda and colleagues (2004) found that the QI interventions (medications or therapy) used in PIC significantly improved for all patients the rates of receiving guideline depression care by 9% to 20% at 6-month follow-up. At 12 months, Latinos in the QI interventions were more likely to receive appropriate depression care than those in usual care (39.4% vs. 26.4%, respectively), with the difference reaching statistical significance (Miranda, Duan, et al., 2003). However, Latino patients still lagged behind non-Latino Whites receiving QI interventions, 62.1% of whom were receiving appropriate depression care at 12 months (Miranda, Duan, et al., 2003).

In IMPACT, patients in the CC group by 12 months used more guideline-congruent depression services than those in the usual care group and reported greater satisfaction with care (Areán et al., 2005). Latinos in the CC group were more likely to use antidepressant medications and psychotherapy than their counterparts in the usual care group.

## Cost-Effectiveness Findings

Two studies reported cost-effectiveness findings of depression treatments programs in primary care for Latinos. Schoenbaum and colleagues (2004) compared the societal cost-effectiveness of PIC for Latinos and non-Latino Whites during 24 months. They found that, compared to usual care, the QI-therapy group that enhanced resources for psychotherapy (i.e., CBT) was more cost-effective for Latinos than was the QI-medication group, which provided resources to receive medication-based care for depression. Latinos in QI-therapy had significantly fewer depression burden days compared to those in usual care, and the cost per quality-adjusted years (QALY) was $6,100 or less. This cost per QALY estimate is well below those found in established medical interventions (Gold, Siegel, Russell, & Weinstein, 1996). Latinos in the QI-medication group reported no significant improvements in depression burden days compared to those in usual care and had an estimated cost per QALY of $90,000 or more, thus making this intervention not cost-effective for this group of Latinos. For non-Latino Whites, those in QI-medication and QI-therapy groups reported lower depression burden days compared to those in usual care, but the differences were not statistically significant. Whites in the QI-therapy reported a significant increase in the days employed, a finding not observed in Latinos. The estimated cost per QALY for Whites on both interventions was around $30,000 or less.

Revicki and colleagues (2005) examined the cost-effectiveness of Miranda, Chung, et al.'s (2003) Women Entering Care clinical trial during a 12-month period. They found that compared to women who received community referrals, both intervention groups (CBT and pharmacotherapy) reported significantly more depression-free days. Furthermore, the cost per QALY was $16,068 for the pharmacotherapy group and $17,624 for the CBT group. The authors concluded that "investment in depression interventions, including the additional outreach, educational attainment, and supportive services (i.e., transportation and babysitting), consistently improves these women's depression and functional outcomes" (pp. 872–873). Therefore, both pharmacotherapy and CBT were cost-effective compared to community mental health services referral for these low-income minority women.

## Discussion and Applications to Social Work

Studies included in this review were rigorous randomized controlled trials of high methodological quality. Findings from these studies indicate that depression treatment programs for Latinos delivered in primary care under a CC model were more effective than usual care in reducing depressive symptoms, improving functioning, and increasing accessibility to guideline-congruent care. Two trials (PIC and Women Entering Care) included in this review also reported that these treatment programs were more cost-effective than usual care, even with the added costs associated with cultural and linguistic adaptations and supportive services (e.g., transportation, child care; Revicki et al., 2005; Schoenbaum et al., 2004). Depression treatments for Latinos in primary care appeared most effective when enhanced treatment was provided. These treatment programs shared the following features: (a) screening or case-finding measures were systematically used to identify depressed patients; (b) patient-education materials that were culturally and/or linguistically adapted for Latino groups were used at the beginning stages of treatment; (c) trained clinicians (e.g., nurses, social workers, clinical psychologists) delivered manualized psychosocial treatments (CBT or PST) and/or coordinated medication management based on published treatment guidelines; (d) a collaborative, interdisciplinary approach among primary-care physicians, clinicians, and consultant psychiatrists was used to manage and make treatment decisions; and (e) standardized, symptom-based depression measures were systematically used to monitor treatment progress and guide treatment decisions.

Several differences between the effectiveness of medication and psychosocial treatments were noted in these trials. In the PIC, QI-therapy was significantly more cost-effective and alleviated depressive symptoms at a significantly higher rate than QI-medication treatment for Latinos compared to non-Latino Whites (Schoenbaum et al., 2004). The QI-therapy treatment gains were sustained at the 57-month follow-up, lowering rates of probable depression and unmet needs for appropriate care and improving health outcomes, but they showed little effect for non-Latino Whites (Wells et al., 2004). These findings support the use of culturally and linguistically tailored CBT as an effective treatment option for depression among PIC Latinos.

The effectiveness of CBT over medication was not supported in the Women Entering Care Trial. In this trial, both treatments (CBT and medication) showed comparable cost-effectiveness when compared to community referrals for these low-income, minority women (Revicki et al., 2005), yet medication-based care was found to increase functioning and decrease depression symptoms more so than CBT. Miranda, Chung, et al. (2003) attributed the effectiveness of medication over CBT to the fact that more women engage in sufficient duration of medication treatment than CBT. However, even with limited exposure and engagement to CBT, these women achieved similar remission rates at 12 months as those in the medication group (56.6% vs. 50.9%, respectively) and were significantly better than their counterparts referred to community mental health services (Miranda et al., 2006).

The differences observed across these trials highlight how similar treatment approaches (CBT and medication management) may have different outcomes depending on the Latino community being served and suggest that a one-size-fits-all approach to treating depression in primary-care settings may not be appropriate for this diverse population. PIC findings suggest that culturally and linguistically adapted CBT may be more appropriate for Latinos served in managed-care organizations that have a regular source of care. The Women Entering Care trial showed enhance medication management may be more appropriate than eight sessions of individual or group CBT to treat depression among low-income, minority women served in county health and welfare services. Supplementing depression care with case management may also be an appropriate approach to help Latinos, particularly those who are monolingual Spanish speaking, overcome access barriers, improve treatment retention, decrease depressive symptoms, and improve functioning (Miranda, Azocar, et al., 2003). The combination of case-management services and depression care may be particularly helpful and effective for low-income and/or low-acculturated Latinos who may need assistance in navigating the health care system and face multiple social and economic demands that prevent them from accessing and engaging in treatment. More studies testing the effectiveness of supplementing depression treatments with case-management programs are needed to understand the clinical and economic benefits of this combination of services in reducing mental health care disparities among Latinos.

Other strategies used in these trials to accommodate the needs of diverse Latino communities included employing bilingual clinicians, providing supportive (e.g., child care, transportation) and case-management services, culturally and linguistically adapting depression education materials, and adding flexible educational meetings to the treatment protocols to increase patients' understanding of depression and its treatment and enhance trust and acceptance of depression treatment. To develop effective depression care programs in primary-care settings for the diverse Latino population, treatment programs need to be carefully adapted and modified to fit the social, cultural, and economic realities of the targeted population.

Cultural and linguistic adaptations employed in these trials can be placed within a continuum ranging from minimal to comprehensive modifications of depression treatments. The IMPACT trial stands at one end of this continuum because few cultural and linguistic adaptations were made to their treatment model, and it was the only trial to use a manualized, short-term psychotherapy (i.e., PST) that had not been previously adapted for Latinos. Moreover, the exclusion of Spanish-speaking individuals limits the generalizability of this trial. Even with these limited adaptations, IMPACT showed better depression outcomes and improved accessibility to guideline-congruent depression care than usual care for African American and English-speaking Latino elders. The remaining trials included in this review stand at the other end of the continuum reporting multifaceted efforts to accommodate the linguistic and cultural variance in their sample.

One key question these trials did not address that deserves further research is the following: How are these cultural and linguistic adaptations linked to treatment effectiveness? These trials provide initial evidence indicating that different degrees of cultural and/or linguistic adaptations of depression treatments in primary care significantly improved the quality, effectiveness, and cost-effectiveness of mental health care for Latinos. To move the findings generated from these trials into real-world ethnically and racially diverse practice settings and inform clinical practice, more studies are needed to clarify which adaptation or combination of adaptations produce high-quality and cost-effective depression care for Latinos. The goals of these studies are to examine and understand the causal relationships between cultural and linguistic adaptations and treatment effectiveness. Dismantling and additive intervention designs can be used to empirically test these causal relationships (Borkovec & Miranda, 1999). Bridging this gap in knowledge will help clarify what culturally competent innovations and clinical skills are necessary to produce high-quality mental health care services (Vega, 2005). Evidence generated from these studies will provide practitioners and policy makers a better understanding of which key ingredients are needed to develop effective depression treatment programs in primary-care settings that meet the linguistic and cultural needs of Latino clients.

Our review is limited because of the small number of clinical trials published, the subjective nature of evaluating the methodological quality of studies, our stringent study-selection criteria, and the scarcity of controlled clinical trials testing the effectiveness of other psychotherapeutic approaches (e.g., family therapy, interpersonal therapy) adapted for Latinos to treat depression in primary-care settings. Notwithstanding these limitations, more randomized controlled trial studies are needed to enhance our understanding of how to provide effective and cost-effective depression care to Latino adults in primary care. These trials need to continue drawing diverse Latino samples that include both English- and Spanish-speaking Latinos who vary in acculturation levels and are drawn from different socioeconomic groups. Future studies should also report effect sizes to facilitate comparison across trials and help build a better empirical understanding of how effective these treatment programs are for this diverse population when compared to usual depression care. More research is also needed on how to translate and diffuse the evidence generated from these trials into primary-care settings serving Latino populations. As the Latino population in the United States continues to grow, more research is needed to develop, test, and implement effective and sustainable depression treatments for Latinos in primary health care. The trials included in this review generate initial evidence supporting the use of evidence-based treatments in primary care as an effective and cost-effective strategy to reduce the inequities Latino primary-care patients face in the accessibility and quality of depression care.

# References

Areán, P., Ayalon, L., Hunkeler, E., Lin, E. H. B., Tang, L., Harpole, L., et al. (2005). Improving depression care for older, minority patients in primary care. *Medical Care, 43,* 381–390.

Areán, P., Hagel, M. T., & Unützer, J. (1999). *Problem solving therapy for older primary care patients: Maintenance group manual for Project IMPACT.* Los Angeles: University of California.

Bernal, G., Bonilla, J., & Bellido, C. (1995). Ecological validity and cultural sensitivity for outcome research: Issues for the cultural adaptation and development of psychosocial treatments with Hispanics. *Journal of Abnormal Child Psychology, 23,* 67–82.

Borkovec, T. D., & Miranda, J. (1999). Between-group psychotherapy outcome research and basic science. *Journal of Clinical Psychology, 55,* 147–158.

Brown, C., & Schulberg, H. C. (1995). The efficacy of psychosocial treatments in primary care: A review of randomized clinical trials. *General Hospital Psychiatry, 17,* 414–424.

Burke, B. L., Arkowitz, H., & Menchola, M. (2003). The efficacy of motivational interviewing: A meta-analysis of controlled clinical trials. *Journal of Consulting and Clinical Psychology, 71,* 843–861.

Cabassa, L. J., Zayas, L. H., & Hansen, M. C. (2006). Latino adults' access to mental health services: A review of epidemiological studies. *Administration and Policy in Mental Health and Mental Health Services Research, 33,* 316–330.

Gold, M. R., Siegel, J. E., Russell, L. B., & Weinstein, M. C. (Eds.). (1996). *Cost-effectiveness in health and medicine*. New York: Oxford University Press.

Lagomasino, I. T., Dwight-Johnson, M., & Simpson, G. M. (2005). Psychopharmacology: The need for effectiveness trials to inform evidence-based psychiatric practice. *Psychiatric Services, 56,* 649–651.

Lewis-Fernández, R., Das, A. K., Alfonso, C., Weissman, M. M., & Olfson, M. (2005). Depression in US Hispanics: Diagnostic and management considerations in family practice. *Journal of the American Board of Family Practice, 18,* 282–296.

Lipsey, M. W., & Wilson, D. B. (2001). *Practical meta-analysis*. Thousand Oaks, CA: Sage Publications.

Miller, W. R. , Brown, J. M., Simpson, L. M., Handmaker, N. S., Bien, T. H., Luckie, L. F., et al. (1995). What works? A methodological analysis of alcohol treatment outcome literature. In R. K. Hester & W. R. Miller (Eds.), *Handbook of alcoholism treatment approaches: Effective alternatives* (2nd ed., pp. 12–44). Boston: Allyn & Bacon.

Miranda, J., Azocar, F., Organista, K. C., Dwyer, E., & Areáne, P. (2003). Treatment of depression among impoverished primary care patients from ethnic minority groups. *Psychiatric Services, 54,* 219–225.

Miranda, J., Chung, J. Y., Green, B. L., Krupnick, J., Siddique, J., Revicki, D. A., et al. (2003). Treating depression in predominantly low-income young minority women: A randomized controlled trial. *Journal of the American Medical Association, 290,* 57–65.

Miranda, J., Duan, N., Sherbourne, C., Shoenbaum, M., Lagomasino, I., Jackson-Triche, M., et al. (2003). Improving care for minorities: Can quality improvement interventions improve care and outcomes for depressed minorities? Results of a randomized, controlled trial. *Health Services Research, 38,* 613–630.

Miranda, J., Green, B. L., Krupnick, J. L., Chung, J., Siddique, J., Belin, T., et al. (2006). One-year outcomes of a randomized clinical trial treating depression in low-income minority women. *Journal of Consulting and Clinical Psychology, 74,* 99–111.

Miranda, J., Schoenbaum, M., Sherbourne, C., Duan, N., & Wells, K. (2004). Effects of primary care depression treatment on minority patients' clinical status and employment. *Archives of General Psychiatry, 61,* 827–834.

Muñoz, R. F., & Mendelson, T. (2005). Toward evidence-based interventions for diverse populations: The San Francisco general hospitals prevention and treatment manuals. *Journal of Consulting and Clinical Psychology, 73,* 790–799.

Olfson, M., Shea, S., Feder, A., Fuentes, M., Nomura, Y., Gameroff, M., et al. (2000). Prevalence of anxiety, depression and substance abuse disorders in an urban general medicine practice. *Archives of Family Medicine, 9,* 876–883.

Revicki, D. A., Siddique, J., Frank, L., Chung, J. Y., Green, B. L., Krupnick, J., et al. (2005). Cost-effectiveness of evidence-based pharmacotherapy or cognitive behavior therapy compared with community referral for major depression in predominantly low-income minority women. *Archives of General Psychiatry, 62,* 868–875.

Robins, L. N., Wing, J., Wittchen, H. U., Helzer, J. E., Babor, T. F., Burke, J., et al. (1988). The Composite International Diagnostic Interview. An epidemiologic instrument suitable for use in conjunction with different diagnostic systems and in different cultures. *Archives of General Psychiatry, 45,* 1069–1077.

Schoenbaum, M., Miranda, J., Sherbourne, C., Duan, N., & Wells, K. (2004). Cost-effectiveness of interventions for depressed Latinos. *The Journal of Mental Health Policy and Economics, 7,* 69–76.

Spitzer, R. L., Williams, J. B. W., Gibbon, M., & First, M. B. (1990). *Structured Clinical Interview for DSM-III-R: Patient education* (SCID-P Version 1.0). Washington, DC: American Psychiatric Association.

U.S. Department of Health and Human Services. (2001). *Mental health: Culture, race, and ethnicity: A supplement to mental health: A report of the Surgeon General.* Rockville, MD: Author.

Vaughn, M. G., & Howard, M. O. (2004). Integrated psychosocial and opioid-antagonist treatment for alcohol dependence: A systematic review of controlled evaluations. *Social Work Research, 28,* 41–53.

Vega, W. A. (2005). Higher stakes ahead for cultural competence. *General Hospital Psychiatry, 27,* 446–450.

Vega, W. A., Kolody, B., & Aguilar-Gaxiola, S. (2001). Help seeking for mental health problems among Mexican Americans. *Journal of Immigrant Health, 3,* 133–140.

Wells, K. B. (1999). Treatment research at the crossroads: The scientific interface of clinical trials and effectiveness research. *American Journal of Psychiatry, 156,* 5–10.

Wells, K. B., Klap, R., Koeke, A., & Sherbourne, C. (2001). Ethnic disparities in unmet needs for alcoholism, drug abuse, and mental health care. *American Journal of Psychiatry, 158,* 2027–2032.

Wells, K. B., Sherbourne, C., Schoenbaum, M., Ettner, S., Duan, N., Miranda, J., et al. (2004). Five year impact of quality improvement for depression: Result of a group-level randomized controlled trial. *Archives of General Psychiatry, 61,* 378–386.

Young, A. S., Klap, R., Sherbourne, C. D., & Wells, K. B. (2001). The quality of care for depressive and anxiety disorders in the United States. *Archives of General Psychiatry, 58,* 55–61.

# Changing Heterosexuals' Attitudes Toward Homosexuals

## A Systematic Review of the Empirical Literature

Edmon W. Tucker and Miriam Potocky-Tripodi

Antigay attitudes in the form of heterosexism and homophobia are pervasive (Yang, 1997) and create significant sources of stress and/or pain for those in the sexual minority (Herek, 1992). The ideological system of heterosexism, which "denies, denigrates, and stigmatizes any non-heterosexual form of behavior, identity, relationship, or community" (Herek, 1990, pp. 316–317), has been promulgated by societal institutions in this country, such as the courts, religion, medicine, and the mass media. This heterosexism has historical roots that suggest that homosexuality is perceived as a threat to Western society (Fone, 2000).

Although American society remains divided on lesbian, gay, and bisexual (LGB) issues, including whether antigay attitudes should be changed, the official position of the profession of social work is unambiguous. Social workers are prohibited from discriminating against clients or colleagues based on their sexual orientation (National Association of Social Workers, 1999). The social work code of ethics also states that social workers should work to "prevent and eliminate domination of, exploitation of, and discrimination against any person . . . on the basis of . . . sexual orientation" (National Association of Social Workers, 1999). The National Association of Social Workers has released various public policy statements concerning sexual orientation, including that "same-gender

Originally published in *Research on Social Work Practice* 2006; 16; 176. DOI: 10.1177/ 1049731505281385 The online version of this article can be found at: http://rsw.sagepub.com/ cgi/content/abstract/16/2/176 sexual orientation should be afforded the same respect and rights as other-gender orientation" (National Association of Social Workers, 2002). Furthermore, schools of social work should be teaching their students to practice without discrimination and "with respect, knowledge and skills related to clients' . . . sexual orientation" (Council on Social Work Education, 2001).

It is not surprising that antigay attitudes are highly correlated with antigay behaviors, including physical attacks (Franklin, 2000; Patel, Long, McCammon & Wuensch, 1995; Roderick, McCammon, Long, & Allred, 1998; Whitley, 2001). In fact, alarming numbers of LGB people are subjected to discrimination, harassment, and violence because of their sexual orientation (Berrill, 1992; D'Augelli & Grossman, 2001; D'Augelli, Pilkington, & Hershberger, 2002; Herek, Gillis, Cogan, & Glunt, 1997; Rose & Mechanic, 2002; Thurlow, 2001; Waldo, Hesson-McInnis, & D'Augelli, 1998). The exact extent of this victimization cannot be known for certain.

Official reports of hate crimes represent only a small fraction of the actual number of incidents motivated by the victim's sexual orientation. Many of these crimes go unreported, and when reported, there are problems with the collection and assimilation of the data (Federal Bureau of Investigation, n.d.; Kuehnle & Sullivan, 2003; Rose & Mechanic, 2002). Moreover, LGB victims often do not notify law enforcement, because they expect an unsympathetic or even hostile response from the police. This expectancy may be based on either their own prior experiences with law enforcement personnel, the shared experiences of others, or both (Berrill & Herek, 1992; Herek, Gillis, & Cogan, 1999).

We do know, however, that the empirical research reveals that homosexuals are much more likely than heterosexuals to be the victims of violent crimes (Berrill, 1992; Bontempo & D'Augelli, 2002; DuRant, Krowchuk, & Sinal, 1998; Herek, Gillis, Cogan, & Glunt, 1997). Similarly, LGB individuals endure far more discrimination and harassment than their heterosexual peers (Bontempo & D'Augelli, 2002; D'Augelli, 1992; Lewis, Derlega, Berndt, Morris, & Rose, 2001; Thurlow, 2001). Pervasive antigay attitudes also mean that the sexual minority is often denied equal access to housing, employment and/or promotions, education, and health care (Hunter, Joslin, & McGowan, 2004). Furthermore, same-sex couples in the United States are refused the fundamental right to marry and are, therefore, deprived of all the social, legal, and financial benefits that marriage conveys to heterosexual couples.

The psychological consequences and other attendant effects of this victimization and discrimination should not be overlooked. Given the correlation between antigay attitudes and behaviors, this systematic review was conducted to determine what, if any, empirically validated interventions exist for improving heterosexuals' attitudes toward homosexuals. This review entailed analysis of selected studies in relation to their methodological characteristics and findings.

# Method

## Selection Criteria

Studies for inclusion in the analyses were identified through searches of the PsycINFO, Social Services Abstracts, and Sociological Abstracts electronic databases from January 1994 to August 2004. Only studies that included at least one intervention designed to improve the heterosexual participants' attitudes toward homosexuals and that were published in peer-reviewed journals were included. Search parameters were broad and included wild cards. Specifically, the search terms were *attitude** and *homosexual** or *gay** or *lesbian** and *experiment** or *intervention** or *outcome** or *change**.

As particular attitudes are often culture bound (Stycos, 1998; Evans, 1997), we limited our inquiry to studies conducted within the United States. Furthermore, a study must have assessed the participants' personal attitudes toward homosexuals or homosexuality generally to be included. Thus, a study that used participant opinions regarding a specific, politically controversial issue (e.g., gays in the military, gay marriage, etc.) to assess attitudes would not suffice for purposes of this analysis. Only one study was eliminated for this reason.

## Rating Criteria

Level of empirical support was assessed using criteria developed by the American Psychological Association's Division 12 task force for evaluating empirically validated therapies (Chambless et al., 1998; Chambless & Hollon, 1998). None of the studies reviewed herein used single-case designs; therefore, only the criteria for group designs were used. Only interventions that have been demonstrated to be superior (statistically significantly so) to a placebo or another intervention or to be equivalent to an already established treatment in at least two good, between-group design experiments with adequate sample sizes (at least 25 participants per condition) are considered well established (Chambless et al., 1998).

A good between-group design means that participants were randomly assigned to the intervention of interest or to one or more comparison conditions (i.e., randomized, clinical trials; Chambless & Hollon, 1998). Additionally, the experiments must have been conducted with treatment manuals, unless the intervention was relatively simple and adequately specified in the procedure section of the journal article reporting on its efficacy. Furthermore, the characteristics of the participants must have been clearly specified, and the experiments must have been conducted by at least two different investigators or investigating teams. If an intervention met the criteria above, unless it was demonstrated to be superior in only one experiment or it was demonstrated to be superior in two or more experiments conducted by the same investigating team, it was considered probably efficacious. Alternatively, if two or more experiments demonstrated that an intervention was superior to a waiting-list control group, it was considered probably efficacious if the experiments met all of the other criteria.

There are other important elements of establishing efficacy. Demonstrating superiority assumes that the outcome assessment tools have demonstrated reliability and validity (Chambless & Hollon, 1998). Multiple methods of assessment are preferable, although not required, and participant self-reports are suspect. Evaluators are also cautioned to check that researchers have interpreted their outcome data correctly. In other words, assessing outcomes and interpreting data appropriately are critical components of good between-group design experiments (Chambless & Hollon, 1998, p. 8).

A study rating sheet was created in accordance with the criteria outlined above. A random sample of six of the eligible studies was selected to test for interrater reliability between the first and second authors. With a reliability of 83.3% established, the first author rated the remaining studies for empirical soundness.

## Findings

Table 12.1 summarizes the 17 studies that met our selection criteria. This section presents the pertinent findings and summarizes the commonalities across studies with regard to participants, interventions, methodologies, attitude measures, and outcomes. Finally, the studies are evaluated for their level of empirical support.

## Summary of the Studies' Participants

Interventions are often efficacious for only a specific problem or population; therefore, it is important that investigators adequately describe any characteristics of the participants that might affect the generalizability of their findings (Chambless & Hollon, 1998). Specifically, it is the participants who completed all aspects of the experiment and about whom postintervention data are available who should be described rather than some larger prescreening pool. In many cases, only the larger pool of eligible participants is described; therefore, attrition, dropout, and/or missing data information should be explained so the reader can make a judgment about whether the final sample is representative of the described participants. Because more than half (nine) of the studies here under review either did not adequately address attrition (four studies) or experienced so much attrition (attrition rates greater than 10% on five studies), we cannot be confident that the final respondents were adequately described in those articles. All of the reviewed studies used convenience samples comprised of either undergraduate or graduate students in U.S. schools. The remainder of our comments about the participants, however, will focus on the eight studies where the final respondents were adequately described.

All of the studies presently under review reported participants' gender. Overall, there were wide disparities in gender representation. Of the eight studies where participants were adequately described, four had large (60% or more) majorities of females (Black, Oles, Cramer, & Bennett, 1999; Cotton-Huston & Waite, 2000; Guth, Lopez, Clements, & Rojas, 2001; Probst, 2003). Two of the studies had less than a 10% difference in gender disparity among participants (Corley & Pollack, 1996; Grutzeck & Gidycz, 1997), and two had male majorities (Grack & R ichman, 1996; Wallick, Cambre, & Townsend, 1995).

Of the eight participant-described studies, six addressed the ages of the participants by providing either a range, median, or mean. Given that all participants were pursuing either undergraduate or graduate degrees, the age range was limited. With few exceptions, the participants were between the ages of 18 and 35.

Five of the eight participant-described studies addressed participants' ethnicity. One of these (Guth et al., 2001) reported only the percentage of Caucasians, which, as with all of the studies, was the overwhelming majority. The remaining four studies reported percentages of participants in five ethnic categories that included Caucasian or White, African American or Black, Hispanic, Asian American or Pacific Islander, Native American, and Other (Black et al., 1999; Grutzeck & Gidycz, 1997; Probst, 2003; Wallick et al., 1995).

With regard to other participant characteristics, all of the eight participant-described studies reported the type of undergraduate or graduate courses from which the respondents were recruited. Six of the eight reported participants' sexual orientation. Two reported marital status. One reported on participants' contact with homosexuals, and another included whether participants had gay or lesbian friends. Finally, one reported on participants' income, religion, region, and parental acceptance of lesbians and gay men, and one reported number of participants with a disability.

## Summary of the Studies' Interventions

The vast majority of the 17 articles devoted substantial attention to the theoretical bases of their investigations. Most focused on two main justifications for their studies: (a) a cognitive and/or educational function of the intervention (e.g., to dispel myths and stereotypes attributed to homosexuals), and (b) contact theory—that exposure to and shared positive experiences with homosexuals will help to change heterosexuals' prejudices. In fact, only three of the studies did not rely to some extent on one or both of these rationales (Pratarelli & Donaldson, 1997; Probst, 2003; Wallick et al., 1995).

**Table 12.1**     Summary of Studies' Characteristics

| Authors | Participants | Interventions | Methodologies | Attitude Measures | Outcomes |
|---|---|---|---|---|---|
| Cramer, 1997 | 107 MSW students in six foundation practice sessions.<br><br>% Female: 82<br>Median age: 27<br><br>Ethnicity:<br>83% White<br>15% Black<br>1% Asian American<br>1% Hispanic<br><br>E1: 39<br>E2: 33<br>C1: 33 | E1: Instructor self-disclosed her lesbian status while conducting educational unit focusing on lesbian identity development<br><br>E2: Same educational unit as E1 but taught by a self-disclosing heterosexual woman of similar age and race<br><br>C1: No intervention | Pre- and posttest. Posttest given 6 weeks after intervention. Attrition reported. Baseline comparisons not reported. | Modified version of ATLG. Modifications somewhat specified. Reliability reported for instrument and subscales (Attitudes Toward Lesbians [ATL] and Attitudes Toward Gay Men [ATG]) but not for modified versions. | Students in E1 had significantly lower mean score (more positive attitudes) than those in C1 on the ATG at posttest. |
| Cramer, Oles, & Black, 1997 | Started with 110 undergraduate and graduate social work students at four different schools.<br><br>% Female: 89<br>Average age: 26<br><br>Ethnicity:<br>84.5% White<br>6.4% Black<br>4.5% Hispanic<br>4.5% Asian American<br><br>Participants per group not reported. | Four different educational interventions, using the information-plus-exposure model and varying disclosure or nondisclosure of instructor sexual orientation, given during the course of one semester. No control. | Pretest given during first 2 weeks of classes. Posttest given during last 2 weeks of classes. Amount of attrition not reported, but missing data were excluded from analyses. | Modified version of ATLG. Modifications somewhat specified. Reliability reported for instrument and subscales (ATL and ATG) but not for modified version. | There was significant change in all four classes from pretest to posttest on ATLG scores. Comparison between the four educational approaches is problematic, as the instructors varied on several dimensions. No significant differences between groups were found. Sufficiency of power for analyses questionable. |

| Authors | Participants | Interventions | Methodologies | Attitude Measures | Outcomes |
|---|---|---|---|---|---|
| Finkel, Storaasli, Bandele, & Schafer, 2003 | 48 graduate students at University of Denver's Graduate School of Professional Psychology.<br><br>% Female: 78<br><br>Median age: 25<br><br>Ethnicity: 78% White | Two 2-hour "Safe Zone" diversity training sessions separated by 6 months. Treatment manuals mentioned. No comparison. No control. | Posttest at end of second session that required participants to (a) rate current level of homophobia and (b) retrospectively rate level of preintervention homophobia. Attrition reported. | Riddle Homophobia Scale (Wall, 1995). Authors reported that the psychometric properties of the scale were unknown. | No significant differences between current and retrospective ratings. |
| Grack & Richman, 1996 | 37 undergraduate psychology students who had scored above the 50th percentile on the Gay and Lesbian Attitude Scale (GLAS; Grack & Richman, 1996).<br><br>% Female: 40<br><br>Age: Not reported<br><br>Ethnicity: Not reported.<br><br>Groups ranged from 4 to 6 participants. | All groups instructed to solve series of logic problems.<br><br>E1: 2 actors self-identifying as homosexual participants and group received extra credit reward<br><br>E2: 2 actors self-identifying as homosexual participants and group did not receive reward<br><br>E3: 2 actors self-identifying as heterosexual participants and group rewarded<br><br>E4: 2 actors self-identifying as heterosexual participants and group did not receive reward.<br><br>No control. | Pretest given 8 weeks prior to the 1-hour intervention. Posttest immediately following intervention. Attrition not reported. Baseline comparisons not reported. | GLAS, which was reportedly based on Hudson and Ricketts' (1980) Index of Homophobia Scale[a]. Reliability for the Index of Homophobia Scale was reported, but authors do not explain how their scale differs from the original, nor is the validity or reliability of the GLAS itself reported. | There was a significant difference reported between groups based on the sexual orientation of the actors. Insufficient power to support analyses. |

(Continued)

**Table 12.1** (Continued)

| Authors | Participants | Interventions | Methodologies | Attitude Measures | Outcomes |
|---|---|---|---|---|---|
| Grutzeck & Gidycz, 1997 | 200 undergraduate introductory psychology students from a moderately sized midwestern university.<br><br>% Female: 54<br><br>Age: Not reported<br><br>Ethnicity:<br>85% White<br>11% Black<br>1% Asian American<br>1% Native American<br>2% Other<br><br>E1: 63<br>E2: 64<br>C1: 73 | E1: 1-hour speaker panel presentation of 4 undergraduates (2 gay males, 2 lesbians), who gave brief biographical sketches followed by question-and-answer period.<br><br>E2: Participants were given a handout with basic facts and harmful stereotypes associated with homosexuality.<br><br>C1: Participants were told that more than expected had shown up for the experiment, so it was not necessary for them to participate but that they would still receive credit. | Random assignment. Pretest given 2 weeks prior to intervention. Posttest given 4 weeks after intervention. Attrition not reported. | Modified version of the IAH (modifications not specified) and the HATH. Psychometric properties of both instruments and of modified IAH were reported. Behavioral measure developed by the authors (psychometric properties indeterminate). | Panel presentation did not have a significant effect on either instrument; however, the entire sample had more tolerant scores on the IAH at posttest. Likely pretest effect. Behavioral measure outcomes indeterminate. |
| Guth, Lopez, Clements, & Rojas, 2001 | 47 upper-level undergraduate psychology students at a southeastern university.<br><br>% Female: 78.7<br><br>Median age: 29.5<br><br>Ethnicity: 88% White<br><br>E1: 17<br>E2: 15<br>C1: 15 | Both E1 and E2 were 2-hour workshops that contained myths and facts about homosexuality and everyday issues faced by gays and lesbians.<br><br>E1: Content was presented "rationally"<br><br>E2: Content was presented "experientially"<br><br>C1: Workshop that focused on finding psychology-related material on the Internet. Guidelines for interventions mentioned. | Random assignment. Pre- and posttest. Posttest given 3 weeks after intervention. Attrition reported. | Thought-listing procedure developed by authors that involved having participants spontaneously list thoughts elicited by a stimulus (six hypothetical scenarios dealing with homosexuals). Three raters (all with doctorates in psychology) judged the pre- and posttests to create categories, then a panel of three graduate students categorized the thoughts. Interrater reliability was reported. Validity not reported. | Thought categories changed significantly at posttest only for E2 group. No between-group comparisons. Insufficient power to support analyses. |

| Authors | Participants | Interventions | Methodologies | Attitude Measures | Outcomes |
|---|---|---|---|---|---|
| Hood, Muller, & Seitz, 2001 | 150 undergraduate students in five sections of an organizational behavior course.<br><br>% Female: 49.5<br><br>Mean age: 24.8<br><br>Ethnicity:<br>55.7% White<br>28.1% Hispanic<br>6.8% Asian American<br>1% Black<br>1% Native American<br>3.5% Other | Course content promoting diversity competency. Vague description of intervention. No comparison. No control. | Pretest given at beginning of semester. Posttest given during one of the last two classes. Attrition reported. | A five-item Attitude Toward Gay Men and Lesbians Scale developed by the authors. Coefficient alphas for the pre- and postintervention surveys were reported. No other psychometric properties reported. | Change for entire sample was reportedly significant. No significant change by racial group. |
| Nelson & Krieger, 1997 | 190 psychology students from six separate classes surveyed across three semesters at a mid-size southeastern university.<br><br>% Female: 72.6<br><br>Average age: 21<br><br>Ethnicity: "Predominantly Caucasian" | 50-minute panel presentation by 2 gay male and 2 lesbian students attending the same university, who gave personal narratives followed by question-and-answer period. No comparison. No control. | Pretest given approximately 2 weeks prior to intervention. Posttest given 6 weeks after intervention. Attrition not reported. | Modified version of the Attitudes Toward Homosexuality Scale (ATHS; MacDonald & Games, 1974). Modifications somewhat specified. Psychometric properties not reported. | Change in sample's posttest score reported as significant. Females demonstrated more change in attitude than males. |
| Pratarelli & Donaldson, 1997 | 80 heterosexual students at a large midwestern university.<br><br>% Female: 50<br><br>Age: 18–24 | E1: Written educational scenario supporting a biological explanation for homosexuality<br><br>E2: A second scenario indirectly supporting an environmental explanation | Random assignment. Baseline survey given 1 week prior to intervention. Posttest immediately following intervention. Attrition not reported. | Two matched, prenormed surveys designed to assess changes in participants' attitudes toward homosexuals, developed by first author. Reliability reported. | No statistically significant differences between groups were reported. |

(Continued)

**Table 12.1** (Continued)

| Authors | Participants | Interventions | Methodologies | Attitude Measures | Outcomes |
|---|---|---|---|---|---|
| | Ethnicity: Not reported.<br>E1: 32<br>E2: 34<br>C1: 34 | by focusing on the weaknesses of the biological evidence<br><br>C1: A control scenario containing no information about sexual orientation | | | |
| Probst, 2003 | 57 undergraduate students in a workplace diversity psychology course at Washington State University made up the experimental group.<br>% Female: 62<br>Mean age: 28.85<br>Ethnicity:<br>87% White<br>7% Asian American<br>3% Native American<br>2% Black<br>2% Hispanic<br>E1: 57<br>C1: 37 | E1: A semester long (17 weeks) upper-level undergraduate workplace diversity psychology course that included content on gay, lesbian, and bisexual issues.<br><br>C1: An elementary statistics course taught by the same instructor during the same semester. | Pre- and posttest given during the first and last weeks of the semester, respectively. No significant differences between groups on pretest. Attrition reported. | Homonegativity Scale (six items; Morrison, Parriag, & Morrison, 1999). Reliability reported. | There was a significant improvement in the attitudes of E1 at posttest, whereas C1 attitudes were slightly worse (more negative), suggesting that a between-group comparison would be significant. No between-group comparisons. |
| Riggle, Ellis, & Crawford, 1996 | 72 students in introductory psychology courses.<br>% Female: 58<br>Age: Not reported<br>Ethnicity: Not reported.<br>E1: 44<br>C1: 28 | E1: An 88-minute documentary, *The Times of Harvey Milk*, about one of the first openly gay elected officials in the United States<br><br>C1: Completed the posttest prior to viewing the documentary | Pretest 3 weeks prior to intervention. Posttest immediately following. Attrition reported and notable (from 314 down to 72). Between-group differences at prescreening reported (not significant). | ATHS developed by Herek, 1984.[b] Citation given for psychometric properties. | E1 had significantly fewer prejudicial attitudes at posttest. |

| Authors | Participants | Interventions | Methodologies | Attitude Measures | Outcomes |
|---|---|---|---|---|---|
| Waldo & Kemp, 1997 | 156 undergraduate students in introductory psychology course<br><br>% Female: 37.8<br><br>Age: Approximately 18–21<br><br>Ethnicity: "Predominantly White/European-American."<br><br>E1: 40<br>C1: 116 | E1: In one section of the course, the instructor came out (self-identified as gay) to the class midway through the semester while presenting educational unit about sexual orientation.<br><br>C1: Four sections of the same course that were taught by self-identified heterosexual instructors and covered same material regarding sexual orientation. | Pre- and posttest at the beginning and end of the semester, respectively. Attrition not reported. Baselines reported. | Short form of ATLG and embedded in a 30-question "controversial issues survey." Psychometric properties reported. | E1 scores changed significantly at posttest compared to controls. |
| Wallick, Cambre, & Townsend, 1995 | Three consecutive 1st-year classes of medical students at Louisiana State University in New Orleans (exact number of participants provided only for the class entering 1991).<br><br>% Female: 34<br><br>Mean age: 22.5<br><br>Ethnicity:<br>Approximately 78% White<br>10% Black<br>7.5% Asian American or Pacific Islander<br>4% Hispanic<br>.5% Native American | 3-hour panel presentation by 3 gay and lesbian physicians, who provided autobiographical sketches, and a faculty member, who shared his son's coming out story, followed by a question-and-answer period; then, students broke into smaller groups for discussion. No comparison. No control. | Of the 186 students in the 1991–1992 cohort, 180 completed the IAH at the beginning of their freshman year, 168 at midyear (2 weeks following intervention), 114 at year's end, and 185 following their required psychology clerkship in their 3rd year. Participation rates were reportedly similar in the two subsequent years, but the IAH was given on entrance and following the intervention only. | IAH. Psychometric properties not reported, but citation provided. | An overall 6.3% decrease in homophobic attitude within the pooled (all three classes) data was reported (p < .03). On follow-up for the '91 class, there was a rebound effect following the junior clerkship. |

NOTE: E = experimental group condition; C = control group condition.

a. The Index of Homophobia Scale is the same instrument cited by other authors in this study as the IAH. The creators of this instrument suggested the name change to IAH to reduce potential bias in response to the original name (Hudson & Ricketts, 1980).

b. Riggle et al. either incorrectly identified Herek as the developer of the ATHS or correctly cited to Herek but called the scale by the wrong name. The name of the instrument developed by Herek (1984, 1988) is the ATLG. An instrument entitled the ATHS was developed by MacDonald and Games (1974).

Pratarelli and Donaldson (1997) were short on theory, but they were investigating whether a biological explanation for sexual orientation influenced attitudes toward homosexuals. Probst (2003) made reference to the increase in diversity courses on college campuses and to the paucity of empirical assessment regarding the extent to which such courses actually change students' attitudes and behaviors. Wallick et al. (1995) saved their rationale for the conclusion, where they simply cited a policy paper adopted by the American Medical Association calling for physicians to demonstrate a nonjudgmental attitude toward gay men and lesbians and for medical schools to increase their focus on how to appropriately address the needs of this population.

As for the interventions themselves, 11 of the studies infused course content with or held workshops presenting educational information about homosexuality. Formats varied and included verbal, written, and audiovisual communications. Typically, the stigmatization and discrimination experienced by LGB people were addressed, as were common myths and stereotypes. Most of the interventions took place within the time span of one class period.

Five of the studies used gay and/or lesbian speaker panels as interventions. Three involved the coming out (disclosure of homosexual status) of the classroom instructor to the student participants in combination with an educational unit about sexual orientation. Other interventions included a nonstereotypical written description of a lesbian couple, a logic problem-solving exercise in which two actor participants self-identified as homosexuals to the other participants, and a written biological explanation for sexual orientation.

As previously mentioned, with the exception of relatively simple interventions that have been adequately explained in the journal article reporting their efficacy, treatment manuals have been deemed essential to empirically validated interventions (Chambless & Hollon,1998). Without them, other researchers cannot know precisely what treatment was tested, nor can the intervention be replicated. Only 2 of the 17 reviewed articles mentioned the use of treatment manuals or their equivalents (Finkel, Storaasli, Bandele, & Schafer, 2003; Guth et al., 2001).

## Summary of the Studies' Methodologies

Only 4 of the 17 studies reviewed were true experimental designs in which participants were randomly assigned to intervention, comparison, and/or control conditions. Unfortunately, 3 of the experiments also used a pretest. Compounding this problem, none of the 3 used a design to account for any possible pretest effects.

Thirteen of the 17 studies were quasi-experimental designs that did not randomly assign participants to comparison groups. In fact, in 6 of the 13, there were no comparison or control groups, which precluded the possibility of between-group comparisons. In 5 of these no comparison–no control studies, there was simply one group of participants who were given one or more pretests, interventions, and posttests. The remaining study simply used a posttest that asked participants to rate their current level of homophobia and to also retrospectively rate their level of homophobia prior to the intervention (Finkel et al., 2003). Of the 7 quasi-experiments that used comparison and/or control groups, 6 of them conducted pretests, but only 3 of them discussed the issue of baseline differences between groups. Of these, only 1 had reported a low level of attrition that did not compromise the equivalency of the groups (Probst, 2003).

## Summary of the Studies' Attitude Measures

It should be noted that many of the 17 reviewed studies were assessing participants on multiple variables. For example, 1 study assessed participants' masculinity or femininity, attitudes regarding women's rights and roles, demographics, and attitudes toward homosexuals (Cotton-Huston & Waite, 2000). Our discussion is limited to those instruments that measured participants' attitudes toward homosexuals.

Six of the 17 studies used measures of heterosexuals' attitudes toward homosexuals developed by other investigators in previous research. Two used an index developed by Hudson and Ricketts (Cotton-Huston & Waite, 2000; Wallick et al., 1995), and one used a scale developed by Herek (Riggle, Ellis, & Crawford, 1996). Both of these measures have established validity and reliability. One investigating team, however, used the Riddle Homophobia Scale developed by Wall (1995; Finkel et al., 2003). This instrument simply asks participants to concurrently (postintervention) rate their current level of homophobia on an 8-point Likert-type scale and rate what their level of homophobia had been prior to the intervention using the same scale. These authors reported that the psychometric properties of the Riddle Homophobia Scale were unknown but that they deemed it to have acceptable face validity.

One of the studies used the Homonegativity Scale developed by Morrison, Parriag, and Morrison (1999; Probst, 2003). This measure contains six items using a 5-point Likert-type scale. The investigator reported the test-retest reliability, but we would like to have seen some discussion regarding the instrument's validity. In this regard, however, a reference for the instrument's psychometric properties was cited in the study.

Grutzeck and Gidycz (1997) were the only investigators to use multiple measures to assess participants' attitudes toward homosexuals. They implemented the Heterosexual Attitudes Toward Homosexuality Scale (HATH) developed by Larsen, Reed, and Hoffman (1980) and a modified version of Hudson and Ricketts' Index of Attitudes Toward Homosexuals (IAH; Hudson & Ricketts, 1980), both of which have previously established validity and reliability. The modifications to the IAH were not specified, but the psychometric properties of the modified version were reported. Grutzeck and Gidycz also used a behavioral measure that they developed for the study to assess tolerance for homosexuals. We have serious doubts about the validity of the behavioral measure, the limitations of which are clearly articulated by the investigators themselves.

Nine studies used modified or adapted versions of previously established measures. These studies varied regarding the extent to which the modifications were specified and whether the psychometric properties of the modified versions were reported. Most, however, were vague about the modifications and did not report on their properties. Of the 14 studies that used either full or modified (or both, i.e., Grutzeck & Gidycz, 1997) versions of preestablished instruments, 6 utilized measures originally developed by Herek, and 4 used some version of Hudson and Ricketts's (1980) IAH. The only other instrument used or adapted by more than one of the studies was Larsen et al.'s (1980) HATH, used by 2 of the studies. Finally, three of the studies used an instrument developed by the investigators of those studies as the sole measure of attitudes toward homosexuals (Guth et al., 2001; Hood, Muller, & Seitz, 2001; Pratarelli & Donaldson, 1997). Guth et al. (2001) developed an instrument using a thought-listing technique for their pretest and posttest measures. They provided a rationale for this type of measurement, supporting reference citations, and documentation of the interrater reliability. Absent, however, was any discussion of validity for this particular instrument.

Hood et al. (2001) developed their own scale because they were interested in attitudes toward gay men and lesbians specifically with regard to workplace issues.

This instrument was composed of five questions on a 5-point Likert-type scale. Coefficient alphas for the pretest and posttest scores were provided, but again, there was no discussion of the validity of this scale.

Pratarelli and Donaldson (1997) used "two matched prenormed surveys" (p. 1412) previously developed by the first author with another investigator to assess changes in participants' attitudes. Two reference citations presumably regarding the development of this instrument were provided, but one referenced a paper presented at a convention, and the other referenced a manuscript submitted for publication. In the present article, reliability was reported, but there was no discussion of the validity of this instrument.

## Summary of the Studies' Analyses and Outcomes

The methodological limitations of the studies summarized above renders a discussion of their analyses and outcomes practically moot. That is, statistical significance is irrelevant when a model has been misspecified or an assumption has been violated. Statistical computer programs are not able to correct for research design and/or methodological shortcomings

(Pedhazur & Schmelkin, 1991). There were, however, additional limitations concerning the studies' analyses that are worth mentioning.

Of the nine studies that analyzed differences between experimental and comparison or control groups, only four used either random assignment without a pretest (one) or nonrandomly assigned groups with baseline comparisons on pretests reported (three). Of these four, only one (Waldo & Kemp, 1997) had enough participants per group to power the analyses. This study, however, did not report the amount of attrition.

None of the reviewed studies discussed effect size or clinical significance. Reports of statistical significance alone are of limited utility (Chambless & Hollon, 1998; Pedhazur & Schmelkin, 1991). We hope that as this area of study expands, there will emerge meaningful units of measures for antigay attitude change. Ultimately, scholars will want to know how much of a change in attitude is required for a measurable change in behavior.

## Evaluation of the Level of Empirical Support of the Interventions

None of the interventions qualified as well established, as no single intervention was subjected to two independent experiments (Chambless et al., 1998; Chambless & Hollon, 1998). Nor did any of the interventions meet the criteria for probably efficacious treatments. Most fell short at this level because they were not tested in a between-group design experiment.

Random assignment serves to equate the comparison groups on all variables except for the intended manipulations. Without it, many researchers believe that the comparison groups are inherently and immutably nonequivalent (Chambless & Hollon, 1998; Pedhazur & Schmelkin, 1991). Nevertheless, investigators will employ various methods (e.g., establishing no significant differences between groups on a pretest) in an attempt to accomplish valid comparisons.

As previously mentioned, four of the reviewed studies used random assignment (Corley & Pollack, 1996; Grutzeck & Gidycz, 1997; Guth et al., 2001; Pratarelli & Donaldson, 1997). Two of these used outcome measures that were developed by one or more of the investigators, and the validity of these instruments was not sufficiently established (Guth et al., 2001; Pratarelli & Donaldson, 1997). Additionally, one of these did not conduct between-group comparisons, and there was insufficient power to support such analyses (Guth et al., 2001). The other one did not report participant attrition, nor did it control for possible pretest effects (Pratarelli & Donaldson, 1997).

Of the two randomized studies that used measures with previously established validity and reliability, one did not have sufficient power to conduct its analyses (Corley & Pollack, 1996). The other did not report using treatment manuals for the experimental group that was exposed to a speaker panel presentation. Additionally, this study did not report attrition, nor did it control for possible pretest effects, and the results indicated that such effects were in operation (Grutzeck & Gidycz, 1997).

# Discussion and Applications to Social Work Research and Practice

This evaluation for empirical validation revealed that none of the interventions was adequately tested by these studies. Optimum design and methodology are an expensive proposition, sometimes prohibitively so. Therefore, investigators can hardly be faulted for making do with their limited resources.

That said, some of the problems reported in our findings warrant further discussion. With regard to participant characteristics, the investigators properly reported that all respondents were university or college students. At a minimum, we thought that investigators should also report on participants' gender, age, ethnicity, and religiosity and/or religion.

Prior research has shown that there are significant differences in attitudes and behaviors toward homosexuals across gender (Franklin, 2000; Whitley, 2001; Yang, 1997). Logic dictates that the outcomes of interventions designed to change attitudes might also differ by gender. Therefore, it is imperative that investigators conducting such studies report on the gender makeup of their samples and any significant differences in outcomes between male and female participants.

Like gender, age could be a distinguishing participant characteristic. From a developmental perspective, we know that attitudes can evolve throughout the life span (Pillari, 1998). Specifically, surveys have demonstrated that there are generational disparities with respect to attitudes toward homosexuals (Ricci & Biederman, 2004). Therefore, it would not be surprising if intervention effects varied by age group.

There is little empirical evidence one way or the other regarding the effect of ethnicity on attitudes toward homosexuals. Ethnicity has, however, had a demonstrated effect on outcomes for therapeutic interventions (Arroyo, Miller, & Tonigan, 2003; Markowitz, Spielman, Sullivan, & Fishman, 2000). Therefore, even if there were not enough participants of various ethnicities in the present studies to demonstrate between-group effects, we would still want to know their ethnic makeup so that we can make a judgment about the generalizability of the findings.

Antigay attitudes have been consistently correlated with religion and religiosity (e.g., Hinrichs & Rosenberg, 2002; Laythe, Finkel, Bringle, & Kirkpatrick, 2002; Snively, Kreuger, Stretch, Watt, & Chadha, 2004). Specifically, studies have found that the participants who score high on measures of antigay attitudes also tend to be those who are the most religious. Similarly, those who belong to fundamentalist churches score higher, overall, on measures of homophobia and/or heterosexism. Therefore, it is important to know how intervention effects vary by religion and religiosity. It is notable that only four of the seventeen reviewed studies attempted to investigate these effects (Black et al., 1999; Cotton-Huston & Waite, 2000; Cramer, 1997; Cramer, Oles, & Black, 1997).

The investigators of at least one study (Waldo & Kemp,1997) purposely did not request demographic information other than gender from participants in an effort to ensure anonymity and to reduce demand effects. Anonymity can be ensured, however, through study design elements while still collecting valuable demographic information. Participants should be instructed that the surveys are designed to be anonymous and to avoid writing their names or other identifying information on their answer sheets. Additionally, research assistants unknown to the participants could administer the surveys and instruct the respondents that the assistant will not be personally analyzing the data. A slotted, locked box could be placed in the room where participants deposit their surveys when completed. Furthermore, it is best if investigators can obtain participants with whom they have no other contact (e.g., as a course instructor).

There were multiple methodological limitations reported in our findings, but the issue of pretests should be further explained. Although pretests are integral to many quasi-experimental designs, investigators conducting experiments with random assignment should generally avoid them (Pedhazur & Schmelkin, 1991). Unless measures are taken to control for the possible effects of the pretest (sensitization of participants to or interaction with the intervention), it is an unnecessary threat to validity.

We also had many concerns about the reporting of instruments used by the investigators to measure antigay attitudes. We were particularly skeptical about the validity of the Riddle Homophobia Scale used by Finkel et al. (2003). In general, however, the investigators of the reviewed studies did not adequately report on the validity and reliability of the instruments they used.

Overall, we applaud the investigators of the reviewed studies for their groundbreaking work in this understudied area. If attention is drawn to the victimization stemming from widespread homophobia and heterosexism, perhaps funding sources will recognize the need for devoting adequate resources to continued study of this pervasive problem. The remainder of this section examines the political and ideological challenges facing researchers who pursue the development of interventions addressing antigay attitudes and concludes with applications to social work practice.

Up to this point, we have focused on the design and methodological issues involved in the intervention studies we reviewed. Our review would be incomplete, however, if we did not address the political and ideological context within which the research occurred and how this is likely to affect future investigations consistent with the reviewed studies. Specifically, it should be noted that the pervasiveness of antigay attitudes in our society, including heterosexism and homophobia, could have a chilling effect on research about these very issues. Although we are hopeful that researchers will be able to secure the funding and resources necessary to conduct well-designed and methodologically sound experiments to further this line of investigation, we suspect that there will be many obstacles.

Not everyone agrees on how homophobia and heterosexism should be addressed. A substantial and apparently politically powerful proportion of the population believes that homophobia and/or heterosexism should be embraced rather than challenged. There are numerous recent reports attesting to the ongoing culture war regarding gay and lesbian issues. For example, an Alabama lawmaker recently introduced a bill in that state's House of Representatives that would prohibit public funds from being spent on any written material that portrays homosexuality as an acceptable lifestyle and would prohibit educators from bringing speakers or any written material to the classroom that includes content on LGB issues (Snorton, 2004).

At the national level, the political climate in the current administration seems particularly unfriendly toward the LGB population generally and specifically toward research designed to study this population. A study that examined the sexual and health risk behaviors of LGB Native Americans was one of five peer-reviewed National Institutes of Health grants targeted by Rep. Pat Toomey for defunding in 2003 (Winerman, 2004). The principal investigator of that study stated that she had been informed by political insiders that Toomey's actions were representative of the many tactics, including the attack on gay marriage, adopted by Republicans to use the LGB population to create wedge issues in the 2004 presidential campaign (LaSala et al., 2005).

More recently, officials from the Substance Abuse and Mental Health Services Administration (SAMHSA) informed the Suicide Prevention Resource Center (SPRC) that SAMHSA's administrator would not be attending the SPRC's conference on suicide prevention unless conference organizers removed the words *gay, lesbian, bisexual,* and *transgender* from the title and descriptor of a planned workshop (R. Bloodworth, J. Liljeholm, & R. Vanderburgh, personal communication, February 15, 2005). The workshop presenters had to change the title from "Suicide Prevention Among Gays, Lesbians, Bisexuals, and Transgender Individuals" to "Suicide Prevention in Vulnerable Populations" in order for the workshop to be offered. Additionally, the offending words in the descriptor had to be replaced with a general reference to sexual orientation, but any reference to gender identity was not permitted.

Societal views about marginalized groups are usually slow to evolve; however, the studies reviewed herein represent attempts to speed that process. First, however, societal views had to progress enough to permit these studies to happen. As few as 20 years ago, studies of this kind would not be allowed on many college campuses. Indeed, not long ago, professors risked their employment at most universities if they came out (Taylor & Raeburn, 1995). From this historical perspective, the reviewed studies also represent pioneering research. We expect, however, that those espousing greater acceptance of the LGB population will continue to encounter significant resistance, particularly from the religious right.

Although official policy toward the LGB population in the field of social work is decidedly progressive and supportive, there are other indicators that suggest that these policies are not effectively put into practice. A study of gay and lesbian content in social work textbooks suggests that social work education programs continue to perpetuate heterosexist bias and discrimination (Morrow, 1996). Other studies have reported moderate to high levels of homophobia and heterosexist attitudes among social work students and little or no attention to practice with LGB populations provided in their social work training (Krieglstein, 2003; Snively et al., 2004).

There are only a few rudimentary studies examining the effects of homophobia on social work practice. For example, homophobia among social workers and counselors has been correlated with discomfort in working with LGB clients (Hayes & Gelso, 1993; Weiner & Siegel, 1990). Missing, however, are studies examining the impact of homophobia and heterosexism on the treatment outcomes of sexual minority clients. There is also a need for research on best practices with LGB individuals and on how to prepare social workers to implement effective interventions with this population (Snively et al., 2004).

Finally, a review of the social work literature indicates a paucity of information regarding LGB issues in general (Van Voorhis & Wagner, 2002). Content analysis of the journals *Social Work, Child Welfare, Social Service Review,* and *Families in Society* for the 10 years spanning 1988 to 1997 was conducted. These particular journals were reportedly selected because of their national audience and because they are not limited to one area of social work.

Only 3.92% of the articles (77 of 1,964) addressed homosexuality at all, and the vast majority of these (more than 65%) addressed HIV or AIDS. That is, less than 1.37% of the articles addressed aspects of practice with LGB clients other than HIV or AIDS. The finding most striking to the researchers, however, was that only 4 of the 77 articles had a macro focus, and none of the non–HIV or AIDS articles focused on macro issues. The researchers concluded that the sparse coverage in these journals of issues addressing the LGB population contributed to the oppression of this group, and they questioned the commitment of the profession to its espoused principles of the ecological perspective and person-in-environment approach (Van Voorhis & Wagner, 2002).

In conclusion, it remains to be seen whether any short-term interventions can create lasting shifts in attitudes that translate into behavioral changes toward LGB individuals. It seems likely that attitude shift is a cumulative process resulting from repeated exposure to consistent information that is deemed credible. The interventions discussed herein may contribute to that process, but they should be further tested with well-designed, methodologically sound experiments. This area of research should also be expanded beyond the university or classroom setting. We would like to see future research test interventions to change antigay attitudes in other settings with other populations (workplaces, community centers, churches, etc.). Most of all, however, we would like to see an overall expansion of research designed to address the pervasive victimization, discrimination, and marginalization experienced by the LGB population in this country.

# References

Arroyo, J. A., Miller, W. R., & Tonigan, J. S. (2003). The influence of Hispanic ethnicity on long-term outcome in three alcohol-treatment modalities. *Journal of Studies on Alcohol, 64,* 98–104.

Bassett, J. D., & Day, K. J. (2003). A test of the infusion method: Emphatic inclusion of material on gay men in a core course. *Journal of Teaching in Social Work, 23,* 29–41.

Berrill, K. T. (1992). Anti-gay violence and victimization in the United States: An overview. In G. M. Herek & K. T. Berrill (Eds.), *Hate crimes: Confronting violence against lesbians and gay men* (pp. 19–45). Newbury Park, CA: Sage Publications.

Berrill, K. T., & Herek, G. M. (1992). Primary and secondary victimization in anti-gay hate crimes: Official response and public policy. In G. M. Herek & K. T. Berrill (Eds.), *Hate crimes: Confronting violence against lesbians and gay men* (pp. 289–305). Newbury Park, CA: Sage Publications.

Black, B., Oles, T. P., Cramer, E. P., & Bennett, C. K. (1999). Attitudes and behaviors of social work students toward lesbian and gay male clients: Can panel presentations make a difference? *Journal of Gay & Lesbian Social Services, 9,* 47–68.

Bontempo, D. E., & D'Augelli, A. R. (2002). Effects of at-school victimization and sexual orientation on lesbian, gay, or bisexual youths' health risk behavior. *Journal of Adolescent Health, 30,* 364–374.

Chambless, D. L., Baker, M. J., Baucom, D. H., Beutler, L. E., Calhoun, K. S., Crits-Christoph, P., et al. (1998). Update on empirically validated therapies II. *The Clinical Psychologist, 51,* 3–16.

Chambless, D. L., & Hollon, S. D. (1998). Defining empirically supported therapies. *Journal of Consulting and Clinical Psychology, 66,* 7–18.

Corley, T. J., & Pollack, R. H. (1996). Do changes in the stereotypic depiction of a lesbian couple affect heterosexuals' attitudes toward lesbianism? *Journal of Homosexuality, 32,* 1–17.

Cotton-Huston, A. L., & Waite, B. M. (2000). Anti-homosexual attitudes in college students: Predictors and classroom interventions. *Journal of Homosexuality, 38,* 117–133.

Council on Social Work Education. (2001). *Educational policy and accreditation standards.* Retrieved February 21, 2005, from http://www.cswe.org/accredita tion/ EPAS/ EPAS_start.htm

Cramer, E. P. (1997). Effects of an educational unit about lesbian identity development and disclosure in a social work methods course. *Journal of Social Work Education, 33,* 461–472.

Cramer, E., Oles, T. P., & Black, B. M. (1997). Reducing social work students' homophobia: An evaluation of teaching strategies. *Arete, 21,* 36–49.

D'Augelli, A. R. (1992). Lesbian and gay male undergraduates' experiences of harassment and fear on campus. *Journal of Interpersonal Violence, 7,* 383–395.

D'Augelli, A. R., & Grossman, A. H. (2001). Disclosure of sexual orientation, victimization, and mental health among lesbian, gay, and bisexual older adults. *Journal of Interpersonal Violence, 16,* 1008–1027.

D'Augelli, A. R., Pilkington, N. W., & Hershberger, S. L. (2002). Incidence and mental health impact of sexual orientation victimization of lesbian, gay, and bisexual youths in high school. *School Psychology Quarterly, 17,* 148–167.

DuRant, R. H., Krowchuk, D. P., & Sinal, S. H. (1998). Victimization, use of violence, and drug use at school among adolescents who engage in same-sex sexual behavior. *The Journal of Pediatrics, 133,* 113–118.

Evans, J. H. (1997). Worldviews or social groups as the source of moral value attitudes: Implications for the culture wars thesis. *Sociological Forum, 12,* 371–404.

Federal Bureau of Investigation. (n.d.). *2001 Hate Crime Statistics.* Retrieved June 27, 2003, from http://www.fbi.gov/ucr/01hate.pdf

Finkel, M. J., Storaasli, R. D., Bandele, A., & Schaefer, V. (2003). Diversity training in graduate school: An exploratory evaluation of the safe zone project. *Professional Psychology: Research and Practice, 34,* 555–561.

Fone, B. (2000). *Homophobia: A history.* New York: Henry Holt.

Franklin, K. (2000). Antigay behaviors among young adults. *Journal of Interpersonal Violence, 15,* 339–362.

Grack, C., & Richman, C. L. (1996). Reducing general and specific heterosexism through cooperative contact. *Journal of Psychology & Human Sexuality, 8,* 59–68.

Grutzeck, S., & Gidycz, C. A. (1997). The effects of a gay and lesbian speaker panel on college students' attitudes and behaviors: The importance of context effects. *Imagination, Cognition, and Personality, 17,* 65–81.

Guth, L. J., Lopez, D. F., Clements, K. D., & Rojas, J. (2001). Student attitudes toward lesbian, gay, and bisexual issues: Analysis of self-talk categories. *Journal of Homosexuality, 41,* 137–156.

Hayes, J. A., & Gelso, C. J. (1993). Male counselors' discomfort with gay and HIV-infected clients. *Journal of Counseling Psychology, 40,* 86–93.

Herek, G. M. (1984). Attitudes toward lesbians and gay men: A factor analytic study. *Journal of Homosexuality, 10,* 39–51.

Herek, G. M. (1988). Heterosexuals' attitudes toward lesbians and gay men: Correlates and gender differences. *Journal of Sex Research, 25,* 451–477.

Herek, G. M. (1990). The context of anti-gay violence: Notes on cultural and psychological heterosexism. *Journal of Interpersonal Violence, 5,* 316–333.

Herek, G. M. (1992). Psychological heterosexism and anti-gay violence: The social psychology of bigotry and bashing. In G. M. Herek & K. T. Berrill (Eds.), *Hate crimes: Confronting violence against lesbians and gay men* (pp. 149–169). Newbury Park, CA: Sage Publications.

Herek, G. M., Gillis, J. R., & Cogan, J. C. (1999). Psychological sequelae of hate-crime victimization among lesbian, gay, and bisexual adults. *Journal of Consulting and Clinical Psychology, 67,* 945–951.

Herek, G. M., Gillis, J. R., Cogan, J. C., & Glunt, E. K. (1997). Hate crime victimization among lesbian, gay, and bisexual adults. *Journal of Interpersonal Violence, 12,* 195–215.

Hinrichs, D. W., & Rosenberg, P. J. (2002). Attitudes toward gay, lesbian, and bisexual persons among heterosexual liberal arts college students. *Journal of Homosexuality, 43,* 61–84.

Hood, J. N., Muller, H. J., & Seitz, P. (2001). Attitudes of Hispanics and Anglos surrounding a workforce diversity intervention. *Hispanic Journal of Behavioral Sciences, 23,* 444–458.

Hudson, W. W., & Ricketts, W. A. (1980). A strategy for the measurement of homophobia. *Journal of Homosexuality, 5,* 357–372.

Hunter, N. D., Joslin, C. G., & McGowan, S. M. (2004). *The rights of lesbians, gay men, bisexuals, and transgender people: The authoritative ACLU guide to a lesbian, gay, bisexual, or transgender person's rights.* Carbondale: Southern Illinois University Press.

Krieglstein, M. (2003). Heterosexism and social work: An ethical issue. *Journal of Human Behavior in the Social Environment, 8,* 75–91.

Kuehnle, K., & Sullivan, A. (2003). Gay and lesbian victimization: Reporting factors in domestic violence and bias incidents. *Criminal Justice & Behavior, 30,* 85–96.

Larsen, R. S., Reed, M., & Hoffman, S. (1980). Attitudes of heterosexuals toward homosexuality: A Likert-type scale and construct validity. *Journal of Sex Research, 16,* 245–257.

LaSala, M., Parks, C., Elze, D., Gorman, M., Walters, K., Fredriksen-Goldsen, K., et al. (2005, January). *LGBT research priorities: Opportunities and strategies to access federal funding.* Workshop conducted at the annual conference of the Society for Social Work and Research, Miami, Florida.

Laythe, B., Finkel, D. G., Bringle, R. G., & Kirkpatrick, L. A. (2002). Religious fundamentalism as predictor of prejudice: A two-component model. *Journal for the Scientific Study of Religion, 41,* 623–635.

Lewis, R. J., Derlega, V. J., Berndt, A., Morris, L. M., & Rose, S. (2001). An empirical analysis of stressors for gay men and lesbians. *Journal of Homosexuality, 42,* 63–88.

MacDonald, A. P. & Games, S. (1974). Some characteristics of those who hold positive and negative attitudes toward homosexuals. *Journal of Homosexuality, 1,* 9–27.

Markowitz, J. C., Spielman, L. A., Sullivan, M., & Fishman, B. (2000). An exploratory study of ethnicity and psychotherapy outcome among HIV-positive patients with depressive symptoms. *Journal of Psychotherapy Practice and Research, 9,* 226–231.

Morrison, T. G., Parriag, A. V., & Morrison, M. A. (1999). The psychometric properties of the Homonegativity Scale. *Journal of Homosexuality, 37,* 111–126.

Morrow, D. F. (1996). Heterosexism: Hidden discrimination in social work education. *Journal of Gay and Lesbian Social Services, 5,* 1–16.

National Association of Social Workers (1999). *Code of Ethics* (Rev.). Retrieved February 8, 2005, from http://www.naswdc.org/pubs/code/code.asp

National Association of Social Workers. (2002). *Lesbian, gay, and bisexual issues.* Retrieved February 8, 2005, from http://www.naswdc.org/resources/abstracts/abstracts/ lesbian.asp

Nelson, E. S., & Krieger, S. L. (1997). Changes in attitudes toward homosexuality in college students: Implementation of a gay men and lesbian peer panel. *Journal of Homosexuality, 33,* 63–81.

Patel, S., Long, T. E., McCammon, S. L., & Wuensch, K. L. (1995). Personality and emotional correlates of self-reported antigay behaviors. *Journal of Interpersonal Violence, 10,* 354–366.

Pedhazur, E. J., & Schmelkin, L. P. (1991). *Measurement, design, and analysis: An integrated approach.* Hillsdale, NJ: Lawrence Erlbaum.

Pillari, V. (1998). *Human behavior in the social environment: The developing person in a holistic context* (2nd ed.). Pacific Grove, CA: Brooks/Cole.

Pratarelli, M. E., & Donaldson, J. S. (1997). Immediate effects of written material on attitudes toward homosexuality. *Psychological Reports, 81,* 1411–1415.

Probst, T. M. (2003). Changing attitudes over time: Assessing the effectiveness of a workplace diversity course. *Teaching of Psychology, 30,* 236–239.

Ricci, J., & Biederman, P. W. (2004, March 30). Acceptance of gays on rise, polls show. *Los Angeles Times.* Retrieved October, 22, 2004, from http://www.latimes.com/news/printedition/california/la-me-change30mar30,1,7069010.story?ctrack=1&cset=true

Riggle, E. D., Ellis, A. L., & Crawford, A. M. (1996). The impact of "media contact" on attitudes toward gay men. *Journal of Homosexuality, 31,* 55–69.

Roderick, T., McCammon, S. L., Long, T. E., & Allred, L. J. (1998). Behavioral aspects of homonegativity. *Journal of Homosexuality, 36,* 79–88.

Rose, S. M., & Mechanic, M. B. (2002). Psychological distress, crime features, and help-seeking behaviors related to homophobic bias incidents. *American Behavioral Scientist, 46,* 14–26.

Snively, C. A., Kreuger, L., Stretch, J. J., Watt, J. W., & Chadha, J. (2004). Understanding homophobia: Preparing for practice realities in urban and rural settings. *Journal of Gay and Lesbian Social Services, 17,* 59–81.

Snorton, R. (2004). *GLSEN decries Alabama lawmakers' homophobic bill to ban and destroy books* [Press release]. Retrieved January 28, 2005, from the Gay, Lesbian, and Straight Education Network Web site: http://www.glsen.org/cgi-bin/iowa/all/news/record/1755.html

Stycos, J. M. (1998). Population knowledge and attitudes of Latin American adolescents: Impact of gender, schooling, and culture. *Cross-Cultural Research, 32,* 378–399.

Taylor, V., & Raeburn, N. C. (1995). Identity politics as high-risk activism: Career consequences for lesbian, gay, and bisexual sociologists. *Social Problems, 42,* 252–273.

Thurlow, C. (2001). Naming the "outsider within": Homophobic pejoratives and the verbal abuse of lesbian, gay and bisexual high-school pupils. *Journal of Adolescence, 24,* 25–38.

Van Vooris, R., & Wagner, M. (2002). Among the missing: Content on lesbian and gay people in social work journals. *Social Work, 47,* 345–354.

Waldo, C. R., Hesson-McInnis, M. S., & D'Augelli, A. R. (1998). Antecedents and consequences of victimization of lesbian, gay, and bisexual young people: A structural model comparing rural university and urban samples. *American Journal of Community Psychology, 26,* 307–334.

Waldo, C. R., & Kemp, J. L. (1997). Should I come out to my students? An empirical investigation. *Journal of Homosexuality, 34,* 79–94.

Wall, V. (1995). *Beyond tolerance: Gays, lesbians, and bisexuals on campus. A handbook of structured experiences and exercises for training and development.* Washington, DC: American College Personnel Association.

Wallick, M. M., Cambre, K. M., & Townsend, M. H. (1995). Influence of a freshman-year panel presentation on medical students' attitudes toward homosexuality. *Academic Medicine, 70,* 839–841.

Weiner, L. S., & Siegel, K. (1990). Social workers' comfort in providing services to AIDS patients. *Social Work, 35,* 18–25.

Whitley, B. E., Jr. (2001). Gender-role variables and attitudes toward homosexuality. *Sex Roles, 45,* 691–721.

Winerman, L. (2004). Toomey targets speak out. *Monitor on Psychology, 35*(9), 38. Retrieved January 20, 2005, from the American Psychological Association Web site: http://www.apa.org/monitor/ oct04/toomey.html

Yang, A. S. (1997). Attitudes toward homosexuality [Electronic version]. *Public Opinion Quarterly, 61,* 477–507.

# 13

# A Systematic Review of the Empirical Literature on Intercessory Prayer

*David R. Hodge*

Intercessory prayer is commonly defined as prayer offered for the benefit of another person (Tloczynski & Fritzsch, 2002). Typically, either a silent or verbal request is made to God, or some other type of transcendent entity, which the petitioner believes is able to effect change in another person's life (Halperin, 2001; Roberts, Ahmed, & Hall, 2003; Targ, 2002). Accordingly, intercessory prayer differs from other types of prayer, such as personal prayer, in which an individual prays for himself or herself. Although a considerable amount of research has explored the effects of personal prayer (Koenig, McCullough, & Larson, 2001), this article focuses on intercessory prayer because of its apparent widespread usage as a therapeutic intervention.

A surprisingly high percentage of social workers appear to use intercessory prayer in their work with clients (Heyman, Buchanan, Musgrave, & Menz, 2006; Stewart, Koeske, & Koeske, 2006). One national survey of direct practitioners affiliated with the National Association of Social Workers (NASW; N = 2,069) found that 28% of respondents had engaged in verbal prayer with their clients, whereas 57% prayed privately for their clients (Canda & Furman, 1999). Similarly, among a national sample of NASW affiliated gerontological workers (N = 299), 43% reported praying verbally with their clients either "sometimes" or "often." In terms of their private prayer interventions, two thirds of respondents indicated they prayed either sometimes (43%) or often (24%) for their clients (Murdock, 2004). In short, although the use of prayer as a therapeutic intervention

Originally published in *Research on Social Work Practice* 2007; 17; 174. DOI: 10.1177/1049731506296170 The online version of this article can be found at: http://rsw.sagepub.com/cgi/content/abstract/17/2/174

remains controversial (Canda, Nakashima, & Furman, 2004; Praglin, 2004), the extant data suggest that most social workers use intercessory prayer as a professional intervention.

The widespread use of intercessory prayer in clinical settings implicitly raises questions about the effectiveness of prayer as an intervention strategy. Even in newly emergent areas such as spirituality, the NASW Code of Ethics (1999, sec. 1.04 [c]) stipulates that social workers should employ interventions only after conducting the necessary research to ensure the competence of their work. Qualitative research, however, suggests that many social workers hold strong beliefs, both in favor of and against, on using prayer in therapeutic settings (Canda et al., 2004). Consequently, it is unsurprising that concerns have been expressed in the social work literature that practitioners' personal metaphysical beliefs rather than established professional protocols maybe guiding therapeutic decisions (Sahlein, 2002).

In keeping with the premise that professional practice should be based on empirical knowledge rather than a priori, personally held beliefs (Rosen, Proctor, & Staudt, 1999), this study explores the effectiveness of intercessory prayer as an intervention strategy. It is important to note at the onset that the purpose of this article is not to suggest that God, or some other transcendent entity, does or does not exist. Although it is theoretically possible that a transcendent being exists and responds to prayer, it is also possible that prayer taps into presently undiscovered natural mechanisms that produce change (Hodge, 2000; Leder, 2005). In other words, intercessory prayer may effect change supernaturally, naturally, or not at all. The discussion of various mechanisms lies beyond the purview of this article. Rather, the purpose of this article is to examine the empirical literature that is capable of informing and guiding practice decisions regarding the use of intercessory prayer.

# Method

## Search Protocol

Toward this end, a keyword search of *Social Work Abstracts, PsycINFO,* and *MEDLINE (latest years)* was conducted in July 2006 using the term *prayer.* Titles and abstracts were reviewed and pertinent articles obtained. Major reviews of the spirituality and religion literature were also examined (Astin, Harkness, & Ernst, 2000; Halperin, 2001; Harris, Thoresen, McCullough, & Larson, 1999; Johnson, 2002; Koenig et al., 2001; Masters, Spielmans, & Goodson, 2006; McCullough & Larson, 1999; Ramondetta & Sills, 2004; Tolson & Koenig, 2003; Townsend, Kladder, Ayele, & Mulligan, 2002). Potentially relevant articles were read and the reference sections examined for other studies that might be pertinent to the present review.

As might be expected given the subject matter, studies on intercessory prayer have been controversial, especially if positive outcomes are reported (Halperin, 2001; Sicher, Targ, Moore, & Smith, 1998; Targ, 2002).

Perhaps the most controversial study has been conducted by Cha and Wirth (2001), and the interchange between Cha (2004) and Flamm (2005) illustrates some of the issues in play. No attempt was made to assess the validity of the various arguments in deciding which studies to include in this review. In at least some cases, the central issues seem to be rooted in differing metaphysical assumptions about the nature of reality, a subject that is beyond the scope of the present article. Thus, all studies featured in academic journals that meet the search criteria were included in this study.

## Inclusion and Exclusion Criteria

Because the purpose of the review was to examine research capable of informing and guiding practice decisions, studies had to meet the following criteria to be included in the review: (a) use intercessory prayer as an intervention, (b) implement the intervention with a population of clients or patients, and (c) test the efficacy of the intervention, preferably using standardized measures and a double-blind randomized control trial (RCT) methodology.

RCTs are widely considered to represent the "gold standard" for empirically validating interventions; although, concurrently, it is important to note that this method involves a number of debatable epistemic assumptions (Slife & Gantt, 1999). In a double-blind RCT design, participants are randomly assigned to either a control group or an experimental group, which is sometimes referred to as a treatment or intervention group. Both the participants and the experimenter are kept uninformed regarding who is receiving the experimental intervention. Some observers have argued that RCTs are particularly important in studies of intercessory prayer because they help control for important confounders such as hope and expectation effects (Chambless & Ollendick, 2001; Targ, 2002). In other words, RCTs help minimize various extraneous effects that might foster false positives or negatives, clarifying whether the experimental treatment, in this case intercessory prayer, is responsible for the observed outcome.

Studies were included regardless of whether participants knew they might be receiving prayer. Some institutional review boards (IRBs) have waived informed consent procedures on the grounds that no known risks exist for receiving intercessory prayer, whereas others have required them. In the latter case, it is possible to argue that the administration of informed consent creates expectancy effects, although as discussed directly above, the RCT design helps mitigate any effects created.

Studies were held to be outside the parameters of the review if they employed nonclinical/patient samples (O'Laoire, 1997; Tloczynski & Fritzsch, 2002) or featured less rigorous designs, such as single case studies (Kowey, Friehling, & Marinchak, 1986; Sajwaj & Hedges, 1973) or nonrandom, voluntary assignment to control and treatment groups (Carson & Huss, 1979). As implied in the introduction, the relatively extensive research on the effects of personal prayer fell outside the study's scope

(Bernardi et al., 2001; Fabbro, Muzur, Bellen, Calacione, & Bava, 1999; Sistler & Washington, 1999). Similarly, cross-sectional research on prayer was deemed beyond the purview of the study (Ellison, 1993).

In addition to intercessory prayer, other methods of distance healing also exist that are designed to foster client well-being (e.g., bioenergetic healing). Because the purpose of this study was to examine the effectiveness of prayer interventions, studies that employed other types of distance healing were also deemed to be outside the parameters of the present study (Beutler et al., 1988; Carvalho, 1995). One study, however, incorporated secular methods along with prayer but used a rotating schedule so that clients were exposed to intercessory prayer (Sicher et al., 1998). Because prayer seemed to be the primary intervention used, a decision was made to include this study in the review.

## Analysis

To assess the research on intercessory prayer, three methods were used. First, studies were critically assessed in keeping with reviews conducted in the field of medicine (Townsend et al., 2002). Second, in accordance with other systematic reviews conducted in social work (Hodge, 2006a; Tucker & Potocky-Tripodi, 2006), the studies were evaluated in light of the standards developed by Division 12 of the American Psychological Association (APA) for determining empirically supported treatments (Chambless et al., 1995; Chambless & Ollendick, 2001).

Finally, a meta-analysis was conducted. The studies that emerged from the search exhibited substantial clinical diversity. In such situations, a meta-analysis is commonly considered inappropriate (Higgins & Green, 2005). Although recognizing this limitation, earlier reviews in medicine have conducted meta-analyses to provide some type of qualitative measure of clinical effects (Astin et al., 2000; Masters et al., 2006). Consistent with this practice, a meta-analysis was performed using Comprehensive Meta-Analysis V.2.

# Results

## Critical Assessment

Seventeen studies met the criteria for inclusion. These studies, which examined the effects of prayer on a wide variety of physical and psychological outcomes, are summarized in Table 13.1. Included in the table is information on the study's design, whether expectancy effects may have been created by the use of informed consent, the experimental sample and intervention, whether intercessors were directed to pray in a specific manner, the control group, and the results. These studies are discussed in more detail below, beginning with those studies in which no positive findings were obtained, through those studies with various mixed findings, to those studies reporting significance across all outcomes at the other end of the continuum.

## Studies Featuring No or Marginal Prayer Effects

In perhaps the most rigorous study to date, Benson and associates (2006) examined the effects of prayer among cardiac bypass patients in six hospitals. Individuals were informed of the study's purpose and randomly assigned to an experimental group, which received intercessory prayer ($n = 604$), and a control group, which received no prayer ($n = 597$). The study also included a third arm ($n = 601$), in which members were told they would be receiving prayer. This three-group design allowed investigators to examine the effects of being certain of receiving prayer. The intervention was provided by three Christian prayer groups who agreed to pray for a successful surgery, no complications, and quick recovery.

At the 30-day follow-up point, a comparison of the experimental and control groups revealed no significant differences on any of the three outcomes (mortality, complications, and major events). Interestingly, an examination of the experimental group and the third group revealed that being certain of receiving prayer was associated with negative outcomes. Individuals certain of receiving prayer were 14% more likely to experience complications than individuals who were uncertain of receiving prayer but did, in fact, receive prayer.

A somewhat similar design was used by Walker, Tonigan, Miller, Comer, and Kahlich (1997) to explore the effects of intercessory prayer among clients receiving treatment for alcohol dependence. Potential participants were informed of the purpose of the study and randomly assigned to a control group ($n = 18$), which received the standard treatment, and an experimental group ($n = 22$), in which the standard treatment was supplemented with daily prayer from a diverse group of Protestants, Catholics, and Jews. Positive, nondirective prayer was suggested.

In addition, a normative, comparison sample ($n = 123$) was included in the study to control for any placebo or expectancy effects that existed as a result of being informed that someone might be praying for them. No significant differences emerged between the experimental or the control group during the course of the 6-month study, with both groups achieving a substantial reduction in alcohol consumption. Because the standard treatment was largely successful, it is possible to argue that little margin exists for the experimental treatment to record better results. Although no differences emerged between the experimental and the control groups, both groups recorded a 3-month delay in the reduction of alcohol consumption after entering treatment relative to the normative, comparison sample.

Consistent with the previous study, the belief that someone might be praying seemed to produce negative effects—increased alcohol consumption relative to the comparison sample. Although the adverse outcome disappeared
by the end of the study, the finding raises the possibility that engendering
expectancy of prayer may have detrimental effects.

The effects of expectancy were directly explored by W. J. Matthews,
Conti, and Sireci (2001), who informed potential participants that they
would receive either prayer or positive visualization. However, after creating the expectation that all volunteers would receive some form of distant
healing, one third of participants ($n = 33$) were randomly assigned to
a treatment group that received no prayer or visualization. The researchers
were thus able to examine if prayer, positive visualization, or the effect of
expectancy was associated with better physical or psychological outcomes
among patients receiving kidney dialysis. In this study, the 5- to 15-minute
daily prayer, offered during the course of 6 weeks, was provided by a group
of six Catholics using scripted prayers that requested emotional and physical healing. No significant differences emerged among the three groups,
suggesting that the effects of prayer and positive visualization cannot be distinguished from expectancy. Nonsignificant results were also obtained by
Mathai and Bourne (2004) using a triple-blind design. These individuals
investigated the effectiveness of intercessory prayer among children coping
with psychiatric disorders. Prayer was offered weekly by a committed
group of 6 individuals selected by the chief investigator. No difference in
outcomes emerged at 3 months between the experimental group ($n = 16$)
and the control group ($n = 17$).

Two studies, apparently based on the same sample, explored the effectiveness of four approaches—stress relaxation, imagery, touch therapy, and
prayer—with patients ($N = 150$) receiving heart surgery for unstable coronary symptoms (Krucoff et al., 2001; Seskevich, Crater, Lane, & Krucoff,
2004). After being informed about the nature of the study, volunteers were
randomly assigned to one of the four treatment groups or the control group.
Off-site prayer was provided by diverse theological groups (e.g., Buddhist,
Jewish, Baptist) from around the globe (Nepal, Israel, United States). Both
studies reported that prayer was unrelated to outcomes. In the initially published study, however, the authors reported that quadrupling the sample size
would have likely produced significant findings in favor of the experimental
prayer group.

In response, Krucoff and associates (2005) essentially replicated their
design in a larger, nine-center study ($N = 748$). Of particular interest, was
the use of a two-tier prayer intervention modeled after the Cha and Wirth
(2001) study. Although all cardiac patients in the intervention group ($n = 371$) received a single "dose" of prayer, a subgroup ($n = 84$) received an
additional dose of prayer. More specifically, a second set of prayer groups
prayed for the efficacy of the prayers offered by the other groups, so as to
compound their effectiveness. No significant differences emerged between

**Table 13.1** Overview of Studies on Intercessory Prayer

| Authors | Design | Expectancy Effects | Sample (n) | Experimental Intervention (n) | Directed Prayer | Control (n) | Result |
|---|---|---|---|---|---|---|---|
| Benson et al. (2006) | Prospective, double-blind RCT | Y | 604 primarily White Protestant and Catholic males receiving cardiac bypass surgery | An unspecified amount of daily, distant IP for each client, for 14 days starting the night before surgery, by 2 Catholic and 1 Protestant prayer groups (n?) | Y | Usual treatment (597) | ns |
| Walker, Tonigan, Miller, Comer, and Kahlich (1997) | Prospective, double-blind RCT | Y | 22 primarily Hispanic males of unknown religion receiving treatment for alcohol abuse | An unspecified amount of daily, distant IP for each client, for 6 months, by experienced Protestant, Catholic, and Jewish intercessors (n?) | N | Usual treatment (18) | ns |
| W. J. Matthews, Conti, and Sireci (2001) | Prospective, double-blind RCT | Y | 15 primarily Black Protestant males receiving kidney dialysis | 5–15 min. of daily distant IP for each client, for 6 weeks, by an experienced Catholic prayer group (6) | Y | Usual treatment (33) | ns |
| Mathai and Bourne (2004) | Prospective, triple-blind RCT | N | 16 children of unknown religion coping with psychiatric disorders | An unspecified amount of distant IP for clients in the intervention group, once a week, for 3 months, by a committed group (6) | N/A | Usual treatment (17) | ns |
| Seskevich, Crater, Lane, and Krucoff (2004) | Prospective, double-blind RCT | Y | 19 likely males of unknown religion receiving heart surgery in a VA medical center | An unspecified amount of distant IP for each client, by 8 prayer groups from different traditions: Unity, Moravian, Baptist, Jewish, evangelical, Buddhists (2 of), and Catholic | N/A | Usual treatment (18) | ns |

(Continued)

**Table 13.1** (Continued)

| Authors | Design | Expectancy Effects | Sample (n) | Experimental Intervention (n) | Directed Prayer | Control (n) | Result |
|---|---|---|---|---|---|---|---|
| Krucoff et al. (2001) | Prospective, double-blind RCT | Y | 23 males of unknown religion receiving heart surgery in the Bible Belt | An unspecified amount of daily distant IP for each client, for 30 days, by 8 groups: Unity (?), Moravian (8), Baptist (3 congregations), Jewish (?), evangelical (1 congregation), 2 Buddhists (18 and 150), and Catholic (17) | N/A | Usual treatment (21) | ns trend favors prayer group |
| Krucoff et al. (2005) | Prospective, double-blind RCT | Y | 84 primarily males of unknown religion, of various degrees of religious commitment, receiving heart surgery | Two-tier prayer intervention: tier 1—an unspecified amount of distant IP for each client, for 5 to 30 days, by 12 diverse prayer groups; tier 2—an unspecified amount of distant IP for the 12 prayer groups by an additional 12 prayer groups | N/A | Usual treatment (88) | ns trend favors prayer group |
| Aviles et al. (2001) | Prospective, double-blind RCT | Y | 400 primarily males of unknown religion wrestling with heart disease | An unspecified amount of distant IP, offered at least weekly for 26 weeks, for each client, by 5 Christian prayer groups (1-65; *Mdn* = 1 intercessor) | N | Usual treatment (399) | ns trend favors prayer group |
| Joyce and Welldon (1965) | Prospective, double-blind sequential matched design | N | 16 primarily female Anglicans with progressively deteriorating rheumatic disease | Approximately 5 minutes of daily distant IP for each client, for 6 months (approx. 15 hours of prayer total), by 19 Quakers and nondenominational Christians | N | Usual treatment (16) | ns trend favors prayer group |

| Authors | Design | Expectancy Effects | Sample (n) | Experimental Intervention (n) | Directed Prayer | Control (n) | Result |
|---|---|---|---|---|---|---|---|
| Collipp (1969) | Prospective, triple-blind | N | 10 children of unknown religion with leukemia | An unspecified amount of daily distant IP for each client, for 15 months, by 10 families in a Protestant church | N/A | Usual treatment (8) | ns trend favors prayer group |
| D. A. Matthews, Marlowe, and MacNutt (2000) | Quasi-experimental using pre- and posttests | Y | 26 primarily White, elderly, born-again females with arthritis | 6 hours of in-person verbal prayer over 3 days for each client by "several" Charismatic Catholics | N/A | Wait-listed and then received prayer (14) | Sig. (in person) ns (dist.) |
| Byrd (1988) | Prospective, double-blind RCT | Y | 192 patients of unknown religion in coronary care | An unspecified amount of daily distant IP for each client, until discharged, by 3 to 7 born-again Protestants and Catholics | Y | Usual treatment (201) | Sig. |
| Harris, Thoresen, McCullough, and Larson (1999) | Prospective, double-blind RCT | N | 466 primarily elderly cardiac patients of unknown religion | An unspecified amount of daily distant IP for each client, for 28 days, by 15 teams composed of 5 Christians | Y | Usual treatment (524) | Sig. |
| Furlow and O'Quinn (2002) | Prospective, double-blind RCT | Y | 21 primarily male, elderly, Christian cardiac patients | Approximately 3 to 6 minutes of daily distant IP for each client, during their hospital stay (27 to 88 minutes total) by 5 female church members | Y | Usual treatment (17) | Sig. |
| Sicher, Targ, Moore, and Smith (1998) | Prospective, double-blind RCT | Y | 20 primarily White middle-age males of unknown religion with AIDS | 1 hour per day of distant IP, per client, for 10 weeks, rotating among a total of 40 Buddhist, Christian, Jewish, Native American, Shamanistic, and secular healers, all with experience healing AIDS | Y | Usual treatment (20) | Sig. |

(Continued)

Table **13.1** (Continued)

| Authors | Design | Expectancy Effects | Sample (n) | Experimental Intervention (n) | Directed Prayer | Control (n) | Result |
|---|---|---|---|---|---|---|---|
| Leibovici (2001) | Retroactive RCT | N | 1,691 primarily elderly patients of unknown religion with bloodstream infection | A list of names was given to a single person of unknown religion who said a "short prayer" for the group | Y | Usual treatment (1,702) | Sig. |
| Cha and Wirth (2001) | Prospective, double-blind RCT | N | 88 women of unknown religion receiving treatment for infertility | Two-tier prayer intervention: Tier 1—an unspecified amount of daily distant IP for groups of 5 clients, for approx. 4 weeks, by groups consisting of 3 to 13 Christians; Tier 2—an unspecified amount of prayer offered for the above groups by additional Christian groups | Y | Usual treatment (81) | Sig. |

NOTE: RCT = randomized control trial; IP = intercessory prayer.

the intervention and control groups among those receiving the single dose or the double dose. Yet although no trend was apparent among recipients of the single-tier prayer, recipients of the two-tier prayer exhibited a trend in favor of the experimental group across three of the four outcomes at the 6-month follow-up. Most notable was the lower rate of death and readmission (25% vs. 35%, $p = .0979$).

Similar results were obtained in an examination of the effects of intercessory prayer on cardiovascular disease progression (Aviles et al., 2001). Potential participants were informed of the study's purpose and randomly assigned to control ($n = 399$) and treatment groups ($n = 400$), with the latter group receiving nondirected prayer at least once a week for 26 weeks following discharge. The prayer was provided by professing Christians, with each intercessor praying for anywhere from 1 to 100 patients ($Mdn = 5$). No significant differences emerged between the control and treatment group on any of the outcomes studied; however, a pattern of positive findings existed across outcomes for the prayer group.

In perhaps the earliest double-blind study on prayer, Joyce and Welldon (1965) explored the effects of prayer on patients with progressively deteriorating rheumatic disease. Individuals, who were not informed of the study's purpose to control for expectancy effects, were matched on a number of demographic characteristics and then randomly assigned to treatment ($n = 16$) and control groups ($n = 16$). A sequential study design was used, resulting in matched patients being enrolled in the study over a period of time. Nondirective, meditative prayer was offered daily by Quakers and an interdenominational group, who were told that the study would last for 6 months and that they would not be contacted until the study was completed. Although no significant differences emerged between the two groups, the researchers suggested that the nonsignificant findings may have been because of the excessive length of the study. Because of delays in enrolling matched pairs into the study, many patients were not evaluated until at least 12 months had elapsed, more than twice as long as the study was intended to last. The researchers reported that they did not know if the intercessors continued to pray beyond the 6 months they had committed to, but they observed a distinct trend in results. Consistently positive results were obtained during the first 12 months, at which point the trend changed. If the time period of the analysis was changed to reflect the first 12 months, then significant results would have been obtained in favor of the group receiving prayer.

The final study in this subsection focused on children wrestling with leukemia (Collipp, 1969). Neither the children, their families, the service providers, nor the Protestant group that agreed to pray for the children were informed of the study. At the study's 15-month conclusion, 7 of the 10 children in the experimental group were still alive, whereas only 2 of the 8 children in the control group were living. The difference was significant at the nontraditional level of .10, and 1 child in the control group was atypical.

This study may represent the midpoint of the continuum because it is arguable that the study belongs in the next subsection, which delineates significant findings. If the atypical child is removed from the analysis, the results are significant at the traditional .05 level.

## Studies Featuring at Least Partially Significant Results

Although all the studies in this review examined the effects of distance or remote intercessory prayer, D. A. Matthews, Marlowe, and MacNutt (2000) also explored the effects of in-person, verbal intercessory prayer. Patients with rheumatoid arthritis served as the study's participants, all of whom were informed of the study's purpose. Because of insufficient volunteers, randomization did not occur for the in-person prayer component of the study. The first 26 volunteers functioned as the experimental group, whereas the next 14 served as a wait-list control group for 6 months, after which they also received the 3-day, in-person prayer intervention. Pretests and posttests were conducted for the whole group 1 year after the intervention $(N = 40)$. For the study's distance prayer component, a double-blind RCT protocol was used in which participants were randomly assigned to either a control group or a treatment group. In addition to the 3-day, in-person prayer, the treatment group received supplemental distance prayer for 10 minutes a day for 6 months. Charismatic Catholics provided all prayers, which incorporated requests for healing. Although analysis revealed that the supplemental distant prayer had no effect, in-person prayer yielded significant differences. The first group receiving in-person prayer did significantly better than the wait-list control group at 6 months on a number of the 10 outcomes. The wait-list control group also demonstrated significant improvement 6 months after receiving the 3-day in-person prayer. These gains were maintained for the entire sample at the final follow-up, 12 months after the in-person prayer intervention.

Three studies have explored outcomes among patients in coronary care settings using generally similar methodologies (Byrd, 1988; Furlow & O'Quinn, 2002; Harris et al., 1999). Among the outcomes of interest were (a) length of hospital stay, (b) length of stay in the coronary care unit, and (c) various global measures of patient progress, outcomes, or complications. During the patient's hospital stay, devout Christians offered daily prayer for rapid recovery with no complications.

Using relatively large samples, Byrd (1988; $N = 393$) and Harris and associates (1999; $N = 990$) recorded similar results, even though the former study used informed consent and the latter did not. Although no significant differences emerged regarding length of stay, the experimental group recorded significantly better global progress or outcomes. Conversely, Furlow and O'Quinn (2002), who did inform participants of the study's purpose, found the exact opposite—no difference in the area of complications, but the prayer group ($n = 21$) recorded significantly shorter stays in the hospital and the coronary care unit relative to the control group ($n = 17$).

Patients with advanced AIDS ($N = 40$) have also been the subject of study (Sicher et al., 1998). The 10-week intervention incorporated prayer offered from members of a variety of traditions (e.g., Buddhist, Christian, Jewish, Native American) and some secular forms of distant healing (e.g., bioenergetic healing). A rotating schedule randomized healers across the 10-week intervention so that participants were exposed to 10 different healers, most of whom appeared to use prayer. Healers were asked to facilitate the participants' health and well-being, working on the task for 1 hour per day for 6 consecutive days. Informed consent was used. Of 11 outcomes measured, significant differences emerged on 6 at the conclusion of the study at 6 months. Relative to the control group, the experimental group experienced significantly fewer hospitalizations, outpatient visits, and new illnesses; fewer days of hospitalization; and less severe new illnesses. The mood of the experimental group also improved significantly, with significant differences occurring on four of the measure's six subscales (e.g., lower levels of depression, tension, confusion, and fatigue among the intervention group).

Although all other studies in the review employed a prospective design, following individuals through time, Leibovici's (2001) study used a retroactive design. Arguing that it cannot be assumed, a priori, that time is necessarily linear or that God is limited by what we perceive as linear time, Leibovici explored the effectiveness of prayer offered in the present for events that took place in the past, namely patients hospitalized 4 to 10 years previously. A 6-year list of adults consecutively admitted to an Israeli hospital with bloodstream infections was randomized into intervention ($n = 1,691$) and control groups ($n = 1,702$). A list of first names of individuals in the intervention group was given to a person who then said a short prayer, requesting full recovery and well-being for the whole group.

Three outcomes were examined: mortality while in the hospital, length of hospital stay, and length of the infection-induced fever. Significant differences emerged for the latter two outcomes, and mortality was lower in the intervention group, although the difference was not significant. In other words, the length of time in the hospital and the duration of the fever were significantly lower for the group that received retroactive prayer, 4 to 10 years after hospitalization. In this case, it is clear that expectancy effects are inoperative. Study participants could not have expectations about an intervention that was not conceived until years later.

In contrast to Leibovici's (2001) study, which employed a seemingly minimal dose of prayer, the final study in the section used two-tier or "compounded" prayer. Cha and Wirth (2001) examined pregnancy rates among Korean women ($N = 219$), aged 26 to 46, undergoing in vitro fertilization–embryo transfer. To compound or increase the effect of the prayer intervention, those in the first tier prayed that women in the experimental group would get pregnant, whereas those in Tier 2 prayed that the efficiency of the intervention would be enhanced. Prayer was offered during the course of the fertilization schedule by Christians in Australia, Canada, and the United States, without the knowledge of the providers or patients (i.e., informed consent was not used).

Compared to the control group, women in the experimental group were significantly more likely to become pregnant (50% vs. 26%). When results were broken down and analyzed by age group, no significant differences emerged among the below-30 group, in which the pregnancy rates were extremely high for both groups. Differences were pronounced, however, among the 30- to 39-year-old group (51% vs. 23%) and the older-than-39 group (42% vs. 23%).

## Intercessory Prayer as an Empirically Supported Intervention

As the above assessment implicitly illustrates, intercessory prayer does not meet the criteria established by the APA's Division 12 for classification as an empirically supported treatment (Chambless et al., 1995; Chambless & Ollendick, 2001). To achieve such classification, studies must meet a number of criteria, including the use of a clearly defined intervention (ideally delineated in a treatment manual), which is administered by therapists, with clients wrestling with a specific, classifiable problem. To be considered effective in addressing a problem, the findings must be replicated by at least two different research teams.

These criteria were rarely met. The prayer interventions reviewed were typically not administered by therapists, and, in many cases, relatively little information was provided about the nature of the interventions. It is also noteworthy that most of the interventions were employed with clients wrestling with a variety of medical, rather than psychological, problems.

In short, intercessory prayer cannot presently be considered an empirically supported intervention for any psychological problem. Even within the evidence-based practice movement, however, the Division 12 criteria have been controversial (APA Presidential Task Force on Evidence-based Practice, 2006). A meta-analysis represents an alternative method for synthesizing results from multiple studies by providing a quantitative estimate of the size of an intervention's effects.

## Meta-Analysis

To calculate an omnibus effect size for intercessory prayer, outcomes were weighted and averaged across studies. In studies with multiple dependent measures, outcomes were pooled to create one effect size for each study. Although some previous meta-analyses have been based on selecting a single significant outcome (Astin et al., 2000), the pooled outcome approach is more conservative. Thus, for example, with Harris and associates' (1999) study, the effect size was calculated using all 40 outcomes rather than the primary global measure of complications that the research team expected might illustrate the effects of prayer.

Of the three dependent measures in Leibovici's (2001) study, insufficient information was reported to calculate effect sizes for the two significant outcomes (i.e., length of hospital stay and fever). Thus, only the non-significant mortality outcomes were used. With Krucoff and associates' (2005) study, effect sizes were calculated based on the outcomes achieved using the two-tier prayer intervention. The authors implied that the compounded dose of prayer might more effectively illustrate the incremental effects of intercessory prayer provided in the study (89% of patients knew of additional, outside intercessory prayer that was being offered on their behalf during the study). Supplementary analysis using the outcomes obtained with the single-tier intervention did not affect whether any of the models reported below achieved significance. Masters et al. (2006) suggested that both fixed- and random-effects models be used to calculate effect size. The heterogeneity and limited number of studies argue in favor of a fixed-effects model, which allows for greater generalization. Conversely, the fact that the fixed-effects model is more conservative, in conjunction with the fact that research on prayer is still in its infancy, argues in favor of a random-effects model.

As can be seen in Table 13.2, both models were significant. Based on commonly accepted conventions, the .171 effect size for intercessory prayer recorded using the random-effects model is considered small (Vaughn & Howard, 2004). The classic fail-safe $N$ is 32. In other words, 32 additional studies with a mean effect of zero are needed for the combined two-tailed $p$ value to exceed the traditional .05 level of significance.

**Table 13.2**    Effects of Intercessory Prayer Across Studies

| Model | Studies Included in Analysis | $g^{a}$ | Z | p |
|---|---|---|---|---|
| Random effects | All | −.171 | −2.436 | .015 |
| Fixed effects | All | −.095 | −2.724 | .006 |
| Random effects | Without Cha and Wirth (2001) | −.109 | −1.866 | .062 |
| Fixed effects | Without Cha and Wirth (2001) | −.077 | −2.154 | .031 |

a. All effect sizes are converted to Hedges's g, which corrects for a small bias in Cohen's d. Negative values for g and Z indicate a positive effect for intercessory prayer.

Additional analysis was also conducted in which perhaps the most controversial study featuring positive outcomes was removed from the models. Without the Cha and Wirth (2001) study, the effect size diminished, and the random-effects model was no longer significant ($p = .062$). The fixed-effects model, however, remained significant.

# Discussion and Applications to Practice

In light of the widespread use of intercessory prayer, this study examined the empirical literature on the topic to provide practitioners with some guidance regarding the use of intercessory prayer in practice settings. Three methods were used to analyze the 17 studies that emerged: an individual assessment of each study, an evaluation of intercessory prayer as an empirically supported intervention using the APA's Division 12 criteria, and a meta-analysis. The results are summarized below. This synthesis is followed by a discussion of implications for practice, which is informed by the APA's Presidential Task Force on Evidence-based Practice (2006).

## Findings Supportive of Prayer

Individual assessment revealed that patients who received intercessory prayer demonstrated significant improvement compared to those who received standard treatment devoid of prayer in 7 of the 17 studies. Furthermore, in an additional 5 studies, the trend favored the prayer group. This raises the possibility that an increase in power would yield significant findings.

As Abbot (2000) observes, an extended period of years is often necessary to establish the empirical effectiveness of new interventions. It is not uncommon to achieve positive effects that do not reach the level of significance, as occurred with some of the studies in this review. With the use of similar methodologies, such studies can be combined, a process that often yields significant results.

For example, the use of aspirin with patients with certain heart problems has been associated with a 23% reduction in death from heart attack. Yet as Abbot (2000) notes, these effects only became apparent after six studies ($N = 10,859$) conducted over the course of a number of years were combined. Given that a majority of the studies in this review evidenced a trend in favor of the experimental group, it is not inconceivable that similar results will eventually be found for prayer.

The results from the meta-analysis support this thesis. The synthesis of outcomes across studies produced small, but significant, effects for intercessory prayer. These results are consistent with earlier meta-analyses conducted in medicine (Astin et al., 2000; Masters et al., 2006).

## Findings Unsupportive of Prayer

Conversely, in 10 of the studies, prayer was unassociated with positive improvement in the condition of clients. In addition, in many of the studies in which significant results were obtained, the results were not uniformly positive across outcome variables. For instance, in the Byrd (1988) study, only six positive outcomes were recorded among 26 specific problem conditions. This type of inconsistent pattern raises the possibility of Type I errors. Individual assessment also revealed nonsignificant findings among some of the most methodologically rigorous studies. Studies by Benson et al. (2006) and Krucoff et al. (2005) employed a multicenter randomized methodology with relatively large sample sizes. Yet both studies failed to produce significant findings.

In addition, intercessory prayer cannot be classified as an empirically supported intervention for any psychological problem based on the criteria established by the APA's Division 12 (Chambless et al., 1995; Chambless & Ollendick, 2001). The Division 12 criteria also help illustrate the heterogeneous nature of the current literature. The methodological similarity needed to make informed assessments across studies is lacking.

Interventions, for instance, should be clearly specified so that practitioners can implement them. Yet so many questions exist about the nature of the interventions, it would be difficult for practitioners to replicate the intervention with any degree of confidence. For example, little agreement exists regarding the amount of prayer required for an intervention to be effective. A minimal amount of prayer by a single person has been effective, whereas more extensive prayer by groups has been ineffective, although this cannot be considered a consistent pattern because extensive group prayer has also been effective in some cases as well. Similar questions also exist about the type of prayer (direct requests for healing and well-being vs. nondirective positive affirmations) and the person or persons providing the prayer (Is one's level of personal spirituality related to effectiveness?). Even if replication were possible, many interventions were so time-consuming that it would be unfeasible to use them in many clinical settings.

## Implications for Practice

For practitioners who adhere to the protocols established by the APA's Division 12, the implications are clear. Intercessory prayer must be classified as an experimental intervention. For such practitioners, further research is needed involving practitioners using specific prayers offered on behalf of clients wrestling with problems classifiable by the *Diagnostic and Statistical Manual of Mental Disorders* (*DSM*). Until such research is conducted, the use of intercessory prayer should generally be avoided in practice settings.

Evidence-based practice, however, is widely understood in more expansive terms than the criteria established by Division 12. The APA's Presidential Task Force on Evidence-based Practice (2006) has defined evidence-based practice as "the integration of the best available research with clinical expertise in the context of patient characteristics, culture and preferences" (p. 273). The best available research is defined broadly. In addition to evidence from RCTs and meta-analyses, it includes a wide range of scientific results, including epidemiological studies, qualitative research, and case studies, to list just some.

This appreciation for multiple forms of scientific evidence addresses many of the concerns of those operating from what might be called postmodern epistemic assumptions. As implied above, the epistemological assumptions on which RCTs are based have been extensively criticized (Lincoln & Guba, 2003; Nakashima, 2003; Slife, Hope, & Nebeker, 1999; Tangenberg, 2000; Walker, 2001). Observers operating from postmodern understandings have argued that RCTs are based on modernistic approaches that provide only a partial understanding of existence and, consequently, should be supplemented by more qualitatively oriented approaches. In addition, some commentators argue that the assumptions on which RCTs are based are particularly unsuited for assessing spiritual phenomena (e.g., Slife et al., 1999).

Accordingly, some practitioners may feel that the best available research supports the use of intercessory prayer. The general trend in favor of the prayer group in 12 of the 17 studies, in conjunction with the positive findings from the meta-analysis, suggests that intercessory prayer may be effective. This understanding is supported by research on prayer using non-experimental designs, in which generally favorable outcomes have been obtained (Koenig et al., 2001).

Consequently, some practitioners may feel that the present level of research satisfies the NASW Code of Ethics (1999, sec. 1.04 [c]) competency requirements for emerging areas of practice. In other words, the current evidence indicates that the use of prayer is consistent with competent service provision. In particular, practitioners who interact with hospital patients, children dealing with leukemia, adults wrestling with advanced AIDS, and older women hoping to become pregnant may believe that the current research supports the use of intercessory prayer.

## The Role of Client Preferences

As the above definition of evidence-based practice implies, the APA's Presidential Task Force (2006) emphasizes the importance of client preferences in the selection of interventions. In other words, clients' beliefs and values must also be considered along with practitioners' assessment of the best available evidence. This stance is fully consistent with the NASW Code of Ethics' (1999) affirmation of client autonomy.

Given the importance of client preferences, it may be helpful to know that many members of the general public use prayer to address their health concerns (McCaffrey, Eisenberg, Legedza, Davis, & Phillips, 2004). In addition, African Americans, women, people with disabilities, and the elderly are more likely to pray (Bell et al., 2005; Hendershot, 2003; Levin & Taylor, 1997). In short, for many clients—particularly those from disadvantaged populations—prayer is a significant strength (Pargament, 1997).

In recognition of this reality, the nation's predominant health care accrediting body, the Joint Commission on Accreditation of Healthcare Organizations (JCAHO), now requires the administration of a spiritual assessment (Hodge, 2006b). In the context of conducting a spiritual assessment, or even a general assessment, social workers may find that clients report that intercessory prayer is a significant strength.

A number of options may be appropriate in such situations, depending on the circumstances. For instance, in some cases, practitioners might explore the possibility of clergy or friends who share clients' spiritual orientation conducting intercessory prayer on clients' behalf. In other cases, it may be appropriate for social workers to pray either with or for clients, particularly if requested by clients.

## The Use of Informed Consent for Private Intercessory Prayer

Another area the results address is the debate about informed consent regarding private intercessory prayer. Some commentators believe that clients should be informed and their consent obtained before practitioners engage in private prayer. Others believe that it is unnecessary to obtain consent in such situations (Canda et al., 2004; Magaletta & Brawer, 1998).

Yet the process of obtaining informed consent may engender expectancy effects (W. J. Matthews et al., 2001). Although expectancy effects are usually assumed to enhance the provided treatment, this did not occur across the studies surveyed. As seen in the study of clients undergoing therapy for alcohol dependency, informing clients that they may be recipients of prayer may have fostered detrimental outcomes (Walker et al., 1997). Similarly, cardiac bypass patients certain of receiving intercessory prayer were 14% more likely to experience negative outcomes compared to those who were uncertain of receiving prayer (Benson et al., 2006).

These findings raise questions about the appropriateness of obtaining informed consent for private intercessory prayer. The NASW Code of Ethics (1999) requires practitioners to avoid interventions that may cause harm to clients. Although permission should typically be sought before engaging in verbal intercessory prayer, securing informed consent to pray privately for clients may foster detrimental outcomes because of the expectancy effects created by securing consent. Conversely, little evidence exists suggesting private intercessory prayer engenders negative outcomes, particularly if clients are unaware that prayer is being offered on their behalf. With the exception of one small pilot study (i.e., Mathai & Bourne, 2004), all six studies in which clients were completely unaware of the intervention yielded positive outcomes or exhibited a trend in favor of the group receiving intercessory prayer. This finding held irrespective of when the prayer was offered (prospective vs. retrospective) or the spiritual tradition of those providing the prayer (Quakers vs. Catholics).

## Study Limitations

The preceding discussion must be considered in the light of the study's limitations. Many individuals believe that studies with positive outcomes are more likely to be submitted and published, whereas those with nonsignificant results are filed away and never seen (Crisp, 2004; Rosenthal, 1979). Although research confirms that many studies are not published in peer-reviewed journals, the extent to which researchers favor submitting significant findings rather than nonsignificant findings remains unclear (Weber, Callaham, Wears, Barton, & Young, 1998). Interestingly, some authorities suggest that studies linking prayer with salutary outcomes may be more likely to be rejected during the peer-review process because of their controversial nature (Koenig et al., 2001).

Research also suggests that computer searches may not be as effective as manual searches of individual journals in locating relevant articles (Bareta, Larson, Lyons, & Zorc, 1990). The breadth of the literature covered in this search, however, precluded a manual examination of the literature. Another limitation is the small number of participants in some of the studies reviewed, a fact that underscores the emerging nature of this area of study. Some individuals may also consider the study's prioritization of RCTs at the expense of more qualitatively oriented case studies to interject some degree of bias into the findings (Slife & Williams, 1995). Indeed, future researchers should employ diverse methodological strategies to map the effects of intercessory prayer.

# Conclusion

Intercessory prayer offered on behalf of clients in clinical settings is a controversial practice, in spite of its apparent frequent occurrence. The topic is one that engenders both support and opposition, often passionately held. This study has attempted to shed some light on the controversy by examining the empirical literature on intercessory prayer.

Practitioners who adhere to Division 12 criteria have little basis for using intercessory prayer, in spite of a meta-analysis indicating small, but significant, effect sizes for the use of intercessory prayer. Most practitioners, however, are likely to affirm the broader understanding of evidence-based practice articulated in the APA's Presidential Task Force on Evidence-based Practice (2006). Such practitioners may believe that the best available evidence currently supports the use of intercessory prayer as an intervention.

Thus, at this juncture in time, the results might be considered inconclusive. Indeed, perhaps the most certain result stemming from this study is the following: The findings are unlikely to satisfy either proponents or opponents of intercessory prayer.

# References

Abbot, N. C. (2000). Healing as a therapy for human disease: A systematic review. *The Journal of Alternative and Complementary Medicine, 6,* 159–169.

APA Presidential Task Force on Evidence-based Practice. (2006). Evidence-based practice in psychology. *American Psychologist, 64,* 271–285.

Astin, J. A., Harkness, E., & Ernst, E. (2000). The efficacy of "distant healing": A systematic review of randomized trails. *Annals of Internal Medicine, 132,* 903–910.

Aviles, J. M., Whelan, E., Hernke, D. A., Williams, B. A., Kenny, K. E., O'Fallon, W. M., et al. (2001). Intercessory prayer and cardiovascular disease progression in a coronary care unit population: A randomized controlled trial. *Mayo Clinic Proceedings, 76,* 1192–1198.

Bareta, J. C., Larson, D. B., Lyons, J. S., & Zorc, J. J. (1990). A comparison of manual and MEDLARS reviews of the literature on consultation-liaison psychiatry. *American Journal of Psychiatry, 147,* 1040–1042.

Bell, R. A., Suerken, C., Quandt, S. A., Grzywacz, J. G., Lang, W., & Arcury, T. A. (2005). Prayer for health among U.S. adults: The 2002 national health interview survey. *Complementary Health Practices Review, 10,* 175–188.

Benson, H., Dusek, J. A., Sherwood, J. B., Lam, P., Bethea, C. F., Capenter, W., et al. (2006). Study of the therapeutic effects of intercessory prayer (STEP) in cardiac bypass patients: A multicenter randomized trial of uncertainty and certainty of receiving intercessory prayer. *American Heart Journal, 151,* 934–942.

Bernardi, L., Sleight, P., Bandinelli, G., Cencetti, S., Fattorini, L., Wdowczyc-Szulc, J., et al. (2001). Effect of rosary prayer and yoga mantras on autonomic cardiovascular rhythms: Comparative study. *British Medical Journal, 323,* 22–29.

Beutler, J. J., Attevelt, J. T. M., Schouten, S. A., Faber, J. A., Mees, E. J. D., & Geijskes, G. G. (1988). Paranormal healing and hypertension. *British Medical Journal, 296*(6635), 1491–1494.

Byrd, R. C. (1988). Positive therapeutic effects of intercessory prayer in a coronary care unit population. *Southern Medical Journal, 81,* 826–829.

Canda, E. R., & Furman, L. D. (1999). *Spiritual diversity in social work practice: The heart of helping.* New York: Free Press.

Canda, E. R., Nakashima, M., & Furman, L. D. (2004). Ethical considerations about spirituality in social work: Insights from a national qualitative survey. *Families in Society, 85,* 27–35.

Carson, V., & Huss, K. (1979). Prayer: An effective therapeutic and teaching tool. *Journal of Psychiatric Nursing & Mental Health Services, 17*(3), 34–37.

Carvalho, M. M. (1995). A healing journey in Brazil: A case study in spiritual surgery. *Journal of the Society for Psychical Research, 60*(838), 161–167.

Cha, K. Y. (2004). Clarification: Influence on prayer on IVF-ET. *The Journal of Reproductive Medicine, 49,* 944–945.

Cha, K. Y., & Wirth, D. P. (2001). Does prayer influence the success of in vitro fertilization-embryo transfer? Report of a masked, randomized trial. *The Journal of Reproductive Medicine, 46,* 781–787.

Chambless, D. L., Babich, K., Christoph, P. C., Frank, E., Gilson, M., Montgomery, R., et al. (1995). Training in and dissemination of empirically-validated psychological treatments: Report and recommendations. *The Clinical Psychologist, 48*(1), 3–23.

Chambless, D. L., & Ollendick, T. H. (2001). Empirically supported psychological interventions: Controversies and evidence. *Annual Review of Psychology, 52,* 685–716.

Collipp, P. J. (1969). The efficacy of prayer: A triple blind study. *Medical Times, 97,* 201–204.

Crisp, B. R. (2004). Evidence-based practice and the borders of data in the global information era. *Journal of Social Work Education, 40,* 73–86.

Ellison, C. G. (1993). Religious involvement and self-perception among Black Americans. *Social Forces, 71,* 1027–1055.

Fabbro, F., Muzur, A., Bellen, R., Calacione, R., & Bava, A. (1999). Effects of praying and a working memory task in participants trained in meditation and controls on the occurrence of spontaneous thoughts. *Perceptual and Motor Skills, 88,* 765–770.

Flamm, B. L. (2005). Prayer and the success of IVF. *The Journal of Reproductive Medicine, 50,* 71.

Furlow, L., & O'Quinn, J. L. (2002). Does prayer really help? *Journal of Christian Nursing, 19*(2), 31–34.

Halperin, E. C. (2001). Should academic medical centers conduct clinical trails of the efficacy of intercessory prayer? *Academic Medicine, 76,* 791–797.

Harris, A., Thoresen, C. E., McCullough, M. E., & Larson, D. B. (1999). Spiritually and religiously oriented health interventions. *Journal of Health Psychology, 4,* 413–433.

Hendershot, G. E. (2003). Mobility limitations and complementary and alternative medicine: Are people with disabilities more likely to pray? *American Journal of Public Health, 93,* 1079–1080.

Heyman, J., Buchanan, R., Musgrave, B., & Menz, V. (2006). Social workers' attention to clients' spirituality: Use of spiritual interventions in practice. *Arete, 30*(1), 78–89.

Higgins, J. P., & Green, S. (2005). Cochrane handbook for systematic reviews of interventions 4.2.5. In *The Cochrane Library* (Issue 3). Chichester, UK: Wiley.

Hodge, D. R. (2000). Spirituality: Towards a theoretical framework. *Social Thought, 19*(4), 1–20.

Hodge, D. R. (2006a). Spiritually modified cognitive therapy: A review of the literature. *Social Work, 51*(7), 157–166.

Hodge, D. R. (2006b). A template for spiritual assessment: A review of the JCAHO requirements and guidelines for implementation. *Social Work, 51*(4), 317–326.

Johnson, B. R. (2002). *Objective hope.* Philadelphia: Center for Research on Religion and Urban Civil Society.

Joyce, C. R. B., & Welldon, R. M. C. (1965). The objective efficacy of prayer: A double-blind clinical trail. *Journal of Chronic Diseases, 18*, 367–377.

Koenig, H. G., McCullough, M. E., & Larson, D. B. (2001). *Handbook of religion and health*. New York: Oxford University Press.

Kowey, P. R., Friehling, T. D., & Marinchak, R. A. (1986). Prayer-meeting cardioversion. *Annals of Internal Medicine, 104*, 727–728.

Krucoff, M. W., Crater, S. W., Gallup, D., Blankenship, J. C., Cuffe, M., Guarneri, M., et al. (2005). Music, imagery, touch, and prayer as adjuncts to interventional cardiac care: The Monitoring and Actualisation of Noetic Trainings (MANTRA) II randomised study. *The Lancet, 366*(9481), 211–217.

Krucoff, M. W., Crater, S. W., Green, C. L., Maas, A. C., Seskevich, J. E., Lane, J. D., et al. (2001). Integrative noetic therapies as adjuncts to precutaneous interventions during unstable coronary syndromes: Monitoring and actualization of noetic training (MANTRA) feasibility pilot. *American Heart Journal, 142*(5), 119–138.

Leder, D. (2005). "Spook actions at a distance": Physics, psi, and distant healing. *The Journal of Alternative and Complementary Medicine, 11*, 923–930.

Leibovici, L. (2001). Effects of remote, retroactive intercessory prayer on outcomes in patients with bloodstream infection: Randomized controlled trial. *British Medical Journal, 323*, 1450–1451.

Levin, J. S., & Taylor, R. J. (1997). Age differences in patterns and correlates of the frequency of prayer. *The Gerontologist, 37*, 75–88.

Lincoln, Y. S., & Guba, E. G. (2003). Paradigmatic controversies, contradictions, and emerging confluences. In N. K. Denzin & Y. S. Lincoln (Eds.), *The landscape of qualitative research: Theories and issues* (2nd ed., pp. 253–291). Thousand Oaks, CA: Sage Publications.

Magaletta, P. R., & Brawer, P. A. (1998). Prayer in psychotherapy: A model for its use, ethical considerations, and guidelines for practice. *Journal of Psychology and Theology, 26*, 322–330.

Masters, K. S., Spielmans, G. I., & Goodson, J. T. (2006). Are there demonstrable effects of distant intercessory prayer? A meta-analytic review. *Annals of Behavioral Medicine, 32*, 21–26.

Mathai, J., & Bourne, A. (2004). Pilot study investigating the effect of intercessory prayer in the treatment of child psychiatric disorders. *Australasian Psychiatry, 12*, 386–389.

Matthews, D. A., Marlowe, S. M., & MacNutt, F. S. (2000). Effects of intercessory prayer on patients with rheumatoid arthritis. *Southern Medical Journal, 93*, 1177–1186.

Matthews, W. J., Conti, J. M., & Sireci, S. G. (2001). The effects of intercessory prayer, positive visualization, and expectancy on the well-being of kidney dialysis patients. *Alternative Therapies, 7*(5), 42–52.

McCaffrey, A. M., Eisenberg, D. M., Legedza, A. T. R., Davis, R. B., & Phillips, R. S. (2004). Prayer for health concerns: Results of a national survey on prevalence and patterns of use. *Archives of Internal Medicine, 164*, 858–862.

McCullough, M. E., & Larson, D. B. (1999). Prayer. In W. R. Miller (Ed.), *Integrating spirituality into treatment* (pp. 85–110). Washington, DC: American Psychological Association.

Murdock, V. (2004, February-March). *Religion and spirituality in gerontological social work practice: Results of a national survey.* Paper presented at the Council on Social Work Education, Anaheim, CA.

Nakashima, M. (2003). Beyond coping and adaption: Promoting a holistic perspective on dying. *Families in Society, 84,* 367–376. *NASW code of ethics.* (1999). Retrieved July 28, 2003, from http://www.socialworkers.org/pubs/code/code.asp

O'Laoire, S. (1997). An experimental study of the effects of distant, intercessory prayer on self-esteem, anxiety, and depression. *Alternative Therapies, 3*(6), 38–53.

Pargament, K. I. (1997). *The psychology of religion and coping.* New York: Guilford.

Praglin, L. J. (2004). Spirituality, religion, and social work: An effort towards interdisciplinary conversation. *Journal for Religion and Spirituality in Social Work, 23*(4), 67–84.

Ramondetta, L. M., & Sills, D. (2004). Spirituality in gynecological oncology: A review. *International Journal of Gynecological Cancer, 14,* 183–201.

Roberts, L., Ahmed, I., & Hall, S. (2003). Intercessory prayer for the alleviation of ill health. *The Cochrane Library, 4.*

Rosen, A., Proctor, E. K., & Staudt, M. M. (1999). Social work research and the quest for effective practice. *Social Work Research, 23,* 4–14.

Rosenthal, R. (1979). The file drawer problem and tolerance for null results. *Psychological Bulletin, 86,* 638–641.

Sahlein, J. (2002). When religion enters the dialogue: A guide for practitioners. *Clinical Social Work Journal, 30,* 381–401.

Sajwaj, T., & Hedges, D. (1973). A note on the effects of saying grace on the behavior of an oppositional retarded boy. *Journal of Applied Behavioral Analysis, 6,* 711–712.

Seskevich, J. E., Crater, S. W., Lane, J. D., & Krucoff, M. W. (2004). Beneficial effects of noetic therapies on mood before percutaneous intervention for unstable coronary syndromes. *Nursing Research, 53,* 116–121.

Sicher, F., Targ, E., Moore, D., & Smith, H. S. (1998). A randomized double-blind study of the effects of distant healing in a population with advanced AIDS: Report from a small scale study. *The Western Journal of Medicine, 169,* 356–363.

Sistler, A., & Washington, K. S. (1999). Serenity for African American caregivers. *Social Work with Groups, 22*(1), 49–62.

Slife, B. D., & Gantt, E. E. (1999). Methodological pluralism: A framework for psychotherapy research. *Journal of Clinical Psychology, 55,* 1453–1465.

Slife, B. D., Hope, C., & Nebeker, R. S. (1999). Examining the relationship between religious spirituality and psychological science. *Journal of Humanistic Psychology, 39,* 51–85.

Slife, B. D., & Williams, R. N. (1995). *What's behind the research? Discovering the hidden assumptions in the behavioral sciences.* Thousand Oaks, CA: Sage Publications.

Stewart, C., Koeske, G. F., & Koeske, R. D. (2006). Personal religiosity and spirituality associated with social work practitioners' use of religious-based intervention practices. *Journal of Religion and Spirituality in Social Work, 25*(1), 69–85.

Tangenberg, K. (2000). Marginalized epistemologies: A feminist approach to understanding the experiences of mothers with HIV. *Affilia, 15*(1), 31–48.

Targ, E. (2002). Research methodology for studies of prayer and distant healing. *Complementary Therapies in Nursing and Midwifery, 8*(1), 29–41.

Tloczynski, J., & Fritzsch, S. (2002). Intercessory prayer in psychological well-being: Using a multiple-baseline, across-subjects design. *Psychological Reports, 91,* 731–741.

Tolson, C. L., & Koenig, H. (2003). *The healing power of prayer.* Grand Rapids, MI: Baker Books.

Townsend, M., Kladder, V., Ayele, H., & Mulligan, T. (2002). Systematic review of clinical trials examining the effects of religion on health. *Southern Medical Journal, 95,* 1429–1434.

Tucker, E. W., & Potocky-Tripodi, M. (2006). Changing heterosexuals' attitudes toward homosexuals: A systematic review of the empirical literature. *Research on Social Work Practice, 16,* 176–190.

Vaughn, M. G., & Howard, M. O. (2004). Adolescent substance abuse treatment: A synthesis of controlled evaluations. *Research on Social Work Practice, 14,* 325–335.

Walker, S. (2001). Tracing the contours of postmodern social work. *British Journal of Social Work, 31,* 29–39.

Walker, S. R., Tonigan, J. S., Miller, W. R., Comer, S., & Kahlich, L. (1997). Intercessory prayer in the treatment of alcohol abuse and dependence: A pilot investigation. *Alternative Therapies, 3*(6), 79–86.

Weber, E. J., Callaham, M. L., Wears, R. L., Barton, C., & Young, G. (1998). Unpublished research from a medical specialty meeting: Why investigators fail to publish. *Journal of the American Medical Association, 280,* 257–259.

# Mental Health and Well-Being

## *Important Practice Points*

**Chapter 9**

• Many intervention areas (e.g., outreach, linkage, advocacy) are elemental to case management service provision, which was the intervention associated with the largest effects.

• Greater linkages between mental health and substance abuse service delivery systems should be developed in order to foster improved treatments for the dually diagnosed.

• Recommended interventions based on this synthesis are intensive case management and standard aftercare with specialized outpatient psychoeducational treatment groups.

**Chapter 10**

• Preliminary findings indicate that medication, alone or in combination with CBT; group therapy with cognitive behavioral, educational, and transactional analysis components; interpersonal therapy; and CBT produce the largest effect sizes.

• Physicians may be reluctant to prescribe medication during pregnancy and the postpartum because absolute safety cannot be assured, despite some selective serotonin reuptake inhibitors (SSRIs) and other antidepressant medications affording relative safety during pregnancy. Furthermore, many women may not wish to take medication during pregnancy and the postpartum. Thus, the need for effective alternative treatments is urgent.

## Chapter 11

• The present reviews indicate that depression treatment programs for Latinos in primary care settings within a CC framework were more effective than usual care in reducing symptoms of depression, improved functioning, and, importantly, increasing accessibility to guideline-congruent care.

• Differences across intervention trials reveal how similar treatment approaches (e.g., CBT and medication management) may have different outcomes depending on the particular Latino community being served. This finding reinforces the principle that one kind of treatment is unlikely to be effective given the diversity of this population.

• Supplemental case management services may be especially helpful for monolingual Spanish speakers in order to overcome barriers to care and navigate the myriad potential service options.

## Chapter 12

• There is a lack of consensus on how homophobia and heterosexism should be addressed. There exists a large and politically powerful proportion of the population that believes that homophobia should be embraced.

• Despite there being general support within social work for the LGB population, there is evidence that this support is not always effectively put into practice.

• It is an open question whether any short-term interventions can create lasting changes in attitude formation that facilitates behavioral changes toward LGB individuals.

## Chapter 13

• For practitioners who adhere to the protocols established by the American Psychological Association's Division 12, intercessory prayer must be regarded as an experimental treatment.

• Although some social work practitioners may feel that the best available research supports the use of intercessory prayer, the evidence does not support this notion, despite a general trend favoring the prayer group in 12 of the 17 studies. Given the importance of client preferences, it may be helpful to know that many members of the general public use prayer to address their medical concerns. For many persons, prayer is a significant strength, and this should be respected.

# Conclusion

## The Way Forward: Translating Research Findings Into Practice Settings

### Bruce A. Thyer, Michael G. Vaughn, and Matthew O. Howard

It is obvious from the collection of readings presented in this volume that the profession has made considerable advances in developing an empirical foundation of research-based interventive knowledge. Of course the selection herein is limited to articles published in one disciplinary journal, and social workers should keep abreast of related credible information appearing in print across a number of journals and Web sites. In many important domains of practice, there are now an array of psychosocial interventions possessing a reasonable evidentiary base of sufficient credibility as to be able to assist social workers and their clients in deciding what approaches to treatment should be undertaken. Readers will be reassured to know that evidence-based practice (EBP) does *not* assert that empirical research alone is sufficient to determine the proper course of therapy. Rather, the original EBP model contends that although it is necessary to consider scientific considerations, this research evidence must be appraised in light of one's clinical expertise, client preferences and circumstances, ethical issues, and available resources. EBP is not a dinner-table monologue wherein the scientist lectures practitioners and clients about what to do. Rather, it is a multifaceted conversation that ensures that the voice of science *is* heard, along with these other equally important perspectives, all of which go into decision making, with no one factor automatically trumping the others (except perhaps ethical considerations).

Contemporary social workers abreast of current developments in EBP find themselves in a situation similar to that of Ignaz Semmelweis, a Hungarian obstetrician of the middle 1800s, who discovered that postnatal maternal infections were caused by contamination from septic material conveyed by doctors from the dissecting room and other sources while examining living patients (Carter, 1994). Semmelweis made this landmark discovery, and indeed provided very credible evidence that his theory was correct, but his findings were largely ignored by the medical profession until decades later, when Louis

321

Pasteur more fully developed the germ theory of disease and more effectively translated these research findings into everyday clinical practice via the introduction of antiseptic procedures into medicine and surgery. For an array of clinical conditions, social workers now have access to a variety of interventions that have shown great promise in providing clients with significant benefits, up to and including complete relief, remission, or cure. Our failure to adequately translate or disseminate these important findings into practice is the human services equivalent to the Semmelweis dilemma.

The Web sites of the Cochrane (www.cochrane.org) and Campbell (www.campbellcollaboration.org) Collaborations are excellent places to begin locating this information on effective treatments, as are some contemporary texts (e.g., Nathan & Gorman, 2007, Roth & Fonagy, 2005) and selected journals (e.g., *Research on Social Work Practice, Evidence and Mental Health*). The principles of EBP are being extended into macro-level practice (see Brownson, Baker, Leet & Gillespie, 2003; Davies, Nutley & Smith, 2000; Thyer, 1996, 2008), and a search of electronic databases using "evidence-based management" or "evidence-based administration" keywords will reveal a surprising amount of literature.

Regrettably, there is a very long lag between advances in research on effective interventions and adoption within the community of practitioners, and reducing this lag is the topic of this concluding chapter. We (social workers) are not alone in having a problem in being slow to adopt treatment advances. Persons (1995, pp. 142–153) presents six reasons that this delay in adoption lag occurs within the discipline of psychology, reasons we suspect are applicable to social workers as well. These causes are:

1. Psychologists receive little training in methods that are supported by empirical evidence of efficacy (see Bledsoe et al., 2007 for an analogous social work exemplar).

2. Psychologists often receive extensive training in methods that are not supported by empirical evidence of efficacy (see Bledsoe et al., 2007).

3. Many clinicians do not read the outcome literature (see Rosen, 1994).

4. Research findings are often difficult for clinicians to use (see Sheldon & Chilvers, 2004).

5. Many clinicians believe that all psychotherapies are equally effective (see Reid, 1997, for a discussion of this error).

6. Consumers are uninformed.

Assuming that the above problems and obstacles also pertain to social work, let us focus on what can be done to more effectively translate empirical research findings into practice settings.

We can be content to publish our work in our profession's journals and books, maybe make some presentations at disciplinary conferences, and hope that a receptive community will listen, learn, and adopt. This does not seem to be too effective (see Point 3 above). Learning and applying empirically supported techniques is hard work, and such efforts are not typically reinforced by agency administrators. And we know that that which is not reinforced does not endure. Training opportunities in empirically supported interventions, with appropriate supervision, are also rare (Bledsoe et al., 2007), which further impedes successful dissemination.

Another approach, borrowed from the pulpit, is exhortations to learn and use empirically supported interventions, and condemnations aimed at shaming those who provide treatments of unknown effectiveness, or, as often happens, treatments known to be ineffective or to be harmful (Gambrill, 2001, 2003). And like other messages from the pulpit, such sermons are mostly heard by those already converted and fail to reach the ears of the heathen.

Some of us have faith that the answer will consist of reforming social work education and that these emerging cohorts of more effectively educated social workers will reform the profession. Social work programs at Washington University and the University of Oxford have adopted an evidence-based orientation toward their professional curricula (Howard, McMillan & Pollio, 2003), and it is hoped that more will follow this example. Others seek improvement via a gradual strengthening of the social work accreditation standards promulgated by the Council on Social Work Education, and in promoting more of an empirical orientation in the content of what is provided, in the form of continuing education for licensed social workers. These pedagogical approaches may have some positive effects, but it is unlikely they will produce either rapid or dramatic improvements, especially given the well-noted problems with the social work accreditation system (Stoesz & Karger, in press) and the general lack of utility of CEU programs to alter practitioner behavior.

Others look to changes in the ethical standards produced by the National Association of Social Workers. Some years ago, the NASW issued the following condemnation of one form of psychosocial treatment:

> Proponents of reparative therapies claim—without documentation—many successes. They assert that their processes are supported by conclusive scientific data, which are in fact little more than anecdotal. NCOLGI protests these efforts to 'convert' people through irresponsible therapies . . . empirical research does not demonstrate that . . . sexual orientation (heterosexual or homosexual) can be changed through these so-called reparative therapies. (NCOLGI, 1992, p. 1)

Some of us experienced a ripple of excitement reading this. If reparative therapies were deemed unethical due to their lack of empirical evidence, then by implication we could look forward to such a standard being applied to other forms of psychosocial treatment similarly unfounded. Ever the optimist, Thyer (1995) subsequently suggested inclusion of the following ethical standard for the NASW Code of Ethics:

Clients should be offered as a first choice treatment, interventions with some significant degree of empirical support, where such knowledge exists, and only provided other treatments after such first choice treatments have been given a legitimate trial and been shown not to be efficacious. (Thyer, 1995, p. 95)

Oddly, this helpful suggestion was never adopted. More recently (9 February 2008), Thyer sent the NASW's Office of Ethics and Professional Review a letter seeking ethical guidance on the following questions:

1. Is a social worker who provides an intervention that lacks any scientifically credible evidence that it helps clients, acting unethically?

2. Is a social worker who provides an intervention that scientifically credible studies have shown to be ineffective, acting unethically?

3. Is a social worker who provides an intervention that scientifically credible studies have shown to be harmful to clients, acting unethically?

After several anxious weeks, he received a reply. The answer was that the Office of Ethics and Professional Review did not provide ethical consultation in writing, only over the phone! Well, a phone-based conversation is not a very authoritative foundation to provide guidance to practitioners seeking clarification related to the above three questions, especially if one was interested in filing an ethics complaint against a member of the NASW practicing a harmful therapy. Perhaps, if the profession's ethical codes were to more clearly address these issues, we would not have MSWs smothering little girls to death while practicing so-called rebirthing therapy (Mercer, Sarner, & Rosa, 2003), or assisting, some years ago, in facilitating the lobotomizing of psychiatric patients (Margolin, 1997). More recently, social workers have adopted the technique called Critical Incident Stress Debriefing (Spitzer & Neely, 1992), despite strong evidence that the method is not helpful (van Emmerik, Kamphuis, Hulsbosch, & Emmelkamp, 2002) and may indeed actually impede natural recovery from trauma (McNally, Bryant & Ehlers, 2003). As of now, there is little in the way of ethical prohibitions dealing with such practices, apart from the obvious admonitions to promote the well-being of clients and to protect clients from harm. Perhaps the professional associations are concerned about alienating those social workers who receive payment for providing ineffective or pseudoscientific treatments. This concern is misplaced. Such individuals need to remove themselves from membership in our major organizations.

Apart from the above lacunae in our Code of Ethics, there is also the continuing puzzling lack of a legal right to effective treatment. Right now, social workers have no apparent legal obligation to provide clients with interventions that have demonstrated effectiveness, where these are known to exist (Myers & Thyer, 1997; Corcoran, 1998). Most lawsuits against social workers alleging improper practice are settled out of court, without establishing a legal precedent. It would be a dramatic, and in our view positive, development for the profession if a client who was provided a known ineffective treatment (e.g. CISD) for a particular problem (e.g., post-traumatic stress disorder), for which effective treatments were established (e.g., cognitive behavior therapy), successfully sued his or her clinical social worker on the grounds of malpractice. The use of CISD would rapidly decline, and social workers who provide treatment to clients with PTSD would rush to learn about effective interventions. This would be a good thing. Need we wait until a client is killed by a social worker, as in the case of Candace Newmaker, before a state legislature is moved to ban harmful techniques (Mercer, Sarner & Rosa, 2003)?

It would also be helpful if social work education stopped promoting a primarily relationship-focused approach to clinical social work, in favor of one more balanced between learning both relationship-building skills *and* specific skills in empirically supported psychosocial interventions. The former position has been most recently articulated in an important article by Simpson, Williams and Segall (2007), and the latter view by Thyer (2007). We believe that Margolin's (1997) statement is broadly representative of the generic clinical perspective taught by many social work programs: "Workers are taught early not to superimpose their own opinions, wishes, or decisions upon their clients, and to see themselves as offering help and support *rather than intervention*" [emphasis added] (Margolin, 1997, p. 114).

If specific interventions are seen as irrelevant to treatment outcome, the process of evidence-based practice will make little headway. This must change (see Reid, 1997). If relationship factors are the *primum mobile* of therapy, of what point are the differential theories, models, and techniques to which graduate social work students devote years of learning? Do these truly make no difference at all in outcome? If they do have a role, then we are obligated to teach those of greater validity and demonstrable effectiveness, as well as empirically supported findings related to therapist and client variables related to treatment outcomes (Beutler et al., 2004).

There are powerful forces aligned against the promotion of evidence-based practice. Those committed to existing ineffective models of helping are threatened by EBP's focus on empirical evaluative research. The advocates of postmodernism find the philosophical assumptions of EBP anathema. Professional inertia cannot be discounted. Our texts are replete with unsupported claims about treatment effectiveness (Stone & Gambrill, 2007). Public agencies are evaluated in terms of inputs, services provided, and clients seen, not people actually helped. Tweed-jacketed academics quake in their Birkenstocks when they hear calls for professional accountability. Social activists propagandize using spurious statistics to support their claims (Sarnoff, 1999), with each such example of "fake" research weakening the public trust in legitimate science. New BSW programs can be established with only two full-time faculty. MSW programs require only six! Respected social work programs teach so-called energy therapies, and psychotherapies known to not be helpful and to be based on erroneous theories to their MSW students (Pignotti, 2007).

The situation may be seen as analogous to medical education 100 years ago. There was a proliferation of underfunded programs with poorly qualified faculty, admitting large numbers of badly educated students; pseudoscientific treatment methods were commonly taught, clinical supervision was poor, and programs were sometimes located in substandard teaching facilities. The solution? The Carnegie Foundation for the Advancement of Teaching commissioned Abraham Flexner to undertake a comprehensive review of medical education in the United States and Canada and to make recommendations to improve the situation. Flexner personally visited every such program, evaluating its faculty, students, library and laboratory resources, training facilities, funding, and relationship to the larger university environment, if any. One proposed (and discarded) solution was as follows:

> If, in a word, scientific method and interest are of slight or no importance to the ordinary practitioner of medicine, we shall permanently establish two types of school—the scientific type, in which enlightened and progressive men may be trained; the routine type, in which "family doctors" may be ground out wholesale. (Flexner, 1910, p. 54)

This approach was not recommended. Instead, Flexner said:

> The one person for whom there is no place in the medical school, the university, or the college, is precisely he who has hitherto generally usurped the medical field—the scientifically dead practitioner, whose knowledge has long since come to a standstill . . . (Flexner, 1910, p. 57)

Following Flexner's report, the higher-quality medical programs banded together and adopted more rigorous standards for faculty, students, training facilities, and curricula. Pseudoscientific techniques such as chiropractic, homeopathy, and magnetic healing were in effect excluded from medical education. A formal and strong system of accreditation was enacted. The number of medical schools dropped dramatically, for, as Flexner observed:

> The improvement of medial education cannot therefore be resisted on the ground that it will destroy schools and restrict output: that is precisely what is needed. (Flexner, 1910, p. 16)

These positive changes took place over decades, accompanied by much hand-wringing and angst. But the result was our current system of medical education in North America, which is the envy of the world, and more important, of demonstrably greater effectiveness than the practices provided to clients 100 years ago. Can social work make the same claim?

Evidence-based practice has the potential to exert a cleansing and leavening effect on social work education, practice, and policy. We resist overly cynical and critical appraisals of the status of our profession, believing that there is much that is good, indeed noble, within the field. But there is a dramatic need for improvements in what we teach and practice. The process of evidence-based practice is one approach to achieving such improvements.

# References

Bledsoe, S. E., Weissman, M. M., Mullen, E. J., Ponniah, K., Gameroff, M. J., Verdeli, H., et al. (2007). Empirically supported psychotherapy in social work training programs: Does the definition of evidence matter? *Research on Social Work Practice, 17*, 449–455.

Beutler, L. E., Malik, M., Alimohamed, S., Harwood, T. M., Talebi, H., Noble, S., & Wong, E. (2004). Therapist variables. In M. J. Lambert (Ed.). *Bergin and Garfield's handbook of psychotherapy and behavior change* (5th ed., pp. 227–306). New York: John S. Wiley & Sons.

Brownson, R. C., Baker, E. A., Leet, T. L., & Gillespie, K. N. (2003). *Evidence-based public health.* New York: Oxford.

Carter, K. C. (1994). *Childbed fever: A scientific biography of Ignaz Semmelweis.* Westport, CT: Greenwood Press.

Corcoran, K. J. (1998). Clients without a cause: Is there a legal right to effective treatment? *Research on Social Work Practice, 8*, 589–596.

Davies, H. T. O., Nutley, S. M., & Smith, P. C. (2000). *What works: Evidence-based policy and practice in public services.* Bristol, UK: The Policy Press.

Flexner, A. (1910). *Medical education in the United States and Canada.* New York: Carnegie Foundation.

Gambrill, E. (2001). Social work: An authority-based profession. *Research on Social Work Practice, 11*, 166–175.

Gambrill, E. (2003). Evidence-based practice: Sea change or the emperor's new clothes? (editorial). *Journal of Social Work Education, 39*, 3–23.

Howard, M. O., McMillan, C. J., & Pollio, D. (2003). Teaching evidence-based practice: Toward a new paradigm for social work education. *Research on Social Work Practice, 13*, 234–259.

Margolin, L. (1997). *Under the cover of kindness: The invention of social work.* Charlottesville, VA: University Press of Virginia.

McNally, R. J., Bryant, R. A., & Ehlers, A. (2003). Does early psychological intervention promote recovery from post-traumatic stress? *Psychological Science in the Public Interest, 4*(2), 45–79.

Mercer, J., Sarner, L., & Rosa, L. (2003). *Attachment therapy on trial: The torture and death of Candace Newmaker.* Westport, CT: Praeger.

Myers, L. L., & Thyer, B. A. (1997). Should social work clients have the right to effective treatment? *Social Work, 42*, 288–298.

Nathan, P. E., & Gorman, J. M. (Eds.) (2007). *A guide to treatments that work* (3rd ed.). New York: Oxford University Press.

National Commission on Lesbian and Gay Issues. (1992). *Statement on reparative therapies.* Washington, DC: National Association of Social Workers.

Persons, J. B. (1995). Why practicing psychologists are slow to adopt empirically validated treatements. In S. C. Hayes, V. M. Follette, R. M. Dawes, & G. E. Grady

(Eds.). *Scientific standards of psychological practice: Issues and recommendations* (pp. 141–157). Reno, NV: Context Press.

Pignotti, M. (2007). Questionable interventions taught at top-ranked school of social work. *Scientific Review of Mental Health Practice 5(2)*, 78–79.

Reid, W. J. (1997). Evaluating the dodo's verdict: Do all interventions have equivalent outcomes? *Social Work Research, 21,* 5–16.

Rosen, A. (1994). Knowledge use in direct practice. *Social Service Review, 68,* 561–577.

Roth, A., & Fonagy, P. (2005). *What works for whom: A critical guide of psychotherapy research* (2nd ed.). New York: Guilford Press.

Sarnoff, S. K. (1999). "Sanctified snake oil": Ideology, junk science, and social work practice. *Families in Society, 80,* 396–408.

Sheldon, B., & Childers (2004). Evidence-based practice in England. In B. A. Thyer & M. A. F. Kazi (Eds.). *International perspectives on evidence-based practice in social work* (pp. 45–80). Birmingham, UK: Venture Press.

Simpson, G. A., Williams, J. C., & Segall, A. B. (2007). Social work education and clinical learning. *Clinical Social Work Journal, 35,* 3–14.

Spitzer, W. J., & Neely, K. (1992). Critical incident stress: The role of hospital-based social work in developing a statewide intervention system for first-responders delivering emergency services. *Social Work in Health Care, 18,* 39–58.

Stoesz, D., & Karger, H. J. (in press). *Curbside academics: Reforming social work education.* New York: Oxford University Press.

Stone, S., & Gambrill, E. (2007). Do school social work textbooks provide a sound guide for education and practice? *Children & Schools, 29,* 109–118.

Thyer, B. A. (1995). Promoting an empiricist agency within the human services: An ethical and humanistic imperative. *Journal of Behavior Therapy and Experimental Psychiatry, 26,* 93–98.

Thyer, B. A. (1996). Behavior analysis and social welfare policy. In M. A. Mattaini & B. A. Thyer (Eds.). *Finding solutions to social problems: Behavioral strategies for change* (pp. 41–60). Washington, DC: American Psychological Association.

Thyer, B. A. (2007). Social work education and clinical practice: Towards evidence-based practice? *Clinical Social Work Journal, 35,* 25–32.

Thyer, B. A. (2008). Evidence-based macro practice: Addressing the challenges and opportunities. *Journal of Evidence-Based Social Work, 5(3–4),* 453–472.

Van Emmerik, A. P., Kamphuis, J. H., Hulsbosch, A. M., & Emmelkamp, P. M. G. (2002). Single-session debriefing after psychological trauma: A meta-analysis. *The Lancet, 360,* 766–771.

# Index _____

# About the Editors _____

**Michael G. Vaughn, PhD,** is Assistant Professor in the School of Social Work at Saint Louis University, where he also holds appointments in the Departments of Community Health and Public Policy. He is the author of more than 70 articles and book chapters. Currently, he has four funded projects, two of which involve developing databases of empirical studies for quantitative synthesis on adolescent substance abuse treatment and adolescent antisocial behavior. In addition, he is writing numerous articles on the topics of serious juvenile offending, transitions to adulthood for foster youth, and applications of a biosocial dynamic framework to antisocial behavior and substance abuse.

**Matthew O. Howard, PhD,** is the Frank Daniels Distinguished Professor of Social Work at the University of North Carolina. Nationally acknowledged as an expert in psychiatric comorbidity of substance use disorders and evidence-based practice, he has published more than 100 articles in these areas and has served as principal investigator or co-PI on several federally funded grants. His recent research has examined predictors of major depression and anxiety disorders in adolescent inhalant and ecstasy users; racial and gender differences in the prevalence and predictors of substance-induced psychiatric disorders; self-medication of psychiatric disorders with alcohol and illicit drugs; and long-term health outcomes of polydrug-dependent adults with comorbid mental health disorders.

**Bruce A. Thyer, PhD,** is Professor of Social Work with Florida State University, and he founded and continues to serve as editor of the journal *Research on Social Work Practice*. Dr. Thyer has authored or coauthored more than 200 articles in peer-reviewed journals in the fields of social work, psychology, psychiatry, behavior analysis, and evaluation, as well as more than 50 book chapters and about 20 books in these areas. He is a Fellow of the American Psychological Association and one of the founders of the Society for Social Work and Research. In 2005, one of his articles on evidence-based practice in social work received a Pro Humanitate Award from the North American Center for Child Welfare.

# List of Contributors_____

Ashley M. Austin, Florida International University

Sarah E. Bledsoe, University of North Carolina at Chapel Hill

Leopoldo J. Cabassa, University of Southern California

Jacqueline Corcoran, Virginia Commonwealth University

Patricia Ann Craven, Florida State University

Patrick Dattalo, Virginia Commonwealth University

Marian L. Dumaine, Florida International University

Nancy K. Grote, University of Washington

Marissa C. Hansen, University of Southern California

David R. Hodge, Arizona State University, West Campus

Matthew O. Howard, University of North Carolina at Chapel Hill

Robert E. Lee, Florida State University

Mark W. Lipsey, Vanderbilt University

Brad W. Lundahl, University of Utah

Mark J. Macgowan, Florida International University

Janelle Nimer, University of Utah

William R. Nugent University of Tennessee

Bruce Parsons, University of Utah

Miriam Potocky-Tripodi, Florida International University

Haluk Soydan, Center for Evaluation of Social Services, Stockholm, Sweden

Bruce A. Thyer, Florida State University

Edmon W. Tucker, Florida International University

**Mark S. Umbreit,** University of Minnesota

**Michael G. Vaughn,** Saint Louis University

**Eric F. Wagner,** Florida International University

**Mona Williams** University of Tennessee

**Sandra Jo Wilson,** Vanderbilt University